□ Third Edition

The Dynamics of Sex and Gender

A Sociological Perspective

Laurel Richardson

Ohio State University

1817

HARPER & ROW, PUBLISHERS, New York
Cambridge,   Philadelphia,   San Francisco,   Washington,
London,   Mexico City,   São Paulo,   Singapore,   Sydney

For Ben and Josh

Sponsoring Editor: Alan McClare
Project Coordination: Caliber Design Planning, Inc.
Cover Design: 20/20 SERVICES, INC.
Compositor: Keystone Typesetting
Printer and Binder: R. R. Donnelley & Sons Company

THE DYNAMICS OF SEX AND GENDER: A SOCIOLOGICAL PERSPECTIVE, Third Edition.

Copyright © 1988 by Harper & Row, Publishers, Inc.

All rights reserved. Printed in the United States of America. No part of this book may be used or reproduced in any manner whatsoever without written permission, except in the case of brief quotations embodied in critical articles and reviews. For information address Harper & Row, Publishers, Inc., 10 East 53d Street, New York, NY 10022.

Library of Congress Cataloging-in-Publication Data

Richardson, Laurel Walum.
    The dynamics of sex and gender.

    Bibliography: p.
    Includes indexes.
    1. Sex role. 2. Socialization. 3. Sex differences
(Psychology) 4. Sexism—United States. I. Title.
HQ21.R46 1987   305.3   87–25112
ISBN 0–06–047291–X (pbk.)

    89 90 9 8 7 6 5 4 3 2

□ □ Contents □ □

Preface   *vii*

Section One   Learning the Culture   1

1   **Culture, Sex, and Gender**   3

Sex and Gender   4
Learning Gender: The Case of Agnes   7
Masculinity/Femininity   9
Transsexualism: Incarnating Sex Stereotyping   12

2   **Language: The Inescapable Socializer**   16

Verbal Communication   18
Nonverbal Communication   24
Sex Differences in Speech   28
Reevaluating the Speech Standard   33

3   **Early Socialization**   35

Infant Socialization   38
Preschool Socialization   43

4   **Education**   50

School Policies and Practices   51
The Male School Experience   56
The Female School Experience   59
Mathematics: An "Instructive" Case   61
Higher Education   64

5   **Mass Media**   69

Newspapers and Magazines   70
Advertisements   75
Television   77
Effects of Television   81

Section Two Institutions of Social Control: Ideational
        Elements   83

6 Religion   85

   Biblical Heritage: Traditionalism   86
   Church Structure   90
   Religious Visions   94
   Potential Outcomes   99

7 The Law   101

   The Legal System   102
   Domestic Relations   104
   Nontraditional Domestic Relations   106
   Employment   107
   Education   109
   Criminal Law   111
   Reproductive Rights   117
   Equal Rights Amendment   119

8 Medical and Mental Health Systems   121

   The Body   122
   Reproduction   123
   Sexuality   127
   Childbirth and Lactation   129
   Medical Practice   131
   Alternative Views and Practices   131
   Clinical Psychology and Psychiatry   134
   Alternative Therapies: The Case of Eating Disorders   138

Section Three   The Structure of Sex-Based
        Inequality   141

9 Sex-Based Stratification   143

   Biogenetic and Biocultural Theories: An Overview   145
   Physiology and Gender   147
   Primate Research   149
   Human Social Evolution   151
   Biocultural Approach   154

10 Inequalities of Power, Property, and Prestige   159

   Power   159

Property   *163*
Prestige   *170*

11   **The Work World: Organization and Process**   **172**

Status Inconsistency   *173*
Sex Segregation   *175*
Hierarchical Networks   *178*
Sponsor-Protégé System   *180*
Socioemotional Bonding   *182*
Work Lives of Men   *186*
Who Benefits?   *188*

12   **The Linkages Between Home and Work**   **191**

Marriage   *193*
Child Care   *197*
Single Parenting   *201*

Section Four   **Social and Political Change**   **205**

13   **Changing Intimate Relationships**   **207**

Being Single   *208*
Being Heterosexually Coupled   *213*
Lesbian Alternatives   *219*
Gay Male Alternatives   *223*

14   **Social Movements**   **227**

Feminist Social Movement   *229*
Antifeminism   *236*
Passive Feminism   *237*
Race and Gender   *238*
Black Women and the Feminist Movement   *240*
Men's Movement   *245*
The Future of the Feminist Movement   *248*

References   *251*
Indexes   *283*

□ □ **Preface** □ □

"It is only at the end that we know where we have been; and only by ending that we can once again begin." These words introduced the first and second editions of *The Dynamics of Sex and Gender.* I am drawn to them again to introduce this third edition. These words continue to deepen for me, reminding me again of why I recommit my energies to the dissemination of knowledge about gender: Our work as gender scholars and teachers does make a difference. Because of our efforts, forthcoming generations of males and females can, and do, enjoy greater gender freedom and greater gender equality.

Since the publication of *The Dynamics of Sex and Gender* ten years ago, our knowledge of sex and gender has continued to flourish, happily making this third edition necessary. Like the earlier editions, the third edition of *The Dynamics of Sex and Gender* links the private experiences of individuals, the structure of institutions, and the interests of the powerful. I have integrated a diverse body of gender knowledge, discussed sociological concepts within a gender dynamics context, illustrated and documented the salience of gender in everyday lives, and provided extensive referencing. This edition, therefore, can serve as the major text in gender and women's studies courses and as an adjunct in other courses such as marriage and family, introductory sociology, and social problems.

The third edition of *The Dynamics of Sex and Gender* consists of four sections. Section One delineates the process by which people are socialized into the culture through language, family, education, and the mass media. Section Two analyzes religion, law, and the medical and mental health systems as institutions of social control. Section Three focuses on sex-based inequality, critically appraises alternative explanations for it, and discusses how sex-based inequality affects home and work. The final section, Section Four, considers social and political change, including changing intimate relationships, and the Women's and Men's Movements. The organization of the book, therefore, helps the student to grasp the unifying power of the sociological perspective: The student moves from the more familiar world of socialization to the more abstract one of institutions and social change.

This revised edition updates demographic, policy, and legal materials; incorporates new research on previously discussed topics; and offers new topics and organization. These changes include:

> more material on men and how gender intersects with race and class

> more integration of materials on gay men, lesbians, and homophobia throughout the text

> more integration of materials on minorities throughout the text

> consolidation of some chapters and reorganization of the last section

Specific additions include: a detailed discussion of gender as a situated accomplishment; a discussion of sex differences in speech strategies, talk as "interaction work," and an evaluation of the speech standard; peer socialization into gender; discussion of the new reproductive technologies; an analysis of categories of mental illness (DSM III) and the treatment of eating disorders; extended discussions of different explanations of sex segregation in the labor force, the "feminization of poverty," and sexual harassment; discussion of dual providers and single-parent homes; extended discussion of the diversity in the Women's Movement, antifeminism and "passive feminism," black feminist history, and the contemporary Men's Movement.

Many people have contributed to the manuscript, and I thank them all. Several people have helped in the revisions, and I gratefully acknowledge the coauthorship of several parts of this manuscript: Karen Schwartz for second and third edition revisions of Chapter 6, "Religion"; Harriet Ganson for additions to the second edition of Chapter 7, "The Law"; Judith A. Cook and Willa Young for additions to Chapter 8, "Medical and Mental Health Systems"; Mary Margaret Fonow and Lisa Ransdell for additions to Chapter 10, "Inequalities of Power, Property, and Prestige"; and Lisa Ransdell for contributions to the third edition of Chapter 9, "Sex-Based Stratification," and Chapter 11, "The Work World: Organization and Process."

In addition, Karen Erickson, Professor of Law, Ohio State University, and Joan Black provided extensive criticism and legal references for Chapter 7, "The Law." Tim Diamond, Nona Glazer, Joan Huber, and many anonymous reviewers have critically read different versions of the manuscript. Graduate and undergraduate students have given excellent feedback. Still others have helped in the editing and preparation of this edition, including Alan McClare, sponsoring editor, and Lois Lombardo, managing editor.

There are some people to whom I am especially thankful. My sons, Ben and Josh Walum, to whom this book has again been dedicated, grown to men, continue to delight me with their views and visions. Verta Taylor again has been an extraordinarily helpful friend and colleague. Many an hour we spent discussing how to shape this revision, and her insights, knowledge, and feedback have lightened my labor. Betty Kirschner again has demonstrated her exceptional capacity for friendship. And there is Ernest Lockridge, whom, once again, I thank again and again.

Laurel Richardson

SECTION

□ *1* □

Learning the Culture

In the beginning, the human fetus is female. When embryos with the XY chromosomal patterns emit the hormone androgen, they become male. The clitoris is transformed into a penis, the ovaries to testes, and the vaginal tract closes over. If the differentiation proceeds without error, the child is recognized at birth as male or female and assigned to one of these two categories, which are used universally to designate sexual differences within the human species.

Commonly, it has been assumed that everything else about the child flows naturally from its anatomy. A boy's disposition, role in child rearing, choice of sex partner, and desires for achievement are frequently viewed as naturally and normally different from a girl's. Such biological determinism has a long history in both scholarship and folklore. Part of the attractiveness of this belief has been its relative truth. Up until quite recently, men have led qualitatively different lives than women have. It has, therefore, seemed natural to explain these differences as a consequence of biology.

More recently, however, the research efforts of many different scientists—physiologists, psychologists, sociologists, endocrinologists, ethologists, and anthropologists—have brought into serious question the import of biology for the subsequent social and sexual development of the child and adult. Researchers from disparate disciplines have come to stress the importance of *social shaping*—of learning to be a ''masculine'' or ''feminine'' person.

In the chapters that follow, we will examine the processes by which children are socially shaped into *gendered* persons. We will look at the major ways in which young children acquire various aspects of the culture in which they live—through language, interaction with parents, the school, and the media. We will begin our exploration by looking at the relationships between culture, sex, and gender.

□ □ *1* □ □

Culture, Sex, and Gender

After a millennium of wandering, the Gynandroids have returned to their originating planet. Inured as they are, and accustomed as they have become to life forms strange and wondrous and cultures peculiar and unexpected, nothing in their travels has prepared them for this bizarre world. Here, for the first time, they encounter a world that purposefully constrains its members by placing them in one of two categories. The category designated is predicated upon the role played in the biological reproduction of the species. This life form builds its culture and socialization processes as well as its social, economic, and political institutions on these biological differences. Most peculiar of all, this world judges the category of life form unable to bear or nurse children more valuable than the category that does!

The world that the Gynandroids visited so briefly is, of course, Earth, and the life form they encountered was us—Americans on the edge of the twenty-first century. The world they found so odd is the one we have taken for granted, for we have been born into it.

Scattered across the earth are other real societies that take for granted different ideas about the nature of the sexes. The Manu, for example, believe that only men can enjoy taking care of children; the Toda see housework as a sacred task and therefore entrust it to men; and the Tcambuli consider men emotionally dependent and irresponsible. On the other hand, the Mundugomor and Arapesh see males and females as possessing essentially similar personalities—violent, competitive, and aggressive by nature, argue the Mundugomor; gentle, kind, and loving, propose the Arapesh.

Everyone is born into a *culture*—a set of ideas shared by a group of people, ideas that are symbolically expressed in their behavior and artifacts. These ideas comprise beliefs about the nature of reality, moral judgments about what is right or wrong, and evaluations of what is desirable and attractive or disgusting and to be avoided. Some people take for granted, as a cultural belief, that men are naturally superior to women; some take for granted that women are naturally superior to men;

and some cannot understand the dispute at all. In each case, the culture is defining for its members that which is to be taken for granted as factual, inalienable, and proved.

A culture also gives a system of ideas for judging how things *ought* to be; for example, according to 300 cultures (out of 1170 sampled) women should be virgins at marriage. These societies have a *proscriptive norm* (a thou-shall-not rule) concerning premarital coitus. In the United States, men should be financially responsible for their families. This is an example of a *prescriptive norm* (a thou-shall rule) governing the role of men.

In addition, the culture includes ideas about what is preferable or enjoyable. In our society, often that which is defined as pleasurable is in direct conflict with that which is defined as right. The old shibboleth, "Everything I like is either immoral, illegal, or fattening," exemplifies this conflict. It is no wonder that we frequently experience considerable stress in making decisions.

Culture, then, is ideational. Behavior, arts, and artifacts are merely symbolic representations of the culture. High heels, lipstick, skirt, and pantyhose are artifacts that symbolize certain attitudes toward women, just as the pinstripe suit, wing tips, and jockstrap symbolize particular attitudes toward men. Each of these items of attire is culturally approved and consistent with the culture's ideas about the nature of men and women, judgments about what is morally appropriate for men and women to do, and evaluations of what is attractive and desirable in each of the sexes.

Any complex society has a great number and variety of ideas, some of which are shared by only a few of its members. But despite the diversity, there does exist a cultural perspective that is unconsciously shared; for example, we believe that we really do exist and are not actors in another person's dream, that fertilization of ova is required for pregnancy, that time can be measured, and that if we drop a pencil, it will fall. We have a general understanding of what a newscaster is talking about and why it is newsworthy—that is, we understand each other's words.

SEX AND GENDER

Similarly, there is a dominant cultural attitude toward sex and gender—a set of ideas we take for granted regardless of our own gender, ethnicity, or family background. An adult member of our society, for example, sees the population as composed of two and only two sexes, male and female. We do not permit, as the Navajo do, the sex status, *nadle*, or hermaphrodite (male *and* female). "Real nadle" are those born hermaphroditic, but others may "pretend they are nadle" and subsequently be released from the sexual division of labor and permitted to take a spouse of either sex. In our culture, from before the cradle to beyond the grave, a person is supposed to be inextricably and forever male or female.

There has been a great deal of confusion in both scholarly and popular discussions concerning the meaning of the concepts, sex and gender. In this book, *sex* refers to the biological aspects of a person, such as the chromosomal, anatomical, hormonal, and physiological structure. It is an *ascribed status* in that a person is assigned to one sex or the other at birth. *Gender* refers to psychological, social, and cultural components. Unlike sex, it is *accomplished* in social contexts (cf. West and Zimmerman, 1987). How gender is accomplished will concern us shortly, but first, we will address the issue of *sex* as an ascribed status.

We are so accustomed to thinking of all aspects of one's *sex* as consistent that it may be difficult to accept inconsistency. However, the chromosomal, anatomical, and hormonal sex within a given individual may in fact be inconsistent. Sex chromosome variations cannot be detected visually, but require the use of laboratory equipment. Although it has been generally taken for granted that a newborn who anatomically looks like a boy carries the male chromosome pattern, XY, and that a newborn who anatomically looks like a girl carries the female chromosome pattern, XX, this is not always the case. Some anatomical males have a double Y pattern, while others have extras of both the X and Y chromosomes; some anatomical females have triple X patterns, while others carry the Y chromosome (Probber and Ehrman, 1978). In a recent Olympics, for example, anatomical females were excluded from participation because they did not have the female chromosomal pattern.

Anatomically, a person's gonads—the sperm- or egg-producing organ (testicles in the male, ovaries in the female)—may not be fully developed, or they may be composed of both ovarian and testicular cells. Similarly, both the internal sex organs (seminal vesicles and prostate gland in males; uterus, fallopian tubes, and vagina in females) and the external sex organs (penis and testicles in the male; vulva including the clitoris in females) may be atrophied or ambiguous. A large clitoris, for example, can be mistaken for a penis, or testicles may not have descended at birth. These cross-sex anatomical anomalies are actually not that rare. Estimates are that between two and three newborns in every 100 live births have some kind of genital anomaly, although most of these are minor. Moreover, approximately four million people in America have genitalia that are neither or both male and female, but are sex assigned either male or female (*Science News*, 1972:376). Finally, sex hormone proportions in some adults conform more to the other sex than to their own. Consequently, it is entirely conceivable for a child to be chromosomally, anatomically, and/or hormonally sex inconsistent.

Further, one's biological sex (even if consistent on all indicators) may be independent of one's *gender identity*—awareness that "I am a boy" or "I am a girl." Indeed, the evidence from a continuing series of studies on sex and gender by John Money, Anke Ehrhardt, and their associates at Johns Hopkins Medical Center overwhelmingly supports the conclusion that biological sex is overridden by the gender of rearing.

In one particularly illustrative example, a set of identical male twins was born without any congenital malformation or sex assignment ambiguity. At seven months, one of the twins lost his penis through a surgical error. (An overpowerful current of electricity during a routine electrocautery circumcision burned the entire tissue of the penis.) When the twin was 17 months old, the decision was reached to rear the child as a girl. The parents "were given confidence that their child . . . (could) be expected to differentiate a female gender identity, in agreement with her sex of rearing" (Money and Ehrhardt, 1975:47). The first steps were changing the child's name, clothing, and hairstyle, followed by plastic surgery to construct female genitalia. The mother reported that she kept the girl in dresses and frilly blouses, that she emphasized neatness and encouraged her daughter to imitate her own domestic interests. By age 5, the mother was happy to report that her daughter preferred dresses to slacks, was proud of her long hair, liked to be cleaned up, and enjoyed imitating her mother's behavior patterns. The mother stated during an interview, "One thing that really amazes me is that she is so feminine. I've never seen a little girl so neat and tidy. . . . She is very proud of herself when she puts on a new dress or I set her hair" (Money and Ehrhardt, 1975:48). As might be expected, the other twin did not exhibit these traits. According to the mother's report, he was active, messy, rejected housework, and liked to copy his father. Although these twins were identical males at birth, their gender-rearing experiences differentiated them. One twin has the gender identity, girl; the other the gender identity, boy.

Gender is a complex notion, too. Rather than thinking of people as simply having a particular gender—as one has a suit of clothes—sociologists think of gender as situationally accomplished. Gender "takes shapes in concrete, historically changing relationships" (Thorne, et al., 1983:16). Learning to identify with one sex only or gender identity is a lasting and abstract achievement, but gender, itself, is not. Rather, people learn how a girl/woman or boy/man should feel, think, and act in different social roles in different social settings. Depending on such things as the sex of the other actors and the norms governing the situation, gender is accomplished differently. A woman lawyer, for example, who is a single mother displays her gender differently when she is talking with her female friends than when she is presenting a case before a jury, or while on a date with a man, or while tending to her children. Not only will she act differently in these different situations, she will feel different pressures on her as a woman regarding her behavior. Similarly, a male lawyer will display his gender differently when he is interacting with his male friends than when he is interacting with a woman on a date or with his children. Gender affects how one plays different roles, as well as what roles one will be assigned, including economic, domestic, and sexual ones.

Consider for a few moments how you achieve your gender in different settings—how you prove to others that you are, indeed, the sex you claim to be. What did you do this morning to prove to yourself and others that your sex is male or female? As a female, did you put on makeup, jewelry, formfitting clothes, "female" shoes? Do you pay more attention to the presentation of self as a female-gendered person when you are going on a date than when you are studying? As a male, did you skip cosmetics this morning, as you do every morning, and concentrate on the simple things in life—pants, shirts, and "male" shoes? Are you sitting now as you read this with your legs crossed at the knee, or are they spread out? Do you pay more attention to your presentation as a male-gendered person when you are out with the guys than you do when you are studying?

If we were to list all the things men and women do to achieve their gender in a given setting, the list would be outrageously long. People do not, obviously, sit down and follow such a list point by point. Rather, because they learn what the culturally appropriate ways to act are, they simply act. If they follow our culture's rules, women will feel feminine and men will feel masculine, because so many of our rules prescribe different behavior for males and females. What is confusing for many people today is entering new settings—settings that were previously the domain of only one sex—and not knowing how a person of your sex should behave to achieve gender—or, indeed, whether the new role should be "gender free."

Cultural stereotypes of masculinity and femininity, moreover, should not be confused with gender identity. They are different concepts and raise different issues. A boy who plays with dolls may be rejecting cultural definitions of what constitutes "masculinity," but he knows his gender identity—boy; a tomboy may not be conforming with traditional expectations of "femininity," but she knows she is a girl. Few people worry about knowing what gender they are, although many struggle with whether they are "masculine" or "feminine" *enough*. Some of the confusion arises because in the process of teaching a child his/her gender identity, the child is also being taught how a person of that gender should behave and think in a multitude of situations. However, the two concepts are and should be kept analytically distinct.

Similarly, we are accustomed to assuming that one's gender identity is linked to one's sex object preference. However, sexual arousal by a member of one's own gender or the other gender is independent of one's gender identity, as well as of one's "masculinity" or "femininity." Homosexuals and lesbians know what sex they are. Further, some see themselves as masculine; others, as feminine. And some see no relationship between their masculinity or femininity and their sexuality; that is, they do not differ in these regards from the heterosexual population.

In summary, *sex* categorization within the cultural context that everyone is (should be) either male or female is determined at birth. Anatomical differences are the basis upon which a child is placed into a sex category. This sex identification is decided by others. Gender identity is one's identification with a sex category, male or female. *Gender*, what it means to be male or female in terms of appropriate role performances, personality structures, attitudes, and behaviors, is accomplished in concrete settings. A child with a given anatomical structure is socialized or taught to think, feel, and act in ways considered natural, morally appropriate, and desirable for a person of that sex. These are the lessons that individuals take on in learning to achieve a given gender.

LEARNING GENDER: THE CASE OF AGNES

The case history of "Agnes," described by Garfinkel, vividly underscores how gender is achieved (Garfinkel, 1967). When Agnes at age 19 first appeared at the UCLA sex change clinic, she appeared to be a very attractive, well-endowed young woman. Medical inspection revealed she possessed normal-sized male genitalia, no female genitalia, and only feminine secondary sexual characteristics (developed breasts and subcutaneous fat, pelvic girdle, lack of facial and body hair, etc.). A long series of interviews with her ensued, during which it was learned that she had been identified as a boy at birth and raised as such until she was 17. At that age, she decided to "pass" as female. She had come now to the sex change clinic to have her "tumor" removed and a vagina constructed, so that she could have what nature had intended all along. She insisted it was both moral and correct for her to be a female.

In the presentation of her biography, she insisted that she really was a female, misunderstood, and mislabeled. Any questions concerning her past identification as a boy were rejected. According to her account, she never had to line up with the boys in school, never had to undergo a physical examination with boys, and so on. She had taken the stance of any normal adult in this culture. For her, there were only two sexes and she was female and was always meant to be female.

Once she had decided to pass as a woman (although in her terms once she had decided to *be* the sex she was always intended to be), she had to *learn* how women *are* and at the same time avoid being found out. She had to discover, in the process of doing the womanly thing, what the features of the womanly thing were and at the same time keep her genitalia and biography a secret. Put another way, the elements of natural behavior for women, the features women take as given, became continuously problematic for Agnes. The daily taking for granted of one's identity and of knowing how to present that identity to others became an ongoing problem for her. She devised certain practices for withholding information, such as evading questions, speaking in generalities or of impersonal cases, and shifting the conversation away from areas that might potentially disclose her secret. She devised a series of techniques by which she could avoid situations or conversations in which her secret might be revealed; for example, when going swimming with her friends, she wore tight underpants and a skirted suit. Or, when asked for a urine sample during a physical exam for a job and not knowing whether male and female urine are different, she claimed an inability to urinate and later took back her female roommate's sample.

But she also had to learn how to reveal that she was a woman. Much of her learning about the practices of womanhood was developed in the context of the claim that she already knew what they were. Her future mother-in-law, a seamstress, taught her, for example, how to sew and in the process taught her what styles were becoming to her figure, what colors went with her complexion, and how clothing could be used to present the desired image. Much of the learning of gender role behavior, according to her own account, came from the lectures and behaviors of her fiancé. Thus, when he arrived home and found her sunbathing in front of the apartment, he reprimanded her that "nice girls" don't show off that way. He was teaching her not to appear indiscriminately seductive.

The case of Agnes, although extreme, illustrates the manner in which each of us demonstrates that we have achieved a particular gender, that we are naturally what we claim to be. Women in our culture frequently report feeling undressed without mascara or lipstick. Although they are literally dressed in their clothing, they feel undressed as women; that is, the process of "putting-on" one's face is a behavior through which some women *achieve* their gender. Similarly, the baggy-eyed middle-aged man can stand in rumpled pajamas and say to the mirror, "You are the chairman of the board of trustees. Be patient. I'll have you looking the part in half an hour."

One young man said he had been unwilling to buy an iron because he thought the salesclerk would think "he was acting like a girl." Male students have refused to take women's studies courses for fear their masculinity would be questioned.

Similarly, women students report fears that their femininity will be questioned if they do too well in math courses or perform too well against male opponents on the racquetball court.

We all go through a multitude of behaviors daily—from opening doors for a friend to sitting with crossed knees—that are symbolic cues to those around us that we wish to be treated as belonging to one gender or the other. And as we are cuing others about our gender, we are reinforcing our own sense of identity. If one cannot perform the expected gender role behaviors one has set for oneself, one feels demasculinized or defeminized.

This leads us to a very important insight: Gender behavior is both *prescribed* and *chosen*. On the one hand, appropriate behavior is socially shared and transmitted through the culture: People learn what is appropriate for their gender. But, on the other hand, they choose how to present themselves. Therefore, persons have the option to accept or reject cultural definitions of appropriate gender behavior and, consequently, the ability to change either themselves or the culture. The processes by which the culture can (and is) being changed will concern us later. Now, let us look at what American culture defines as natural, normal, appropriate, and preferable for men and women. Let us see what the stereotypes for "masculinity" and "femininity" are. By so doing, we will begin to understand why Agnes, and others like her, chose to have her sex changed surgically—a topic to which we shall shortly return.

MASCULINITY/FEMININITY

In our society, masculinity and femininity have been thought of as *traits* that people have—components of personality. Ideas of "masculinity" and "femininity" have been rather rigid, so rigid that we can talk about them as *sex stereotypes*. The important thing about sex stereotypes—or any stereotypes for that matter—is that they influence how one sees oneself, how one sees others, and how one actually behaves. They have the power to become what Robert Merton referred to as "self-fulfilling prophecies" (1968). If a little girl, for example, expects girls to write neatly, she is likely to work on her penmanship; if a little boy, on the other hand, expects boys to have a messy hand, he will eschew neatness. Indeed, the boy who is neat in his work, a feminine stereotype, may be called a "sissy," and may come to think of himself as nonmasculine.

Psychologists and social psychologists have done a great deal of research over the past 40 years on sex stereotyping (cf. Fernberger, 1948; McKee and Sherrifs, 1957; Rosenkrantz, et al., 1968; Broverman, et al., 1970; Spence and Helmreich, 1978; Deaux and Lewis, 1984; Eagly, 1983). Surprisingly, the results have been fairly consistent: We do have set ideas about how typical males and typical females differ. We have associated different traits with males than we have with females. Let us look at some of this research.

Rosenkrantz and his associates (1968) asked college students to look at a list of bipolar traits—such as "Not at all Aggressive" versus "Very Aggressive" and "Not at all Talkative" versus "Very Talkative." They were asked to check which trait they associated with either an adult male or an adult female and to assess the social desirability of each trait. The students saw adult males as more typically aggressive, independent, objective, self-confident, and so on, and saw females as more typically submissive, dependent, sneaky, illogical, and so on. The researchers noted there were two different *clusters* of traits: a competency cluster associated with males and a warm-expressiveness cluster associated with females. Table 1.1 gives the list of attributes that are found to be stereotypically associated with masculinity and femininity. Of the 38 items that are judged "socially desirable," 70 percent (27) are masculine items.

Following Rosenkrantz's lead, Broverman, et al. (1970) wanted to see whether mental health clinicians held these stereotypes. The researchers wanted to know whether the clinicians associated certain personality traits with mentally healthy females and other traits with mentally healthy males. The mental health clinicians were divided into three groups, with three different sets of instructions. The first group was asked to indicate for each item the pole toward which a normal, healthy, mature, and competent man would tend; the second group was asked to evaluate a mature, healthy, normal, competent woman; and the third group, a mature, healthy, competent adult (sex unspecified).

The researchers found that there were no statistically significant differences in the judgments between male and female clinicians and that there was substantial agreement as to what constituted a healthy male, a healthy female, and a healthy adult. The clinicians also agreed that the socially desirable items were those to be found in a healthy mature adult. Further, they shared the societal consensus about sex role stereotypes and social desirability. Male-valued stereotypic items were more often ascribed to healthy males than to healthy females. Females were associated with characteristics that, in our culture, are considered negative: submissive, easily influenced, not adventurous, dependent, feelings easily hurt, excitable in a crisis, conceited, disliking math and science, subjective. Broverman comments, "This constellation seems a most unusual way of describing any mature, healthy individual" (1970:5).

But perhaps the most significant result of the study was the differentiation clinicians made between women, on the one hand, and men and adults, on the other. These clinicians agreed that the mature adult was substantially equivalent in personality structure to the mature man, but that maturity for a woman was different from that of an adult; that is, there is a double standard of mental health. Put simply, according to these clinicians, for a woman to be considered mature and healthy in this culture, she must behave in ways that are considered socially undesirable and immature for a competent adult. There exists, then, a culturally constructed conflict situation for women. If they choose to act in the more socially desirable and adult ways preferred by their culture, they risk having their femininity questioned. If, however, they choose to act in the prescribed feminine way, they may not be treated as adults. These clinicians, who are highly educated and presumably more sensitive and informed than the general population, sex stereotype; we would expect the general population's thinking to be even more stereotypical.

More recently, researchers interested in sex stereotyping have been concerned with it along a number of different dimensions—traits, role behaviors, occupations,

Table 1.1   CLINICAL JUDGMENTS OF MENTAL HEALTH*

Competency cluster: Masculine pole is judged more socially desirable	
Feminine Pole	**Masculine Pole**
Not at all aggressive	Very aggressive
Not at all independent	Very independent
Very emotional	Not at all emotional
Does not hide emotions at all	Almost always hides emotions
Very subjective	Very objective
Very easily influenced	Not at all easily influenced
Very submissive	Very dominant
Dislikes math and science very much	Likes math and science very much
Very excitable in a minor crisis	Not at all excitable in a minor crisis
Very passive	Very active
Not at all competitive	Very competitive
Very illogical	Very logical
Very home-oriented	Very worldly
Not at all skilled in business	Very skilled in business
Very sneaky	Very direct
Does not know the way of the world	Knows the way of the world
Feelings easily hurt	Feelings not easily hurt
Not at all adventurous	Very adventurous
Has difficulty making decisions	Can make decisions easily
Cries very easily	Never cries
Almost never acts as a leader	Almost always acts as a leader
Not at all self-confident	Very self-confident
Very uncomfortable about being aggressive	Not at all uncomfortable about being aggressive
Not at all ambitious	Very ambitious
Unable to separate feelings from ideas	Easily able to separate feelings from ideas
Very dependent	Not at all dependent
Very conceited about appearance	Never conceited about appearance

Warm-expressiveness cluster: Feminine pole is judged more socially desirable	
Feminine Pole	**Masculine Pole**
Very talkative	Not at all talkative
Very tactful	Very blunt
Very gentle	Very rough
Very aware of feelings of others	Not at all aware of feelings of others
Very religious	Not at all religious
Very interested in own appearance	Not at all interested in own appearance
Very neat in habits	Very sloppy in habits
Very quiet	Very loud
Very strong need for security	Very little need for security
Enjoys art and literature very much	Does not enjoy art and literature at all
Easily expresses tender feelings	Does not express tender feelings at all

*Adapted from Broverman, et al., 1970:3, with permission of authors and publisher.

and physical appearance (Deaux and Lewis, 1984; Eagly, 1983). Each of these has associated with it "masculine and feminine versions," which are "significantly more strongly associated with males and females, respectively," but not exclusively so (Deaux and Lewis, 1984:992); that is, the emphasis of this new research is on the *relative* rather than on the *absolute* nature of sex stereotyping. Looked for are probability judgments as to whether the average person of a given sex would or would not possess a particular characteristic, rather than rigid categorization.

Using this probability approach to sex stereotyping, Deaux found that college students, nevertheless, still differentially associate particular traits and behavior with males and females (1984); for example, men were seen as more likely to be competitive and independent, women as warm and emotional. Men were viewed as the financial providers and initiators of sex, whereas women were assigned to child care and food preparation. Although this was true, however, she also discovered that the rigid stereotyping was breaking down: Students could imagine independent, competitive, muscular women and warm, child-tending, graceful men.

Although sex stereotyping is breaking down in the society, it has not disappeared. Perhaps one of the best ways to grasp the impact of it is to return to the issue of transsexualism. *Why* would a person find it necessary to have a sex change operation, and why would clinicians and surgeons condone it?

TRANSSEXUALISM: INCARNATING SEX STEREOTYPING

Sex change operations have become increasingly frequent and a complex medical technology has been developed to treat those with "gender dysphoria" or "the belief that they are trapped in the wrong (sex) body." Biological explanations of transsexualism have blamed "hormones" (cf. Money and Ehrhardt, 1972), while psychological explanations have blamed mothers, especially "mother-smothering" and/or "mother-neglect" (cf. Stohler, 1975). Neither explanation seems adequate (cf. Raymond, 1978). Rather, it is highly likely that a culture "which generates rigid stereotypes of masculinity and femininity is itself the *primary* cause of transsexualism; the 'essence' of 'masculinity' and 'femininity' become reified and incarnated in the organs and body of the other sex" (Raymond, 1978). Persons choose to exchange bodies and to exchange one stereotype for another because gender stereotyping is deeply embedded and ambiguity not tolerated. Within a society with rigid sex stereotyping, it seems perfectly reasonable to change a person's body to adjust to the mind, if the mind refuses to adjust to the body.

The goal of "sex reassignment surgery" is to turn a man as much as anatomically possible into a woman, or a woman as much as anatomically possible into a man. The surgery is expensive, time-consuming, arduous, and *painful*. A male-to-female transsexual will be treated with hormones, his excess hair removed through electrolysis, his face altered through plastic surgery and hair implants, and his breasts enlarged with silicones. Following these medical experiences, he lives as a female for six months to two years, during which time he is taught how to "pass" as a female. If successful in fulfilling the stereotype, his male sex organs are removed and an artificial vagina constructed (cf. Money and Wiedeking, 1980).

To sex reassign a female is even more expensive and complicated. After she is treated with hormones to stimulate facial hair growth, lower her voice, and stop her ovulation cycle, her breasts and uterus are surgically removed. After a period of living like a man, and acting stereotypically like one, she can request an artificial penis; if fitted with an hydraulic device, the penis can become erect.

Given the pain, the complexity, and the expense, persons who voluntarily choose sex reassignment surgery must be very determined—so determined that they are willing to undergo "body mutilation—the willful destruction of physically healthy" tissues and organs "for purely *social* reasons" (Eichler, 1980:87). Furthermore, clinicians and surgeons must be very committed to proper gender behavior to justify to themselves and to the medical community the removal of healthy tissues for basically *cosmetic* reasons. For no matter how good the surgery, the transsexual can never fully function *sexually* after reassignment surgery. A constructed female does not lubricate, wears a vagina "spacer," and cannot bear children or lactate; a constructed male cannot ejaculate or sire a child.

Transsexuals request these operations because they have an excessively narrow idea of what constitutes sex-appropriate behavior, and there are surgeons and clinicians who share their narrow vision. As Eichler suggests, "were the notions of masculinity and femininity less rigid, sex change operations would be unnecessary" (1980:75).

Striking in the accounts of transsexuals are their inflexible attribution of "masculine" traits to males and "feminine" traits to females and their strong beliefs that men *should* act like men, women like women. Jan Morris, a transsexual, expresses this sex stereotyping in her autobiography, *Conundrum*, as the following excerpt illustrates: ". . . my own opinion of the female principle was one of gentleness as against force, forgiveness rather than punishment, give more than take, helping more than leading" (1974:12). In other words, Jan Morris could not conceive of a male as gentle, forgiving, giving, and helping, or of a female as forceful, punishing, taking, and leading. She believes in rigidly identifying character traits with biological sex.

Moreover, it is likely that male-to-female transsexuals also rigidly subscribe to the cultural belief in the superiority of men. In Jan Morris' autobiography, for example, we find the following homage to masculinity:

> It is the feeling of unfluctuating control, I think, that women cannot share, and it springs from the body. . . . I look back at these moments of supreme male fitness as one remembers champagne or a morning swim. . . . I never mind the swagger of young men. It is their right to swank, and I know the sensation (1974:89–91).

Morris lived, when she was James, what might be considered a supermacho life. He was trained in military school, partook in competitions, climbed Mt. Everest. Yet, according to the autobiography, no matter what feats he set himself as a male or what his accomplishments, the high ideals of masculinity were never attained. By placing masculinity on a pedestal, the male-to-female transsexual finds himself unworthy and unable to live up to the honor of being a male; not meeting the ideal, he becomes a woman. By becoming a *heterosexual* woman, he gains entry into that exalted masculine world, a world he basically respects and cherishes, but for which he was unworthy when he was a man.

Valuing the "masculine" above the "feminine," the male-to-female transsexual acts and appears like a stereotypical man's idea of a woman—fancy coiffures, heavy makeup, precise speech, strong identification with housewifery and domesticity, and dedication to finding and pleasing "Mr. Right" (Raymond, 1978). Jan Morris' exaltation of "femininity"—"her frailty is her strength, her inferiority is her privilege"—does not sound at all like a woman, but like a male-stereotypical *idea* of womanhood (cf. Rebecca West's 1975 review of Jan Morris' *Conundrum*).

Transsexuals elect surgery so that they can fulfill their rigid definitions of sex-appropriate behaviors. That greater sex role rigidity is expected of men in this society may explain, in part, why most of the sex reassignment surgeries are male-to-female.[1] Satisfaction after surgery is measured by fulfilling sex-typed *roles*, not by fulfilling oneself *sexually* (Eichler, 1980:87); the greatest satisfaction postoperative transsexuals report is being socially accepted as women by women and others.

Such surgery is a testimony, then, to the depth of sex stereotyping. Individuals who seek sex reassignment surgery are judged "treatable"—*not treated* is the *cultural* rigidity that produces transsexuals. The surgery assumes that an individual cannot achieve certain *social* goals while "trapped" in a particular body. This identification of personality characteristics and anatomy is so strong that patients and doctors collude to treat transsexualism as a medical-technical and psychiatric problem, rather than as the social and political issue it is.

In the last analysis, however, it is important to recognize that transsexualism is one extreme and obvious result of sex stereotyping; however, less extreme and more subtle results of gender typing are common in our everyday worlds. There is no way for us fully to escape sex stereotyping ourselves and others, for we have inherited a culture that continues to categorize and stereotype people based on their sex.

In this culture, males and the "masculine" are considered superior to females and the "feminine." Indeed, *androcentrism* (also sometimes referred to as *sexism*, *male chauvinism*, or *patriarchalism*) exists in all industrialized societies—socialist and capitalist, democratic and authoritarian. Patriarchalism is to culture as a rhythm section is to a band. Sometimes it overrides the melodic theme and sometimes it is hushed—but it is always there. When we have been listening to a band for hours and hours, we lose awareness of the rhythm as distinct from the totality of the music. Similarly, the principle of male superiority after hundreds of years has become so embedded in the culture that we unconsciously behave and think in ways that perpetuate it.

---

[1]Some other reasons why more males elect to become females than vice versa are:(1) less cost and complexity; (2) fewer social movement alternatives for men (a woman who rejects gender stereotypes can find support in the feminist movement; a man does not have that option to the same degree and is more likely to view the problem as an *individual* and personal one); (3) socialization of men to see sexuality as resting in one's genitals, which are *objects*. As such, to change one's sexuality, it makes "sense" to remove one set of genitals and to add the other kind.

How is it that persons learn so thoroughly the values of the culture that they unquestionably consider them to be natural? They do so through a process called *socialization*. Socialization is accomplished through communication; it is through communication that our ideas about gender are learned and perpetuated. It behooves us, therefore, to look rather closely at what our language has taught us about the sexes.

☐ ☐ 2 ☐ ☐

Language:
The Inescapable Socializer

"Smile, honey. Be nice. Look good. But, be careful. Don't act like 'you're asking for it.' Do well in school, but not better than your boyfriend! Don't be too successful or no man will want you. Anyway, you'll find your greatest joy in being a mother and wife." All women in this society have heard these messages.

"Go get'em Tiger. Prepare yourself for a good job so you can be a good provider for your wife and kids. Choose a wife who will be a good helpmate and good mother, but, it's okay if you have a little fun on the side. All work and no play makes Jack a dull boy. Get it! Ha! Ha!" All men in this society have heard these messages.

You may protest, "People don't expect *me* to be like that." As one woman student wrote in a journal kept for a sociology class, "I consider myself fortunate. My parents never told me to act like a girl; they wanted me to have a career and always talked to me like I would." Or, as a male student wrote, "I don't understand what the fuss is about. My parents never hassled me about being a big career man. They just wanted me to be a good person, happy, and contented with my life."

Unfortunately, despite the protestations and claims to a gender-free rearing, it is impossible for a person who is socialized into this culture to escape the culturally prescribed gender stereotyping. This is so because we all have learned verbal and nonverbal language that encapsulates gender stereotyping.[1]

The world can be thought about in many different ways. The language that we acquire as children provides the lens through which we see and, therefore, structure the world. Language is not a piece of clothing we put on and take off at will; rather, it is more like a mold into which young minds are poured. In the process of learning the language, the child learns how to think like other members of the society.

This means that much of what we define as reality is merely that portion of life

[1]For an excellent annotated bibliography, see Kramarae, et al., 1983.

that we have learned to identify verbally. Through language, we abstract and select from the myriad of sensory impressions those elements that are considered relevant; by means of our categories, we make sense out of the world and assimilate our experiences.

A few examples might clarify the relevance of language for the structuring of thought. In English, we take for granted such notions as causality, temporal sequence, and the existence of the individual. It is almost impossible for us to think in noncausal ways, to imagine life *without* the concept of time, or an ''I'' as inseparable from a ''we.'' Yet, societies do exist where these ideas are incorporated into the language and are taken for granted. Similarly, ideas about gender are deeply embedded in our language and become nonconscious, taken-for-granted elements of our thought structure—for example, the idea that the two sexes are absolutely distinct from one another.

Language, however, does more than reflect thought patterns—it also structures in great part the nature of our social relations. In acquiring language—both verbal and nonverbal—we are learning to be the kinds of people judged appropriate in our society.

Communication is a complex ''multichanneled system . . . of behavior'' (Scheflen, 1974:3) in which persons of a common culture share a common code for conveying messages. Much of communication is communication *about* the communication process itself (metacommunication) and is conveyed nonverbally through gestures, postures, and facial expressions. These are used to perpetuate or alter the ongoing communication; that is, the communication system itself transmits the culture and thereby constrains behavior. It is a ''means of regulating *all* types of behavior and/or maintaining social order and social control'' (Scheflen, 1974:4). With the acquisition of language, we learn *how* to interact with others; with this acquisition, we become communicating human beings.

The life of Helen Keller, born blind and deaf, amply illustrates the point. Before she learned to communicate, she was considered incorrigible, alone in a sightless, soundless world. Through the patient work of her teacher, she not only learned how to communicate but also how to be a social human being; the kind of social human being she became was the one appropriate to her cultural milieu.

Language perpetuates the thought structure and social patterns by continuously reiterating them. When parents, teachers, or television programs communicate to the young, they use both the verbal and nonverbal languages of the culture; indeed, even when we dream, we communicate to ourselves in these languages. It is inescapable. The consequence of this omnipresence is that we are perpetually being labeled by ourselves and others along gender-stereotypic dimensions.

When people are *labeled*, they are treated in accordance with that label, and consequently they learn to see themselves as persons who deserve that label and come to act accordingly (Scheff, 1966; Becker, 1970). Men and women ''come to see themselves as others see them'' (Cooley, 1902:151). They nonconsciously apply labels to themselves and, then, subsequently act in ways compatible with the labels.

Because verbal and nonverbal languages can be so subtle and pervasive, we need to look closely at the ideas about gender within them. In addition, we will explore sex differences in speech patterns and strategies, and reevaluate the male speech practices as the appropriate standard for judging female speech practices.

VERBAL COMMUNICATION

Everyone in our society regardless of class, ethnicity, sex, age, or race is exposed to the same language—the language of the dominant culture.

Analysis of verbal language can tell us a great deal about a people's fears, prejudices, anxieties, and interests. A rich vocabulary on a particular subject indicates societal interests or obsessions (e.g., the extensive vocabulary about cars in America). Also, different words for the same subject (such as *freedom fighter* or *terrorist*, *passed away* or *croaked*, *make love* or *ball*) show that there is a range of attitudes and feelings in the society toward that subject.

It should not be surprising, then, to find rooted in the linguistic structure differential attitudes and feelings about men and women. Although language has not been completely analyzed, six general propositions concerning ideas about males and females that are inherent in the language can be made.

First, in terms of grammatic and semantic structure, women do not have a fully autonomous, independent existence; they are part of man. Our language is not divided into male and female with distinct conjugations and declensions as is characteristic of many other languages. Rather, women are supposedly included under the generic *man*. Grammar books specify that the pronoun *he* can be used generically to refer to he or she. Further, *man*, when used as an indefinite pronoun, grammatically supposedly refers to both men and women. So, for example, when we read *man* in the following phrases, we are to interpret it as applying to both men and women: "man the oars," "one small step for man, one giant step for mankind," "man, that's tough," "man overboard," "man the Toolmaker," "alienated man," "garbage man." Our rules of etiquette complete the grammatical presumption of inclusivity. When two persons are pronounced "man and wife," Miss Susan Jones changes her entire name to Mrs. Robert Gordon (Vanderbilt, 1972: chapter 6). In each of these correct usages, women are a part of man; they do not exist autonomously. The exclusion of women is well expressed in Mary Daly's ear-jarring slogan "the sisterhood of man" (1973:7–21).

However, there is some question as to whether the theory that man means everybody is carried out in practice (cf. Kramerae, et al., 1975; Bendix, 1979; Martyna, 1980); for example, an 8-year-old interrupts her reading of *The Story of the Cavemen* to ask how we got here without cavewomen. A 10-year-old thinks it dumb to have a woman post*man*. A beginning anthropology student believes (incorrectly) that all shamans (witch doctors) are males because her textbook and professor use the referential pronoun *he*.

However, beginning language learners are not the only ones who visualize males when they see the word *man*. Research has consistently demonstrated that when the generic *man* is used, people visualize men, not women (Schneider and Hacker, 1973; DeStefano, 1976; Mackay, 1983; Martyna, 1978; Hamilton and

Henley, 1982). DeStefano, for example, reports that college students choose sil-houettes of males for sentences with the word *man* or *men* in them. Similarly, the presumably generic *he* elicits images of men, rather than women. The finding is so persistent that linguists have begun to refer to the generic *he* as a prescriptive *he* and they doubt whether there actually is a semantic generic in English (cf. Mackay, 1983).

Man, then, does not suggest humanity, but rather *male images*. Moreover, over one's lifetime, an educated American will be exposed to the prescriptive *he* over one million times (Mackay, 1983). One consequence is the exclusion of women in the visualization, imagination, and thought of males and females. Most likely, this linguistic practice perpetuates in men their feelings of dominance over and responsibility for women—feelings that interfere with the development of equality in relationships.

Second, in actual practice, our pronoun usage perpetuates different person-ality attributes and career aspirations for men and women. Nurses, secretaries, and elementary school teachers are almost invariably referred to as *she*; doctors, engi-neers, electricians, and presidents as *he*. In one classroom, students referred to an unidentified child as *he* and then, interestingly, shifted to *she* when discussing the child's parent. In a faculty discussion of the problems of acquiring new staff, architects, engineers, security officers, faculty, and computer programmers were all referred to as *he*; maids, secretaries, and file clerks were referred to as *she*. Martyna (1978) has noted that speakers consistently use *he* when the referent is a high-status occupation (e.g., doctor, lawyer, judge), but they shift to *she* when the occupations are of lower-status (e.g., nurse, secretary).

Even our choice of sex ascription to nonhuman objects subtly reinforces different personalities for males and females. It seems as though the small (e.g., kittens), the graceful (e.g., poetry), the unpredictable (e.g., the fates), the nurturant (e.g., the church, the school), and that which is owned and/or controlled by men (e.g., boats, cars, governments, nations) represent the feminine, whereas that which is a controlled forceful power in and of itself (e.g., God, satan, tigers) primarily represents the masculine. Even athletic teams are not immune. Men's teams are called, for example, *Wolverines* and *Cougars*, while the women's are disempowered and tagged *Lady Wolverines* and *Lady Cougars*. In one college, the men's teams are called the *Bearcats*, and the women's teams, the *Bearkittens*.

Some of you may wonder how much it matters that the female is included in the male. The inclusion of women under the pseudo-generic *man* and the prescrip-tive *he*, however, are not trivial issues. Language has tremendous power to shape attitudes and influence behavior. Indeed, Mackay (1983) argues that the prescriptive *he* "has all the characteristics of a highly effective propaganda technique": frequent repetition; early age of acquisition (before age 6); covertness (*he* is not thought of as propaganda); use in high-prestige sources (including university texts); and indirect-ness (presented as though it was a matter of common knowledge).

As a result, the prescriptive affects females' feelings of well-being and sense of life options. For example, Adamsky (1981) found that women's sense of power and importance was enhanced when the prescriptive *he* was replaced with *she*.

Furthermore, female children (McArthur and Eisen, 1976) and high schoolers (Bem and Bem, 1973) were found less likely to choose career achievement after reading text with the prescriptive *he*.

Awareness of the impact of the generic *man* and prescriptive *he* has generated considerable activity to change the language. One change, approved of by the Modern Language Association, is to replace the prescriptive *he* with the plural *they*—which was the usage prior to the eighteenth century (Bodine, 1975); another is the use of "he or she." Although at first sounding awkward, the "he or she" designation is increasingly being used in speech practices in the media and among people who have recognized the power of the pronoun to perpetuate sex stereotyping. When a professor, for example, talks about the occupation, lawyer, and refers to the lawyer as "he or she," a speech pattern that counteracts sex stereotyping is modeled. This drive to neutralize the impact of pronouns is evidenced, further, in the renaming of the occupations in the United States, such as the replacement of policeman with police officer, postman with mail carrier, stewardess with flight attendant.

Third, linguistic practice defines females as immature, incompetent, and incapable and males as mature, complete, and competent. Apparently, the words *man* and *woman* tend to connote sexual and human maturity. Consequently, in common speech, organizational titles, public addresses, and on bathroom doors, *lady* is frequently substituted for *woman*. Simply contrast the different connotations of *lady* and *woman* in the following common phrases:

> Luck, be a lady (woman) tonight.
>
> Barbara's a little lady (woman).
>
> Ladies' (Women's) Air Corps

In the first two examples, the use of *lady* desexualizes the contextual meaning of *woman*. So trivializing is the use of *lady* in the last phrase that it sounds wholly anomalous. The male equivalent, *lord*, is never used; and the synonym, *gentleman*, is used infrequently. When *gentleman* is used, the assumption seems to be that certain culturally condoned aspects of masculinity (e.g., aggressivity, activity, and strength) should be set aside in the interests of maturity and order, as exemplified in the following phrases:

> A gentlemen's (men's) agreement
>
> A duel between gentlemen (men)
>
> He's a real gentleman (man).

Rather than requiring males to set aside the stereotypes associated with *man*, the opposite frequently occurs. The contextual connotation of *man* places a strain on males to be continuously sexually and socially potent, as the following examples illustrate:

I was not a man (gentleman) with her tonight.

This is a man's (gentleman's) job.

Be a man (gentleman).

Whether males, therefore, feel competent or anxious, valuable or worthless in particular contexts is influenced by the demands placed on them by the expectations of the language.

Not only are men rarely called *gentlemen*, but they are seldom labeled *boys*. The term *boy* is reserved for young males, bellhops, car attendants, and as a put-down to those males judged inferior. *Boy* connotes immaturity and powerlessness. Only occasionally do males "have a night out with the boys." They do not talk "boy talk" at the office. Rarely does our language legitimize carefreeness in males. Rather, they are expected, linguistically, to adopt the responsibilities of manhood.

On the other hand, women of all ages may be called *girls*. Grown females "play bridge with the girls" and indulge in "girl talk." Although they are allowed to remain childlike, the implication is that they are basically immature and without power. Men can become men, linguistically, putting aside the immaturity of childhood; indeed, for them to retain the openness and gamefulness of boyhood is linguistically difficult.

Further, the presumed incompetence and immaturity of women are evidenced by the "linguistic" company they keep. Women are categorized with children— "women and children first"; the infirm—"the blind, the lame, the women"; and the incompetent—"women, convicts, and idiots" (New York's old franchise law).

The use of these categorical designations is not accidental happenstance; ". . . rather these selectional groupings are powerful forces behind the actual expressions of language and are based on distinctions which are not regarded as trivial by the speakers of the language" (Key, 1975:82). A total language analysis of categorical groupings is not available, and yet it seems likely that women tend to be included in groupings that designate incompleteness, ineptitude, and immaturity. On the other hand, it is difficult for us to conceive of the word *man* in any categorical grouping other than one that extends beyond humanity, such as "Man, apes, and angels" or "Man and Superman"; that is, men do exist as an independent category capable of autonomy; women are grouped with the stigmatized, the immature, and the foolish. Moreover, when men are in human groupings, males are invariably first in the list—"men and women," "he and she," "man and wife" (Iritani and West, 1983). This order is not accidental, but it was prescribed in the sixteenth century to honor the worthier party (Bodine, 1975).

Fourth, in practice women are defined in terms of their sexual desirability (to men); men are defined in terms of their sexual prowess (over women). Most slang words in reference to women refer to their sexual desirability to men (e.g., *dog, fox, broad, piece, ass, chick*, etc.). Slang about men refers to their sexual prowess over women (e.g., *dude, stud, hunk*, etc.). The fewer examples given for men is not an oversight. In an analysis of sexual slang, for example, more than 1000 words and phrases that derogate women sexually were listed, while there were "nowhere near this multitude for describing men'' (Kramerae, 1975:72). Farmer and Henley (cited in Schulz, 1975) list 500 synonyms for *prostitute*, for example, and only 65 for *whoremonger*. Stanley (1977) reports 220 terms for a sexually promiscuous woman and only 22 for a sexually promiscuous man. Shuster (1973) reports that the passive verb form is used in reference to women's sexual experiences (e.g., *to be laid*, *to be had*, *to be taken*), whereas the active tense is used in reference to the male's (e.g., *lay*, *take*, *have*). Being sexually attractive to males is culturally condoned for women and being sexually powerful is approved for males. In these regards, the slang of the street is certainly not counterculture; rather, it perpetuates and reinforces different expectations as sexual objects and performers.

Further, we find sexual connotations associated with neutral words applied to women. A few examples should suffice. A male academician questioned the title of a new course, asserting it was ''too suggestive.'' The title?—''The Position of Women in the Social Order.'' A male *tramp* is simply a ''hobo,'' but a female *tramp* is a ''slut.'' And consider the difference in connotation of the following expressions:

It's easy.

He's easy.

She's easy.

In the first, we assume something is ''easy to do''; in the second, we might assume a professor is an ''easy grader'' or a man is ''easy-go-lucky.'' But when we read ''she's easy,'' the connotation is ''she's an easy lay.''

In the world of slang, men are defined by their sexual prowess. In the world of slang and proper speech, women are defined as sexual objects. The rule in practice seems to be, if in doubt, assume that *any* reference to a woman has a sexual connotation. For both genders, the constant bombardment of prescribed sexuality is bound to have real consequences.

Fifth, women are defined in terms of their relationships to men; men are defined in terms of their relationship to the world at large. A good example in our language usage are the words *master* and *mistress*. Originally, these words had the same meaning—''the power held by a person over servants.'' With the demise of the feudal system, however, these words took on different meanings. The masculine variant metaphorically refers to power over something; that is, ''He is the master of his trade''; the feminine variant metaphorically (although probably not in actuality) refers to power over a man sexually; that is, ''She is Tom's mistress.'' Men are defined in terms of their power in the occupational world; women in terms of their sexual power over men.

The existence of two contractions for *Mistress* (*Miss* and *Mrs.*) and but one for *Mister* (*Mr.*) underscores the cultural concern and linguistic practice: Women are defined in relationship to men. The recent preference of many women to be called *Ms.* is an attempt to provide an equivalency title for women that is not dependent upon marital status. Even a divorced woman is defined in terms of her no-longer existing relationship to a man; she is still *Mrs.* Man's Name. Apparently the man's divorced state is not relevant enough to the man or to the society to even require a label. A divorced woman is a *divorcée*, but what do you call a divorced man?

Sixth, there is an historical pattern such that originally neutral words for women acquire obscene and/or debased connotations, a pattern of derogation that does not hold for neutral words referring to men. The processes of *pejoration* (the acquiring of an obscene or debased connotation) and *amelioration* (the reacquiring of a neutral or positive connotation) in the English language regarding terms for males and females have been studied extensively by Muriel Schulz (1975). It is to her work that we now turn.

Leveling is the least derogative form of pejoration. Through leveling, titles that originally referred to an elite class of persons come to include a wider class of persons. Such democratic leveling is more common for female designates than for male. For example, contrast the following: *Lord-Lady* (*lady*); *Baronet-Dame* (*dame*); *Governor-Governess* (*governess*).

Most frequently, what happens to words designating women as they become pejorated, however, is that they come to denote or connote sexual wantonness; for example, *Sir* and *Mister* remain titles of courtesy; however, at some time *Madam*, *Miss*, and *Mistress* respectively have become synonyms for *brothel-keeper*, *prostitute*, and *unmarried sexual partner of a male* (Schulz, 1975:66).

Names for domestic helpers, if they are females, are frequently derogated; for example, *hussy* originally meant "housewife." *Laundress, needlewoman, spinster* ("tender of the spinning wheel"), and *nurse* all referred to domestic occupations within the home, and all at some point became slang expressions for "prostitute" or "mistress."

Even kinship terms referring to women become denigrated. During the seventeenth century, *mother* was used to mean "a bawd"; more recently *mother* (*moth-uh*—) has become a common derogatory epithet (Cameron, 1974). Probably at some point in history, every kinship term for females has been derogated (Schulz, 1975:66).

Terms of endearment for women, also seem to follow a downward path. Pet names such as *Tart, Dolly, Kitty, Polly, Mopsy, Biddy,* and *Jill* all eventually became sexually derogative (Schulz, 1975:67). *Whore* comes from the same Latin root as *care* and once meant "a lover of either sex."

Indeed, even the most neutral categorical designations—girl, female, woman, lady—at some point in their history have been used to connote sexual immorality. *Girl* originally meant "a child of either sex"; through the process of semantic degeneration, it eventually meant "a prostitute." Although *girl* has lost this meaning, *girlie* still retains sexual connotations. *Woman* connoted "a mistress" in the early nineteenth century; *female* was a degrading epithet in the latter part of the nineteenth century; and when *lady* was introduced as a euphemism, it too became deprecatory. "Even so neutral a term as *person*, when it was used as substitute for *woman*, suffered [vulgarization]" (Mencken, 1963:350, quoted in Schulz, 1975:71).

Whether one looks at elite titles, occupational roles, kinship relationships, endearments, or age and sex categorical designations, the pattern is clear. Terms referring to females are pejorated—"become negative in the middle instances and abusive in the extremes" (Schulz, 1975:69). Such semantic derogation, however, is not evidenced for male referents. *Lord, baronet, father, brother, nephew, footman, bowman, boy, lad, fellow, gentleman, man, male*, and so on, "have failed to undergo the derogation found in the history of their corresponding feminine designations" (Schulz, 1975:67). Interestingly, rather than derogating the male referent, a female referent frequently is used to debase a male; for example, a weak man is referred to as a *sissy* (diminutive of sister), and an army recruit during basic training is called a *pussy*. When one is swearing at a male, he is referred to as a *bastard* or a *son-of-a-bitch*—both appellations that impugn the dignity of the man's mother.

In summary, these verbal practices are consistent with the gender stereotypes that we encountered in Chapter 1. Women are thought to be a part of man, non-autonomous, dependent, relegated to roles that require few skills, characteristically incompetent and immature, sexual objects, best defined in terms of their relationships to men. On the other hand, males are visible, autonomous and independent, responsible for the protection and containment of women, expected to occupy positions based on their high achievement or physical power, assumed to be sexually potent, and defined primarily by their relationships to the world of work. For both genders, the use of the language perpetuates the stereotypes and limits the options available for self-definition.

NONVERBAL COMMUNICATION

As important as verbal communication is in the structuring of thought and relationships, there is some evidence to support the hypothesis that *nonverbal* communication is more salient for the transmission of attitudes and the maintenance of interpersonal relationships. One estimate is that the nonverbal cues are approximately four times as strong as verbal ones (Argyle, et al., 1970:222; also see Henley, et al., 1985; Sachs, 1985).

Gender differences in nonverbal communication do exist. Men and women systematically communicate nonverbally in interpersonal distances, gestures and postures, demeanors and etiquette, different self-images and different statuses. These nonverbal signs communicate male dominance, independence, and activity, and female submissiveness, dependence, and passivity.

Let us look at the use of space first.

Space

Social space is not empty or silent, nor is it distributed randomly. Rather, all indications from animal and human research suggest that there is a direct association between the amount of space surrounding a person and his or her dominance (Sommer, 1969). Professors stand behind lecterns on raised platforms, while students are arranged equidistantly side by side, row by row. The size of an executive's desk is directly proportionate to his/her position in the hierarchy of the organization. More space is given to the rich, the titled, the famous, and the powerful than to those who lack those attributes. Not only is more space allotted to higher-status persons, but also that space is more highly evaluated, for with it come "the resources, the privileges, the pleasures of the powerful; that is, what 'position' means in life" (Henley, 1977:42).

The principle of the higher the status, the greater the space, when applied to males and females, suggests that even when their other statuses are ostensibly equal (e.g., both executives, both professors, both parents), greater personal space is given to the male; for example, executive and professional women are often assigned smaller offices in less advantageous areas than their male peers; and husbands are more likely to have a room of their own or a chair of their own, and to use more than their proportionate share of the double bed (Altman and Nelson, 1972, referred to in Henley, 1977).

The status differentiation between males' and females' access to space, however, is especially telling when we consider the nonconscious use of interpersonal distance. Laboratory experiments and field observations yield the same results. Women's space is invaded more than is men's space. People approach women more closely and sit closer to them than they do men. Moreover, men cut across women's paths more frequently than vice versa, and women are more likely to step aside for men (Henley, 1985; Silveira, 1972). Chivalry, apparently, does not extend to relinquishing spatial dominance, and the right to intrude into a woman's space.

The final invasion of personal space is, of course, *touching*. Although touching may symbolize intimacy, it also symbolizes status (Goffman, 1967:75). In general, the principle is that those with higher status touch those with lower status: The physician touches the orderly; the teacher, the pupil; the coach, the football player; the police officer, the accused; the priest, the supplicant. Women as a group—perhaps due to their roles as secretaries, mothers, nurses, and so on, or perhaps due to their status as women—are probably touched by more people in more settings than are men (cf. Henley, 1977:94–117).

Males initiate touching more often than females, and in public settings, the touching routine is fairly standardized. For example, in a movie theater or bar, the male's arm is over the female's shoulder; her response is to cuddle close, as if to have her own personal space wrapped up inside of his. Cuddling, a *submissive* response (Henley, 1973:17), is rarely observed in men in public settings. Further, more of the females' body is routinely touched in public than that of the male's. But perhaps the most subtle dominance differential is in couples walking side by side, hand in hand, apparent equals; invariably the male's hand is clasped in front of the female's so that he is leading. Finally, men touch women, aggressively: Male customers paw at and pinch waitresses; men hold women upside down at the edge of swimming pools, swing them and dunk them; male college students throw water bombs at college women. Women are spanked and restrained by men in "play."

In brief, women are accorded less personal space than are men, are subject to more invasions of it by more persons, and are more likely to be the submissive recipients of the touch of intimacy and the powerless recipients of the touch of "playful" aggression; that is, in terms of one of the primary dimensions of interpersonal relationships—space—(Brown, 1965:78–82), women have lower status and less power.

Demeanor

Goffman describes demeanor as that which is conveyed through one's dress, bearing, and deportment (1967). Many differences between males and females in dress, bearing, and deportment are obvious. Adorned and decorated, women's bodies and faces become virtual art objects, "things" of beauty to be observed and evaluated (cf. Banner, 1983; Brownmiller, 1984). Skirts, high-heeled shoes, and purses restrict freedom of movement and contribute to a bearing of propriety and a quiet and passive deportment. Indeed, a "loose" woman is portrayed in loose clothes, untamed hair, and floppy body postures (Henley, 1977:91). Male dress emphasizes greater ruggedness, greater uniformity (the pinstripe suit, jeans and shirt), and greater freedom of movement (pants, flat-heeled shoes, *pockets*). The male is not a beauty object, his bearing is quasi-military, and his deportment is active and (comparatively) loud.

Despite the appearance of similar professional and casual styles for men and women—fashion in which the female adopts the male standard—major differences in how women and men dress persist. Indeed, some argue that these differences are growing greater, rather than diminishing (Nonkin, 1986). Women's styles are becoming more stereotypically feminine, as witnessed by the "hooker" look (tight jeans, slit skirts, cleavage revealed, gaudy color combinations), the "damsel" look (flounced skirts, lace blouses, teddies, lace slips—showing), and the "femme fatale" look (fitted bodices, tight skirts, black shiny fabrics). In contrast, men's fashion palette is still primarily the gray suit with the conservative silk tie. What is particularly fascinating about men's and women's clothing, though, is that the greatest difference in dress occurs when the situation is defined as a potentially romantic and special one. Visualize for just a moment how different the male and female students look on prom night.

Beneath the clothing of men and women, there are also many differences in demeanor. Between equals, the social norms that govern demeanor are symmetrical (Goffman, 1967:78). As might be expected, the norms that govern the demeanor of males and females are not symmetrical, though; for example, people try to maintain eye contact with persons whose approval they want; women try to maintain mutual eye contact longer with men than men do with women (Henley, et al., 1985:180). The stare, on the other hand, is perceived of as an aggressive act by both animals and humans (Ellsworth, et al., 1972:310). When a woman looks directly at a man, she usually tilts her head, a submissive gesture that renders her stare ambivalent, if not submissive (O'Connor, 1970:9). Furthermore, when a man stares at a woman, she will avert her eyes, drop her eyelids, tilt her head, and perhaps smile—all appeasement gestures (Henley, 1977:176). Indeed, smiling is a strong sign of appeasement used by apes and monkeys, as well as by women and children. It signifies that the subordinate party intends no harm to the dominant party. Women smile more and more expansively than men do, whether they are happy or not. Women smile so much that some have referred to their smile as a "nervous habit" (Henley, et al., 1985:181), and others have analyzed the smile as a necessary component of the "feminine" occupations, such as that of flight attendants (cf. Hochschild, 1983).

Using a demeanor that is self-revealing or self-hiding is another way in which an imbalance between men and women persists. Women tend to be more revealing—in their clothing, in their facial expressions, and in their body gestures than do men. A well-demeaned young woman in this society is expected to be open and self-disclosing, whereas a well-demeaned young man hides his feelings and emotions. The difference has important implications, for in American society, persons with higher status are not expected to reveal much about themselves to persons of lower status (Goffman, 1967:64). The professor, psychiatrist, and social worker can inquire about the personal lives of students, patients, and welfare clients, respectively, but these privileges are not reciprocal. The availability of information about someone can give the knower power over that person.

All small nonverbal communications add up to a larger bearing or "presentation of self" (Goffman, 1959), which is strongly related to perpetuating gender stereotypes. Women are taught to present a demeanor of dependence, frailty, passivity, and submission; men are expected to be nonrevealing, independent, strong, active, and dominant. The personal consequences are feelings of "femininity" *and* vulnerability and powerlessness in women and feelings of "masculinity" *and* dominance and higher status in men.

Etiquette

In our everyday associations, we abide by rules of conduct through which we convey an appropriate demeanor and appropriate *deference* or appreciation and confirmation of others (Goffman, 1967:56). Although there has been considerable talk about how men and women should treat each other differently at this point in history, in reality the same old rules of etiquette are still in force—particularly when men and women are out together socially. Men are still expected to extend certain courtesies to women—such as picking them up for dates, opening doors for them, and steering them across streets. These rules of conduct function simultaneously to support cultural values and reinforce self-images (Richardson [Walum], 1974, 1983).

Masculinity is still associated with activity, dominance, authority, and strength; femininity is associated with passivity, subordination, dependence, and weakness. To the extent that men act according to the prescribed etiquette, they will feel stereotypically masculine because they will be active, dominant, in charge, and strong. To the extent that women act according to the prescribed etiquette, they will feel stereotypically feminine because they will be passive, subordinate, and weak; they will wait for a man to call, to hail a cab, to light a cigarette, to open a door, to discharge a bill. By so waiting, the woman is signaling, nonverbally, that she needs someone to get her through her daily rounds of activities. If men and women perform their parts in the ritual drama between the sexes, they will have *actualized* those stereotypes associated with masculinity and femininity.

Who opens the door for whom, then, along with the other rules of etiquette, is not a trivial issue (Richardson [Walum], 1974). As one woman executive commented, "It's nice to have a male colleague open a door for me—but it's not worth the $12,000 *difference* in our salaries." Etiquette does more than confirm gender identity; it reaffirms cultural values. In a very profound sense, then, these daily etiquette rituals become the living testimony of a basic value of the culture—the superiority of men. As Goffman succinctly states, "The gestures which we sometimes call empty are perhaps, in fact, the fullest things of all" (1967:91).

SEX DIFFERENCES IN SPEECH

There is no doubt, then, that the language teaches us different things about men and women; however, we, also, need to ask whether men and women use the language differently. Is women's speech and men's speech different? If so, what do those differences convey about males and females?

For the past 15 years, linguists, conversational analysts, folklorists, and others have been intensively studying these questions. What they are finding is that the differences in terms of linguistic practices (e.g., use of adjectives, intonation, and inflected speech), are not as great, or as many, or as consistent as had been previously thought. Speech, like gender, is differently displayed depending upon the social role, the topic, the setting, the sex of the other participants, class, ethnicity, and other variables. On the other hand, they are finding that men and women may typically use different *speech strategies* in their communication. Let us look at the isolated linguistic practices, first, and the speech strategies, second.

Although ostensibly males and females share the same culturally prescribed neutral language, in actuality, girls speak in a distinctively feminine style of speech that is not condoned in boys. That speech style is apparently recognizable at an early age; for example, Garcia-Zamor (1973) found that nursery school children associated euphemistic speech and negative value judgments with girls, and aggressive and competitive comments with boys. In a series of carefully controlled studies of the voices of prepuberty children, Sachs (et. al., 1973 and Sachs, 1975) reports that judges can accurately describe the sex of young children by listening to their taped voices. Since there is no average difference in the voice mechanisms in children before puberty, the differences in speech cannot be attributed to anatomy. Sachs suggests that at least part of the reason that boys and girls sound different is that they have learned to use the voice and speech style that is viewed as appropriate for their sex (Sachs, 1975:168).

Intonation (pitch, stress, and melody) appears to be one of the persistent differences between male and female speech. The difference in pitch between the genders, the amount of which is learned (Navajo boys, for example, do not lower their voices at puberty [McConnell-Ginet, 1983]), however, is not the most striking difference: The *melody* or tonal variation and stress are.

Ruth Brend (1975) reports the difficulty that she had in teaching Russian male teachers of English the American-English intonational patterns. Although they were mimicking *her* intonations correctly, she found herself dissatisfied with their pronunciations. This led her to an analysis of different intonational patterns in male and female speech in American English. Brend found that certain intonational patterns "seem to be completely lacking from men's speech, while others are differently preferred by men and women" (1975:85).

Thinking of intonations in speech as tones on a four-note musical scale, the different intonation patterns of men and women can be seen. Men, for example, are more likely to use the "incomplete deliberative," intonating a small upstep from a low vocalization, such as:

```
                kn
     es,  es,      o
(1)  y   y   I      ow.
```

On the other hand, women tend to use the more polite, incomplete, longer upsweep, such as:

```
        es,    es,   kn
        y      y      o
        y      y      o
(2)  y      y    I      ow.
```

Other patterns seem to be virtually absent from men's speech. These include the "surprise" pattern of high voice to low-voice downglide, such as:

```
     O       th      aw
       o       a       w
         o       a       w
           o       a       w
(3)         oh     t's        ful.
```

The hesitation pattern, such as:

```
            stu
(4)  Well, I    died.
```

The "polite, cheerful" pattern, such as:

```
                 ing?
(5)  Are you com
```

In summary, Brend suggests that there are some clear differences in intonation patterns between males and females. Men tend to use only the three lowest notes on the intonation scale, whereas females use four. Unlike women, "men avoid final patterns which do not terminate at the lowest level of pitch, and use a final short upstep only for special effects, incomplete sequence, and for certain interrogative sentences" (1975:86—all examples in the text preceding are from Brend's work); that is, the female intonational patterns are more polite and less definite than those of the males. The female intonational patterns, moreover, tend to be devalued, imitated in a condescending or negative way, and associated with emotionalism. The extreme masculine tonal pattern—the monotone—is a model of control and rationality (McConnell-Ginet, 1983).

In addition to intonation, a second fairly consistent sex difference across race, age, and geography is the female's greater use of correct form (Kramerae, 1975; Thorne, et al., 1983); for example, women are more likely to say "I want to go running with you," whereas men are more likely to say "I wanna go runnin' wid' ja." This tendency to speak properly is very strong among black women, so strong that linguists sometimes refer to the style as "hypercorrect" (Abrahams, 1975; DeStefano, 1976). Researchers (cf. Trudgill, 1972; Thorne et al., 1983) have attributed women's greater concern with correct usage and pronunciation to the fact that women have to counteract their low social status; men, it is conjectured, are more concerned with demonstrating their masculinity by disassociating themselves from the correct "feminine" style.

There are some fairly consistent differences in the vocabulary of men and women as well. There are several important studies that have elicited spontaneous speech from males and females (cf. Wood, 1966; Swacker, 1975). Wood (1966) reports an analysis of 90,000 words of elicited spontaneous speech in relation-ship to photographs of the same person with different facial expressions. Certain spatial and mathematical words, such as *centimeter*, *dots*, *fraction*, *shape*, *intersect*, *parallels*, *protruded*, *right-angular*, are part of the male's vocabulary. Although approximately one-third of the female's vocabulary is of this kind, the female list is characterized by connotative and interpretive words and phrases, such as *death*, *family*, *confused*, *distasteful*, *skeptical*, *enjoying*, *might have just put*, *has been surprised*. Wood suggests that the male vocabulary tends to be more descriptive of the directly observable features, whereas female vocabulary lends itself to interpretative descriptions and greater imagery. Swacker (1975) also reports that males tend to use more numbers in their descriptions than do fe-males, and that the latter tend to precede numerals with approximations (e.g., *about six*).

Other assumed differences in speech, however, have not been supported by recent research (Henley, et al., 1985; Thorne, et al., 1983). Women do not, for example, use more adjectives or intensifiers (*so*, *such*) than men do; nor do they use more tag questions ("Ben's home, isn't he?"); the usages for both males and females depend upon the setting. Finally, despite the long-held myth, women do not talk longer or more often than men do.

In sum, then, linguists are finding few consistent differences between men and women in terms of particular speech components. Folklorists and conversa-tional analysts who study speech contextually, however, are discovering a great deal about the strategies males and females use to communicate. Conversational analysts, for example, assume that people are "rational actors oriented toward communicative goals and employing strategies to achieve those goals" (Brown, 1976:247). Because men and women's status in society is unequal, though, they are likely to have to use different speech strategies to accomplish their communication goals. These differences will become clearer as we examine, first, how hierarchy is perpetuated in male-female interactions and, second, how different spheres for males and females are created and sustained.

Power is defined as the ability to impose one's will upon another (Weber, 1969:152). This imposition can take place in the most intimate of settings, with the more powerful person determining the *definition of reality*, and making it stick (Berger and Luckman, 1967:109; Fishman, 1983). In the dynamics of conversation between male and female intimates, the males are more likely to be powerful—to have their definitions of reality reign. How does this happen?

Fishman (1983) asked a similar question: How is power reflected and maintained in daily interaction? To answer this question, she placed tape recorders in the homes of three heterosexual couples; both partners were graduate students and all of them claimed to be sympathetic to the women's movement; that is, the partners were ostensibly of equal status and sensitive to women's inequalities. Fifty-two hours of naturally occurring conversation were recorded.

Analysis of the taped conversations revealed a number of different strategies to "insure, encourage, and subvert conversations," and that these strategies were differentially used by the males and females (Fishman, 1983:93). There is "an inequality in talk between the sexes": Women work harder to accomplish an interaction than men do, but men have greater control over it (Fishman, 1983:93); for example, women are more likely to use strategies that initiate conversation. Women asked questions two and a half times as frequently as men did. Questions are interactionally powerful because they "deserve" answers; using them strengthens the possibility of getting a response. Women also used "attention getters," such as, "This is interesting," twice as often as men did. The message is "pay attention—I can't assume that you will." Often the conversation strategies used by women did not work, because the men did not respond or they discouraged further interaction by using a minimal delayed response—waiting for several seconds and then saying, "mm" or "uh-huh."

Indeed, men succeeded in controlling the conversations because of the inequality in the interaction work; for example, men made statements twice as often as women did. A statement does not "deserve" an answer, but an assumption is made that the statement will be responded to. Women always responded to the men's statements, but men did not respond to women's statements. In addition, women used "mm" and "uh-huh" as "support work," carefully inserting the supportive "mm" when the male took a breath during his speech, rather than overlapping his words.

Males controlled the topic of conversation, as well. Although women introduced 47 topics, only 17 of these got responses. Of the 29 topics introduced by men, 28 of these succeeded in becoming conversations. The male success rate cannot be attributed to the content of the topic, since both speakers introduced the same kinds of topics—papers, books, vitae. Rather his success is based on the woman's willingness to fulfill her part of the conversational bargain; her failure is a result of his unwillingness to reciprocate. Thus, the definition of what is an appropriate topic becomes the man's decision. He defines reality.

Although Fishman has only looked at three homes, it is likely her findings, to one degree or another, are being replicated throughout the country. Her results are consistent with a large body of research on the interactions between men and women; for example, researchers have found that in natural settings men interrupt women speakers, give minimal responses, change topics, and in other ways treat females as "a class of speakers—whose rights to speak (can be) casually infringed upon by males'' (Zimmerman and West, 1975:115). Add to these, women's tendencies to polite speech styles, melodic speech, and submissive nonverbal display. All together, women, then, use a set of speech strategies that empower men, and men, too, use a set of speech strategies that empower men.

Differences in power between men and women are reflected and maintained in the interactional process. Persons who are interested in achieving more equality in their intimate relationships might, therefore, experiment with changing their speech strategies. Women might, for example, decide to do less of the conversational work that empowers men, and men might choose to do more of that work, thus empowering the women in their lives.

Speech strategies not only perpetuate power imbalances between men and women, they can be used to create and sustain separate spheres. An example of this is found in the speech strategies of Black Americans. Black Americans of various social classes and geographical locations share a distinctive language and speech style (Folb, 1972). Members of the black community correctly learn to speak a language that is structurally complex (Labov, 1972), grammatically ordered (Abrahams, 1972), action-oriented (Kochman, 1972), and capable of finely honed double entendres (Labov, 1972).

A distinction is made between two styles: sweet talk and smart talk. *Sweet talk* is associated primarily with the home, women, children, and respectability; *smart talk* is associated primarily with the street, men, and peer reputation (Abrahams, 1975).

With the exception of a few abbreviated years of adolescent freedom, girls and women are expected to affirm the values of a good home and to be respectable (Abrahams, 1975), and their language patterns are highly compatible with these cultural demands. Women are less abandoned in their talk, less public, less loud (Abrahams, 1975). The voice is modulated close to that of standard English, and the style is sweet talk—so much so that some linguists consider it saccharine. A ''respectable'' woman ''speaks little with the mouth . . .'' (Abrahams, 1975); a ''little momma'' enunciates hypercorrectly (Abrahams, 1975), and her speech pace is slow (DeStefano, 1976).

In addition to sweet talk, a woman must be capable of street talk, even if she does not use the language of the street. To earn respectability, a woman must be able to control the talk in her presence. If her self-image is being threatened, she must be able to talk *smart* or *cold* (the silent treatment); she proves her respectability by contending with the street talk. Success in the confrontation earns her respectability.

In contrast, men tend to reserve the sweet-talk style for hustling women and ''lames'' (nonhip persons). The usual male language style is combative, aggressive, argumentative, and hostile (Abrahams, 1975). In addition, the personal style of the speaker is highly dramatized with more syllabic stress, tonal changes, and rhythmic variations than is found in standard English or in a black woman's speech (Abrahams, 1975). Further, a male's *reputation* is a function of his ability to use street talk. Good mastery indicates not only that he has arrived with his peers, but also that he has succeeded in freeing himself from his home and mother.

Thus, through speech strategies, males and females protect their reputations in two different spheres. Males achieve a public reputation with their peers through their verbal abilities; females, through their strategies, achieve reputations as respectable women. No doubt there are many different speech strategies used by different ethnic and racial groups to separate the men from the women; and, once again, it would be instructive for you to examine some of those strategies that you use in your own life to divide the genders, and to think about them as different and unequal.

REEVALUATING THE SPEECH STANDARD

Much of the research on speech, both cross-culturally and in America, has focused on how men do it. The male mode has been viewed as *the* standard language; women's speech has been considered as the deviation (Henley, et al., 1985). Moreover, recently, women have been encouraged to speak like men—to be more forceful and aggressive in their speech; to interrupt more; to control topics; to talk for longer periods; to be competitive; to modulate their voices; and to change their nonverbal behaviors (cf. Richardson, 1981). Classes in empowering women have focused on changing women so that they talk more like men. There are two problems with this approach.

First, because women are women, they are responded to in terms of their sex status—female. The same behavior in a woman as that in a man may not be evaluated in the same way; for example, a man who speaks in a forceful way may be judged, ''a winner,'' whereas a woman who speaks the same way may be judged ''a castrating bitch.'' Women in professional roles often find themselves in a double bind: If they speak in female sex-stereotyped ways, their competency may be challenged; but if they speak in male sex-stereotyped ways, they may be personally disliked (Richardson, et al., 1983). Since being judged competent and likable are both essential components for job advancement, simply ''talking like a man'' will not guarantee a woman equal access to advancement.

Moreover, there is no guarantee that her male colleagues will *let* her talk like a man—that is, let her interrupt them, control the topic, or be given credit for her ideas—because they will be interacting with her as a female. An example from a faculty meeting is illustrative. Major curriculum changes were being proposed. A woman professor suggested a way of expediting the changes. The Chair, a man who prides himself on fairness, totally ignored her comment; it was as though she had not even spoken. A while later, her husband, also a professor in the department, proposed the same solution. The Chair not only responded, he praised the suggestion. After the meeting, the Chair invited the male professor, along with the male committee chairs, out for lunch to discuss the idea further. The female professor in question talked ''like a man''—forcefully and directly—but she was responded to as a woman, and not as a full-fledged colleague.

Second, the demand that women talk more like men assumes that the male way of interacting is the preferable one, and that it is women who should change, rather than men. Women's styles of communication are denigrated. Because of this, researchers have tried to discover whether women talk differently with each other than they do with men, and, if so, whether there are some benefits to the female speech style that have been overlooked through the hallowing of the male style.

Talk between women is characterized first and foremost by "mutuality of interaction work" (Thorne, et al., 1983). Women's conversations are *collaborative* (Thorne, et al., 1983). Women support each other's conversational ploys, rather than compete for control; they are more flexible in the conversational leadership, rather than establishing a dominant-submissive pattern; they draw each other out through head nodding and supportive "mm's"; they mutually share intimacies and feelings; they tend to be equally vulnerable and open; their style is more discursive and informal, rather than linear—a topic can be returned to over and over again; and they value highly the talk, itself: It bonds women (cf. Richardson, 1985:23–24; Thorne, et al., 1983; Edelsky, 1981).

To dismiss or discount these features of women's talk with each other is certainly to ignore the major benefits that such interactions give to women, on the one hand, and to ignore the potential benefits they could give to mixed-sex and male groupings, on the other. If both men and women were more sensitive listeners and more collaborative in conversational style, major changes toward equity between the sexes could accrue at both the personal and institutional levels.

To summarize, language is both subtle and pervasive. It is an inescapable socializer. It structures our thought and our interpersonal relationships, affirming over and over again in word and gesture the cultural assumptions of sex differences and male dominance. Yet, it is a "living" language; we, the people, are the ones who use it and who can change it. We can change the language, the nonverbal communication, and the speech strategies to reflect and perpetuate fewer meaningless differences between the sexes, and greater equality.

Language is the beginning. We turn now to how the very young are socialized into genders.

□ □ *3* □ □

Early Socialization

The place is the Mercy Hospital maternity ward. Two babies, a male and a female, were born 12 hours earlier and are now resting in the nursery, wrapped in their respective blue and pink blankets. The time is two o'clock, and afternoon visiting hours have begun. The excited grandparents are peering into the glassed-in nursery. Although their conversations may sound as though they are reading a soap-opera script, their lines have *not* been made up. Rather, they are a composite of actual conversations that were overheard and recorded in a maternity ward. Let us eavesdrop:

GRANDMA B: There he is—our first grandchild, and a boy!

GRANDPA B: Hey, isn't he a hefty little fellow? Look at that fist he's making. He's going to be a regular little fighter, that guy is. [Grandpa B smiles and throws out a boxing jab to his grandson.] At-a-boy!

GRANDMA B: I think he looks like you. He has your strong chin. Oh look, he's starting to cry.

GRANDPA B: Yeah—just listen to that set of lungs. He's going to be some boy.

GRANDMA B: Poor thing—he's still crying.

GRANDPA B: It's okay. It's good for him. He's exercising and it will develop his lungs.

GRANDMA B: Let's go congratulate the parents. I know they're thrilled about little Fred. They wanted a boy, *first*.

GRANDPA B: Yeah and they were sure it would be a boy, too, what with all that kicking and thumping going on even before he got here.

And off they go to congratulate the happy parents. Let us listen to the other set of grandparents, though, while we're at the nursery.

GRANDMA G: There *she* is . . . the one with the pink bow taped to her head. Isn't she darling?

35

GRANDPA G: Yeah—isn't she little? Look at how tiny her fingers are. Oh, look—she's *trying* to make a fist.

GRANDMA G: Isn't she sweet? . . . You know, I think she looks a little like me.

GRANDPA G: Yeah, she sorta does. She has your chin.

GRANDMA G: Oh look, she's starting to cry.

GRANDPA G: Maybe we'd better call the nurse to pick her up or change her or something.

GRANDMA G: Yes, let's. Poor little girl. [To the baby] There, there, we'll try to help you.

GRANDPA G: Let's find the nurse and congratulate the parents. I don't like to see her cry.

GRANDMA G: Hmmm. I wonder when they will have their next one. I know Fred would like a son, but little Fredericka is well and healthy. After all, that's what really matters.

GRANDPA G: They're young yet. They have time for more kids. I'm thankful, too, that she's healthy.

GRANDMA G: I don't think they were surprised when it was a girl, anyway . . . she was carrying so low.

Here are two simple conversations by two sets of grandparents. Embedded in the thrill and excitement of a first grandchild are the various cultural beliefs and expectations for grandsons and granddaughters. It is not surprising that the grandparents of the girl infant begin to think, ''well, at least she's healthy,'' and turn their attention to the idea of more grandchildren.

In the United States, as in most societies, sons are preferred over daughters. If there is to be one child, the societal preference is for that child to be a boy; if there is more than one child, the preference is to have the boy first, and to have more boys than girls. In general, the lower the woman's social, legal, and economic status, the greater the tendency for both men and women to prefer male children (Warren, 1985:13–14). With the advent of amniocentesis, which permits the parents to know what sex the unborn fetus is, and the very near real possibility of being able to preselect a baby's sex, some researchers are concerned about what they term *gendercide*, or the curtailment of female live births. One estimate made some years ago, and which has not changed, is that if people could choose the sex of their unborn children, there would be 133 boys born for every 100 girls (Etzioni, 1968).[1] The child, then, even today, is born into a culture that has a preference for boys.

Given that sex identity has been determined, and given the cultural preference for boys, the task of gender socialization—of teaching the child to be a man or a woman—begins. The child must be taught to identify with the appropriate gender.

[1]Nancy Williamson's (1976) cross-cultural data suggest that the ratio of male to female children, particularly in Third World countries, would be even higher if the current technology were used in deciding to terminate a pregnancy. Given that special rights (both real and symbolic) are accorded the firstborn, and given that males are universally preferred as firstborn, if the technology is used, we may find that preselection of the sex of a child is the ultimate form of sex discrimination.

In teaching the child, the parents and grandparents draw upon their culture's under-standings of what is appropriate for males and what is appropriate for females. The conversations between the two sets of grandparents illustrate some of the cultural dictates concerning what the differences are between males and females, what they should be, and what differences are preferable.

Socialization of children begins in the first group with which they live—*the family of orientation* or a substitute for it. Such groups are examples of *primary groups* and are "characterized by intimate face-to-face association and coopera-tion" (Cooley, 1909:23). The family of orientation is primary in three ways: first, it is the first socializing experience; second, it provides the most intense and complete experience of belonging; and third, it teaches the social knowledge necessary to engage in associations outside the familial sphere.

Later, the child will experience other primary groups, such as the play group and the friendship clique. However, it is in this initial primary group that children learn to communicate. They acquire the language of the culture, and with that acquisition, how to think, what to think about, and how to relate to others, are indelibly etched upon them. Most importantly, children learn about their fundamen-tal social nature and the basic social ideals of their culture when they are profoundly psychobiologically dependent upon others. Their needs can be fulfilled only through social interaction. Consequently, the kind of self that develops is a function of the kind of communication that is provided by significant others, tending (or not tend-ing) to their needs.

Within the context of a primary group, the child begins to learn the most central, basic, and gut-level feelings about the nature of gender differences, the importance of such differences, and gender expectations. These ideas and ideals are the most relevant to the child's subsequent gender behavior, and they are the most difficult to contravene. So intense and striking, or subtle and pervasive, are these primary experiences in childhood that to violate them as adults is difficult, uncom-fortable, improbable, and, in some cases, psychologically impossible. To choose to act in ways that we learned were gender inappropriate during our years of greatest vulnerability—childhood—is to potentially choose to lose the sense of self and belonging that we knew as children. So subtle and pervasive are these teachings, we don't even know we are acting in a certain way.

There are different explanatory models regarding how socialization works. Two of these—the *social-learning model* and the *cognitive-development model*—have been particularly concerned with the processes by which gender identity is acquired. Both of these models reject the notion that gender is biologically pro-grammed.

The social-learning model proposes that a child learns appropriate sex-typed behavior through observations, rewards, punishments, and imitation of adult mod-els. Accordingly, sex-typed behavior is learned in the same way as other behaviors. Boys are encouraged to copy their fathers, girls, their mothers. Subsequently, children find that modeling their behavior on the same-sex parent is rewarding in and of itself. According to this perspective, the teaching of appropriate sex-typed behavior and the imitation of it begin quite early in a child's life, and such behavior is very difficult to alter. The child learns to conform to parental and cultural expectations. This viewpoint is widely held in sociology, anthropology, and psychology (Sears, 1965; Bandura and Walters, 1964).

The cognitive-development model of gender and sexuality is almost entirely the work of one scholar, Lawrence Kohlberg (1966), who built upon the seminal ideas of Jean Piaget (cf. 1954). Kohlberg maintains that, unlike the social-learning model, a child's gender identity and sexuality are not directly taught by others; rather, sexual ideas and sex role concepts derive from the child's active structuring of experience. The key experience is the child's categorization of himself or herself as a male or female. This categorization occurs at the same time that language is being acquired, between the ages of 18 months and 3 years. Once children have self-categorized themselves, they begin the process of categorizing the rest of the world on the same basis. At first, the understanding is tentative. It is not until about ages 4 to 6 that children conceptualize the idea of sex constancy—that is, that their sex does not change like their hairstyle, age, and so on. It is not until about age 5 or 6 that they recognize that same-sex persons of different *ages* are part of the same category; that is, the idea of "we male" or "we female" is a late cognitive development. In the development of gender identity and sex-typed behavior, children actively *use* the messages that the culture presents, such as different clothing, hairstyles, and occupational roles for the sexes; and they cognitively rehearse being a fireman and a father, if a boy; a nurse and a mother, if a girl.

Because self-categorization occurs so early in life and forms the basis upon which children categorize and order their experiences, it is nearly impossible to change one's belief about what gender one is after the age of three. If one has defined oneself as a male or a female, that categorization forms the crucial basis for the categorization of others and for self-socialization. We turn now to the specific procedures through which infants and children are socialized into a gender.

INFANT SOCIALIZATION

Before the baby arrives, the probability of its sex has been speculated upon, and the wishes of the parents and grandparents have been at least tentatively vocalized. The months of expectant waiting have been filled with deciding what to name the baby, reading baby manuals, and outfitting a nursery.

Apart from the standard given names and the practice of naming an offspring after a significant relative, there are some unconscious rules that govern the name preferences in middle-class America. Male names tend to be short, hard-hitting, and explosive (e.g., Bret, Lance, Mark, Craig, Bruce, etc.). Even when the given name is multisyllabic (e.g., Benjamin, Joshua, William, Thomas), the nickname tends to imply hardness and energy (e.g., Ben, Josh, Bill, Tom, etc.). Female names, on the other hand, are longer, more melodic, and softer (e.g., Deborah, Caroline, Jessica, Christina) and easily succumb to the diminutive *ie*-ending form (e.g., Debbie, Carrie, Jessie, Christie). Although feminization of male names (e.g., Fredericka, Roberta, Alexandra) is not uncommon, the inverse rarely occurs.

Parents also read baby manuals. Benjamin Spock's all-time best-seller, *Baby and Child Care*, advocated the housekeeper/childrearer mother and the breadwinner/companion father. The influence of his book on generations of families has probably been immense. Due to severe feminist criticism and his subsequent rethinking of the issues, however, in his more recent writings, he argues that "the father—any father—should be sharing with the mother the day-to-day care of the children from birth onward" (Spock, 1974:242), and that fathers should do their share of housework to teach the children that the home is as "vital, worthy and challenging as his job" (Spock, 1974:243). Even a cursory glance at the 50 or so parenting manuals that are currently available in the mass market shows that sex stereotyping is not recognized as a problem for parents to combat and overcome. Without such recognition and remedial action, we can expect infants still to be socialized along specific gender lines.

Special spaces—nurseries and bedrooms—are provided for children. In an ingenious study, Rheingold and Cook (1975) examined the furnishings and toys of boys' and girls' private bedrooms. The children were all under 6, born into affluent and well-educated homes. The researchers proposed that the selection of furnishings and toys would reflect the parents' perceptions of what was appropriate for boys and girls, and would be an indirect indicator of their probable behavior toward the children. These parents did, indeed, provide different environments for boys and for girls. Boys' rooms contained more sports equipment, military items, art and educational materials, toy animals and animal motifs, spatial (building) toys, machines, and substantially more vehicular toys; girls' rooms contained more dolls, especially realistic dolls, objects for doll play, and small-scale domestic appliances, floral designs, and ruffles. Only in numbers of books and musical toys were the sexes equivalently lavished.

The boys were provided more toys in more toy categories at every age than were girls. The differences in two categories—vehicles for boys and dolls for girls—were overwhelming. Indeed, not one girl had a wagon, a boat, or a bus, and baby dolls and toy domestic equipment were rarely found in a boy's room. As the authors conclude, "the boys were provided objects that encouraged activities directed away from home—toward sports, cars, animals, and the military—and the girls objects that encouraged activities toward the home—keeping house and caring for children" (1975:463). Since it is not likely that the parents have one set of attitudes toward furnishing their children's rooms and another toward their children's clothing, language, and behavior generally, we must conclude that these furnishings provide a kind of documentation for sex stereotyping in the children's rearing. Moreover, there is little indication that these differences have abated: Boys are still given more space and more toys than girls are given (Richardson, 1981); and the toys that are given to girls are less interesting to "active, curious, children" (Best, 1985).

There is more to infant socialization, however, than simply deciding on a given name, reading a manual, and decorating a room. The child has to learn to live up to the gender identity and the gender expectations that are embedded in that name. Children learn what they are taught. To the extent that male and female infants are treated differently—to the extent that the same behavior (such as the presentation of a fist) elicits a different response—these same infants are differentially taught or socialized. The discovery of such differential socialization requires intensive and extensive observations of the actual behavior of infants and their parents. Only through such observation might early gender differences that are physiologically dependent be separated from those that are sociologically dependent.

Physiologically, males at birth tend to be heavier (by five percent) and longer (by two percent). However, beyond that, there appear to be few consistent physiological or behavioral differences between the infants during their early months. In a monumental review of the literature on differences between infants by sex, *The Psychology of Sex Differences* (1974), Maccoby and Jacklin conclude that, for most behaviors studied, the findings are either inconclusive or indicate that there are no significant differences attributable to sex. Although more than a decade has passed since this monumental review of the literature, new research, for the most part, has corroborated their conclusions.

In terms of activity level, Korner (1969) reports that the spontaneous activities of the infant male and female are quantitatively the same, although they differ qualitatively. Boys, he reports, engage in more gross-body startle movements; girl's movements are predominately confined to the facial area—sucks, smiles, and rhythmic mouthing. Although the evidence is inconclusive, boys probably spend less time sleeping (Maccoby and Jacklin, 1974:171). However, as follow-up studies suggest, the activity level at one point in time does not consistently predict the activity level at another.

In terms of sensory perception, the research findings are also inconclusive. There is some evidence to suggest that females are more sensitive to smells and taste, but the research is too scanty to permit generalization. In relationship to sensitivity to touch, some research indicates no difference by sex for newborns; that which does report a difference suggests that newborn girls are more tactilely sensitive. Infant boys and girls are similar in their responses to auditory and visual stimuli, as well as in their receptivity to social (faces and voices) or nonsocial stimuli. From the research thus far, there does not seem to be strong empirical evidence to argue that infant boys and girls are naturally different in regard to sensory responsiveness.

Clearly, there is a great deal more to learn about what physiological differences, if any, there are between male and female infants. Once these are better understood, however, we still need to understand how they are related to subsequent social development. If further research, for example, continues to confirm the *similarity* between the physiological states of infants of different sexes, then we can be even more certain about the primary role of socialization for the development of personalities that are gender stereotyped.

Although most parents would probably claim that they do not alter their behavior to suit the sex of the child, there is research evidence to the contrary. In reviewing some of the literature, Lake (1975) reports that mothers described their newborn daughters as tiny, soft, delicate, and fine-featured, shortly after their first glimpse of them, and described their sons as strong, alert, and well-coordinated. Fathers, especially, are likely to describe their newborn son or daughter in gender stereotypes (Rubin, et al., 1974). In an exploratory study, five young mothers were presented Adam, a 6-month-old who was dressed in blue overalls; a second group of mothers were given Beth, a 6-month-old in a pink frilly dress. Compared to Adam, Beth was smiled at more, offered a doll to play with more often, and was viewed as "sweet" with a "soft cry." However, Adam and Beth were in actuality the same 6-month-old child. In another study, a baby's cry was interpreted as "anger" when it was thought to be a boy, and as "fear" when it was thought to be a girl (Condry and Condry, 1976). Furthermore, female college students offered a baby "boy" a football 80 percent of the time, rather than a teething ring or a doll (Russo, 1983).

In addition, observational studies of infants and mothers have discovered some significant differences in the early socialization of males and females. Lewis (1972) has found that during the first six months of life, boys receive more physical contact (being touched, held, nursed) and *less* nonphysical contact (being looked at and talked to) than girls receive. This is true despite the fact that the *amount* of both verbal (Moss, 1967) and nonverbal activity of the 3-month-old male and female was the same; that is, there was early differential reinforcement of males' *physical* activity and of females' *verbal* activity. However, after that initial six-month period, girls receive both more physical and nonphysical contact than do boys.

Moreover, fathers treat their sons and daughters differently, so much so, that by the second year of the infant's life, significantly more interaction exists between father and son than between father and daughter (Lamb, 1977; Rossi, 1984). The research evidence is quite consistent: Parents "elicit 'gross motor behavior' more from their sons than from their daughters" (Maccoby and Jacklin, 1974:307). In addition to Lewis' study, Yarrow (et al., 1971) reports that parents are more likely to play vigorously with their sons. Both fathers (Pederson and Robson, 1969) and mothers (Minton et al., 1971) have been found to be more apprehensive about physical danger to their daughters than to their sons, and to view the former as more fragile. "The form of the motor stimulation undoubtedly changes drastically with the age of the child, but the continuing theme appears to be that girls are treated as though they were more fragile than boys" (Maccoby and Jacklin, 1974:309). Further, more attention is paid to teaching daughters than sons to smile (Lake, 1975: 24). Parents were observed giving 7-week-old infants a social and development test. Although the infant boys and girls performed similarly, their parents did not. More coaxing and terms of endearment were used to elicit a smile or a "coo" from the girls.

Lewis (1972) contends that the physically contiguous, face-to-face relationship between mother and child must be transformed into the visual-verbal relationship of adults. Consequently, mothers detach themselves from their children through such techniques as facing them away and drawing their attention to other objects and persons in the room. In this process of learning "independence" from the mother, boys are moved along much more quickly than girls, so that, by the time the infants are 13 months old, boys venture further out into their environment, look at and talk to their mothers less frequently, and manipulate the environment more aggressively than do girls.

There is no clear evidence to explain why boys and girls are differently socialized in these early months. The reasons may be based on the different physiological states, or on different cultural expectations, or on some admixture of both; for example, the males' developmental immaturity may lead to greater fretfulness and consequently the need to be held and fondled more, or the greater cultural value placed on boys might increase the mother's desire to touch the male infant. Boys' greater gross activity, higher basal metabolism, and greater caloric intake may ready them earlier for independence, or they may be sped on their way due to cultural expectations for dominance and mastery. Clearly, much more evidence is necessary to unravel the nature-nurture controversy embedded in the earliest socialization experiences.

Pogrebin (1983) proposes a sociocultural reason why parents treat male and female children differently. She argues that even parents who have rejected sex stereotyping for themselves have deep, emotional fears that result in their children being reared along sex role lines (Pogrebin, 1983). What are these fears? Parents fear that sex role behaviors are linked to sexuality, and that if their children do not act in sex role appropriate ways, they will become homosexuals.

The idea that prescribed sex roles lead to heterosexuality rests in the assumption that "opposites attract"—that "masculinity" and "femininity" attract each other. Despite the hold of this idea on the consciousness of parents (and others), the fact is one's sex role behaviors and one's sexual preference are independent of each other. Lesbians and homosexual men, as well as heterosexuals, run the gamut in how traditional or liberated they are from the prescribed sex roles.

Second, despite a bevy of theories about homosexuality, no one knows what causes it. Gay and heterosexual children come out of the same homes; heterosexual, intact families have gay children; lesbian mothers have heterosexual daughters, and so on. Further, homosexuality exists in all societies (Ford and Beach, 1951). The estimated ten percent of Americans who are gay (Marmor, 1980) are similar to heterosexuals in terms of gender identity, self-esteem, drinking habits, general life satisfaction, suicide rates, drug use, and relationships with parents and friends (Pogrebin, 1983:38). Despite these facts, parents feel obliged to protect their children from becoming homosexuals: They see homosexuality as one of the worst things that could happen to their child—worse, even, than drug addiction (Pogrebin, 1983:39).

Why does this feeling prevail? It is because the society is *homophobic*— fearful and intolerant of homosexuality. Sexism and homophobia go hand in hand. Boys are especially severely socialized not to be "sissies," not to do "girl things," like play with dolls, or, for that matter, to play with girls. Boys are reared so that many repress their feelings of love for other men, and learn to hate and fear the feminine—both within themselves and in those around them. Indeed, as a recent comprehensive review of the literature has confirmed, as boys develop, they increasingly inhibit the expression of all of their emotions (Brody, 1985); grown to manhood, they are "inexpressive" (Sattel, 1983). As Pogrebin concludes, "While homophobia cannot prevent homosexuality, its power to destroy female assertiveness and male sensitivity is boundless" (1983:39). She advises parents not to worry about how to raise a heterosexual child, but how not to be a homophobic parent.

Most parents, however, continue to socialize their children into prescribed sex roles, and to have different gender expectations for the youngest of children. We see these differences even in the paraphernalia designed for infants. There are different styles and colors for male and female infants in such basics as cribs, potty seats, comforters, changing tables, diaper pins, and toys; perhaps the clearest distinctions between the sexes are reflected in the most personal of possessions—namely, infant clothing.

In a trip through an infant section of any department store, gross imitations of the adult gender-linked styles are easily discernible. On the girls' racks are princess dresses, granny gowns, pink satin pantsuits, and bikinis; on the boys' racks are baseball uniforms, tweed suits with vests and decorative pocket watches, astronaut pajamas, and starched white dress shirts. Often, the differences in style are more subtle; for example, large manufacturers of infant ready-to-wear clothing design male and female variants of the same basic romper. The male variant snaps from left to right, has a pointed collar and a football motif; the female snaps right to left, has a Peter Pan collar with lace trim and embroidered butterflies. (Only diapers and christening dresses seem to be entirely immune to gender typing.)

Although we have witnessed some relaxation of the infant dress codes, the differences still persist. Girls are more readily dressed in boy's play clothes than the reverse. Furthermore, when the children are "dressed up," the distinctions are more pronounced. Choosing different clothing styles not only signifies to others—including the parents and grandparents—what sex the child is and therefore how the child is to be treated, but also facilitates or hampers the activity of the child. The clothing itself reflects the cultural expectations regarding the appropriate behavior of each sex.

In brief, the earliest months of the child's life are not gender role free. Differences in expectations, names, behavioral responses, apparel, toys, furniture styles, and games treat the baby as belonging to either the male sex or the female sex. Indeed, as Stoller, the director of the U.C.L.A. Gender Identity Research Clinic, argues: In the *first two or three years of life*, core gender identity—the sense of maleness or femaleness—is established as a "result of the parents' conviction that their infant's assignment at birth to either the male or female sex is correct" (1967). Despite the potential existence of hormones, chromosomes, gonads, or internal reproductive organs to the contrary, if the parents define a child as belonging to a particular gender during its first few years of life, the child will identify with that gender.

PRESCHOOL SOCIALIZATION

Although the studies of newborns are few, there is a vast literature on the older infant and preschool child, which Maccoby and Jacklin (1974) have also reviewed and summarized. What has psychology found out regarding the differences in personalities of young boys and girls? The two most frequently studied traits are aggression and dependency. *Aggression* is considered a complex "cluster of actions and motives" that share the "central theme . . . the intent of one individual to hurt another" (Maccoby and Jacklin, 1974:227). It may involve physically or verbally lashing out or simply fantasizing hostile activity, and it may be done to gain control or simply to punish another person. Maccoby and Jacklin summarize their research: "The major fact . . . is that males are consistently found to be more aggressive than females. . . . The behavioral sex difference is found in a variety of cultures" (1974:228).

Their research, however, suggests that the differences in aggression between males and females increase as the children grow older: the younger the children, the greater the number of research studies that report no difference between the sexes (see summary table in Maccoby and Jacklin, 1974:230–233). It is only after the 18th month that the greater negative emotional outbursts following frustrations are found in boys (Maccoby and Jacklin, 1974:181). What appears to be happening as the children age is "not that boys are increasing in their emotional volatility . . . but that girls are decreasing in the frequency and intensity of their emotional reactions [to frustration] at a faster rate than boys" (Maccoby and Jacklin, 1974: 182). These differences in aggressive activity as the child ages seem to be related to the willingness of the child to act hostilely; for example, in studies of children in which models of aggressive behavior were presented (through films, tapes, etc.), boys were more likely to imitate the aggressive behavior than were the girls. However, when rewards were offered for imitating the aggressive behaviors, the differences between the sexes diminished (Maccoby and Jacklin, 1974:182).

The evidence still seems inconclusive as to whether greater aggression in the male is a biologically based trait or a learned one. Although Maccoby and Jacklin contend that "it has a biological foundation" (1974:242; for their arguments see 242–247), the extent to which biology is destiny for the male remains unresolved. Boys, for example, show greater aggression when they are in active rough play with other boys and, as we have already noted, boys are played with more physically by their parents than are girls. Does greater activity lead to greater aggression or does greater biologically based aggression lead to greater roughhousing? To what extent and through what mechanism does the society reward aggression in males? However it does so, we might pause for a moment to wonder why a society would choose to reinforce aggression.

Dependency may be defined as a complex behavior system that includes actions that a child performs in order to receive nurturance, help, or caretaking. Such actions as touching or clinging to someone and asking for help, protection, or attention (directly or indirectly) are considered dependent behavior (Maccoby and Jacklin, 1974:191). However, despite the lumping of various activities under the rubric *dependency*, research indicates that they do not exist as a cluster; for example, seeking closeness and seeking attention appear to be quite different activities, "which have distinct courses of development and are responsive to different antecedent conditions" (Maccoby and Jacklin, 1974:191).

The majority of the research concerning young children's dependency on their mothers, as indicated by seeking closeness, touching, or resisting separation, reports no difference in the dependency actions of young (under age 3) boys and girls (Maccoby and Jacklin, 1974:196). Further, seeking proximity to other adults and children is a behavior that both sexes perform equally often (Maccoby and Jacklin, 1974:200). In the early childhood years, both boys and girls will seek comfort or protection through dependency actions. "Clinging to parents or other caretakers or remaining near them under conditions of uncertainty or anxiety is characteristic of human children" (Maccoby and Jacklin, 1974:201).

For some other traits studied, Maccoby and Jacklin report that the findings suggest no differences in the early childhood years. These include such traits as *sociability*, *suggestibility*, *spatial-visual ability*, and *mathematical ability*. For other traits, such as *fear, competitiveness, dominance, compliance, nurturance*, they report that the evidence is too inconclusive to reach any generalizations. Yet, for many of these traits, differences do appear in later childhood and in adulthood; and, for all of these traits discussed so far, there is a cultural belief that males and females are different. The question, therefore, becomes what consequences does the belief system have for the socialization of young children? Do parents treat their sons differently than they treat their daughters?

At this point, the research strategies to help answer this question are just being mapped out. Thus far, persistent findings concerning the differential treatment of boys and girls are that boys receive more physical punishment, more negative feedback, and more positive feedback (praise and encouragement) than do girls; that is, socialization pressures are applied more intensely to boys than to girls, and there is some evidence to suggest that the father is particularly instrumental in this regard.

More demands are made on boys at a younger age than on girls (Hartley, 1974:7). Parents reprimand boys more severely for acting in sex-inappropriate ways (such as acting like "sissies") than they do girls who, for example, act like "tom-boys." Fathers tend to be more concerned than mothers that their sons act in gender-appropriate ways, and are more punitive than mothers to sons who act inappropriately (Lynn, 1976). Further, the demands on boys are defined primarily proscriptively (boys should *not*), rather than prescriptively (boys should). Consequently, young boys must either discover somewhat accidentally what they should do or receive repeated negative sanctions for straying into sex-inappropriate behavior. Hartley suggests these socialization practices—"the demand that the child do something which is not clearly defined to him, based on reasons he cannot possibly appreciate, and enforced with threats, punishments, and anger by those who are close to him"—induce sex role anxiety in boys (1974:7). This anxiety expresses "itself in overstraining to be masculine, in virtual panic of being caught doing anything traditionally defined as feminine, and in hostility toward anything even hinting at femininity, including females themselves" (Hartley, 1974:8). Unfortunately, because this anxiety is produced when boys are young and vulnerable, the behaviors and attitudes—fear of and hostility toward the feminine—often persist into adult life.

However, it would be false to assume, as Weitzman (1979:12–17) so well argues, that the socialization process for girls is without anxiety. Young girls find running and building more interesting than watching and carrying. By the time children are 5, they recognize that what males do in the world is more important and more rewarded than what females do. Yet, girls are expected to imitate their mothers. A girl is expected to behave in ways that are socially devalued. Her internal anxiety must be quite deep "when she realizes her mother, a loved model, receives neither recognition nor satisfaction for such activities, and yet encourages them in her" (Weitzman, 1979:15). In addition, although boys are punished more severely, it is highly possible that girls are punished more subtly (e.g., removing love) but psychologically more deeply. Girls may not be given the opportunity to try out "punishable behaviors" and may be controlled by guilt.

Consequently, it is probably correct to argue that socialization into gender is anxiety producing for both boys and girls. Although girls have the mother available for a role model, they are being asked to conform to a role that is confining and socially devalued. Although boys are punished more severely for deviations and frequently lack an available father, they are, nevertheless, motivated to adopt their assigned role, for with it comes prestige, excitement, and limited domestic responsibility.

Many parents insist that they treat their children the same—that they do not differentiate them by sex. In one study, parents report that they want both their sons and daughters to be equally neat, helpful around the house, able to control their anger and crying, considerate, competitive, and able to defend themselves (Maccoby and Jacklin, 1974:343–344). Similarly, in a class research project where 50 college students interviewed their parents, parents claimed they did not treat their sons and daughters differently. However, when parents were asked "In what ways do you think boys and girls are different?", their responses indicated that they felt that boys were naturally more active, competitive, aggressive, noisy, and messy, and that girls were naturally more gentle, neat, quiet, helpful, courteous, and so on. The students' own reports indicated greater awareness of differential treatment and expectations from that which their parents acknowledged; and the reconstructions of the students were consonant with parental definitions of the nature of boys and the nature of girls. Because the parents believed that boys and girls were naturally different, it is difficult to accept the claim that they treated them the same—despite their protestations to the contrary. "Most parents give them [cues] without conscious effort, routinely" (Money and Ehrhardt, 1975:50).

Unfortunately, nearly all the work done on early-infant socialization has focused on white middle-class families. Consequently, very little is known about the socialization into gender by other groups. Although there is no doubt that ethnic, class, and racial differences in child rearing do exist, until we have more data—the careful, controlled observations of *actual* interactions between child and parent—we cannot know the extent to which children are treated in a nonsexist manner by their parents. Analogous to the studies previously reviewed, what people *say* they do is frequently not in agreement with what they *actually* do.

Consequently, the reports of parents that they treat children the same must be viewed skeptically. We find this skepticism an even more appropriate stance the older the child becomes. This is so because as the child matures, the parent increasingly depends on external agents for socializing the child. Chief among these agents in the preschoolers' world are books, toys, and television. Through them, the infant's core gender identity is translated into appropriate gender image, attitude, and behavior.

Artifacts for Children

Children's artifacts are a particularly cogent source for learning about cultural values. As Margaret Mead has commented, the ideas of the culture have to be presented to children in such simple terms that even a behavioral scientist can understand them. Things as important as the core values of a culture and the role expectations for genders cannot be left purely to the happenstance of parental socializing. Further, these values can be, must be, and are incorporated into material designed for the young; for example, McClelland (1961) found that by doing a content analysis of achievement motivation in children's readers, he was able to predict a nation's economic growth—that is, the values found in children's stories were a sensitive predictor of a society's actual (in practice) value system. Let us look closely, now, at two major socializing materials for young children—picture books and toys. The role of television and other media in socialization will be discussed in Chapter 5.

Weitzman (et al., 1972) analyzed gender roles in the Caldecott Medal Award books and in Little Golden Books, which sold over 3 million copies. The Caldecott Medal is awarded annually by the American Library Association for the best children's picture book of the year. Winning the medal assures these books virtual universal purchase by libraries, central positions in story hours, and wide circulation to homes and schools. Little Golden Books are priced inexpensively and are readily available. The researchers found three major significant differences in gender roles in these preschool books.

First, males were much more prevalent than females in stories and pictures; for example, in the Caldecott Medal books that were studied, the ratio of males who were depicted to females was 11:1 (261 males, 23 females). Second, the activities of the males and females differed. Males engaged in far-out adventures, riotous activities, and various pursuits that required independence and competence. In contrast, most of the girls were passive and remained indoors. Girls were rarely seen working or playing together. In brief, the activities of the boys were directly linked to preferable male values of activity, independence, and achievement, and the activities of girls were linked to passivity and dependence.

Third, the adult roles of men and women were differentially presented. The presentation of adults by sex teaches the children what they might expect for themselves when they grow up, and hence helps inculcate aspirations, goals, and self-images. Not one woman in all the books that were surveyed held a job or had a profession. Motherhood was presented as a full-time, lifelong job. The adult males in these books, on the other hand, displayed a wide range of roles: storekeepers, kings, storytellers, monks, fighters, fishermen, policemen, fathers, preachers, judges, cooks, and adventurers.

Although one may think that picture books are now equalitarian, this is not the case. Using the *Children's Catalog*—the guide librarians use—Grauerholz and Pescosolido (1985) analyzed information about male and female characters in 2216 picture books that were published throughout the century. Their findings are instructive. The overall ratio of male names and male central characters compared to those of females during the 1980s was almost $2\frac{1}{2}$:1; adult male characters outnumbered adult female characters nearly 3:1; and male animal characters outnumbered female animal characters almost $4\frac{1}{2}$:1. Although these ratios are an improvement over the 1970s, a sex-balanced representation has not been achieved. In addition, a recent major "backlash" trend is noticeable, namely, the reduction in the total number of adult female characters. When they are shown, further, they are being shown more often as mothers in the servicing role than they were in the early 1980s (Williams,

1986). Since one of the functions of picture books is to help young children picture, literally, a world beyond the one they inhabit, the lack of adult female role models is a striking omission (Grauerholz and Pescosolido, 1985).

The themes of the children's books are replayed subtly, and more persistently, when we enter the toy worlds of boys and girls. A content analysis of toys in selected categories merchandised in the 1986 Sears *Toys* catalogue shows that toys are still gender linked. I viewed each half page of the catalogue and cross-tabulated the kind of toy that was pictured by the presence of a male child, a female child, children of both sexes, or no children. Then I categorized the various toys into: preparation for spousehood and parenthood; manipulatory toys (e.g., construction toys) and wheeled vehicles; and cultural and educational toys (e.g., books, music, arts and crafts). The results of this content analysis are provided in Table 3.1.

Even the most cursory examination of the table suggests clear differences in the expectations, by gender, for young children. Girls are to play house and take care of babies; boys are rarely depicted engaging in fathering, cooking, or cleaning. As Alice Rossi once remarked, a girl may spend more years playing with her dolls than a mother spends with her children (1964:105). Toys that require manipulation (e.g., blocks, Tinker Toys, erector sets, construction trucks, wheeled vehicles) are the province of boys. When girls are shown with such toys, the actual toy has been feminized; for example, on one page, a boy is shown on a speedster that is "faster than a speeding bullet," "a racy little vehicle that comes loaded with options"; another boy is shown on a "formula racer" sled in which he can "be king of the snow hill"; the lone girl, who is dressed in cuddly pajamas with a bow in her hair, is shown sitting on "Krinkles . . . an adorable dog that's a rocker with a soft acrylic body." Girls are not shown playing with construction equipment, trains, robots, or Rambo. When boys and girls are shown together, they are usually toddlers on swing sets, or the boy is being active, such as hitting a golf ball, while the girl watches.

As though to emphasize that the boys' toy world and the girls' toy world do not overlap—indeed, are not even contiguous—the pages of dolls and the pages of vehicles and construction toys are separated by the more neutral world of educa-

Table 3.1   PERCENT* OF HALF PAGES IN 1986 SEARS *TOYS* CATALOGUE
PRESENTING TOYS FOR CHILDREN IN SELECTED CATEGORIES

Sex	Preparation for spouse/parent roles	Play context (manipulatory and vehicular toys)	Cultural and educational
Male	2% (1)	27% (37)	17% (17)
Female	36% (21)	3% (2)	7% (7)
Mixed genders	3% (2)	19% (26)	13% (13)
No models	59% (35)	52% (71)	63% (63)
Total	59	136	100

*Percent is rounded to nearest whole number.

tional and cultural toys. Both boys and girls may read, listen to music, work with craft sets, and play with educator-designed learning sets.

The adult-designed toy world—the most central and engrossing world of the young—presents different worlds to boys and girls. Although both can use educational toys, the boy is not encouraged to play house or play with baby dolls, and the young girl is not encouraged to play with construction equipment, manipulative or war toys.

Boys *are* to be boys. That means they manipulate their environment. Their toys are designed to encourage this approach to life itself, to develop the necessary manipulative skills, and to prevent them from becoming feminized. Although girls are geared to motherhood through the various agents of preschool socialization, they are allowed greater freedom than are boys to veer from the approved play path. They are allowed *not* to play with dolls, and they are permitted to be tomboys (cf. Thorne, 1986a). Girls may be cautioned and reprimanded for their unfeminine behavior, but, in these earliest years, they are not subject to the same condemnation that meets the boy who would rather dress a doll than hit a ball. One of the results is that girls and boys have different value systems, such that girls tend to value *attachment to others* whereas boys value more highly *individual achievement* (Gilligan, 1983).

Perhaps one of the most subtle but persistent ways, though, that preschool children are socialized into expected stereotyped roles is through the modeling provided by their parents. When a daughter sees her mother taking care of the house, tending to the other children, settling arguments between family members, calling the baby-sitter, making beds, taking care of her parents, choosing clothes, planning menus, deferring to her husband—and working outside the home—the daughter is learning not only what roles a grown woman performs and how she performs them, but what is expected of her. Sons are learning what to expect from their wives. So strong are these role-modeling and rule-giving messages that sociologists see them as a major force in the *reproduction* of the current domestic division of labor in the future (cf. Chodorow, 1978; 1980). Not only are children produced in a home, those children reproduce in their own homes what they learned growing up.

From birth to school age, then, children are treated differently depending upon their gender. By the time they start their formal education, they know what is expected of a member of their gender; the educational system continues the gender education.

□ □ 4 □ □

Education

Many of us still remember that special day in early September, when, dressed in new clothes and new shoes, we entered the school world. Many of us had spent long hours *role playing* or rehearsing pupil and teacher roles; most of us had been socialized by stories from our parents and siblings of the relevance and importance of the goods and evils to befall us in that new world. In addition, probably nearly all of us saw the occasion as a momentous rite of passage: We are now ''big'' girls or boys. Thus, we entered with preconceived notions of what to expect and whether we should and would like it.

However, regardless of what parents tell children about school, they show by their own behavior that they take for granted the societal norm. *Children go to school.* Going to school means that parents are willing to let these other adults (perfect strangers, all named Teacher) discipline, inspire, and evaluate—in short, socialize—their children.

Subjective evaluations, such as ''school must be important—even my parents act like it is,'' are reinforced by the objective reality. For the next 10 or 20 years, with the willing compliance of parents, a child's time is organized around schooling; the major portion of waking hours is spent in school and school-related activities. Days are now structured in order to attend school (e.g., the deferment of doctors' appointments to after school, trips and outings relegated to the weekends and school vacations, etc.); the time to sleep and the time to rise are determined by ''getting to school on time'' and by ''not being tired'' once there. Rather than the laissez faire playtime enjoyed as preschoolers, children now spend an hour or two in travel time, another five or six in the classroom, a few more doing homework, and, as they grow older, they invest the last remaining wakeful hours in extracurricular activities.

Any doubts that might be harbored concerning the parentally approved priority of school are often erased when the student complains about the teacher's methods or assignments. Parents may be sympathetic with the grievances, but the usual message is, ''The teacher is right: Behave yourself!'' Thus, parents accept the

50

schools as having a legitimate right to discipline, evaluate, and inspire. In short, the transfer of authority from the parents to the school is complied with willingly by the parents. Both the parents and the school take for granted that this transfer of authority will occur.

In addition to the parental acceptance of the school as the legitimate educator, the school is formally charged through law to educate the young. The school is one of the few institutions that is recognized as a legitimate agent of socialization. In effect, the school stands not only in *locos parentis* ("in place of the parents"), but also as importantly *in locos societate* ("in place of the society"). Children are required to go to school, and the school is held accountable for teaching what the society values.

Why should a society, however, want a school system? Why is the task of socialization transferred at great public expense from the home to the school? The major reason is that compulsory public education contributes to the survival of complex industrialized societies. First, if any society is to survive, its value system must be transmitted to the next generation. In traditional societies, this transmission is accomplished through the socializing efforts of the entire society. Because what is to be learned remains fairly constant in such societies and because all adults in them are carriers of the general shared culture, there is little need for specialized institutions of education. However, in a complex and rapidly changing society, such as the United States since the late 1800s, the learning of the cultural values cannot be left to happenstance and the efforts of parents. Rather, such a complex society needs to ensure the survival of its culture by systematically teaching all of its future citizens how they should think, feel, and behave. In addition, a major requirement for the survival of industrialized societies is the creation of a particular kind of labor force. Indeed, by 1880, compulsory public education was universal in the industrialized world. The schools fulfill the needs of the labor force in a technological society not only by teaching basic literacy, but also by preparing students to enter occupations upon which a technological economy depends. The public-school system, therefore, is functionally integrative in a complex industrial society, because it transmits core cultural values and teaches the skills that are required in expanding the technological base of the society.

Some of this approved and/or necessary learning is spelled out clearly in the formal curriculum. Students are expected to read (English), write (English), and do arithmetic, as well as to master history, geography, civics, and possibly music, art, and physical education. In addition to this formal curriculum, an *informal* one exists that teaches students about the value preferences of this culture in regard to political, social, racial, economic, familial, gender, and other systems of thought, as well as about what they might expect for themselves. While learning to read, write, and do arithmetic, children are also learning about their culture's attitudes toward gender. What is being taught?

SCHOOL POLICIES AND PRACTICES

Many people seem to think that the social and political climate has changed so radically that children and young adults in our grade schools, high schools, colleges, and universities are being treated in a totally sex-fair way. Some believe that sexism in education is a problem of the past. Unfortunately, that belief does not square with reality. Indeed, Myra and David Sadker, well-known researchers on sex equity issues, and Susan Klein, a researcher with the U.S. Department of Education, argue that in the past few years, the sex equity gains of the 1970s are being eroded (1986).

One of the erosions arises from a major change in federal policy. In 1972, Title IX of the Education Amendment Act was passed. This act required that any school receiving any federal money must, by law, offer equal opportunities for males and females in all the school's programs. But in 1984, the Supreme Court narrowed Title IX to include only those programs that directly received federal aid. Thus, if a school receives only federal lunch program money, it may not discriminate between boys and girls in providing food—but it may, now, discriminate between them in athletics, tutoring, courses, guidance counseling, scholarships, and so on.

Buttressed by this Supreme Court decision and the increasing sentiment against affirmative action in the executive branch of the federal government, along with the false belief that equity has been achieved, schools have become increasingly lax toward creating environments that enhance the educational and occupational lives of all their students, independent of gender.

In addition to the belief that equity has been obtained, there is another belief that many now hold—namely, the belief that achieving sex equity (or any kind of equity for that matter) and achieving excellence are inconsistent goals. Excellence, it is thought, will suffer if we try to treat people equally. Research, however, does not bear out this assumption. Repeatedly, studies show that if an educational activity is introduced to help a targeted population, that program "can raise the quality of education for all" (Sadker, et al., 1986:220). Witness "Sesame Street," which was intended to help poor children, but which helped middle- and upper-class children, as well.

More relevantly, programs that instruct teachers to treat boys and girls equitably have positive consequences not only for the girls, but for the boys, as well. Sadker and Sadker (1984; 1985), for example, found that teachers who were trained to be sex fair in their classroom interactions, became, generally, more effective teachers: They interacted more with their students; talked more about academic and intellectual problems; and offered more precise and constructive feedback, and more praise and remediation. In short, the teachers "became more alert and intentional in their teaching" (Sadker, et al., 1986:220). Although these are positive outcomes for *all* students, because of the change in social climate and federal policy—including the drying up of funds for equity research and demonstration projects—fewer students in the future will be educated by teachers who are themselves trained to be sex fair.

School guidance counselors are, also, unlikely to receive special training in sex equity issues. Because guidance counselors are likely to hold sex stereotypes— seeing girls, for example, as they did in one study (Petro and Putnam, 1979), as easily excitable, home-oriented, indecisive, and passive—they are more likely to advise girls into "feminine" careers, and boys into "masculine" ones. Because girls are unable to see themselves in certain careers, *average test* scores may discourage girls from even considering an atypical career; that is, girls may believe they have to score in the superior ranges in order to be "good enough." In an ingenious study, female students were given the Strong Vocational Test with the regular instructions, and then again with role-playing instructions (to imagine that men liked intelligent women and that women could manage careers and families simultaneously). Under the latter instructions, the career interest of women rose in five occupations: artist, psychologist, lawyer, physician, and life insurance salesperson (Farmer and Bohn, 1970).

If the counselor's role is defined as the "facilitator of adjustment" (Fields, n.d.), students with "deviant" career choices will be discouraged. However, as some argue, if indeed children are to enlarge their horizons and successfully buck the conspiracy of their socialization, the counselor's role should be redefined as one of *advocate*. From this perspective, the counselor's task is to take an active and visible stance throughout the school, providing discussion groups, nonsex-stereotyped career role models, nonsexist library materials, teacher's workshops in nonsexist education, and so on. Such a counseling role recognizes the relevance of changing the environment in order that students can have a greater number of life options, rather than adjusting students to socially prescribed career molds. As complacency and backlash rise, playing this advocacy role has become increasingly difficult in the nation's schools.

The pattern of staffing in the schools, also, tends to reinforce occupational sex stereotyping; for example, custodians are male; lunchroom servers and nurses are female; elementary teachers are female; science and math teachers and principals are male. Indeed, the popular belief that affirmative action has brought a fair proportion of women into school administration is false; in some arenas, the proportion of women has decreased. In the late 1920s, for example, over half of the elementary principals were women; in the 1980s, fewer than a fourth are, although 80 percent of the elementary-school teachers are women (Sadker, et al., 1986). Fewer than ten percent of the high-school principals are women—a proportionate decline since 1950 (Sadker, et al., 1986). Only a handful of women are school superintendents (out of a possible 17,000 positions).

The lack of female administrators in the educational system cannot be attributed to a dearth of administrative competence among females. Schools that are headed by women, in fact, have higher student achievement, better morale, and fewer disciplinary problems than those headed by males (Shakeshaft, 1985). In addition, female educational administrators use techniques that reduce school conflicts, and increase community involvement; know more about curriculum and learning issues; and are more careful about monitoring their students' progress than are their male counterparts (Sadker, et al., 1986). Unfortunately, despite the ability of women to successfully administer schools, school boards repeatedly choose men over women for these positions (Shakeshaft, 1985; Smith, et al., 1982). Despite affirmative action, today, proportionately more men are heading our country's schools—and that trend is only likely to continue.

This pyramidical staffing teaches the teacher and the female students to limit their aspirations: There is little room at the top for women. More subtly, children learn that although their teacher, usually female, is in charge of the room, the school is run by a male, without whose strength she could not cope; the principal's office is where the incorrigibles are sent. This learning, which parallels what many children have already learned in their homes regarding the roles of their mothers and fathers, only perpetuates further the notion that women require the leadership of men and that men should be able to provide that help. This learning is even more intensely taught every day in the classroom itself.

The child spends approximately 1000 hours a year in a particular school environment—the classroom. Within that setting, incidental learning about gender is a major part of a hidden curriculum. Boys and girls are often segregated in different lines, play areas, and classroom lists; are pitted against each other in academic and deportment contests; and are rewarded and punished as groups. Comments from boys that they "don't want to read about any dumb girl" or their refusal to stand near a girl for fear of "getting girl germs" go unnoticed and uncorrected by teachers who would certainly reprimand children for comparable racial or ethnic slurs.

When teachers transmit differential expectations for children's performances, they cause real consequences. Research has born this out repeatedly; for example, Rosenthal and Jackson (1971) told teachers that certain randomly selected children were destined for rapid intellectual growth during the school year. However, these children had the same range of intelligence scores as another group. At the end of the term, the children labeled as high-growth potentials had significantly higher I.Q. standings than those of the other group. The raising of the intelligence level is attributed to the fact that the teachers expected these students to blossom and, therefore, treated them differently than the control group. In terms of gender expectations, there are similar consequences.

By the time children are in the third grade, they know that a boy's life is better and more valued than a girl's. When students in grades 3 through 12 were asked, for example, how would their lives be different if they awakened one morning and were the opposite sex, their answers, at every grade level, confirmed their beliefs in male superiority and male privilege. Boys, for example, said: "I would hope it was a bad dream"; "If I were a girl, everyone would be better than me, because boys are better than girls"; and, "If I were a girl, I'd kill myself." Girls, on the other hand, said: "People would take my decisions . . . more seriously"; "If I were a boy, I'd drop my typing class"; and, "My whole life would be easier" (Tavris and Baumgartner, 1983).

Sex segregation, when it is approved and sanctioned by adults, then, has major and differential consequences for boys and girls. Separate is never equal. When the school supports separate programs, it perpetuates male superiority and female inferiority.

However, it is not only the school and teachers that sex segregate the children: The children sex segregate themselves. Virtually every study that was done of children in mixed-sex schools finds the same pattern; girls primarily interact with girls, and boys primarily interact with boys (Lockheed, 1985). The amount of sex segregation varies by activity and age (Thorne, 1986a). As the children progress through the elementary grades, the amount of segregation increases. Lunchrooms are characterized by "boys' tables" and "girls' tables" (Thorne, 1986b). Playgrounds are becoming increasingly "gendered geography," with boys dominating the playfields and basketball courts, and girls dominating the play equipment and sidewalks (Thorne, 1986b; Phillips, 1982).

What is important to recognize about these gender groupings is that they are constructed by the children: They do it themselves. At one level of analysis, boys and girls create two "separate spheres" with two different kinds of social organization (cf. Thorne and Luria, 1986; Thorne, 1986b; Phillips, 1982; Best, 1985; Lever, 1976; Maltz and Borker, 1983). Girls tend to interact in smaller groups or in friendship pairs, whereas boys interact more publicly and visibly in larger groups. Girls talk about their interactions in terms that stress being "nice" and cooperative, whereas boys talk about teams, contests, and hierarchies. Girls' conflicts are handled through indirection; those of boys are handled through direct verbal and physical assaults. Girls show their affection for each other through compliments, stroking, hairbrushing, and so on, whereas boys show affection through backslapping, hand hitting, nicknames, and so on (Thorne, 1986a).

Some argue that these different childhood experiences affect future work possibilities. It is argued that because men learned as boys to be "team players," they are able to be loyal "team members" of their corporations—a requisite for advancement (Blotnick, 1986). Loyalty and team play are learnings that supposedly have eluded the girls; jumping rope does not count.

Whether women lose out by not playing on football teams, however, is less the problem than providing both males and females with experiences in each other's worlds. If the task of education is truly to teach equality and to help each child achieve his or her full potential, then teachers and other administrators need to *intervene* in the sex segregation that children themselves create: Schools need policies that take into account the self-imposed gender segregation.

There are at least three ways to lessen the children's sex segregation. First, teachers can carefully monitor themselves and not use language—such as "boys and girls"—that underscores differences. Teachers do not have to give children choices that will allow them to sex segregate. Children do not have to be allowed to choose their classroom seats or to make decisions that separate the boys from the girls—such as at "Secret Santa" time, when girls buy gifts for girls, boys for boys. Second, classroom and play activities can be broken down to include only a few children, because, when the numbers are few, children are more likely to interact across sex boundaries (Thorne and Luria, 1986). And third, more teacher appreciation can be given to children who cross the gender boundaries—the children who have learned to interact in both worlds and who offer an alternative to the "separate sphere" model (Thorne, 1986a).

By limiting sex segregation, the first step toward gender equality in the schools is possible. However, because boys and girls are already well on their way toward gender-defined lives by the time they go to school, it will profit us to look at how the school is experienced by boys and girls. Not only are the objective outcomes of their education different, but so are their subjective experiences.

THE MALE SCHOOL EXPERIENCE

Although developmentally, boys are approximately 12 months behind girls at age 6 and approximately 18 months behind by age 9 (Bentzen, 1966), both genders are expected to begin first grade during their sixth year and to progress uniformly from grade to grade. Consequently, in the beginning, a boy is at a decisive disadvantage.

The boy is not ready to acquire the particular skills that are rewarded in the classroom, such as "coloring within the lines." Furthermore, the way he is supposed to behave is in direct contradiction to the autonomy for which he had been rewarded previously (Alwin, 1986). In school, he is to sit still, be quiet, keep his hands and belongings to himself, follow directions, and wait for the teacher to call upon him.

Consequently, the young boy is sent to a classroom for which he is developmentally and psychologically unprepared, and which daily requires him to act in ways that are not encouraged at home. Little wonder that boys are more likely than girls to have learning and behavior problems at school.

Studies of reading, for example, indicate that boys are at least two or three times more likely to have reading difficulties (Frazier and Sadker, 1973:93). These academic problems of boys are routinely addressed and remediated. Reading programs are available in schools and privately. The academic problems of boys are taken seriously (Greenberg, 1985).

One of the reasons boys have more trouble learning to read is traceable to their classroom experiences. In an experiment in which children were removed from the classroom setting and taught by computers that were programmed to give positive reinforcement and to require all children to read the same amount daily, kindergarten boys performed better than kindergarten girls. But when they were returned to their regular classrooms, the boys were soon lagging behind the girls. Analysis of the interaction between the teacher and the children revealed that the boys were much more likely to receive negative comments—such as "Sit up!" "Don't play with your bookmark!"—and were called upon less frequently to read than were the girls (McNeil, 1964).

Observational studies in the classrooms repeatedly find the same pattern of teacher-pupil interaction. Boys are much more likely to receive negative comments, generally, and those comments are likely to be harsher than those addressed to girls who are guilty of the same offenses (Jackson and Lahaderne, 1971). Moreover, studies indicate that boys receive more attention of all kinds: negative comments, positive comments, instruction, and listening (Frazier and Sadker, 1973:91; Sadker and Sadker, 1984, 1985). In half the classes observed by the Sadkers (1984, 1985), the teachers acted as if the class was sex segregated, and they interacted more often and more directly with the boys than with the girls. In 1986, Sadker (et al.) concluded that in American classrooms, "boys are the central figures . . . and girls are relegated to second class participation" (1986: 220). Some educators argue that this greater interaction encourages the boys toward greater independence, because they are interacting actively and directly with the teacher, who in turn is taking them, their questions, and their behavior more seriously than they are taking the girls' (Frazier and Sadker, 1973:91).

Although this greater interaction may indeed lead to greater independence of thought and analytical ability, it certainly does not lead to greater success in terms of grades. Boys with the same intellectual ability as girls, and who score as well on standardized achievement tests, nevertheless, receive lower grades on their report cards (Lipmen-Blumen, 1984).

School, therefore, is often an uncomfortable experience for the boy, and he may end up hating it, dropping out either in body or spirit. He has a constant struggle trying to make sense out of the contradiction between the two worlds of home and school. Despite his initial lack of success, however, as time goes on, he is less likely to be an underachiever (Sadker, et al., 1986). As he moves through high school, his academic achievement improves, and the occupational future looks increasingly bright (Ekstrom, 1985; Cordes, 1986).

In addition to these classroom experiences, an important aspect of the male's school life is the emphasis placed on athletics. Young males, whether they choose to engage in competitive sports or not, are subject to the socializing impact of the societal norm: Athletics are good for boys. As early as fifth grade, the sex differences in the games that children play propel boys toward competitive, sex-homogenous, and complex team sports (Lever, 1976; 1978). By prepuberty, the male student is encouraged by the school (as well as by parents and peers) to take up a sport, to join a team. If he does not, he may be cajoled, shamed, and ridiculed; if he does, he may also be cajoled, shamed, and ridiculed.

Witness the chilly fall afternoon on which a midwestern sixth-grade football team pretended not to be discomforted by the degrading ceremony in which they were the sacrificial lambs. Proclaiming to team and onlookers (of which I happened to be one), their coach shouted: "This isn't just football we're playing. . . . It's Life! Trample and be trampled! The one with the guts is the one who wins—out there in the field and in life. And you're cowards. I want to see you out there: Pop 'em! Hit 'em! This is life, and there's no place here for *losers*."

Although young boys are told that their success as athletes is an indicator of their potential success in life, it is at adolescence that athletic achievement becomes firmly linked to prestige for males. It is one of the most important factors for a male adolescent's social standing in high school.

Not only does athletic participation provide the male with prestige, team membership offers a kind of initiation rite that helps ease the transition from boyhood to manhood (Fiske, 1972). In team sports, for example, boys learn to sacrifice self for the team effort, to develop confidence through public demonstration of their skills, to dedicate themselves to hard work and concentration, and to identify fully with other males through the joint display of aggression, physical prowess, and courage on the playing field (Fiske, 1972; Armstrong, 1980). In effect, team sports socialize males for occupational roles in two important ways. First, they incorporate into their own personalities the traits that are necessary for success on the field— competitive spirit, achievement orientation, courage, aggressiveness, and endurance. Second, they learn to identify with the team—male bonding through aggressive activity toward other males (Felshin, 1974). Team sports, therefore, are seen as developing a boy's ability to cooperate with other males in a competitive framework.

By learning these skills, the adolescent male is helped in his transition to manhood and occupational success. To the extent that he can compete successfully on the field—trample others before they trample him—and to the extent that he can recognize his identification with the team, he is being prepared to be a "man." In short, athletics as taught and practiced in the school posits masculine stereotypes of aggression, competitiveness, strength, and male bonding as ideal and natural for boys, and as relevant to their success.

Embedded in the athletics-is-good philosophy is the notion that there is one highly preferable life that men should pursue. Many boys, however, are not built either physically or psychologically to achieve athletically. The accent on physical prowess during adolescence, therefore, can be extremely disturbing to the nonjock. Although there are social-class differences, "the primary resource the young male has is still his own body" (Gagnon, 1976:173). He measures himself by what he can do physically compared to others his age; and how he stacks up determines to a great extent his social acceptance by others and his own self-esteem. The nonathletic boy is not only less likely to be a leader (Armstrong, 1980), but also more likely to doubt his masculinity and perhaps harbor resentment toward women, as this brief excerpt from Julius Lester's autobiographical comments suggests: "While humiliating myself on the football and baseball fields, the girls stood on the sidelines laughing at me, because they didn't have to do anything except be girls" (1976: 270). Undoubtedly, thousands of boys have sat waiting (and still do) to be picked for a team, questioning their masculinity and believing as Lester did, "As boys go, I'm . . . [not] much" (1976:270).

Although the need for physical strength is decreasing in the technological world and although there is some indication that competitive sports are less valued presently in middle- and upper-class high schools (Gagnon, 1976), the emphasis on them is still visible in school-corridor trophy cases, conversations, daily announcements, and pep rallies. Athletics has traditionally provided a path of upward mobility for working-class males, and it continues to do so. Therefore, despite some changes in adolescent society's concern with competitive sports, the institutional supports for competitive athletics have not particularly diminished. There are still few structural avenues open to the nonjock to learn sports skills for their own sake.

Not only are athletics associated with masculine traits, but also male competitive sports enjoy the greatest organizational and financial support within the school. More money, time allocation, and physical facilities are provided for these activities than for female competitive events or either sex's acquisition of general athletic skills. The recent guidelines for Title IX permit the disparity in financial support to continue. Coaches' salaries, players' uniforms, and the provision of facilities for the male athletic teams are considered legitimate line items in a school's budget. Schools communicate in many ways not only that girls' sports are not as important in the total educational experience as boys' sports, but also that the athletic development of boys who are not interested in competitive sports is of little consequence.

In summary, then, boys tend to experience difficulty in their early years of schooling, but their difficulties are taken seriously. If they remain in school, their academic performance tends to improve, as do their standard achievement scores, and their career goals enlarge. Once in high school, the pressure to perform athletically provides the skillful athlete with prestige and the potential for upward mobility; for the boy uninterested in competitive sports, however, the challenge is how to earn the respect of self and others and to accomplish the transition from boyhood to manhood.

THE FEMALE SCHOOL EXPERIENCE

The classroom world of neatness, docility, and passivity, which boys experience as frustrating, is for girls simply an extension of those virtues for which they have been rewarded previously. Unfortunately, these classroom virtues have little to do with the intellectual enterprise. Although the girl feels subjectively more at home in the classroom and is better able to meet the developmental and behavioral requirements of school, the outcome in the long run may be destructive. If the girl learns well the "stylized version of the feminine role" presented to her in the early grades, then the rewards "can be almost too successful in that in later years it is difficult to move girls beyond the orderly virtues learned in their first school encounters" (Bruner, 1966:123–124).

In one study, Dweck (et al., 1978) examined "learned helplessness"—that state where effort is reduced because failure seems certain. Following a failure experience, Dweck and her associates found that girls are more likely to attribute failure to their lack of ability—an uncontrollable factor—whereas boys attribute failure to a controllable one, such as lack of effort or a "mistake." Believing they cannot alter the situation, girls exhibit "learned helplessness" much more frequently than boys do.

Rather than attempting academically difficult problems, many girls tend to avoid them, fearing failure and the subsequent loss of teacher approval; for example, in one study where failure was experimentally manipulated, girls and boys were asked to put together two 7-piece puzzles in one and a half minutes. As soon as the subjects had completed one puzzle and had two pieces joined on the other, time was called. When given the option to work on the puzzles again, girls were much more likely to choose the puzzle that they had already mastered, whereas boys more frequently chose the one they had not completed. As Frazier and Sadker comment, "For good grades and teachers' praise, the grade-school girl relinquishes the courage that it takes to grapple with difficult material. This naive young bargainer of seven or eight has made an exchange that will cost her dearly" (1973:96).

One of the costs is a declining I.Q.: Children who show declining I.Q.'s are passive, shy, and dependent (Maccoby, 1963). The school, through its reward system for docility, in effect robs the girl of her intellectual abilities. Another cost for the young girl is her perception of limited life options; for example, in a large survey of upper-elementary-school children, practically all career choices made by girls were in one of four categories: teacher, nurse, secretary, mother. Boys' choices were dispersed and often fanciful.

When girls reach puberty, they are more likely to become underachievers (Greenberg, 1985). Even if they receive good grades, they are less likely to see themselves as college material than are boys with similar grades, are likely to do less well on their SAT's, and are less likely to plan to go to college (Frazier and Sadker, 1973:140; Cordes, 1986; Ekstrom, 1985).

If a girl becomes pregnant, she is likely to join ranks with the 200,000 other high-school girls who annually drop out of school due to maternity. Only about one-third of the school districts have any kind of continuing education program for these women.

The school athletic experiences of girls are also different enough from those of boys to warrant discussion. The facilities, conditioning, coaching, and training of the female athletics have been inferior traditionally to that provided for the males. In effect, "learning that she should not be athletic is what makes the female inferior athletically—not the other way around" (Wilmore, 1974:40). In a series of experiments, Wilmore, a board member of the American College of Sports Medicine, concluded that for the three major components of athletics—strength, endurance, body composition (lean-fat ratio)—"there are few actual differences between the best female and male athletes when tested in the laboratory" (Wilmore, 1974:81).[1] The female's inferior performance, however, can be attributed to "the degree to which the sport has been recognized or emphasized for women, and the time and effort given to coaching, facilities, and training techniques" (Wilmore, 1974:80). Where facilities, training, conditioning, and coaching are equalized, the gap between male and female performances has been steadily closing; for example, several female Olympic swimmers in 1984 would have won silver and bronze medals if they had competed in the 1976 men's competition.

In addition to these rather clear and blatantly different treatments of male and female superior athletes, there are more subtle ways in which sports are culturally organized to exclude female participation—subtle ways in which the schools are, perhaps, unwitting dupes.

In order to succeed at a given sport, it is necessary to acquire a set of skills that are used in that sport. Most sports require skills based on certain body movements—"efforts in space" (Grunden, 1973); that is, success in sports requires an ability to use the body in certain ways. Most sports that are available in this culture, for example, require direct, controlled, sudden, and strong motions emanating from a central body core. These movements allow the body to rise and advance in widening spheres and permit the player to move forward, upward, and laterally outward with speed and strength. Nearly all of our sports—hockey, football, bowling, tennis, basketball—require that repertoire of movement. Although the equipment, rules, and playing terrain differ, all of these sports require similar body movements in the penetration of space.

These movements—the ones necessary for success in sports—are "not present in the daily movement vocabulary of most girls" (Grunden, 1973:1). Girls, in learning to be women, learn how to move in a feminine way (Brownmiller, 1984). This means that they learn to move in a light and airy manner. Movements are kept close to the body, and, when projecting outward, girls do so in a kind of "joint-by-joint" manner. (That is presumably what is described by the expression, "You

---

[1]Another aspect of Dr. Wilmore's research bears comment. When he and his colleagues trained nonathletic male and female college students through a ten-week weight-lifting program, the women increased their upper-body strength by 30 percent, *without* increasing their muscle bulk. Although they were still less strong than the newly trained men by body weight (7.6 percent), by lean body weight (weight without fat), they were actually 5.8 percent *stronger*. Incidentally, it is estimated that we use only 20 percent of our muscle power anyway.

throw like a girl.'') The movement of the girl is not a sustained, strong one with the effort flowing from a center core throughout her body; rather, there is either a jerkiness or a giving-into-gravity motion that signals femininity.

Consequently, when girls are exposed to sports, they are ill prepared to be successful for two important reasons. First, they do not have the necessary movement vocabulary that sports require; second, the acquisition of these movements requires that they move in ways culturally defined as masculine. To be successful at a sport means that a woman is (movement-wise) defeminized.

The school sports program does not provide valid athletics for its women students, because it does not take into account the socialization of the female student. Such an athletic program would require teaching her ''to explore movements that are concerned with aggression, the outside world . . . action and reaching out . . . in order that she discover the range of movement and expression'' (Grunden, 1973:13). Only through such an expansion might girls learn to participate successfully in sports as they are now constituted. Furthermore, only through such a program might girls develop a movement vocabulary that can express confidence and strength in their daily lives and, consequently, allow them to act with greater freedom from gender stereotyping

In summary, although the girl experiences the early years of school as more comfortable than does the boy, if she succumbs to the rewards, she is more likely to leave her school experience docile, intellectually unmotivated, and without self-esteem. In addition, if she succumbs to a ''female'' education, she will be unprepared to advance in the most prestigious careers. We can see the consequences of ''female'' and ''male'' educational worlds operate when we look at an especially instructive case—mathematics.

MATHEMATICS: AN "INSTRUCTIVE" CASE

Without a grounding in mathematics, a child is virtually excluded from professional careers in physics, chemistry, medicine, engineering, architecture, economics, business administration, electronics, and computer sciences—all either highly prestigious occupations or rapidly growing fields that offer job placement and excellent salaries. Few girls receive the requisite preparatory math in high school. This is true despite the surprising fact that in the early grades, girls do better than boys in mathematics (Lipmen-Blumen, 1984) and that boys and girls ''like'' it equally well (Ernest, 1976). Boys take more math because they know they need it for subsequent education and careers. When it is time for the boys and girls to take their SAT's, no wonder the boys score higher on mathematics (Benbow and Stanley, 1980; 1983).

Do girls take fewer math classes because they are neurologically unsuited for math, or are there sociological reasons for girls being early math dropouts?

Once in high school, a girl's mathematical achievement goes down (Benbow and Stanley, 1983). Mathematics is still associated with masculinity. Consequently, girls may choose to avoid it and the harsh negative stereotypes (e.g., unattractive, masculine, cold, distant, odd) that are associated with ''female mathematicians'' (Boswell, 1979:15; Tomizuka and Tobias, 1981). Indeed, girls may work hard to disassociate themselves from their math talents (Kaminski, 1985). An example is a high-school senior, a female, who scored in the 95th percentile on her math SAT and in the 70th percentile on her verbal. What was her career choice? "Unknown. . . . Definitely not science—maybe literature or art . . . and, then, marriage."

Math courses are still male biased. Most of the problems, examples, and role models in the math texts involve males (Weitzman, 1979). When adolescents are asked to solve word problems that involve woodworking, geometric spaces, and guns, that is, male-typed activities, the girls do poorly. However, when the problems are about sewing, cooking, and gardening, that is, female-typed activities, the girls do much better. In both sets of problems, the logic required to solve them is the same; only the content varies. Unfortunately, the female-typed activities are not often presented, so the girl does not learn to feel at home (Milton, in Weitzman, 1979:42).

Given that the content of math courses is male biased and that math is associated with "masculinity," it might be possible, nevertheless, that girls simply have less analytical ability than do boys. In a careful review of the literature on sex differences in analytical ability, Sherman (1974) has demonstrated that the term *analytical ability* is misleading, though, since most researchers have studied only *spatial perception*. Spatial perception refers to the ability of a person to perceive an object (figure, shape) independent of its background. Females tend to be *field-dependent*, or not very good at seeing figures out of context, whereas males tend to be *field-independent*. The most frequent test for field dependence or independence is the "rod and frame" test—a test that requires the subject to place a rod vertically in a frame, despite misleading background cues.

On the face of it, this is surely a very narrow skill upon which to claim sex differences in analytical ability. Curious, too, is the fact that although girls tend to do better than boys do on *verbal perception* (Sherman, 1974), verbal ability is not called analytical ability. Is it not likely that if males scored high on verbal perception and females on spatial perception, then, the former would have been labeled "analytical ability?" Clearly, "What the researchers have done is to seize upon one of the few traits in which males score higher and label it analytical ability" (Weitzman, 1979:42).

Indeed, we might even argue that spatial ability, in fact, *really* has very little to do with analytical ability. Since mathematics rests on a language pattern—a particular form of logical argument—we might even propose that, if anything is true, girls *should*, on the average, be better at math than boys are.

However, it must be conceded that spatial ability may relate to certain aspects of mathematical reasoning, especially in "visualizing" problems. Like other abilities, however, spatial ability is acquired, and persons who are good at spatial perception are those who have had *practice* at it through hobbies and training. Since boys are more likely to make model airplanes, set up electronic experiments, and take mechanical drawing and shop than girls are, they have a greater opportunity to enhance their spatial skills than do girls. Indeed, once the number of math courses that are taken is held constant, there are *no* sex differences in boys' and girls' spatial perception abilities (Fennema and Sherman, 1977). In Japan, where boys and girls both explore the world of origami paper folding, there are no sex differences in spatial ability (Lipmen-Blumen, 1984).

As to whether males and females actually do differ in a wide range of math skills (e.g., computational, geometric, algebraic abilities, etc.), the evidence is at least inconclusive (Ernest, 1976) and probably negative (Sherman, 1977). If differences in ability do exist, they are apparently not large. What is true, though, is that females *believe* they are not as good as boys are in math. Girls will explain a poor grade in math by saying, "I'm not good in math. Boys will say, "I didn't try" (Dornbusch, 1974).

Not only does the girl think she lacks math aptitude, apparently the teachers do, too (Kelly, 1984). Ernest (1976), for example, found that 41 percent of the teachers that he interviewed thought boys were better at math than girls were; none thought girls were better (although they thought girls were better than boys in English). Kelly (1984) found that teachers believed that differences were genetic. The self-fulfilling prophecy is at work in the math classroom. If a student is labeled "good," she/he will tend to meet those expectations; and if she/he is labeled "poor," motivation and performance will decline.

So persistent and subtle are these beliefs about the inability of girls to do math, that even when change is attempted, it can be (consciously or unconsciously) sabotaged by the adults in the school. Lynn Fox's dissertation (1974, reported in Weitzman, 1979:72–74) clearly illustrates the process.

Fox created a special summer Algebra I program for girls gifted in mathematics. Women teachers, noncompetitive activities, informal and individualized instruction, and an emphasis on using math to solve social problems were used. At the end of the summer, 18 of the girls scored well enough to place into Algebra II. However, half of them were told by their principal or counselor that they were not ready. Three were convinced that they should repeat Algebra I; one was placed in Algebra II on probation. Many of those who were allowed to enroll were told that they would not perform well; several were told not to come for help when they had trouble. Parents reported that the teachers did not want these girls, since they believed that they would do poorly. Predictably, the attitudes of the adults had consequences for the girls' success. Fox concludes, in fact, that the girls who performed well in Algebra II were those whose school personnel were enthusiastic about the program and supportive of the girls. Negative expectations, on the other hand, produced negative results.

Further, the research clearly shows that the school has to reach girls by junior high school (Boswell, 1979) if they are going to be accorded "free and *informed* choice" (Ernest, 1976). Successful programs "caught" the girls early—by *sixth grade*—before they could learn that "math was male," and soon enough for math to become "natural" and taken for granted. The current low enrollment and high attrition rate constitute an "immorality," resting "precisely in the fact that they are the result of many subtle and not so subtle forces, restrictions [and] stereotypes . . ." (Ernest, 1976:21). For women to achieve occupational equity with men, therefore, it is necessary for the schools to encourage and support young girls to excel at mathematics. Fortunately, the message that "girls can and should do mathematics" is taking hold in the minds and choices of girls. More are enrolling in math classes and are being encouraged to do so by their parents and counselors (Lipmen-Blumen, 1984).

Regardless of what happens to students in high school, some go on to higher education. What happens to them?

HIGHER EDUCATION

In the college classroom, a logic professor (illogically) distinguishes between "logic" and "female logic" (i.e., nonlogic). A statistics professor anthropomorphizes the transformation of a double-peaked curve into a normal bell-shaped one by saying, "a once busty woman who had breast cancer." Most of the students laugh. A woman professor draws all of her examples from her roles as a wife and mother and from her husband's role as a college professor; her husband never mentions his familial relations. An English professor lectures on poetry and "pseudo-poetry," the latter having been written "for or by women." A male student's final rebuttal to a woman who has bested him in a seminar is, "Women just don't understand"; and the male professor laughs. These are but a sampling of incidents in a college classroom reported by students in journals kept for a woman's studies course.

These sex-stereotyping behaviors—combined with professors' proclivities to call on men more often than on women, to allow men to talk longer, and to respond longer to men's comments—create a classroom climate that is a "chilly" one for women, in general (Hall and Sandler, 1982), and a "freezing" one for minority women. Despite the high educational aspirations of black female high-school seniors—higher than those of white females or black men—once in college, they are subject to harassment, devaluation, and invisibility (Benokraitis and Feagin, 1986:127). Even if minority women succeed despite the psychological stress and structural barriers in getting through college, more devaluation awaits them in professional school. Kendall and Feagin (1983) in their study of minority women in medical school found, for example, that minority women are evaluated on their ability to fit the "white-male subcultural model" of studying medicine, rather than on their medical knowledge and skills. One Mexican-American woman, for instance, described her medical school experience as "like walking a picket fence." This required her to fit the " 'Anglo mold,' which sees medicine as . . . impersonal and disease-oriented, [and] the 'male mold,' which is aggressive, competitive, [and] authoritative . . ." (Kendall and Feagin, 1983:21–22). Indeed, Sadker (et al., 1986) proposes that colleges have lagged even farther behind than the elementary and secondary schools in working toward equity in education.

Professors' lowered expectations and open prejudice become self-fulfilling prophecies. If professors consider women innately inferior, less original, and as illogical sex objects who are better off married, might they not find the evidence to support their beliefs? Little wonder that, after four years of college, a woman's aspirations have decreased. Repeatedly, in studies of college women, approval and encouragement are the catalytic agents toward achieving ambitions; for example, one exceptionally talented female senior explained her academic career as follows:

> I came to college planning to get a Ph.D. in mathematics. However, I was disappointed when I didn't make the most advanced math class. I decided to major in astronomy. When I got a B in astronomy, I decided it wasn't for me either. Meanwhile, I was getting A's in psychology, and a woman instructor encouraged me to major in it. Although I really didn't like it, I decided to become a social science major. I'll graduate with a 4-point in my major, but I wish I had stayed in mathematics.

This gifted undergraduate viewed her grades as indicators of approval to such an extent that they determined the course of her college career and her professional one, as well.

First, however, a woman must be admitted to a university. It is estimated that women comprise 75 to 90 percent of the very qualified students who do not go to college. Women receive fewer fellowships and less financial aid than men do. Although most upper-middle-class and upper-class families will assume the financial support of both daughters and sons through college, few consider the financing of a daughter through graduate or professional school as obligatory or desirable. Lower-class parents are likely to consider the education of their sons more necessary than that of their daughters. In fact, the greatest loss of intellectual potential is estimated to come from the lower-class daughters, who are not aspiring and do not receive financial aid.

Despite these structural barriers, for the first time since World War II, there are more women enrolled in colleges than men, and many more women over 35 than men enrolled as part-time students (Sadker, et al., 1986). The female students, however, still tend to be concentrated in female sex-typed departments; for example, 74 percent of the B.A.'s in Education are awarded to women, and 81 percent of the B.A.'s in Social Work (Seager and Olson, 1986:3). Faculty and university administrative positions, nevertheless, remain male dominated, even in these female sex-typed disciplines. One of the reasons for this is that women do not go on to receive Ph.D.'s at the same rate that men do. Despite the preponderance of females at the undergraduate level, for example, only 44 percent of the Ph.D.'s in Education go to women, and only 50 percent of the Ph.D.'s in Social Work. Considering all university faculty positions, less than one-fourth are filled by women, and these women are concentrated in the lower rungs of academia (assistant professors, lecturers, and instructors) and in such traditionally female departments as nursing and home economics.

Discrimination against women in hiring, promotions, and salaries is routine in universities, despite governmental regulations that prohibit it. Fewer than ten percent of the presidents of colleges and universities, including the all-female ones, are women (Sadker, et al., 1986). Ninety percent of the full professors are male, as well as 80 percent of the associates and nearly 70 percent of the assistants (Sadker, et al., 1986). Only at the least well-paid and least job-secure slots (instructors and lecturers) do the proportions of female faculty begin to equal those of the male faculty (AAUP, 1986). As Harris (1970:284) succinctly summarizes it, "The rule is a simple one: the higher, the fewer."

The longer a woman is in academia, the greater the discrimination. Salaries for women assistant professors lag a mere four percent behind their male counterparts, but 15 years after their doctorates, women earn 13 to 23 percent less than their male colleagues (Educational Testing Service, Princeton, reported in *Ms.* magazine, June 1980:25).

University administrators and faculty argue that they would hire, promote, and equally reward women faculty members, if only they could find qualified women. Sometimes, they suggest that the pool of female Ph.D.'s is inferior to the pool of male Ph.D.'s. Following sex equity guidelines, they warn, would endanger academic standards and reduce the quality of higher education in America. Would hiring women be detrimental to the academic health of our universities?

Listening to the vituperations of faculty and administration when they discuss sex equity issues, one might believe that the university is a veritable haven of truth, justice, and excellence; it would lead one to believe that the university is a *Meritocracy*, where individuals are sought and rewarded on purely academic criteria—research and teaching excellence. University spokespersons claim that individuals are rewarded on their merit (the ''merit system'').

The reality of university life, however, stands in contrast to that ideal. University departments, for example, frequently are committed to *Mediocracy*. They choose to remain undistinguished, ensuring themselves a comfortable and non-pressured life tenure. Two examples—one from teaching and one from hiring practices—will illustrate how the ''culture of mediocracy'' can control a university department. The data are drawn from in-depth interviews with faculty, as part of a study funded by the National Institute of Education's research program on sex inequities in higher education (Richardson, et al., 1980).

Excellence in teaching is not only not rewarded (a commonplace practice throughout many universities), but is also actively discouraged in this department, which is committed to mediocracy. During the interviews, several members (males and females) commented on the negative sanctions that they received for teaching well. One woman said, ''I was told (by a friendly colleague) that if I wanted to get tenure, I had to stop teaching so well, because the other faculty didn't like 'being shown up'.'' Another member stated, ''I know if I talk about how much I like teaching—and what a good job I think I am doing—I will be 'punished' by the department.''

Perpetuating the mediocracy depends on hiring mediocre faculty. Among the applicants for a new position in this department was a Ph.D. from a very prestigious department, who was currently teaching at another esteemed university. Her vita included numerous fellowships, honors, publications, and teaching awards. Another applicant was a student at a mediocre university, who had not yet begun his dissertation, had no fellowships, honors, or teaching awards, or, for that matter, independent teaching experience. His publications were coauthored with his advisor and appeared in readers that his advisor edited. The personnel committee of this department rejected the Ph.D. from the prestigious university. Why? ''She hasn't published *all* that much.'' ''Why would she want to leave University X?'' ''I don't think she's married.'' ''I think she's older.'' Invited for the job interview was the predissertation student. Why? ''He's X's student and X always turns out good ones.'' ''He's promising.'' ''He'll make a good colleague.'' ''I think we could all live with him.'' The affirmative action representative who was present at this discussion never questioned the procedures or the criteria. Perhaps, as a tenured member of the culture of mediocrity, he did not recognize that the criteria were *not* academic ones.

The department described above is dedicated, then, to preserving standards of academic mediocrity, not standards of academic excellence. Such departments are not uncommon, even in excellent universities (Bienen et al., 1977). Even when not so extreme, university departments have tendencies to select members who will be ''good colleagues,'' which usually means someone with whom they feel comfortable socially, a part of the ''old boys' network.'' Ergo, a department perpetuates itself in its own image.

The question remains: Are there fewer *qualified* women than qualified men to fill the faculty positions? Research evidence continuously points to the academic superiority and academic motivation of women Ph.D.'s over male Ph.D.'s. Women have higher scores on entrance exams and perform better in graduate school. *Married* women, in fact, are more academically gifted than single women, or married or single men (Bienen, 1977). Given the pressures against women in graduate school, completing a demanding academic program requires strong motivation. The strength of women's motivation is attested to in their ''staying power.'' Despite the belief to the contrary, women are more likely to be employed ten years after their Ph.D. than men are, and they are much more likely to be employed in a field that is related to their degree. Indeed, a decade past their doctorate, only 69 percent of the men are working in an occupation that is related to their Ph.D. (Bienen, 1977:376).

The productivity of women, as measured by research publications, suggests that there are *no* overall sex differences. Women in the natural sciences publish slightly more than their male counterparts do, in the social sciences slightly less, and in the humanities about the same (Bienen, 1977). Given that women are more likely to be hired in less prestigious schools and that they do have home responsibilities, the fact that the productivity rate of males and females is practically identical is rather remarkable.

Finally, women professors teach at least as well as male professors. Statham, Richardson, and Cook (1980) interviewed university faculty regarding their perceptions of and attitudes toward teaching. Then, they observed the actual behavior of professors in classrooms and coded their behavior every five seconds.

The professors, both male and female, agreed that ''good teaching'' involves organization, an interactive model (student input), and intellectual growth. Contrasting the actual classroom practices of male and female professors, we would have to conclude that, based on the faculty's own criteria of ''good teaching,'' women are *better* teachers than men are. Although both males and females are equally organized, ordered, and ''logical'' in their presentations, women professors solicit and receive more student input, provide their students with more evaluative feedback on their contributions, encourage them to think more independently, and interact with them in a more personalized and less authoritarian way.

Women, then, it would appear, are more motivated than are men, equally as productive in research, and surpass them in teaching excellence. All of this is true, despite the cultural pressures not to perform well and despite their responsibilities to homes/husbands/children. The question, therefore, might be: Why aren't men *more* productive than they are? Perhaps a committee should be formed to investigate the "male problem" on campus. Perhaps that committee will find what women already know—that male professors do not have to produce as much as women in order to be rewarded. There are fewer obstacles for them to surmount, and once tenured, they can enjoy the leisurely life of male bonding with their academic brethren, assured in the knowledge that real work is not necessary for their continued financial advancement, power, and prestige in the university.

Perhaps, universities *should* actually institute the *merit* system that they now claim to use. If a merit system was used in universities, not only would the proportion of female faculty rise, but also the quality of American education would improve—for entering the ranks would be scholars and teachers who are motivated and committed to excellence. Not only do *qualified* females suffer from the present indecency, but *all* students—female *and* male—are thereby cheated of the finest faculty and the best education. Only the Brotherhood of Academicians profit.

With few role models and many barriers, many women continue to view college as something to do before they get married. Parental and peer pressures to marry directly after graduation from college are still strong, although young women are increasingly resisting those pressures; for example, in a survey of graduating women that I conducted at Ohio State University, only 31 percent were planning on marrying within a year of graduation, 38 percent were planning lifelong careers, 61 percent believed that women should be financially self-supporting whether they were married or not.

Although men are probably more at home in college and although the demands of the academic program are more in keeping with the kinds of abilities they have already developed, they nevertheless face the increasingly mounting pressure of occupational preparation. If a man chooses to major in sociology, history, fine arts, or English, the usual query is, "But what will you *do* with it?" Pursuing a course of study for sheer intellectual pleasure is not acceptable; as a male, he is expected to prepare himself for a career. If he plans on a postgraduate education, then he has to *make good* grades. As one male student explained when he asked to drop an elective, "I plan to go to dental school and I need a high grade-point average. I took this course out of interest, but I can't afford the C I'll probably earn in it. Can I still sit in?" In addition to the grade pressure, he knows that he must make the right connections for jobs or graduate school during this college period, and that he must make the important friendships that will aid and abet him in his career.

The pressure to perform academically in order to achieve occupational success is exacerbated by social pressures to demonstrate one's "cool" through success in dating, drinking, and so on. The pressure mounts on the male student to finally shape up and take his responsibilities seriously, but at the same time to be a "man." He can choose to lower his aspirations and limit his extracurricular life, but it may cost him social condemnation.

Children, then, are reared in a culture that uses a formal educational system to perpetuate sex stereotypes. As a final building block, to ensure the enculturation of children—and adults—the mass media is called upon. We turn now to an analysis of the role of the mass media in the socialization process.

□ □ 5 □ □

Mass Media

Human existence is sustained through human communication. Through language, socialization, and education, we learn about our society's expectations for us as males or females. Yet, the more complex and heterogeneous a society is, it seems, the greater the need for centralized transmission of the beliefs and values of that society. Standardized public education helps fulfill that function, but, increasingly, so does the mass media.

Through the media, individuals enter a world of symbols that demonstrate to them how society works, by dramatizing its norms and values and by showing its prevailing outlook and social relationships. People perceive the media presentations of their social order as moral, normal, right, and just (Gerbner and Gross, 1976: 173). The media is in the *socialization* business—and it is Big Business. Individual spending on the media is over $40 billion. Commercials and advertising expenditures to get us to buy products go into the multibillions. To violate conventional thought—producers feel—would cost the media and its advertisers the mass market's dollars.

Because the media depend upon their advertisers for financial survival, sponsors control the *content* of the media: "Whoever pays the piper calls the tune." It is argued that because 20 million viewers are necessary to retain a television program (Gerbner and Gross, 1976), a program's content must be as inoffensive as possible. Most likely, television audiences could learn to accept more controversial, artistic, and humane programming; such programming is by and large absent, however. The media are formidable defenders of the *status quo*—as we shall soon see in detail— and a socialization force with which it is hard to reckon. Even if parents want their children to be free of sex stereotypes, that task will be almost impossible if the children are allowed to thumb through and read mass magazines or are permitted to watch television. Television, for example, negatively affects the creativity and sociability (Burton, et al., 1979) as well as the liberalness (Prisute, 1979) of its young viewers. And even if parents carefully control the programs that their chil-

69

dren watch, they should know that children under age 6 cannot distinguish humans from puppets and cartoon characters on television (Quarforth, 1979), nor can they tell where the program ends and the commercial begins (Palmer and McDowell, 1979).

Recently, the media has given the impression that equality between the sexes has been achieved. They do this, in part, by emphasizing superficial changes. One of the favorite topics of the media is the "first woman———"—fill in the blank— astronaut, bank president, district court judge, department chair, television anchor, and so on. By emphasizing the "first," the media give the impression that women, as a class, have achieved equity or are even "taking over," rather than that some doors have been opened to some highly accomplished women in some organizations. If many women were taking new positions, on the face of it, the "first" whatever would not be news. Even more insidious is the idea that because they are the "first," that the second, third and hundredth are sure to follow. Giving the impression that equity has been achieved is a particularly invidious practice, because it creates complacency and false expectations.

Although any form of media could be analyzed in detail, we shall restrict our discussion to newspapers, magazines, advertisements, and television. These forms are easily accessible and available within the home to both children and adults; that is, the media socialize children *and* adults. At each stage of development, young and old are given media images to copy and media messages to emulate.

NEWSPAPERS AND MAGAZINES

The morning coffee and the morning newspaper are well institutionalized in our society. From editorial cartoons (cf. Meyer et al., 1980) to comic strips (cf. Brabant, 1976), obituaries, sports pages, women's pages, and editorial pages (cf. Domhoff, 1978; Epstein, 1978; Tuchman, 1978), newspapers perpetuate differentiation by sex.

Editorial decisions are made—perhaps nonconsciously—that affect how subscribers perceive women and men. Some of these decisions are deceptively insidious, such as those that refer to the looks, marital status, and emotional states of women in "straight reporting," and the writing of headlines that accentuate sex stereotypes, no matter how irrelevant they may be to the news article. The obituaries of men stress their accomplishments, whereas those of women—even those who have had active public lives—stress their familial roles (Benokraitis and Feagin, 1986:94–95). The caption over a picture of a woman on the "FBI's Ten Most Wanted List" queried, "Who would marry her?" The headline over the photo of a male on that same list, however, said, "Have you seen this killer?"

Where a story is placed in a newspaper—front page, editorial pages, women's pages, and so on—is another editorial decision that has consequences for the story's public fame or public oblivion. People read the front page and the editorial pages as "news," whereas stories on women's pages are viewed as "nonnews" and of interest only to women. During this past decade, the formerly women's pages have been renamed "People's" pages, "Life-style," or "Social" pages. The content of these pages, however, has remained that which concerns food, fashion, and furniture, plus news of women's advancements in public life. Placing news of the women's accomplishments on the "life-style" pages says that it is not news, and that the equal-rights issues have as much political, economic, and social significance as the Pillsbury bake-off, Kroger coupon specials, Heloise's household hints, and Erica's needlework instructions. The major issues about women are compartmentalized and trivialized.

The image-making potential of the news media, however, is perhaps best illustrated by the results of the annual Gallop poll that asks Americans, "Which woman do you most admire?" The women that Americans choose for that list testify to the power of the news media to create *images* "worthy" of women (Lang, 1978). Similar to "media events" (nonevents), these "most-admired women" are "media characters" or nonpeople.

Increasingly, these most-admired women—such as the First Lady—are satellites of public male figures. Women who have achieved stature on their own do not stay on the list for long, and are notable primarily for female sex-typed activities, such as arts, nursing, and missionary work.

First Ladies invariably make the most-admired list; the press seems willing to follow diligently the activities and headaches of the president's wife. Moreover, the activities of the First Lady make front-section (i.e., "real") news. Most frequently, these wives are cast into the passive, nonassertive, warm, and supportive "good-wife" image—such as that of Nancy Reagan. Not in the news are any items to mar the "good-wife" image—such as that of Eleanor Roosevelt's intimate relationship with another woman.

By according so much attention to the president's wife, the media creates an interest, rather than reflects one, and their coverage perpetuates sex stereotyping. The self-esteem or motivation of millions of women is certainly not enhanced, since the media have reinforced the idea that the way to fame is to marry a successful man. Little incentive is given to achieve autonomously.

Newspapers exert considerable socialization influence, moreover, in translating the research of the biological, social, and physical sciences into a language that is comprehensible to a general audience. Consequently, it is reasonable to expect some watering down and some overgeneralization. Science as it is imaginatively rendered and interpreted by journalists is somewhat akin to the rumor process. Details drop out, and certain elements are sharpened so that the ideas can be more easily assimilated (Richardson [Walum], 1975). When the research and ideas are about sex and gender, however, a journalist can trivialize the results and sex stereotype the researcher; for example, a feature story on gender research by *The New York Times* on the Op-Ed page (i.e., general news) was picked up and altered by many other newspapers (Richardson [Walum], 1975. In their versions, the research, which was performed by a woman, was transformed into "human interest" and then into a "woman's news" item. The researcher was credited with statements, such as "men—the despicable slobs," which she did not make; and she was assigned attributes, such as "the helpless female professor," which were unfounded, and physical characteristics, such as "the very pretty academic," which were irrelevant. Personalizing and trivializing ideas that concern social and political change, then, are powers journalists have—and use.

Journalistic power is seen in a different way when we consider magazines. For every age and stage—from preschool through retirement—specialized magazines exist to educate, inform, and anticipatorily socialize the public. Like newspapers and television, these magazines depend upon their advertisers for financial success; the subscription and newsstand prices do not cover the cost of the magazines. But, unlike television and newspapers, magazines are directed toward a specific market—such as "model airplane enthusiasts," "adolescent girls," "newlyweds," and so on. Because these intended markets are small (compared to newspaper and television markets), the magazines are, in theory, freer to change their style, coverage, and content.

Browsing through the magazine rack at a well-stocked bookstore or newsstand, one cannot help but notice that some magazines are intended for men and others for women. Men's magazines are apparently of two kinds: finance and sex. The finance magazines, such as *Forbes* and *Fortune*, are "reality," that is, success-oriented. Articles concern investment possibilities, semi-legal activities (such as tax-evasion and loopholes in the bribery law), international business interests (such as the dividends of a Middle-East peace, Japan's computer industry, and the economic emergence of China), and get-rich-quick schemes (such as turning art into money and investing in rare metals). Advertisements for computers, cars, liquor, stocks and bond issues, banks, and data processing systems dominate. The covers are frequently of famous men, such as Rockefeller, Reagan, Iacocca, Henry Ford, or they are stylized drawings of wealth, such as moneybags in a safe, oil wells, and diesel rigs. Scanning *Fortune* for 1986, I found very few women pictured; those who were depicted were predominately in secretarial or nursing roles; two women executives were shown, both of whom were attached to famous men. Playfulness is downplayed. "Jack is (almost) all work" in *Fortune*.

Sex-oriented magazines, on the other hand, such as *Playboy*, *Hustler*, and *Penthouse*, usually show a seminude woman with parted lips and soulful eyes on the cover; she seems to be asking the viewer to relieve her sexual desire. The cover message is buy the magazine and "turn women on," or at least feast your eyes on pages of women who desire you.

Smith's (1976) conclusions from his analysis of "adult-fiction" pornography of the 1970s seem applicable to the content of the 1980s men's porn magazines, as well. The magazines are built around explicit "sex episodes" that are tied together by transition pages in which the reader is treated to male-prowess stories that teach how to "score" more successfully—new (sex) jokes to tell, potent drinks to serve, aphrodisiacal foods to prepare. Typically, the pictured models are females—young, white, attractive, and heterosexually involved. Their genitals are pictured or described in great detail. Lesbian or masturbation scenes are *controlled* or instigated by men. Only physical sex is presented; feelings of caring or emotional involvement are virtually absent.

The advertisements complement the photos and text. On sale along with liquor, cigarettes, motorcycles, and cars are sex enhancers, such as full-sized latex dolls, textured condoms, penis-sized enhancers, climax prolongers, sex videotapes, and *The Easy Way to Get Girls: Through Hypnotism* book (only $10). Sex is *objectified*, depersonalized, and available to any man—in his fantasy, anyway. He can arouse any woman; once aroused, only he can satisfy her. (For an excellent historical analysis of *Playboy* and the double standard, see Ehrenreich, 1983).

Clearly distinct from these men's magazines about money and sex are those for women. Traditional women's magazines have at their core getting and/or keeping a man. In both the working-class and middle-class magazines for women, women are defined in terms of their relationships with men. Traditional values are asserted; for example, these magazines declined publishing articles about single women who are involved with married men because, as one magazine editor summarized it, "Our readers—wives—don't want to be disturbed by reality."

The sales appeal of the standard mass magazines for middle-aged, middle-class women is epitomized in the following poem by Ellin Carter. Imagine a woman at a supermarket's magazine rack. One cover catches her eye and holds her attention. Each of the nonitalicized sentence fragments appear on the cover of the magazine; the italicized words are her thoughts.

November Issue

Harvard nutrition expert's
calorie-control diet plan
      do I want this magazine
pretty afghans to keep you cozy
      that preys upon my needs

16 best hair styles
      insecurities

elegant decorating ideas
at do-it-yourself prices
      incapacities

everything-in-a-dish party meals
      loneliness

fabulous food gifts
      dullest yearnings

how to shape and tone your body
      innermost fears

10 at-home tests to guard your health
      I seem to be buying it

With the advent of the women's movement and changing demographics (e.g., more unmarried people and more working women), new potential consumer markets have arisen. To reach those markets, new magazines have appeared (e.g., *Ms.*, *Working Woman*, *New Woman*, *Living Single*, etc.), and established magazines (e.g., *Glamour*, *Mademoiselle*, *Woman's Day*) have been updated in some ways and have retained their traditionalism in other ways. Let's look briefly at the established women's magazines for the young adult, and then at the newer breed of magazines.

Look at a cover—any cover—of *Glamour*, *Mademoiselle*, or *Cosmopolitan* from the past decade or more. You see the same picture—different face, different model—but the overall effect is the same. The cover girl is always a full-face photo of an attractive, smiling, bland, and cheerful young woman, looking directly at you, as though she is *your* reflection in a mirror. The cover photo is saying, "Don't you want to look like me? Buy the magazine and you will find out how. Come with me into the wonderful world of womanhood, where everyone is beautiful and happy." Once the pages are entered, the woman is given some apparently contradictory messages; for example, she will be told what to wear to look sexy as well as what to wear to be successful. She will be told how to get and keep a man, as well as how to move up in a career. She will be told how to control flyaway hair, as well as how to lift weights. The editorial will invariably propound a women's rights issue; the pronoun *she* will be assiduously used to refer to doctors, lawyers, and other professionals. An article advocating women's rights will appear sandwiched between full-page spreads of semi-nude women who are narcissisticly admiring their diamonded fingers and wrists, and their red-foxed shoulders.

Thus, what these traditional young women's magazines are doing is adding women's career and social issues to their usual fashion and femme fatale format. By doing so, the magazines keep up with their target market and increase the number and kinds of advertisers. More kinds of clothes and other products are salable; the new "Cosmo Girl" needs a career wardrobe and a weekend wardrobe, as well as more kinds of makeup, exercise programs, success courses, rest and relaxation spas, and so on. The young woman can be sold products that help her believe that she is happy and beautiful like the cover girl and, simultaneously, that she is an independent career woman.

Barbara Ehrenreich (1986) sees the image of women in the modern woman's magazines as one that heightens the demands on women to be superlative in all arenas. Today's magazine woman has a "black belt" in aerobics and a child who is enrolled in an ivy league nursery school; she dresses for success and has power lunches during the day, and lounges in her Dior robe in front of her mesquite logs in her new condo at night, discussing tax shelters with her husband, who is also lounging in his Dior robe.

Traditional mass magazines for women, then, have softened their disapproval of employment outside the home and have become more sympathetic to working women and less sexist in their editorial content. What then about the newer magazines, such as *New Woman* and *Working Woman*, that are especially targeted to gainfully employed women? Do they prefer new ideas, or do they reinforce old ones and create new problems for women? To answer these questions, Glazer (1980) analyzed *Working Woman*, a magazine specifically intended for women who are employed outside the home. She looked for any references to domestic labor—childcare, cooking, (including shopping), consumption, and house maintenance (including repairs, decorating, and cleaning). Her results still stand.

Working Woman perpetuates the "double-duty" woman—a woman who is employed for pay outside the home, and for no pay inside the home. The solutions to her double-duty day that are preferred by the magazines are *personal* solutions, that is, being better organized, changing her standards of cleanliness for success, hiring a baby-sitter, training her husband to be cooperative, and reorganizing her use of time, money, and leisure. Not offered by the magazine are *social* solutions to her problems, such as state- or business-provided day care, after-school childcare sites, flexible work schedules, communal living, and neighborhood cooperatives.

Suggestions that might alter the traditional relationships between employee and employer, and between men and women, are not given in the magazine's pages. Rather, tremendous efficiency is required if a woman is to succeed at work and at home. Nearly every aspect of her life needs to be managed, according to the magazine. Thus, for example, in order to be on time at work, the usual morning jobs should be scrutinized and those found unnecessary should not be done or should be relegated to others; other morning chores should be done the night before, "added to cooking ahead, to supervising children's homework and spending 'quality' time with them . . . relaxing with one's husband, studying to improve oneself for the job"—and all this after staying late at the office to impress the boss (Glazer, 1980:83–84).

According to the image in *Working Woman*, married women should continue to be responsible for domestic chores; husbands are problematical (lazy, inept, intractable) or highly unusual and commendable if they "help" with domestic chores. Of course, a woman may decide to forego marriage and children, leisure and friends, to devote herself to her career just as an "up and coming" man would. If a woman works hard, applies herself, and is dedicated and assertive, she might make it to middle management (in a female sex-typed occupational slot) or she might even own a (very) small business (Glazer, 1980).

Thus, *Working Woman* perpetuates the double standard: women are still responsible for housework and childcare. No protest is raised that women are expected to perform two jobs simultaneously; no note is taken that the problems of the double-duty wife are socially generated and need social solutions (Glazer, 1980).

Consequently, magazines remain sex-typed male or female. Male magazines offer finance and sex. Women's magazines, whether traditional or modern, proclaim that it is all right for a woman to want to work, as long as she retains her "femininity." That "femininity" might be demonstrable through her fashions and wardrobe, or through her domestic wizardry of keeping husband and children well fed and content.

Overall, then, magazines and newspapers as the major representatives of the printed media encourage sex stereotyping and the division of the world into male and female domains. The maintenance of the sex-stereotyped world is furthered, moreover, by the advertisements that are the financial backbone of these magazines and newspapers.

ADVERTISEMENTS

Advertisements not only sell products, but they also sell gender stereotypes. Indeed, selling products, in part, depends upon selling those stereotypes (Farrell, 1974; Lahof, 1975). Marlboro ads, for example, sell the Marlboro Man—tough, aloof, rugged, craggy, mobile, and independent. The Marlboro Man personifies the same values as those that are found in trucker songs—the desire to sow wild oats, to flirt with danger, and to roam free (Lahof, 1975). Virginia Slim ads sell the "neoliberat-

ed'' woman, who has ''come a long way, baby'' without sacrificing her ''femininity.'' Arpège and Johnson's Wax are used by ''feminine'' women; Pabst and
Brylcreem are used by ''masculine'' men. But these portrayals are really quite
obvious compared to the subtle ways advertisements portray gender stereotypes.

Advertisements are carefully designed, photographed, airbrushed, and laid
out. The task of an ad is to get the message across at a glance; thus, considerable
control is exercised to make the picture appear *natural*, no matter how outlandish it
might be. One of the ways that naturalness is created is through the display of
genderisms in the photo.

Look, if you will, at an advertisement in any magazine or newspaper. In your
imagination, change the sex of the model(s). Does the picture still make sense and
appear natural? Chances are that the advertisement you have imaginatively recre-
ated will seem inappropriate and strange. The reason is that the photo has been
carefully constructed to display cultural understandings about the differences, and
the relationships, between men and women.

In a brilliant analysis of ''gender advertisements,'' Goffman (1976) analyzed
some of the concrete visual components in ads that create the appearance of ''gender naturalness.'' He labels these components *gender themes* or *genderisms*, five of
which are: relative size, ritualization of subordination, function ranking, the family,
and feminine touch.[1]

One's authority is directly relative to one's size; in general, the greater one's
size, especially height, the greater one's authority, fame, and prestige. In ads, men
are usually displayed as taller than women, except when the woman is superior in
social status to the man. Thus, when women are shown with lovers, husbands, and
teachers, they are shorter than the men; but when the man is the woman's chef,
chauffeur, mechanic, or waiter, he is shorter than she.

Advertisement women are usually diminished not only in size, but also in
other ways. Deference is shown by physically lowering oneself, and superiority is
shown by standing erect, head held high. Being prostrate makes one vulnerable and
dependent on the goodwill of others; if one is lying on the floor, one's position is
associated with the unclean and the impure, for the floor is ''the place to keep dogs,
baskets of soiled clothes, street footwear, and the like'' (Goffman, 1976:127).
Women (and children) are more likely than men to be pictured lying on floors and
beds. If a woman is shown standing, frequently her knee is bent, her head is cocked,
and she is smiling broadly. She may be posed in a childlike, clownlike posture; or
she may be shown being led around by the hand, helped by an arm hold, or directed
by an arm around her shoulder. She also may be depicted having a marvelous time
as the object of a man's mock assaults, happily being tossed around, carried upside
down, and restrained from movement. All of these portray *subordination*.

Related to the relative size and subordination gender themes, is the *function
ranking* theme. In ads, the male is likely to be depicted in charge, higher in rank
(authority, prestige, knowledge, etc.), and more valuable in function. This is true
whether occupations are exhibited or whether they are not. Moreover, when a male
is presented in female domains (e.g., kitchens, nurseries), he is depicted as per-

---

[1]A sixth theme, *licensed withdrawal*—the woman's greater freedom to be psychologically ''not
there''—I will not discuss.

forming no role at all or else as a somewhat ludicrous and helpless creature who does not really belong in the (trivial) female function world; he knows that—and so do we.

Family as a gender theme also emerges in the ads. The ideal—two children, one of each sex, and two parents, one of each sex—is the typical image. A father stands a little outside the family grouping, just a little bit distant—perhaps to protect his family or perhaps to protect himself from intimacy. Fathers are depicted relating to sons, mothers to daughters. The kind of relationship is different, however. Daughters appear to be simply miniatures of their mothers—same dress, hairstyle, poses. Frequently, the figures are touching or overlapping. Womanhood, apparently, is something that just "happens" to a girl; she just grows into it as she grows into the next clothing size. No special training, no special skills, no special worry: Simply let nature take its course. Unity between sons and fathers is portrayed differently. Sons and fathers are not dressed alike, posed alike, or in physical contact. Continuity between boyhood and manhood is not portrayed; thus, to become a man, the boy will have to *do* something; he will have to achieve it.

The final gender theme, the *feminine touch*, appears frequently in advertisements. Women are shown cradling, tracing, just barely touching, and caressing the surface of objects—including their own bodies—with their fingers and hands. Their hands are not prehensile; they do not grasp, hold, manipulate, or reach. Faces, then, and other parts of the body can touch, and do the work of the "feminine" hands. Carried to extremes, advertisements portray women as narcissists, touchers, and adorers of their own semi-nude bodies; they appear turned inward, relating to men only as "props."

However, although magazines, newspapers, and advertisements are powerful agents of sexist socialization, they are truly welterweight when compared to the impact of television—a subject to which we now turn.

TELEVISION

"Then," asks Socrates in Plato's *Republic*, "shall we simply allow our children to listen to any stories that anyone happens to make up, and so receive unto their minds ideas very often opposite of those we think they ought to have when they grow up?"

Little did Socrates suspect that in the two millennia since the proposed Republic, the danger of hearing a stranger's saga or an enemy's tale would be replaced by a repetitive and ritualized storytelling system that cultivates a homogeneity of consciousness in the most far-flung communities. Little could he know of the videocast or of the potential impact of television. Indeed, most people today who live with television have little grasp of it as a unique and qualitatively different media form.

Television is essentially different from all other media because it is "the central cultural arm—an agency of the established order," whose purpose is to maintain and extend the conventional behaviors and beliefs. Its chief cultural function is "to enculturate and socialize people into standardized roles and behaviors, to cultivate in people resistance to change" (Gerbner and Gross, 1976:175). Television inculcates in its viewers standard and conservative assumptions about "normal/abnormal," "right/wrong," and "good/bad"; like language (see Chapter 2), television tells us what to think about, how to think about it, and how to feel about others who think differently than we (''televisionists'') do. It is the first centralized cultural influence to permeate the first and final years of life, and all those in between. ''The reach, scope, ritualization, organic connectedness, and non-selective uses of mainstream television'' make it a qualitatively different kind of media (Gerbner and Gross, 1976:176).

More American homes have television sets than indoor plumbing. Average viewing is six hours a day. By the time children start school, they will have spent more time in front of a television than they will spend in college classrooms. More than 40 percent of adults' leisure time is spent in front of a television set. Each year, ''Americans spend trillions of hours watching television'' (Tuchman, 1978:10).

Unlike magazines, newspapers, and books, television does not require literacy; unlike movies and theater, it is free, always available, and requires no mobility; and unlike radio, records, and tapes, it can show as well as tell. Not only does it precede reading in a child's life, it also preempts it. Unlike all the other media that bring specialized parochial and private messages to selected audiences, television brings the same message to all—rich and poor, old and young, male and female. The major networks all serve the same social systems, sell to the same markets, and use the same programming formats.

No matter how contrived the plot, viewers assume the story takes place in a real world and against a real background. Even if the action is understood as imaginary, the background seems to be natural and realistic. Thus, television character medical doctors receive millions of letters that ask for medical advice. And although few of us have been in prisons, criminal courts, and operating rooms, we *think* we know what those places are like because *we have seen them on television*.

In the same way, we learn to accept as realistic, natural, normal, and correct, the assignments of sex, race, and personality traits to characters, the roles characters play, and the relationships between them. Although ''TV drama is a mixture of truth and falsehood, of accuracy and distortion'' (Gerbner and Gross, 1976:179), television is the primary ''storyteller,'' the primary medium through which diversity is standardized. Socrates would be speechless if he knew the story that we are repetitively told on television, for television does, indeed, repeat the same message.

Television is an *organic* system of messages and images (Gerbner and Gross, 1976); the system as a whole sets the agenda of issues and opinions, normality and abnormality. Any particular drama, newscast, soap opera, and commercial, should be considered within the total context of television as an organic system. Television is a unity—it is mainstream American culture (Gerbner and Gross, 1976). What does it teach?

Seven days a week, many times a day, the television brings messages into the home through dramatic shows. Being represented in those dramas gives a group social existence; absence from the dramas is ''symbolic annihilation'' (Gerbner and Gross, 1976:182). Who is cast into what parts, then, has meaning and conveys a message.

For the past 35 years, despite the social changes and the occasional television show that reflects those changes, there has been considerable consistency and stability in the presentation of males and females on television. Whether one looks at newscasts, children's programs, prime time, soaps, or commercials, the majority of actors and characters are male. In a recent review of all the research that has been done on role portrayal and stereotyping, Signorelli (1985) summarizes that in "study after study men outnumber women two to three;" in children's programs and cartoons, males outnumber females four or five to one. Moreover, in most programming, women and men are "cast into very traditional and stereotypical roles" (xiv). Television portrays women in few occupational roles, and as unsuccessful at mixing careers, marriage, and child rearing. For the most part, programs that have married women with careers as major characters, focus on their home lives. In daytime serials, career women have a harder time than noncareer women, and they are punished more harshly. Women spend a lot of time on television talking about men, talking with men, and trying to attract men. Women are portrayed as less aggressive than men, and as more affectionate, sociable, and nurturant than men. Men are portrayed in more occupations, as more often in charge and in authority, and as more often aggressive in behavior. Moreover, the majority of these males are middle-upper-class, prime-of-life Americans—the same type who dominate the social order (Gerbner and Gross, 1976).

These stereotypical portrayals are the primary ones on television, and they are repeated day in and day out. It is easy to think that this is not so, because certain programs—like "Cagney and Lacey" and "L.A. Law"—fall outside the norm. These programs do present women and men as complex, and in nonstereotypical roles and relationships. Although romance is often a subtext in the drama, the female is not necessarily the passive sex object, and the male the active suitor. Whatever the week's plot and theme, male and female characters are shown as equals in work and love, or as struggling to accomplish this; and both men and women are shown trying to balance home and work, families and careers. If these are the programs you watch, you may have come to the erroneous conclusion that all television has improved in its portrayal of women and men.

In most of the top-rated television shows, though, males are the prime actors, and women are sexual creatures or manipulative matriarchs; and there is some indication that stereotyping is presently on the increase. "Dallas" is particularly instructive on this count. During the two years that Bobby Ewing was thought dead, the women in the show took on new roles, and both male and female characters enlarged their repertoires. Sue Ellen became a top-notch fund raiser for a medical foundation; Jamie Ewing became the intelligence behind Wentworth Oil; Pamela Ewing coadministered Ewing Oil; Jenna Wade successfully managed her boutique; Donna Ewing adopted a deaf child; and Mandy Winger, J. R.'s mistress, expressed desires for independence and honesty. J. R. Ewing became a "nice" man, warm and loving; and Cliff Barnes gave up some of his old insensitivity, and expressed his love for his wife, Jamie, taking her as a full partner at home and at the office.

When Bobby was brought back into the show, his death was explained as Pam's dream; apparently, so were the changes in the characters. When Bobby returned, Sue Ellen and J. R. resumed their conflict-habituated relationship. Sue Ellen was no longer a force behind a medical-research organization; Cliff separated from his wife, Jamie, who subsequently died; Pam remarried Bobby, and neurotically focused on their son's well-being; Jenna sold her boutique, and became dependent upon Ray; and Donna resumed her career, lost her marriage, and had a baby. Central to the plots were male-bonding issues (the three Ewing brothers); male competition (e.g., between Bobby and Cliff, and their sons); male violence and aggression (e.g., between Miss Ellie's husbands and J. R.'s entanglement with guns-for-hire); and male sexual prowess, including paternity. The stereotypes have returned to "Dallas."

For the most part, then, in television, men are the actors, and women are acted upon. Nowhere do we find the male-female message more chillingly proclaimed than in the portrayal of violence on television. For two decades, Gerbner and his associates have been monitoring television violence.[2] They have found violence to be a consistent and frequent feature on television. Eight out of ten programs have violence in them. Six out of ten major characters engage in violent activity. Nearly one-fifth of these specialize in violence—law breakers or law enforcers. Every six and one half minutes, a violent act occurs on television—every three and one-third minutes on children's programming. By the time a child graduates from high school, she/he will have seen 13,000 violent deaths on television.

Violence on television preserves the social order and socializes the young by generating fear, mistrust, and selective aggression (Gerbner and Gross, 1976). Television symbolically portrays that it is normal to live in a society ruled by violence. To live in such a society requires the cultivation of fear, the acquiescence to power. What television communicates is who can do what to whom with what consequences. What are the rules of the game of life, and who wins? Who will be victim? Who will be victimizer?

Women are more likely to be victims of physical violence—especially women who are unmarried, young, old, employed, lower-class, foreign, or nonwhite. The risk rate for women has steadily increased, especially on programs for children. "Good" women, old women, and black women are powerless; they never kill—but they are killed.

"Good-guys," on the other hand, are killers. They avenge their "good" women, they right wrongs through physical violence. Old, foreign, and lower-class men get killed by the powerful "good-guys" on television.

"By generating among the many a fear of the power of the few, TV violence achieves its greatest effect" (Gerbner et al., 1979:180). *Fear* rather than aggression is the outcome (Gerbner and Gross, 1976:178). The heightened sense of risk and fear generated in women (as well as in the poor, old, and ethnic minorities) is likely to increase their acquiescence to the established order. Force is legitimate when used by the socially powerful. Television violence, therefore, teaches that some people—white, rich, males—are legitimately in control, and others—women, old people, poor people, nonwhite people—are liable to be physically abused, mutilated, and murdered. Physical violence thus symbolizes in an effective and cheap way the psychological and social lives that different categories of people might expect. Its power lies in its ability to foster obedience and acquiescence.

---

[2] They have defined violence as "the overt expression of physical force against self or other compelling action against one's will on pain of being hurt or killed, or actually hurting or killing" (Gerbner and Gross, 1976:184).

EFFECTS OF TELEVISION

In the introduction to this chapter, I mentioned the negative effects of commercial television on children—on such things as their sociability, grades, creativity, independence of thought, and liberal perspective. These are just some of the consequences. Indeed, I would argue that television is dangerous to one's (mental) health, especially to the health of children and adolescents. The evidence is overwhelming.

The domestic and occupational role messages are not lost on children. Children who view stereotypical marriages on television—no matter what their parents' marriages are like—evaluate traditional roles as "correct" (Cheles-Miller, 1975). When presented with women in atypical occupations, children endorse them as "appropriate" (Atkin, 1975; Miller and Reeves, 1976). However, as already indicated, most portrayals are stereotypical ones. So much so that a 5-year-old responded in exasperation to her mother's query as to whether a particular animal on "Sesame Street" was a male by asserting, "Oh, you know! It's always a boy unless it's a mommy!"

In addition to monitoring television programming, Gerbner, Gross, and their associates have investigated whether the programming has had any impact on its viewers. Since television *is* mainstream American culture, it is difficult to sort out exactly *what* is enculturated through television. To resolve this methodological problem, Gerbner and his associates analyzed television content to find out what knowledge television *fosters*, or what they refer to as "television answers"—ideas that are grounded in television's portrayal of life rather than in real life. They then asked heavy viewers and light viewers a series of questions. They found that heavy viewers were more likely to give "television answers" than light viewers were. Heavy viewers, in contrast to light viewers, think there is a much higher proportion of police officers than there actually is, and believe the probability of being involved in violence is much higher than it actually is. Adolescents who are heavy viewers are more likely to condone violence and are more likely to commit violent acts (Gerbner et al., 1979). Most telling is the fact that heavy viewers believe police have to use force, see the world as more violent, and express more *fear* (Gerbner et al., 1979). The television message is being received.

To summarize, children are reared in a culture that assigns one set of traits to males and another set to females. The major agents of socialization—home, language, school, and mass media—teach children what is expected for a member of their sex. The success of this socialization, however, depends in great measure on socially controlling the adults who socialize the young. In the following section, we will explore the nature of some of these social-control mechanisms that maintain the perspective of the culture in the actions and ideas of its adults.

SECTION

□ 2 □

Institutions of Social Control:
Ideational Elements

A child is born, taught a language, reared in a family, led through an educational system, and exposed to the mass media—along the way receiving the messages that define for him or her how to act, how to feel, and what to believe. As we have seen, in order for a culture to be perpetuated, the young must be socialized into the taken-for-granted attitudes, beliefs, and values of the culture. Such socialization is ensured because the child is psycho-biologically dependent upon the adult world. However, because human beings have volition, they can and do stray from prescribed paths, and they can and do think heretical thoughts. Because indoctrination of the young is dependent on adults who are capable of deviant perspectives and behavior, in order for a culture to survive, there must be strategies for enforcing the traditional among the adults. If the adults are not kept in line, the young will not be appropriately socialized. Social control of adults is necessary to perpetuate the culture.

It is *authority structures* that ensure the perpetuation of the culture among the adult population. Authority structures are of several kinds: religious, legal, scientific, economic, and political. In this section, we will examine the first three—the religious, legal, and scientific—with a particular emphasis on their ideational (ideas and values) components. In Section Three, we will focus on politics and economics.

Religion carries with it *moral authority* and, frequently, threatens sanctions beyond the here and now on into eternity. Laws represent the formal codification of certain norms and mores, and they carry the *authority of the state*; to break the law is to risk social sanction, public punishment, and the loss of privileges. Science has the weight of empirical truth or pragmatic authority. To challenge scientific findings or to behave contrary to what has been declared to be normal, subjects one to ridicule or pity. These three authority structures—religion, law, and science—are effective methods of adult social control. Disagreeing with them can result in ostracism (from heaven or friends) or incarceration (in prisons or asylums).

As Marx argued, what is frequently proposed as moral/true/legal is often no more than an ideological rationalization for the interests of the dominant group. Many of the ideas that are posited as authoritative are simply "religionized/ scientized/legalized" restatements of the cultural values that we encountered in Chapter 1. These ideas, rather than representing absolute truth, are culturally relative and culturally dependent statements that in effect justify the social inequality between the sexes.

That this is so should not really surprise us; after all, scholars, scientists, legislators, judges, and clerics are members of the society. As such, they do not act in value-free ways; rather, they bring their own socialization into their professional lives. Their values unwittingly impinge upon the kinds of questions they ask, the priorities they give to research problems, the consensus they reach regarding reasonable proof—and in the most subtle and pervasive way of all—the technical language they use.

In this section, we will look first at religion and law, and then at biological, medical, and psychological knowledge systems. As we will see, religion, law, and science are not at odds with each other or with the culture as a whole in regard to gender role reinforcement in adults. Rather, they stand as three boulders in a retaining wall: authoritative, powerful legitimators of culturally prescribed gender roles.

□ □ *6* □ □

Religion

Although the separation of church and state is an historical principle, such a separation is not evidenced from a sociological perspective. Institutionally, churches[1] are active in education, child welfare, prison reform, care of the aged, social services, mass media, unemployment, political action, as well as in capitalist ventures, such as real estate holdings (Wilson, 1972). The church as an institution, then, plays an active and integrative role in the larger society, rationalizing activities and providing a sense of consistency to the whole. In addition, it receives certain benefits from the state (e.g., tax-exempt status on its financial and real estate holdings). Because the church invests its energies, money, and time, it has a stake in preserving the *status quo* (Wilson, 1971); and because the status quo favors the interests of the more powerful, religion helps perpetuate social inequality. This is not to deny that the church can and does play a role in social change; rather, it is to recognize that one of its primary functions is to maintain the existing order and its own place within it.

Further, not only is there an institutional overlap, but there is also an ideological consistency. Indeed, the legal system uses the doctrines of religion to rationalize legislation and adjudication. Religion, in effect, provides the final moral authority—the divine sanction—for the human values that are enacted into law. The deployment of the divine sanction effectively ensures compliance not only with the legal system, but also with society's norms.

Although the source of the truth is different, the Judeo-Christian tradition—from *Genesis* to the present—parallels rather closely the teachings of the academician and the counsel of the therapist. To disagree with a scientist is to risk being labeled ignorant; to disagree with a therapist is to risk being labeled crazy; to violate the law is to risk being incarcerated. To disagree with the teachings of the church or

---

[1] I am using the term *church* as it is used in sociology to refer to beliefs and rituals about the sacred that bind people together in a moral community.

their interpretation by a "man of God," however, is to risk much more, because religion plays, in the lives of many people, a particular kind of role that science and therapy do not.

In the first place, the doctrines of a religion are usually learned at an early age. As we have seen, socialization of the young is etched deeply. The messages of religion are carved into vivid scenes by a child's literal interpretations of heaven and hell, god and satan, good and evil. The childhood literalness may be finally rejected by the adult, but the feelings and imagery initially associated with those learnings tend to linger. Questioning the moral authority of the church or its spokesperson, therefore, raises the deep-seated childhood images and fears of the transcendental, as well as the adult's images and concerns.

Secondly, religion, unlike law, science, and therapy, fulfills certain psychological functions for the individual. It can answer the unanswerable, rationalize the unreasonable, and predict the unpredictable. Chaos, cruelty, and disaster, as well as inequity, pain, and suffering, can be explained to the individual on the basis of "God's will" or of "purposes of a grander nature." To question the moral authority of the church about its prescriptions for gender performance means to risk losing the reassurance and support that religion can provide at those times of uncertainty, struggle, and suffering.

Third and perhaps most important, in terms of its impact on adult social control, religion is more than just a set of beliefs about the sacred. Religion takes place in the context of a community of believers—friends and relatives who share common lives that extend beyond the stained-glass windows. To challenge the doctrine of the church means, then, to risk the ostracism, rejection, and censure of one's community.

The impact of early socialization, combined with the risks involved in questioning religious teachings—risks at the psychological, interpersonal, and transcendental levels—functions to present the adult with an external control system that is enduring, deep, and forceful. Unlike any other social control system, religion has all bases covered—the here and now and the forever after. Its hold on its parishioners, combined with its own institutional stake in the perpetuation of the status quo, makes it a formidable social force.

BIBLICAL HERITAGE: TRADITIONALISM

There can be little doubt that the parables, stories, teachings, and gospels of the Judeo-Christian tradition that our culture has *chosen* to emphasize are those that perpetuate gender stereotyping. Through the centuries, Judeo-Christian heritage has portrayed the divine sanctioning of a patriarchal system; and translations and interpretations of the biblical message have been androcentrically biased.

Presently, religion is being scrutinized by feminists who question traditional religious principles and practices. Change is a slow process, however, and tradition is deeply etched. From the version of the creation story that is taught, to the prayers uttered, the songs sung, the rituals practiced, and the structure of the church itself, a hierarchy is assumed and perpetuated. First, there is God, then man (men), and at the bottom, women.

The version of the creation story that is taught (there is another version, which will be discussed later) presents a God-ordained sex role hierarchy. The story, in part, is as follows:

> Then the Lord God formed man of dust from the ground, and breathed into his nostrils the breath of life; and man became a living being. Then the Lord God said, "It is not good that the man should be alone, I will make him a helper fit for him." So the Lord God caused a deep sleep to fall upon the man, and while he slept took one of his ribs and closed up its place with flesh and the rib which the Lord God had taken from the man he made into a woman and brought her to the man. Then the man said, "This at last is bone of my bones and flesh of my flesh; she shall be called Woman because she was taken out of Man" (Genesis 2:7, 18, 21–23).[2]

Since this account specifies that God created man first, the theological position has been that man is superior to woman, who was created to be an assistant to man—almost as an afterthought.

The position of man's superiority is found again in Genesis (3), the story of the expulsion from Eden, the garden paradise. Eve, not Adam, some biblical scholars argue, was the cause of sin entering the world, not unlike Pandora and her box in Greek mythology. This story, many believe, reinforces women's already established lower position in the hierarchy—with God's pronouncement that "he (man) shall rule over you (woman)"—and the righteousness of sex roles was predicated: man, the worker, and woman, the childbearer.

Other Old Testament accounts further illustrate patriarchal hierarchy. Genealogies were listed only through the male line since women were considered to be the property of their fathers and then of their husbands. In Exodus (20:17), the commandment is given not to "covet your neighbor's house." The wife is listed among the possessions, along with the servants, the oxen, and the asses. As a possession, of course, she is not entitled to inheritance. So, for example, if a widow were childless, her deceased husband's property was given to his kinsmen; and, although not often carried out, a widow could be forced to marry her husband's brother in order to bear male heirs.

In Jewish law, fornication and adultery were considered serious crimes. Brides were required to be virgins, and tokens of their virginity (e.g., bloody marriage beds) could be demanded. If no proof could be offered, the woman was taken "to the door of her father's house, and the men of her city shall stone her to death with stones, because she has wrought folly in Israel by playing the harlot in her father's house . . ." (Deuteronomy 22:21). But if tokens of virginity could be produced to counter the false charge,

> the elders of that city shall take the man and whip him; and they shall fine him a hundred shekels of silver, and give them to the father of the young woman, because he has brought an evil name upon a virgin of Israel; and she shall be his wife; he may not put her away all his days" (Deuteronomy 22:18–19).

[2]Unless otherwise stated, all biblical passages are from the Revised Standard Version of the Bible.

The falsely accused bride, then, was not allowed to divorce her accuser husband but would have to live with him to the end of her days; nor was she entitled to the hundred shekels of silver. Those went to her father as payment for *his* anguish.

The crime of adultery called for the death penalty for both offenders. What must be understood, then, is that the seriousness of the crimes lies not in the act itself, but in what it represents—the violation of the exclusive right of the husband to his wife's sexuality (Bird, 1974:51; MacHaffie, 1986:8). The man who was involved was punished not for being unfaithful to his wife, but for committing a crime against another *man*. Other punishments were meted out for breaking chastity laws. If a betrothed virgin had sexual intercourse with a man and did not call for help,[3] both would be stoned to death. The engaged virgin was already another man's property.

According to Jewish law, only those persons who were considered clean were granted the right to participate in religious ceremonies. The laws defining unclean-ness and their appropriate atonement were applied to both men and women, but women, by virtue of their biology, were more frequently unclean than men were, since childbirth and menstruation were unclean states. Since it was desirable to have large families and since women menstruate regularly, a woman, because of her biological functions, lived almost continuously with the belief that she was unclean (Bird, 1974, MacHaffie, 1986:8).

When menstruating, a woman was unclean for seven days, and on the eighth day, she was obliged to make an offering of atonement to the priest. The length of time that a woman remained unclean following childbirth was determined by the sex of her infant. If she bore a male child, she was unclean for seven days, but if she bore a female child, fourteen days had to elapse before she could be atoned (Leviticus 12:1–5). The strength of that culture's idea of the filthiness of women's bodies is epito-mized when Job (4:4) asks, "How can he be clean that was born of woman?"

Although the emissions at childbirth were considered unclean, barrenness was a sign of divine displeasure. Since a barren wife was not fulfilling her duty to her husband, he could divorce her or take another wife or slave to have his children, hopefully boys, thereby ensuring the continuation of his family line. So strong were these injunctions, that Sarah (Genesis 16), having had no children for Abraham, impeached him to take her maid Hagar in order to sire children; similarly, Rachel, having borne no children, gave Jacob her maid Bilhah (Genesis 30).

Though Old Testament laws reflect and perpetuate a patriarchal order, it is the New Testament that is often used to fully justify male superiority. One verse seems to stand out; Ephesians (5:22–24) says:

> Wives, be subject to your husbands, as to the Lord. For the husband is the head of the wife as Christ is the head of the church, his body, and is himself its Savior. As the church is subject to Christ, so let wives also be subject in everything to their husbands.

---

[3]This idea, of course, still persists today in the belief that a woman who does not prove she struggled against a rape is responsible for the act.

What was an admonition that was addressed to wives in these verses has been broadened and interpreted to include all women in all situations. I Corinthians (11:3) reinforces this ordained chain of command. The verse says:

> But I [Apostle Paul] want you [Corinthian church members] to understand that the head of every man is Christ, the head of a woman is her husband, and the head of Christ is God.

These verses have been used by religious institutions to legitimize the subordination of women not only within the home, but also in all other areas of life.

St. Thomas Aquinas, in the thirteenth century, carried the message further. Women, by his logic, were no longer made in the image of God. Applying the principles of Aristotelian anthropology, St. Thomas Aquinas argued that semen provided the genetic material for offspring, and that all male seed produced males except "when the lower material principle gains an aberrant dominance over the higher formative principle, producing a 'misbegotten male' or female" (Reuther, 1975:72). Men, therefore, represent the "full image of God," whereas "women by themselves do not possess the image of God, but only when taken together with the male who is their 'head' " (Reuther, 1975:72).

Rather than being "real" people within the Christian tradition, two *images* of women are emphasized: Eve, the first "sinner" and responsible for the loss of paradise, and Mary, "the unattainable ideal combining virginity and motherhood," the epitome of "perfect obedience" (Hole and Levine, 1971:380). Christianity's accent on the Eve-Mary images in the Bible means that women in general are viewed as "symbolic representations of male ideas about sex": the sexual evilness of the temptress, the sexual purity of the virgin, the sexual procreativity of the mother (Hole and Levine, 1971:381). For males, the role models in Christianity are more diverse. Two of these—God the Father, and God the virginal Son—are exceptionally powerful symbols. Analogous to what happens to men in the secular world, male models are offered that are virtually impossible to attain. Even the disciples and angels, including the fallen Lucifer, are exceptional. Whether saints or demons, they are interpreted as epitomizing the highest forms of achievement or power. And the lesser models—kings, leaders, warriors—are fulfilling the traditional male roles, as well.

Granted that the culture decides how to interpret the Bible—which passages to teach the children, and which saints to revere for what—it can, nevertheless, be said that on the whole there are more elements in the religious heritage that favor different role performances and expectations for men and women than there are passages that favor a gender-free society. At one level, this is perfectly understandable because the individuals described in the Bible lived in patriarchal societies, as did the recorders of their history. They taught that which they had learned.

In reviewing these teachings, we find that women are defined primarily in terms of their sexuality—virgins, wives, mothers; men are defined in a wider diversity of roles. In the Catholic tradition, for example, each day of the year is dedicated to one or more saints. Sixty women are so honored—all of them virgins or martyrs. In contrast, 396 men are so honored—bishops, abbots, popes, martyrs, doctors, apostles, and so on (St. Joseph's Daily Missal, 1957). Virginity and death are the role model options for would-be sainted women; achievement or death are those for men. Further, like the stories in the children's readers, an analysis of Jesus' parables reveals that 26 of them are about males; 7 are about females (Ryan and Schirtzinger, 1974).

Indeed, some argue that the Bible itself was written exclusively for men. Examples of this come from the Ten Commandments (e.g., "Thou shall not covet thy neighbor's wife"). Another example can be found in the pact made with God by the Israelites during the exodus: The covenant with God required circumcision; only men, therefore, could have this special relationship with God and take part in the sacred public rituals.

Despite major religious upheavals during the mid-twentieth century, the doctrine of male dominance/female submissiveness has been left virtually intact. In the writings and sermons of the modern clergy, the sex stereotypes persist. Women are still admonished to embrace the "eternally feminine" roles of wife and mother. Further, they are instructed that "True emancipation will not involve false liberty or unnatural equality with their husband (Pope Pius XII, quoted in Daly, 1970:126). Seeking a different kind of liberation and failing to fulfill their duties may create in women the feeling of having failed in their duties to God. And in a parallel fashion, if men see themselves as responsible for the leadership of their families and if they also fail, they, too, may view themselves as less worthy in the eyes of God. However, as epitomized in the daily orthodox Jewish prayer for men, ("I thank Thee, O Lord, that Thou hast not made me a woman"), the strains on the male for fulfilling his religious destiny are any day, and every day, probably preferable in a man's eyes to the alternative—being a woman.

CHURCH STRUCTURE

Religious ideology has consequences for the social organization of religious institutions. That which is taught from the Judeo-Christian heritage is reflected in the hierarchical structuring of the church and the expected performances of males and females within it.

In various surveys that have been reported over the past 20 years, one finding is repeatedly verified: Women have a greater religious orientation than do men; that is, more women than men attend church, are active in church social life, and express a greater need for a religious dimension in their lives (Robertson, 1981).

There are several possible explanations for this phenomenon. Generally, oppressed groups in any society are more likely to be oriented towards the "other world" than is the dominant group. Whether one explains this, as Karl Marx (1964) did—as a method by which the dominant group provides the masses with an opiate—or whether one views religion as providing the oppressed with much-needed relief, it is understandable that more women than men are attracted to religious institutions.

Yinger (1957) suggests that because women have fewer options open to them outside the home, they are less likely to become secularized. Moreover, because women are expected to uphold traditional values, the church provides a setting where they can do so and at the same time engage in extrafamilial, but "safe," social interaction.

Diamond (1976) hypothesizes that a part of the appeal in Christianity is linked to women's sexual attraction to both the biblical superheroes (as illustrated in the song "I Don't Know How to Love Him" from *Jesus Christ Superstar*) and to the clergy themselves. Although totally unresearched, the deflection of a woman's extramarital or premarital sexual interests into safe fantasies about religious personages may contribute to her greater time and emotional investments in the church.

In addition, the values of the church are consistent with the values that are espoused by the family, such as the ultimate authority of the father (God the Father), sacrificial love, the acceptance of another's burden, the power of love. Because it is especially the woman who is expected to carry these virtues into the home, the church provides a divine rationale for her own role in the family. Coupled with the value consistency is the important part the church plays in the life stages of many families—marriage, birth, death. These rites of passage are frequently solemnized or celebrated in religious ceremonies. In that religious tradition encourages women to bring into the home the teachings of the church, an interesting question is: What positions should women hold within the formal church structure? The religious institution has not remained unaffected by the changes concerning the status of women that are occurring in society. Similar to their sisters in the secular world, women are entering into male-dominated religious vocations, though not without controversy and conflict.

One indication of women's movement into the religious structure is the increasing enrollment of women in theological seminaries. In 1972, women comprised 4.7 percent of the total enrollment in the seminary programs that normally lead to ordination. But by the 1980–1981 school year, women became 14.7 percent of the total enrollment—an increase of 340.8 percent compared to only a 25 percent increase for men during the same time period (Carroll, et al., 1983:7). Overall, about one-fourth of the students who are enrolled in graduate divinity programs are women (Lehman, 1985:13). As a result of more women entering seminaries, other facets of seminary life are changing. In 1971, women comprised only 3.2 percent of the full-time seminary faculty, but, by 1980, the percentage increased to 7.9 percent (Lehman, 1985:15). In the same fashion, more women moved into administrative positions on seminary campuses, making up about 18.8 percent of the total in 1980 (Lehman, 1985:15).

The number of women clergy also continues to grow, presently comprising five percent of the total number of clerics (MacHaffie, 1986:141). Although women still remain a minority, the growth has been phenomenal given the fact that most denominations denied ordination for women before the 1970s.

Reformed Judaism did not ordain women until 1972, for example. The Lutheran church in America and the American Lutheran church did not ordain their first women clergy until 1970, and the Protestant Episcopal church did not follow suit until 1976, and only after a long, bitter struggle within the church hierarchy. However, the increasing presence and activism of women in the religious community—both within the professional and lay ranks—has fostered other changes in church operation, such as an emphasis on new biblical interpretations and the elimination of sexist language in biblical translations, liturgies, and hymnals. Even the office of clergy is changing, because women clergy tend to be less authoritarian and hierarchal in their ministry and more willing to use the resources of church members than are male clergy. Clergywomen often bring a new sensitivity to the ministry that helps "others give birth to new talent and dimensions of personality" (MacHaffie, 1985:143).

However, the position of women within formal church structure is neither secure nor totally accepted. When compared to clergymen, women clergy report that they are more likely to serve as assistant or associate pastors; are less likely to experience upward mobility; are more often relegated to small congregations; and receive lower salaries than do their male colleagues (Carroll, et al., 1983:109–138). For many women, ordination is still an unobtainable goal. Conservative and Orthodox Judaism prohibit females in that role, as do the Missouri-Synod-Lutherans; and in 1984, the Southern Baptist Convention passed a national resolution opposing the ordination of women (Mt. Vernon News, 1984). Perhaps most significantly, though, the Roman Catholic and Eastern Orthodox churches, which represent over half of the Christian population, prohibit ordination for women (MacHaffie, 1986:139).

A 1976 pronouncement from the Vatican officially restated the church's traditional stance against admitting women to the priesthood, since a female priest cannot represent a male Christ (MacHaffie, 1986:140). Consequently, women cannot be bishops, cardinals, or popes. The role of a Catholic nun is defined primarily as a service role—to the priest, to the young, and to the sick. Women service the domestic needs of the church, but the sacraments—the communion between God and parishioner—must be mediated through a male. Traditional values are reasserting themselves, moreover. In 1983, for example, women were barred from acting as servers at mass by the Cardinal of Chicago (Greeley, 1984:143). Then, in 1984 in St. Louis, about 25 altar girls were told that they could no longer perform the same duties as male altar boys. Among the activities that were banned for the girls were "holding" the book of prayers, touching the sacramental wafer and wine, and helping in communion (Kash, 1984:21).

In the Eastern Orthodox church in 1976, the subject of the ordination of women was brought before the "Consultation on the Role of Orthodox Women in the Church and in Society" in Agapia, Romania. The Consultation recommended the expansion of the role of women, including allowing them to serve as deacons, readers, and acolytes. However, the Consultation did not take any action on the ordination of women (MacHaffie, 1986:140–141).

The lack of women in high positions in the church is frequently justified on the basis of the religious credo itself. In the more traditional Jewish congregations, the exclusion is based on the interpretation of Talmudic Law. Others argue that, since God is always symbolized in the male form and always referred to as "He," women cannot represent "His" image; indeed, as discussed earlier, some theologians have questioned whether women were even created in God's image. Added to this argument, by some religions, is that God chose a male image—Jesus—when on earth, and that Jesus, in turn, selected only males to be His disciples. Consequently, it is posited that it is God's will that women not represent God. Still others draw upon their interpretation of Paul's admonition to the women of the Corinthian church, namely:

> As in all the churches of the saints, the women should keep silence in the churches. For they are not permitted to speak, but should be subordinate, as even the law says. If there is anything they desire to know, let them ask their husbands at home. For it is shameful for a woman to speak in church (I Corinthians 14:33b–35).

In addition to these doctrinal issues justifying the exclusion of women, secular concerns are marshaled to defend the status quo; for example, it is argued that men in the congregation might become sexually attracted to a woman minister and concentrate on earthly pleasures rather than heavenly principles, or that she might be inadequate as a counselor to males and male problems. Most difficult, however, would be the time and responsibility conflicts that she would experience due to obligations to her husband, children, and parishioners, it is argued. Clearly, these arguments are based on gender stereotypes and the perpetuation of them. Nowhere in these arguments do we see the questioning reversed: What about women being sexually attracted to their ministers, priests, and rabbis? What about males counseling female parishioners? What about males' conflicts between home and work? If we are to take the secular arguments seriously, then the best minister might be a computer-programmed robot.

The result of religious and secular traditionalism is a church that is controlled by men to "appeal" to women. Ironically, two of the outcomes are that the church takes on "feminine" characteristics, and that the male clergy are not expected to be "masculine"; for example, clergy are expected to excel in the traits usually assigned to women—sympathy, humility, obedience, sensitivity to others, and, in some religions, chastity. Seidler (1976) goes further in pointing out, "Childlikeness [is] expected of clergy by laity who don't want or expect clergy to really know the ways of the world, from handling money to knowing how to fix a car"; and, even further, some male church members may view the clergy as men who are unable to succeed in the nonreligious occupational world.

Organized religion, therefore, systematically excludes women from positions of sacramental authority and at the same time tends to devalue those roles (in the eyes of the society) by associating them with feminine skills. Whether based on Scripture, tradition, or modern prejudice, the outcome is the perpetuation of the current system and the devitalization of the church itself. Both males and females are effectively held in line, socially controlled by the imagery presented to them, and "projected into the realm of beliefs, which in turn justify the social [structure of the church]. The belief system becomes hardened and objectified seeming to have an unchangeable, independent existence and validity of its own" (Daly, n.d.:1).

Nevertheless, the winds of change are blowing through some belfries. Recently, alternative theological visions have been proposed.

RELIGIOUS VISIONS

Flowing from humanist and feminist concerns, the traditional and the orthodox in religious precept and practice have been challenged. Women are actively involved in reassessing, redefining, and reinterpreting theology to reflect the experiences of women, and to eliminate the duality and hierarchical view of reality that is inherent in the theology of men (MacHaffie, 1986:149). The adherents of these new religious visions can be considered either reformists or revolutionaries (Christ and Plaskow, 1979).

Religious criticism is not just a contemporary phenomenon, but rather, a continuation of the work that was started by early feminists in the nineteenth century, such as Elizabeth Cady Stanton and Lucy Stone. Stone, beginning the reformist or revisionist tradition, believed "that the Bible, rightly interpreted, was on the side of equal rights for women" (Goldenberg, 1979:13). In contrast, Stanton understood how biblical texts were used to justify the social order and subjugate women, and she challenged the authority of the Bible (Goldenberg, 1982:79–82). Adherents of the Stanton tradition took a more revolutionary stance. We shall first look at the ideas of the reformists, and then turn to those of the revolutionaries.

The Reformists

Although conceding that religious teachings have been used to separate the roles of men and women into different spheres, the reformists firmly believe that the Bible and its heritage can be used to free both men and women from the tyranny of rigid gender stereotyping. Drawing on the principles of liberation theology, reformists emphasize the freeing aspects of the Bible (MacHaffie, 1986:151). The problem, they argue, is not in the Bible itself but in the way patriarchal ideology has controlled its emphases and interpretations. In accordance with prevalent societal norms, certain teachings were upheld as divine principles while others were ignored.

The Genesis creation account is an excellent example, they argue, because the account, which supposedly establishes a male hierarchical order, has received societal endorsement, while another creation account in Genesis has barely been acknowledged. That story reads as follows:

> Then God said, "Let us make man in our image, after our likeness, and let them have dominion over the fish of the sea, and over the birds of the air, and over the cattle, and over all the earth, and over every creeping thing that creeps upon the earth. So God created man in his own image, in the image of God he created him, male and female he created them (Genesis 1:26–27).

This version is particularly interesting for it implies that God is either simultaneously male and female, or neither, and it states clearly that both male and female were created simultaneously. Several interpretations are possible; for example, the passage can be understood to mean that originally mankind ('ādām) contained both sexes within one form and that the taking of the rib separated the entity into two distinct sexes; or it can be interpreted that each sex contains within itself the elements of both sexes.

How then are the two seemingly contradictory stories of creation reconciled? Reformists believe that the two stories are complementary. Although Genesis 2 is a narrative account of creation, both stories emphasize that the creation of man and woman is different from that of the animals, and that only man and woman are created in the image of God. Though it is not known for sure what "created in God's image" really means, it is believed that both men and women were given the rationality and social awareness of God. Humans are social creatures and, as the Scriptures imply, they need one another. Both men and women were also given dominion over the rest of creation. The command in Genesis 1, ". . . fill the earth and subdue it," is given to both without regard to sex.

The most glaring discrepancies between the two creation accounts are the order of creation and the implication in Genesis 2 that woman was created only to be a helper to man. But does it really matter who was created first? Can we logically infer that the first is always the best, the last always inferior? In Genesis 1, the animals are created first; does this make them superior to humans (Scanzoni and Hardesty, 1978)?

Was woman made to be a helper for man? The common interpretations of "helper" have been servant or assistant, which implies the superiority of man. Although the Hebrew word *'ezer* ("helper") is used 21 times in the Old Testament, at no time does it connote subordination; rather, 16 times it means superordinate (Scanzoni and Hardesty, 1978). 'Ezer implies "opposite" or "corresponding to," and in Hebrew 'ezer recognizes the distinctness of the two, but yet their oneness. Man and woman share an essential unity, a sameness of bone and flesh—the two of them one order of creation.

Unlike the traditionalists, the reformists do not believe that Eve bears the sole responsibility for the expulsion from Eden. Adam also disobeyed. He knew very well what God had commanded; yet, he offered no protest when Eve offered him the forbidden fruit. He made no attempt to stop Eve, either. When God confronted the two, Adam tried to shift the blame to Eve, saying, "The woman whom thou gavest to be with me, she gave me the fruit of the tree, and I ate" (Genesis 3:12), but God was not taken in by Adam's finger pointing. Adam, too, was punished for his transgression, as God ordered him to become dependent upon the ground, like the animals.

The reformists point again and again to translations and interpretations that they see as distortions of the original biblical text; for example, the traditional translation of Ephesians (5:22–24) is claimed to reveal God's hierarchy within the home by the command, "Wives be subject to your husbands . . ." A literal translation of the verse, however, reveals the absence of the verb, *be subject*. Rather, the verse reads, "wives to your own husbands . . . ," and is in actuality the end of verse 21. A more accurate translation would be, "Subjecting yourselves to one another, wives to your own husbands . . ." (Gundry, 1977). The reformists argue that Paul is speaking of mutual submissiveness between men and women within a marital bond and that, instead of advocating the superiority of the husband, Paul was calling for a state of mutuality.

Distortion of Paul's writings in I Corinthians (11:3), the reformists posit, also exists. In this verse, the word *head* is used by traditionalists to justify male dominance, but again by studying the original language, another connotation is revealed: the word *head* means "source." But source does not imply superiority. Man was created from the dust of the ground; is he therefore inferior to the earth (Scanzoni and Hardesty, 1978)?

Particularly telling, the reformists argue, are the inconsistent translations of the *same* word, depending on whether a male or female is the subject. A case in point is found in Romans (16:1, 2) when Paul introduces Phoebe to the Roman church. The translated verses read as follows:

> I commend unto you Phoebe our sister, which is a servant of the church which is at Cenchrea: That ye receive her in the Lord, as becometh saints, and that ye assist her in whatsoever business she hath need of you: for she hath been a succorer of many, and of myself also (Romans 16:1, 2, King James).

In this translation Phoebe is referred to as a servant, but in the Greek version the word *diakonos* is used. Paul uses this word 20 times in his writings, and the only time the word is translated *servant* is in reference to Phoebe. In the other instances, when the word refers to men, it is translated *minister* or *deacon* (Gundry, 1977). Since Phoebe did minister in some capacity and was recommended by Paul, would this not contradict Paul's supposed stand on women remaining silent in the church?

Doctrinal reinterpretation of Jesus' life by reformists further reveals alternative ways for the sexes to relate to one another. The amount and kinds of associations that Jesus had with women goes way beyond those permissible in His culture. Included among his close friends, traveling companions, and disciples were Mary Magdalene, Joanna, and Susanna. Such inclusion "must have seemed highly unconventional in that traditional society" (Reuther, 1975:64). Further, Jesus violated Judaic law by touching menstruating women (Mark 5:25–34; Matthew 9:20–22), by speaking alone with a woman not his wife (John 4:27), by vindicating Mary's right to sit at his feet and learn (Luke 10:38–42), and by allowing women to witness and testify to the Resurrection (John 20:1 ff.; Luke 24:10, 22–25). Because Jewish law did not accept women as responsible witnesses, "to make women the first witnesses of the resurrection was to make them the original source of the credibility of the Christian faith" (Reuther, 1975:65). Incidentally, the first witness was Mary Magdalene, a professed harlot. In sum, the reformists argue, "Jesus was a feminist."

Moreover, the reformists point out that the Bible provides many models of women outside the stereotypes. In the Old Testament, among the many wise and strong women, there are: Deborah, a judge and military commander of the Israelites; Jael, a woman who kills Sisera, a principal enemy of Israel (Judges 4; 5:24–26); Abigail, whose intelligence saves her foolish husband from the wrath of King David (I Samuel 25); and Queen Esther, a woman who saved her people from destruction. Even in proverb 31, which describes a good wife, these words are found:

She considers a field and buys it; with the fruit of her hands she plants a vineyard. She girds her loins with strength and makes her arms strong. She perceives that her merchandise is profitable. . . . She opens her mouth with wisdom, and the teaching of kindness is on her tongue (Proverbs 31:16–18a, 26).

In the New Testament, women are mentioned as leaders and teachers. Priscilla's name is mentioned before her husband's, which in Greek usually indicates a place of prominence (Scanzoni and Hardesty, 1978). In Romans (16:7), Junia is mentioned among the apostles in Rome. (Interestingly, translators often use the masculine form of Junia, although evidence exists to uphold the feminine translation.) Lydia was a tradeswoman and the first Christian convert in Asia. The list could go on for pages.

Nontraditional roles are not only assigned to women in the Bible, the reformists point out; they are also assigned to men. Men are urged in some proverbs to humble themselves, to forego competitiveness, and not to follow in the footsteps of those whose success depends on the oppression of others. The New Testament presents many nonmacho messages: Jesus and His disciples are men of emotion—they cry, fear, and agonize; they are able to be weak (Luke 22:54 ff.; John 20:24 ff.; II Corinthians 4:5 ff.), to be controlled by others (John 2; Luke 22–23, 24:13 ff.), and to demonstrate compassion (John 8; Mark 6:34 ff.) and humility (John 13; Luke 6:17 ff.).

Given the orientation of the reformists, it is not surprising that they are vitally involved in the struggles within their churches to ordain women and, if ordination exists, to employ those ordained women as leaders of their congregations. They offer three primary pragmatic arguments to support the ordination of women. First, they argue, "women clergy are vital in order to reassess and counterbalance . . . [the] historically 'male interpretations and teachings' within the church." Second, because clergy play a major role in church policy formation (e.g., where to distribute funds, what curricula to teach, what position to take on social-political issues), "women in the clergy would put women into policy-making positions enabling them to shape the decisions that affect women's as well as men's lives." And third, because only men traditionally have had the privilege to respond to the calling of the ministry, women should be accorded the same right, as well as the right to lead a congregation (Hole and Levine, 1971:385–386).

In addition to these pragmatic reasons, the reformists see important symbolic reasons for ordaining women. First, such ordination would symbolically transcend the dogma of the subordinance of women. "Ordaining women would . . . symbolically . . . purge the church of the 'eternal feminine' . . . and force it to transform its image of women from mysterious and mystical creatures into people" (Hole and Levine, 1971:386). Second, a large proportion of women ministers would "visibly challenge the assumption that leader/follower is the only acceptable male/female relationship within the church structure" (Hole and Levine, 1971: 386). And, third, women in cleric roles would help dispel the latent assumption that only a male can be a direct link to God.

Reformists, then, envision a major reform of existent church belief and structure—but they, nevertheless, believe that the existent structure is salvageable.

Revolutionaries

The revolutionaries, unlike the reformists, do not believe that a reappraisal of
biblical tradition will change religious structure from a male hierarchy to one of
equality between the sexes in a gender-free society. They maintain that an institution that is so thoroughly permeated with male images—beginning with a male God
who reigns supreme and who is represented on earth by men—cannot reform itself
to include women as an integral part of its dominion. People may "speak of the
'spirit' of God" but "at the same time imagine 'him' as belonging to the male sex"
(Daly, n.d.:2). Consequently, they argue, the only way to be free of the male
permeation in traditional Judeo-Christian teachings is to reject those teachings
(Christ and Plaskow, 1979).

The depth of this male imagery is suggested in Diamond's exploratory disser-
tational research (1976). Using the game of charades as the research vehicle, he
reports that when the word *God* is acted out, male charaders tend to take on Godlike
qualities (such as puffing out their chests, looking stern, and pointing a mighty
finger down from on high), whereas female charaders assume the supplicant role by
kneeling before and praying to God. That is, male actors—but not female ones—
become God.

The language of the church, the interpretation of the Scriptures, and the all-
male leadership have perpetuated the "popular image of the great patriarch in
heaven" (Daly, n.d.:2). This imagery has consequences for men and women,
Reuther argues that the image of God-as-Father sanctifies both hierarchism and
sexism. By casting God in a domination-subordination relationship to humanity,
"allowing ruling-class men to identify with the divine father," they are encouraged
"to establish themselves in the same kind of hierarchical arrangement to women
and lower classes" (1975:65); that is, the imagery of God-as-Father not only helps
perpetuate sexism, but also perpetuates the hierarchical arrangement of people.

Some argue that the notion that "*the* Supreme Being is male is the quintes-
sence of sexism" (Hole and Levine, 1971:379) and call for "the death of God the
Father" (Daly, n.d.). These men and women recognize that the solution is not to
introduce an image of God-as-Mother, but to delete the notion of paternity, maternity entirely by conceptualizing God-as-Spirit.

The recognition that theology perpetuates hierarchism of *all* kinds—not just
the gender one—is an even more radical view than those thus far discussed. It is
proposing that the traditional theology perpetuates a class system in which not only
women lose, but many men do, too.

Though revolutionaries agree on a disavowal of the traditional Judeo-Christian heritage, many still believe that the religious or spiritual element is important in
the lives of people. These women are searching for and finding alternative avenues
for spiritual experience. Goddess worship arising from a study of prebiblical history
is a source of spiritual experience for many feminists (Christ and Plaskow, 1971:
10–11). Other women find meaning in witchcraft. Covens that consist exclusively

of women or those with men playing only minor roles counteract the image of a male God and allow women to celebrate internal feelings of spirituality in a ritual fashion. Menstruation, childbirth, lactation, and menopause—the biological experiences of women—are celebrated in ritual and symbol. Other women find an alternative to religion in dream analysis, psychic phenomena, and other self-explorations. Spiritual growth has replaced religious affiliation.

The single factor that binds the revolutionary point of view together is an emphasis on women's experience within feminism. Feminism becomes theology, transcending a need for an image of a male God; women relating to women on a spiritual level creates experiences that cannot be bound by traditional religious thought. More closely aware of nature and less attuned to the duality of the church (e.g., soul vs. body, spirit vs. flesh, etc.), these revolutionaries argue that a religion that is spiritually fit for womankind must "express a combination of rootedness in nature and freedom that feminists experience in their lives" (Christ and Plaskow, 1979:12). In truly revolutionary fashion, these women are rejecting the old and are creating new spiritual visions, new religious experience.

POTENTIAL OUTCOMES

The transformation of the church is an exceptionally complex theological and structural question. It is difficult to assess just what the consequences would be if the radical alterations that are proposed were to be enforced. Many church feminists believe that these changes would have a revolutionary effect on religion, and that, because of religion's investment in the larger social order, the impact would have major ramifications for the entire society. They envision a church that would be divested of the oppressiveness of sexism and hierarchism—a church that would be dedicated to the individual's rights, and that would allocate its energies and financial resources toward humanizing the society—stripping it of its worship of violence, cutthroat competition, and hierarchical arrangement of individuals.

However, because the question is so complex, we might ask what some of the unexpected and negative outcomes of such a revision would be. Speculatively, if the theological and structural changes did occur, one potential consequence might be the total devaluation of the church and the virtual exclusion of the male laity. As was discussed earlier, the church fulfills many functions in the everyday lives of its members by providing solace and comfort, explanation of the unknown, a social community, a ceremonial marking of important familial events, and so on. It already services more women than men in these ways. Further, it currently has an aura of the "feminine." The church is a place where feminine values are sanctified. These values are not highly regarded socially and are not socially ascribed to men.

If the theology was altered to limit God to spirit and, in the Christian tradition, to divest Jesus of His special divinity, and if the prestigious positions within the church were in actuality filled in substantial numbers by women, might not one of the out-comes be that males would view it as even a less desirable place for them than they already do? Because males now have few structural supports for incorporating the "softer" values and behaviors in their lives, and few institutions in which they can seek aid, comfort, and communion, might the transformation of the church, in effect, remove even this source of support from the male? Is it not possible that the church would become even more insulated and isolated from the "real" world by closing off even that institution to the male? It is possible, therefore, that the changes that are envisioned would only serve to further devalue the church, making it truly a female ghetto and inaccessible to males.

Whether one is a traditionalist, reformist, or revolutionary, all would concede that the church is a major force in controlling and molding adult behavior. But the church does not stand alone in defending societal controls and roles. It is buttressed by the law, to which we now turn.

7

The Law[1]

A paradox is the law, simultaneously freeing and constraining. Without rules of order and mechanisms for their enforcement, anarchy would result. The most powerful would be safe, but everyone else would be subject to terror. And yet laws lessen individual autonomy. Most scholars would agree that some laws are necessary to preserve a semblance of social order; hence the paradox: Only through constraints can there be freedom.

The task of preserving social order belongs to the state; and, as such, the state has the right to determine the nature of the constraints, that is, to legislate. Further, the state is expected to enforce those laws—to arrest, prosecute, judge, and punish offenders. Since it has a legitimate right to violence, the state is a powerful agent of adult social control.

The power of the legal system as a social control mechanism, however, does not primarily rest in its ability to deter crime or to reduce recidivism. Indeed, in some studies, crime rates were found to vary directly with the severity and frequency of punishment (Wilson, 1966:567). Rather, the power and importance of the legal system is its impact on the law-abiding—the offended rather than the offender. As Durkheim argued a century ago, the function of punishment is to reconfirm the culture's values, to kindle in the law-abiding a renewed commitment to conduct consistent with the value system. "Punishment is only the symbol—a language through which either the general social conscience or that of the authorities expresses the feeling inspired by the deviant behavior" (Wilson, 1966:568).

As for what laws are righteous, there is an unquestionable association among legal statements, a society's norms, and the interests of the powerful. Laws stand as the formalized and enforceable symbolic representations of the culture's preferences, ideological stances, mores, and norms. Perhaps, nowhere are the norms and

[1]I wish to heartily thank Nancy Erickson, Professor of Law, Ohio State University, and Joan Black for their help on this chapter.

101

laws more "intimate and reciprocally influential" than in the area of male and female relationships (Kanowitz, 1969:4). As Kanowitz argues, laws that pertain directly to the sexes "inevitably produce far-reaching effects . . . upon male-female relationships beyond the limited confines of legislative chambers and courtrooms" (1969:4). Differences that are emphasized in the law influence the content and tone of the social and power relationships between the sexes, as well as their legal relationships.

Although there is a mirroring of social norms and legal norms, in a changing society this reflection is far from perfect. Old laws remain on the books, unenforced and perhaps unenforceable—such as those that specify the positions of married partners during intercourse. And new laws that are inconsistent with the culture's norms are sometimes introduced. However, because a major function of the law is to bind together the law-abiding, a change in the law can have a substantial impact on changing the norms. Thus, the law can serve as a mechanism of social control, as well as a catalyst of social change. Once enacted, a new law carries symbolic and literal weight and affects the behavior and attitudes of the people.

To understand how laws both control and change behavior and attitudes that concern sex equality, it is necessary to discuss, briefly, how laws are made and enforced. As we shall soon see, sex differentiation is pervasive within the legal system; the results of this legal differentiation are detrimental to both men and women, although the negative effects are more severe for women. As we shall also see, there have been major changes in the laws toward sex equity.

THE LEGAL SYSTEM

Thomas Jefferson, "democrat," had the following to say about women's rights under the Constitution:

> Were our state a pure democracy there would still be excluded from our deliberations women, who, to prevent depravation of morals and ambiguity of issues, should not mix promiscuously in gatherings of men" (quoted in Ginsberg, 1978:22).

Jefferson's views reigned in this century for almost 150 years when in 1920, women gained the right to vote. Judeo-Christian tradition, English law, and the Constitution of the United States have viewed women as chattel or *property*, who were unable to administer estates or to be a *person*, legally. The father "giving" away the bride, by custom, socially displays the "owned-owner" relationship.

However, laws are not only inherited; they are made. In our society, law is made in three different ways: through legislative action, administrative action, and judicial review. *Legislative action* through legislative bodies goes on at the local, state, and federal levels. These lawmakers are susceptible to pressure groups and lobbyists, since their tenure in office depends upon reelection. Women have only recently become an effective or unified interest group with legislative influence (see Chapter 14).

Once laws have been passed, *administrative action* can influence the effectiveness of the law. The bureaucracy that is charged with "keeping the law" sends down guidelines, regulations, and interpretations about it. Depending on the policies, interests, and priorities of the bureaucracy, they can establish guidelines that strengthen or weaken the law. Most of the agencies responsible for sex discrimination guidelines have not strengthened the law, and they have been slow in interpreting them or reluctant to do so in favor of women.

When individuals question the *legality* of the law, they can take their concern to court. Through *judicial review*, precedent is set and subsequent cases rely upon such precedent. If the court, however, refuses to hear cases that regard discrimination on the basis of sex, confronting those issues is delayed. The primary judicial pattern, though, has been to find the laws constitutional.

Federal, state, and local legislators—as well as government administrators in policy-making positions—are overwhelmingly male. In addition, the proportion of women judges is quite low, although it has been increasing. Of an estimated 12,000 judges, only four percent are women (Cook, 1978).[2] One woman now serves on the Supreme Court, and few sit on the highest courts at the state level.

The fact that most lawmakers—legislators, administrators, and judges—are males cannot help but affect the way men and women are viewed in the legal system. The day-to-day reality of a woman's life does not influence lawmaking. For the most part, the male lawmakers are guided by their own *personal* experiences; and for the most part, these men maintain traditional relationships with their wives and, thus, also maintain traditional views of what relationships should be between men and women. When thinking about "women's" legislation, they are likely to ask their wife's opinion and to accept her opinion as representative of "what women want" and "what is good" for them.

The enforcement of the law is in large part the responsibility of the police. Most police officers are male and take for granted the male's point of view. Intervention, arrest, and determination of charges, therefore, depend on the police officer's gender-based expectations for behavior. Thus, for example, in domestic violence cases, police have traditionally been sympathetic to the husband, allowing him to stay in the home or to walk around the block to "cool off," and discouraging the wife from pressing charges (Glass, 1980). Similarly, prostitutes are treated differently than their customers, and "immoral" women who are assaulted are dealt with differently than "moral" ones (Holstrom, 1974).

More women are enrolling in police academies and more are being trained to handle crimes against women. However, the number of female officers remains low because the physical strength and agility tests make it difficult for a woman to qualify. Whenever the legality of these "tests" has been tried in the courts, they have been found unconstitutional because they are "unreasonable and unrelated to job requirements"; each ruling, however, has had only local, rather than national, effect. Consequently, police forces have few women officers.

If a case goes to trial, attorneys, judges, and perhaps a jury become actors within the legal system. Attorneys, including female ones, are trained in a highly patriarchal institution—law school—and carry those values into the courtroom.

[2]This estimate excludes justices of the peace.

Advice that is offered to their clients will often be based on stereotypes about sex rather than on the particulars of the case. Thus, an attorney may discourage a male from seeking custody of his children and encourage a female to ''fight'' for custody. Judges are given discretion in determining the outcome of a case, which means many judicial decisions are based on the individual judge's personal morality. Thus, a woman who is known to have sexual relationships may be denied custody of children. If the judge views a woman's extramarital relationships as immoral, they become effectively illegal. The jury system, finally, is supposed to ensure a trial by one's peers. However, only recently have special restrictions on women's jury duty been subject to legal challenge.

Overall, four basic assumptions pervade the creation and differential application of the law. First, women are viewed as incompetent, childlike, and in need of protection. Second, and closely related, males are seen as the protectors and financial caretakers of women. Third, husband and wife are treated as ''one'' under the law—and that ''one'' is the male. Finally, the double standard of morality that is based on biological deterministic thought is built into the legal process. These assumptions have negative consequences for men and, particularly, for women, and these assumptions pervade all areas of the law, leading to continued sex discrimination.

Sex discrimination exists in both civil and criminal law. Civil law refers to that body of law that is concerned with resolving private conflicts (e.g., contracts, divorce) and results in some type of remedial resolution or monetary compensation. Criminal law denotes an offense against the state, rather than an offense against an individual. At issue is the restoration of public order, with the resolution being punitive. Thus, a rape case could involve both civil and criminal action. The crime of rape is a crime against the state. The victim is the state's witness. However, the victim may file a civil suit, demanding compensation for physical or emotional injuries.

In the last 15 years, much progress toward sex equity has been made, especially in the areas of case law and administrative rulings. The following sections focus on legal issues that demonstrate how the four assumptions that previously have been delineated lead to sex-based discrimination in the law, and how the legal system responds to challenges to this discrimination.

DOMESTIC RELATIONS

Since the individual states make laws that govern marriage and other domestic issues, there is considerable variation from state to state. Although, generally, there has been a movement toward sex equality, domestic law is still based upon the premise that women and men fulfill different functions in the home. The outcome is that both men and women are discriminated against in ways that are consistent with the culture's presuppositions about men and women.

The law requires that the husband support his wife and family; however, what constitutes such support is usually not specified until a marriage is dissolving (Kanowitz, 1969). Thus, during the marriage, the husband can choose *where* to live, how much ''allowance'' to give his wife, the amount of the food budget, and so on; if his wife feels the support is inadequate, she has no recourse—save filing for divorce for gross neglect. In some states, wives have the duty of secondary support *if* their husbands become incapacitated, but the rationale for these laws is not to alter sex stereotyping; rather, the purpose is to keep people off welfare (Kanowitz, 1969).

If divorce occurs, in most states men are responsible for their own and their ex-wives' legal fees and temporary alimony. Permanent alimony can be awarded only if a state statute specifically prescribes it. Only since 1979 (*Orr* v. *Orr*) have states laws that prohibited alimony to men been struck down. Although people think that the laws on alimony and support obligations discriminate against men, women actually suffer more under the laws. First, alimony is generally available only to a woman who is unable to support herself, and usually only if there has been a long-term marriage; thus, a woman who has a low-paying job (which characterizes most of the jobs that women hold) may be considered ineligible for alimony because she has some means of support. Second, fewer than 12 percent of the women are awarded alimony. Enforcement is so lax, however, that fewer than half of these women receive their support regularly. Thus, only about seven to eight percent of divorced women actually receive alimony (Weitzman, 1985). In 90 percent of the cases, child custody goes to the mother, mostly because custody is not contested. Child support legally continues to be the responsibility of the father. However, the husband's support payments are rarely enough to cover the child-rearing expenses. Divorced women and children suffer an immediate 73 percent drop in their standard of living, while their ex-husbands enjoy a 42 percent increase in theirs (Weitzman, 1985). Further, enforcement of support payments is lax. Weitzman (1985) found 58 percent of the fathers paid nothing; five years later, 67 percent had defaulted; and ten years later, 87 percent were not in compliance with the court order. The women who were involved still had minor children. Griffiths (1976) reported that fewer than half of the mothers who were awarded child support received it on a regular basis. Weitzman's (1985) recent major work on divorce summarizes these data: Divorce has negative financial consequences for women and children.

In addition, the value of the mother's unpaid contributions—that is, the actual task of child rearing—is discounted in computing support payments. To summarize, under current custody and support laws, males may appear to be discriminated against, yet is seems to be the women who suffer.

Discrimination against women also begins with a wedding license. In some states, she is required to accept her husband's choice of domicile, to service him sexually, to clean house, and to care for their children. In some states, men can be granted divorces based on their wives ''gross neglect of duty''—interpreted as dirty houses, unkempt children, and refusal to have intercourse. Approximately half of the states disallow that a husband can rape a wife, if she is living with him.

The issue of protection from one's own spouse is becoming a widely recognized social problem, as more and more studies document the prevalence of domestic violence—specifically wife beating (Strauss, et al., 1979). Although there has been some attention given to ''husband beating'' (Steinmetz, 1977), the major problem is wife battering (Flemming, 1979).

Battered women exist because women as a class lack political, economic, and social power. This limits their options, because of the culture of (male) violence, and because the legal system has condoned the husband's right to physically "punish" his wife (Eisenberg, 1977). In some states, the first beating is legal; in others, based on the ancient "rule of thumb" or the right of a husband to strike his wife with a stick not thicker than his thumb, the severity of the beating is the criterion (Gringold, 1976). Wives report that calling the police only serves to escalate a husband's violence, because the husband normally is not arrested but is left at home with his wife (Gringold, 1976). Further, abusive husbands span the entire social-class system; wife beating is a phenomenon common to all age, racial, social, and economic groups. In the second wealthiest county in this country, for example, 600 cases of wife assault were brought to police attention during 1975 ("Weekend," ABC television, March 6, 1976.

State legislatures have begun to address the problem of domestic violence and currently many have laws that deal specifically with spouse abuse. Some of these laws simply acknowledge that spouse abuse is a crime and that the victim can pursue either civil remedies or criminal action. Other states have been more progressive in providing protection, as well as in authorizing services; for example, Ohio, Montana, and Florida have a marriage license tax; the monies that are collected through these taxes are used to provide services to victims (i.e., homes for battered women, medical and psychological help, etc.). However, the problem is far from resolved.

NONTRADITIONAL DOMESTIC RELATIONS

The law has paid scant attention to domestic relations that do not conform to the traditional model—wife/husband/(legitimate) children. There is no body of case law that specifies the rights of individuals in nontraditional families, such as heterosexual and homosexual cohabitation; rather, cohabitants experience problems that are related to child custody, insurance, real and personal property, and wills and estates (Bernstein, 1977:366).

Marvin v. *Marvin* (1976), a case involving the rights of nonmarried cohabitors to property and economic support, was well publicized in the media. "The California Supreme Court held that either party to a nonmarital relationship may enforce an expressed or implied agreement dividing accumulated property" (Rivera, 1979:905). Although many felt this case would be a breakthrough for individuals in nontraditional living arrangements, other states have not followed California's lead. It is doubtful, in spite of this California ruling, that courts in other states will change their traditional view of cohabitation as simply a meretricious relationship.

Gay male and lesbian couples who have expressed a desire to become legally married have not been able to do so. "The ability to marry is regulated by the state. Once validated, the marriage relationship confers upon its participants . . . right of action with regard to a fatal accident of the spouse, lower automobile insurance, and the ability to hold real estate by its entirety" (Rivera, 1979:874). Homosexual couples are thus denied the rights to these benefits. The courts in several states consistently have refused to recognize the right of homosexuals to be married; they hold that marriage, by definition, can be entered into only by persons of the opposite sex (Rivera, 1979).

Because the law does not recognize nontraditional living arrangements, those engaging in them may have to forfeit other rights, such as child custody; for example, a lesbian, simply because of her sexual preference, may be found to be an unfit parent. A homosexual father would be even less likely to gain custody than a heterosexual father, and his homosexuality may even be used to deny him visiting privileges.

To summarize, although nontraditional living arrangements are increasing in this country, the laws are not keeping pace. By choosing these nontraditional forms, both males and females can be denied certain legal, social, economic, and child custody benefits.

Whether one chooses a traditional or nontraditional life-style, the legal system perpetuates sex inequities in domestic relationships.

EMPLOYMENT

Of all the tenets of feminism, the one that has the most public approval is the idea of "equal pay for equal work." This idea has been expanded to include equal opportunity in employment generally. These demands have not really altered the economic power structure in this country, but they did become a law of the land when in 1963 the Equal Pay Act was passed.

In 1964, an omnibus Civil Rights Act was passed. One of its provisions was designed specifically to prevent discrimination in employment based on sex—and that included discrimination against either men or women. The key provision of the most important statue—Title VII—states:

> It shall be an unlawful employment practice for an employer (1) to fail or refuse to hire or discharge any individual, or otherwise to discriminate against any individual with respect to his compensation, terms, conditions, or privileges of employment, because of such individual's race, color, religion, sex, or national origin (42.U.C.S.A. 1974 2000 [e]–2[a]).

Under this law and later additions to it, litigations that concern discriminatory practices in hiring, promotion, and salaries have been heard by the courts. Only those occupations for which it can be shown that sex is a bona fide qualification of employment are excluded from the act. However, it is worthy of note that sex is the only classification upon which discrimination in hiring can be legally defended. Laws that have the effect of condoning sex-discriminatory hiring practices are upheld; these would be unconstitutional if they pertained to color, religion, race, or national origin. If the complaints were processed *solely* on the basis of biological sex differences, the only excludable occupations would be wet nurse, semen donor, and so on.

One outcome of the legislation has been an invalidation of many restrictive state labor laws and employment practices. Requiring women but not men to wear revealing costumes as a condition of their employment has been overturned. "Customer preference'' has been ruled invalid, and Pan American Airways was ordered to hire and train men as flight attendants, despite claims that clients preferred women. Similarly, in that ruling, ease of administering a training program for one sex was held as invalid grounds for discrimination. And in the first major sex discrimination litigation brought by the Equal Employment Opportunity Commission (EEOC), the Federal Communication Commission (FCC) denied a rate increase to American Telephone and Telegraph Company—the single largest commercial employer of women in the United States—on the grounds that the corporation's discriminatory employment practices were not in the public interest. After a year of testimony and hearings, a final settlement of back pay of $38 million was awarded. However, when that amount is contrasted with the $3.5 billion that was due to women from the corporation since unequal pay became illegal, the economic gains are quite minor. Indeed, the adjudication of this case illustrates rather clearly how the law in practice protects the interests of the powerful.

"Protective labor legislation," which has excluded women from the better-paying jobs, has also been struck down; for example, in 1969, a circuit court of appeals ruled that under Title VII, weight-lifting restrictions on women, and the exclusion of women from night work, were illegal.

Differential employee benefits have effectively operated to discriminate against men and women simultaneously. As these cases that regard the differences in work week, overtime pay, retirement, and fringe benefits go through the court, they are usually held unlawful under Title VII. A policy that specifies the number of hours a woman can work, for example, not only discriminates against her by limiting her overtime, but also puts the male at a disadvantage, making it difficult for him to refuse extra hours without jeopardizing his job. Similarly, a policy that requires women be paid more for overtime disadvantages the male; however, the effect of the policy can limit the woman's potential earnings—because she costs more, she is not hired. In these cases, the court has ruled the policies unlawful.

Health plans that cover only the wives of male employees but not the husbands of female employees have been held unlawful. Similarly, plans that allow widows to automatically collect death benefits, but that require widowers to demonstrate incapacity for self-support have been struck down. Each of these differential benefit systems discriminates against both sexes. Women are discriminated against, because, in most instances, they receive fewer fringe benefits from their employment; men are discriminated against, because they do not receive the same survivor and health benefits from their wives' work.

One of the common grounds for sex discrimination in hiring and benefits cases has been that of motherhood (*not* parenthood). In the first case concerning sex discrimination under Title VII that was heard by the Supreme Court in 1971, the role of mother was ruled extraneous to the right to work. In *Phillips* v. *Martin Marietta Corporation*, the Supreme Court ruled that the corporation did not have a right to refuse to hire women with preschool children, because its hiring policy for men did not include such restrictions. Only since 1972 has the EEOC established pregnancy as a ''temporary,'' rather than permanent, disability and therefore not grounds for termination, forced maternity leave, or refusal to hire or promote.

Finally, in 1979, Congress passed the Pregnancy Discrimination Act, which bans discrimination in employment due to pregnancy.

Although some of the laws that have been found to be sex discriminatory have been repealed, the process has been slow. There is an enormous backlog of cases— over 130,000 of them. Consequently, although Title VII does provide the basis for equal employment opportunity, these rights are determined on a case-by-case basis at a very slow rate.

More recently, sexual harassment on the job has been recognized as a form of sex discrimination that is prohibited under the employment protection provisions of Title VII; and in March 1980, guidelines were issued to prevent sexual harassment. "Sexual harassment exemplifies and promotes employment practices which disadvantage women" and "degrade and objectify (them)—sexual harassment at work undercuts a woman's potential for social equality in two interpenetrated ways: by using her employment position to coerce her sexually, while using her sexual position to coerce her economically" (MacKinnon, 1979:7). Precise figures on the prevalence of sexual harassment are not known; however, because of women's inferior and vulnerable position in the workforce, it is estimated that it is widespread. In a (nonrandom) survey conducted by *Redbook* magazine, nine out of ten working women reported experiencing sexual harassment (Safron, 1976). Other studies report similar findings (The Project on the Status and Education of Women, 1978). However, such harassment has been held illegal and women now have legal recourse, although many women have lost cases even with strong evidence (Martin, 1984).

To summarize, the old laws and policies are based on stereotypical assumptions about men as breadwinners and women as dependents. But it is nevertheless striking how immersed these cultural stereotypes are in minute interstices of employment practices. To the extent that these policies remain unchallenged, employment discrimination will affect both males and females. It is remarkable, though, how sex equity in employment is becoming the law of the land.

EDUCATION

Closely related to the potential for economic well-being is the opportunity for equal educational opportunities. Although any random 37 words will *not* change the world, the 37 words contained in Title IX of the Education Amendments Act of 1972 had the potential to strongly impact the educational institutions of this country. The provision reads:

> No person in the United States shall, on the basis of sex, be excluded from participation in, be denied the benefits of, or be subjected to discrimination under any educational program or activity receiving federal financial assistance.

The federal agency that was charged with interpreting and enforcing the provision, wrote guidelines requiring that *all* programs (with some major exceptions regarding athletics), whether they receive direct aid or not, within *any* educational institution that does receive federal aid, must meet the standards of Title IX. Because nearly all educational institutions in this nation—from preschools to postgraduate training centers—receive federal assistance, virtually all educational institutions were subject to prosecution under Title IX. Furthermore, the ultimate weapon—the withholding of funds—had been specifically approved. Sex-segregated classrooms, admission quotas, differential admission standards, dress codes, propriety rules that apply to only one sex, and discriminatory promotion and tenure policies are illegal.

The enforcement of affirmative action compliance has been chronically lax. It took three years for the Department of Health and Human Services to develop regulations for the enforcement of Title IX, and actual enforcement activities did not begin until 1977. Under Title IX, all institutions with federal contracts over $50,000 must evaluate themselves on sex discrimination issues and have a written affirmative action plan. If the institution finds itself discriminating, then it must take restitutive actions. Yet in 1977, HHS reported that approximately two-thirds of the universities had failed to submit the required compliance forms or assurance statements (WEAL, 1980). Despite the affirmative action violations, federal contracts to these universities have not been slowed or terminated (Freeman, 1975:199). Instead, a major backlog of unprocessed complaints from academic women has resulted, and HHS is using the "resulting logjam as an excuse for inaction" (WEAL, *Washington Report*, 1978). Recent executive attitudes have made it clear that enforcing affirmative action is not a priority.

Two particular sex equality questions have received attention in the courts and the media; namely, the tenure and promotion of women faculty and women in sports. Women have not won much in the courts on promotion and tenure issues; for example, a woman professor was denied tenure by her university on the grounds that her research was unacceptable because it was concerned with the role of women, a "trendy" issue and an "unworthy topic for research" (*The Equal Employer*, 1979). The judge refused to rule this an act of sex discrimination, and deferred to the judgment of the tenure committee (*Lynn* v. *Regents of the University of California*, 1979). By refusing to intervene, the court perpetuated the male domination of universities (see Chapter 4). Moreover, recently in the Grove City case, the court ruled that only the discriminating unit or program within an educational institution could be penalized. This means that if the science program favors boys, federal funds can be withheld *only* from that program. In response to this new, restricted judicial interpretation of Title IX, the Civil Rights Restoration Act has been introduced into Congress.

Title IX has, unquestionably, helped women's intercollegiate athletic programs by increasing their budgets and scholarship funds. However, there still is great disparity between budgets and scholarships for women's athletics and those for men's athletics. In some cases, men's athletic programs receive 30 times more money than women's programs (WEAL, Sports Fact Sheet, 1978). Despite the obvious sex discrimination, HHS remains reluctant to do anything about it; apparently, not offending (men's) sports interests is more important than achieving sports equity. Overall, Title IX has not made a major impact because its provisions have not been enforced. Further, the widespread notion that there has been "reverse discrimination" (the preferential hiring of women and minorities over white males) is not born out in the facts. There have been practically no changes in the academic world in terms of pay, employment, or promotion resulting from affirmative action (Huber, 1976a). Some argue, the situation is even worse today than it was (see Chapter 11).

Consequently, because discriminatory policies in education have continued *after* legislation, it is doubtful that they will suddenly cease.

CRIMINAL LAW

According to the ideology that underlies the law, men and women are different in terms of their sexuality and their propensity to violence. These beliefs about gender differences have consequences for the structure of criminal law.

Early beliefs and theories imputed the kind of criminal behavior that was engaged in as explainable by inherent differences in the physiology and psychology of males and females (Klein, 1973:4). More recently, these differences have been explained by their social roles. Males who are maladjusted or blocked in their instrumental roles resort to criminal behavior; females who are maladjusted or blocked in their expressive roles turn to crime, delinquency, and prostitution (Heidensohn, 1968:166–167). These theorists argue that, because women are not required to perform instrumentally, they act through men who incite them to crime or who use their sex to engage in crimes against morality.

For some of these theorists, the kinds of crime committed were explainable by the biology of sexual intercourse. Pollak, for example, argued that "Man must achieve an erection in order to perform the sex act and will not be able to hide his failure. . . ." On the other hand, women can make a pretense of orgasm, and "neither her pretense or lack of orgasm prevents her from participation" (1950:10). Therefore, man's crimes are overt, manifest, obvious; women's crimes are hidden, secret, deceitful. Indeed, Pollak argued further that because "our sex mores" require women to "conceal their menstrual periods every four weeks," they are conditioned to hold a "different attitude toward veracity than men" (1950:11).

Pollak's viewpoint would have us conclude that male crimes such as bribery, embezzlement, kickbacks, price-setting, "cover-ups," and fraud are not hidden, secret, or deceitful. Obviously, such a conclusion is as unwarranted as the assumption upon which it is based—namely, that one's sexual apparatus determines the kind of crime one will commit.

Although most modern sociologists and criminologists no longer adhere to the physiological explanations of crime, these ideas still inform our legislation and policy decisions. As late as 1967, for example, Reckless and Kay, both distinguished criminologists, reported to the President's Commission on Law Enforcement and the Administration of Justice:

> A large part of the infrequent officially acted upon involvement of women in crime can be traced to the masking effect of women's roles, effective practice on the part of women of deceit and indirection, their instigation of men to commit their crimes (the Lady Macbeth factor), and the unwillingness on the part of the public and law enforcement officials to hold women accountable for their deeds (the chivalry factor) (1967:13).

In these few sentences, the criminologists—without empirical evidence—reported to the President that women have a lesser moral character that is inherited from their Mother Eve whose life-style they emulate by seducing (lesser) men to misconducts and (better) men to protect them from punishment. Not only are they impugning women, but they are also implying that men are suckers—fools led around by their penises.

These ideas intrude upon the sensibilities of governmental commissions and invade the processing of the offender. As Cicourel and Kitsuse (1963) have demonstrated, the social organization of justice is such that the probation officers, social workers, counselors, police officers, and other specialists process cases that are based on normative assumptions about female and male crime and delinquency. The ideas become self-fulfilling prophecies.

Crimes of Violence

Apart from rape, which we shall discuss later, crimes of violence such as murder, manslaughter, and assault are presumed under the law to be committable by members of either gender. Yet, the processing of men and women in such cases differs; for example, although Nagel and Weitzman (1962) found that men were more likely to be awarded counsel and a jury trial than women—a due process consideration—they also found two other patterns of treatment that discriminate against men. The first, the "disadvantaged" pattern, results in greater harshness to the black and the indigent. The second, the "paternalistic," involves greater leniency to women and children. Male acts of violence—and especially black males' violence—are perceived as somehow more violent and dangerous than females' and, therefore, require greater punishment. Men, as a class, then, are likely to receive harsher sentences and more convictions for their violence than are women.

Prostitution

The traditional double standard of morality is well represented in the laws that govern prostitution and in their administration. Prostitution is variously defined in many states, as "the practice of the female offering her body to an indiscriminate sexual intercourse with men for compensation" or "common lewdness of a woman for gain" (Kanowitz, 1969:16). Obviously, the law makes guilty only one partner—the female—and, further, is written in such a way as to exclude the possibility of a male being a prostitute.

Although it is legally possible to punish men for patronizing prostitutes, in most states no such direct provisions are provided. Only recently have states written direct provisions. Where indirect provisions are given—such as fornication, lewdness, solicitation, or associating with a prostitute—the interpretations of the laws have led to the exoneration of the male. Thus, various courts have ruled that visiting a house of prostitution does not constitute "open and gross lewdness," that occasional intercourse outside of marriage is not "adultery or fornication" (providing there is no pretense of living with the woman), and that, if a male solicits a prostitute to achieve personal gratification, he is not convictable for "solicitation" (Kanowitz, 1969:16–17).

Most importantly, of course, is the fact that the decisions regarding the processing of the crime are made by police officers and prosecuting attorneys who are usually male. Consequently, although males could be charged with a direct or indirect crime that involves their visiting a prostitute, this rarely occurs. Males are arrested to induce their cooperation in convicting women.

The sex bias in the processing of prostitution is only too obvious. In effect, only women are held criminally accountable. As Flexner argued in 1941, to undo this inequity, "the stigma and consequence of the crime—must—be either removed from the woman or affixed to the man" (quoted in Kanowitz, 1969:18).

Some states have recently revised their criminal statutes to define prostitution as committable by either males or females. However, prostitutes, led by Margo St. John (president of COYOTE, for "Cut Out Your Old Tired Ethics"), have organized to challenge *any* criminal legislation concerning prostitution. They are not interested in "affixing the stigma" to the male, but in removing the stigma *entirely* by decriminalizing prostitution *entirely*—viewing it as a professional service (sex therapy) that is voluntarily sought and rendered.

Statutory Rape and Rape

Historically, common law has been concerned with the protection of innocent—that is, virginal—women from the sexual advances of older men. No parallel concern with protecting the innocent male from the mature female existed—presumably because females were considered incapable of sexual aggression. The existence of these protective laws was based on the presumption that families were unable to adequately shield their young women from the temptations and abuses of the adult male and on the grounds that the state had an interest in such protection. In a society that valued a girl's virginity as a "sexual treasure" not to be unwisely disposed of (62 *Yale Law Journal*, 55 quoted in Lopez, 1974:1) and that was concerned with the legitimate inheritance of property from father to sons, such laws were seen as necessary to protect "the society, the family, and the infant" (judicial decision quoted in Kanowitz, 1969:25).

Until recently, statutory rape law specified sexual intercourse with a female under the age of consent. The seriousness of the crime was determined by the age of the female, her previous chasteness, and/or the age differential between the male and the female. Most states now have statutes that permit as a crime the statutory rape of a young male by an adult female; but, for example, in *Michael M.* v. *California Superior Court*, the Supreme Court ruled that defining statutory rape as an offense only against a female was not sex discriminatory because the purpose of the law was to prevent teenage pregnancy. (Incidentally, the first and only female Supreme Court Judge wrote the opinion.)

The laws are written specifically to protect underage females, not males, and to specifically deny to females the right to consent to sexual intercourse. Such intercourse is legally defined as rape, while a male's ability to consent to an adult female is not questioned. Only underage females are protected by the legislation and only underage males are deemed capable of a voluntary, consensual union. The argument presumes that if a female was capable of making a right decision, she would refuse sexual intercourse; because she did not, *ergo*, she was not capable of making the right decision.

Legal thinking transforms the innocent girl who is incapable of consenting to intercourse into a woman at age 16 (or 18, depending on the state) who is capable of—indeed desirous of—sexually seducing and tricking men. This ideological belief in woman as a sexual seducer is perhaps most evident in the legal processing of the victims of rape.

Although the mass media have depicted the police as insensitive and threatening to the rape victim, in a social-scientific study in which rape victims were interviewed while being processed through the judicial system, the women did not see the police as the culprits (Holmstrom and Burgess, 1974). Rather, they saw themselves as victimized first by the rape, and secondly by the court. "Going to court for the women is as much a crisis as the rape itself" (Holmstrom and Burgess, 1974:8).

First, some of the feelings of being a victim of the court system arise from the interminable delays that are arranged by defense lawyers; 12 to 18 months can easily elapse between the rape and the final verdict, during which time the women report feeling their lives have been suspended. Secondly, women report feeling victimized by the public setting of the court—a setting in which they must face the accused, and speak into a microphone before thrill-seeking strangers who vicariously "witness the rape." The women relive the event at each stage of the court processing—the preliminary hearing, the Grand Jury, and the actual trial. Thirdly, women report feeling as though they are treated as the offender.

Although the male is on trial, the rape laws of most states are structured to protect the accused. In many states, a man cannot be convicted solely on the testimony of the alleged victim; corroborative evidence is required. This includes proof of penetration, proof of the identity of the assailant, and proof that the act occurred without consent.

Penetration is not always possible to prove because women frequently wait before going to the police; proof of the identity of the assailant is also sometimes problematic due to the settings in which some rapes occur—such as parks, alleys, dark streets, and dark rooms. Proof of nonconsent is the one kind of corroborative evidence that especially marks the sex bias of the legal processing of rape. A woman can be seen as instigating the crime—and, therefore, guilty of seduction—by her involvement in such activities as going to a bar alone, walking on the streets at night, and hitchhiking. It is the only crime where the *victim* is held responsible; for example, if a woman went to the bank and carried money out in her purse, she would not be accused of precipitating a robbery. A woman who walks alone at night or hitchhikes, however, has to prove in court that she was not out looking for sex. Further, if her previous history has included extramarital relationships (or in some cases even "familiarity with alcohol"—that is, working as a cocktail waitress), there is *prima facie* evidence that she is of low moral character. Ironically, although a man's previous convictions for rape or assault cannot be used as evidence against him in a new case, a defense attorney can pry into the private life of the female victim and use this information to undermine her moral credibility. In fact, the defense attorney's questioning can be so vicious that, according to Holmstrom and Burgess (1974), women feel those attorneys are like the rapists—twisted, degraded, offensive. Only recently have states passed "rape shield" laws to protect the victim from assaultive lines of questioning.

Rape, according to Griffin, is the "all-American crime" (1973). Not only is rape the most frequently committed violent crime (Griffin, 1973:2), but also rape is thought of as natural and not raping, learned (Griffin, 1973:3). This belief is held despite the fact that most rapes are not spontaneous, but *preplanned* (Amir, 1971). A companion myth, that all women secretly want to be raped, completes the basis for the legal reasoning: Women precipitate the inevitable. Further, given that in our culture normal heterosexuality involves a dominant male and a submissive female, the courts have difficulty distinguishing rape from mutual consent. "Rape is simply at one end of the continuum of male-aggressive, female-passive patterns, and an arbitrary line has been drawn to mark it off from the rest of such relationships" (Medea and Thompson, 1974:11–12, quoted in Hudnell and Dunham, 1974:1).

Although there is no statistical evidence, it is quite probable that males and females have different conceptions of what constitutes rape; for example, in one case a polygraph (lie detector test) was administered to both the accused and the accuser. The results showed *both* were telling the truth; that is, the female defined her refusal as a bona fide "no"; the male perceived her "no" as "c'mon, yes" (Hudnell and Dunham, 1974). As long as women are trained to act coy and expect to be chased, subdued, and seduced, and as long as males are taught to view these female behaviors as enticements—as part of the normal romantic foreplay—it will be difficult for the law to sharply demarcate rape from normal heterosexual intercourse.

Moreover, because the law requires proof that the accused had knowledge of wrongful action, the fact that men do not view their behavior as rape (i.e., "the women wanted it") exonerates them. What is needed, and what is happening, is that the society is being reeducated, and female definitions of rape are becoming part of the court process. Rape is an act of violence, not sex.

"Male sexuality and violence in our culture seem to be inseparable" (Griffin, 1973:3). In a society "where James Bond alternately whips out his revolver and his cock" (Griffin, 1973:3), rape represents an archetypal model of eroticism—the blending of sex and violence in one act. Despite the myths to the contrary, "the typical rapist might be the boy next door. Especially if the boy next door happens to be about 19 years of age and the neighborhood you live in happens to fit the socioeconomic description of lower class or bears the appellation 'ghetto'" (Brownmiller, 1975:174). Statistically, the male who is convicted of forcible rape has the same attitudes toward sexuality as the "normal, well-adjusted male," differing "only in having a greater tendency to *express* [emphasis mine] violence and rage" (Amir, 1971, referred to in Griffin, 1973:538). As a final example of the attraction to rape that is taught to males in this society, Hudnell and Dunham (1974) report the following episode from a documentary movie (*Rape: Law, Justice and Public Opinion*):

[A defense lawyer] . . . related the story of a local prosecutor who belonged to a businessmen's luncheon group in which it was customary for the members to give gifts to each other. The prosecutor decided his gift would be indictment forms with the members' names filled in as defendants for the crime of rape. This would . . . signify the masculinity and prowess of these men (1974:16).

When these ideas of eroticism are located within the more general legal and social ideology that views women as "sexual objects," the rationale for the processing of rape in the courts becomes clear. Illustrative of this is an explanatory opinion of rape laws that appeared in the *Yale Law Review*. The authors stressed that the rape laws both foster and bolster "a masculine pride in the exclusive possession of a sexual object." Consequently, by establishing a consent standard in the law, men are assured that the women they do possess are personal prizes. Further, sole ownership of the sexual object enhances their status. If other males forcibly rape his possession, they are threatening *him*. Accordingly, "The law of rape provides an orderly outlet for . . . [male] vengeance" against other men (quoted in Griffin, 1973:6).

Therefore, historically, rape is not seen so much as a crime that a man perpetuates against a woman as one that a man perpetuates against another *man*. Rape laws were not written to protect the rights of females over their own bodies; rather, their purpose was to protect the rights of men as owners of females (Griffin, 1973:6).

Women continue to structure their employment opportunities and social activities around their fears of rape. They remain prisoners by night, at home "where they belong." The threat of rape and the knowledge of how it will be processed in the court are effective deterrents to female freedom of movement. The law continues to hold in line the law-abiding—and, in this case, the line is drawn at the front door.

What is to be done? Obviously, rape will not cease until the views that are held toward women are altered and until men are no longer socialized to revere violence. In the meantime, there are possible changes that would contribute to greater justice and equity. In some states, some legal changes have already occurred; for example, in Ohio, the current criminal code defines rape as:

sexual conduct (i.e., vaginal and anal intercourse, fellatio and cunnilingus) between persons, regardless of sex, when the offender uses threat of force or when s/he administers any drug or intoxicant to the other person for the purpose of impairing the person's judgment in order to prevent resistance, or when the other person is less than thirteen (13) years old (Hudnell and Dunham, 1974:7).

First, the new rape law, which exists in only a few states, has moved away from the archaic concept of viewing a woman's virginity as the property of her father and her sexuality as the property of her husband, and has placed it in the context of modern criminal violence (Brownmiller, 1975:377). Viewed as such, "the crime retains its unique dimensions, falling midway between robbery and assault. It is in one act both a blow to the body and a blow to the mind and a 'taking' of sex through the use of threat or force'' (Brownmiller, 1975:377).

Secondly, the revised rape law has become less sex activity specific (intercourse) and become more gender free. It recognizes that "acts of sex forced on unwilling victims," whether male or female, "deserve to be treated in concept as equally grave offenses in the eyes of the law" (Brownmiller, 1975:378). Sexual assault does not occur only genitally, nor is it solely a male-on-female offense. "As men may invade women through other orifices, so, too, do they invade other men" (Brownmiller, 1975:378). Is the assault to the dignity of the male any less than that to the dignity of the female? Is forced oral or anal penetration any less a violation "of the personal, private inner space, a lesser injury to mind, spirit and sense of self?" (Brownmiller, 1975:383).

States are adopting model laws concerning rape. Although these new laws rectify much of the abusiveness of the old ones, the crime of rape will not disappear until the socialization of males and females and our socialization toward sexuality are radically altered.

REPRODUCTIVE RIGHTS

Until the 1960s, the word and practice—abortion—lay sealed in silence. Although there are few accurate statistics, there were probably more than one million illegal abortions annually in the United States. Most of these were performed on married women in the upper socioeconomic classes who wanted no more children. Legal abortions were permitted in most states only to "save the life of the mother" or, in some states, if the pregnancy "endangered the health of the mother." In court cases, 10-year-old victims of rape, menopausal mothers, mentally ill girls, and intellectually slow girls were denied the right to a legal abortion.

Then, after many years of controversy on complex moral, religious, and legal issues, the Supreme Court ruled on abortion in January of 1973. Its seven-to-two ruling stated that during the first trimester of pregnancy, the decision to abort was a matter between the woman and her physician—a matter in which the state could not intervene. During the second trimester, when abortion is more dangerous to the woman, however, the court ruled that the state has a legitimate interest in the woman's health; thus, the state can legislate statutes concerning where abortions may be performed. The court also reasoned that when the fetus was viable, the state could prohibit abortion during the third trimester, unless the life or health of the mother was threatened.

The *right* to abortion still rests with the woman and her physician. Yet, the goal of the proabortion activists to gain the absolute right to abortion for all women was not accepted by the court. Rather, the grounds upon which the ruling was based was the Fourteenth Amendment's concept of "personal liberty and the right to privacy."

As a consequence of the ruling, therefore, abortions are legally available to women, although the state has some leeway to legislate pregnancies during their last six months. Predictably, however, because abortions are expensive, they are more obtainable by women in the upper socioeconomic classes.

In 1976, the court ruled that neither the father of the fetus nor the parents of an underage girl have the right to prevent an abortion if she chooses one. Both of these rulings are effectively further removing the ''property value'' that was attached to women and children. Only the state is seen as having a vested interest in the issue. The continued extension of ''personal liberty and the right to privacy'' that is extended to minors and married women may have additional ramifications.

Very deep emotional and moral concerns have been generated by the abortion ruling (cf. Luker, 1984). Judging from the continued growth of the antiabortion groups and the antiabortion stance of many political leaders, the controversies and legal issues surrounding it are far from over; for example, in 1977, the Supreme Court, by ruling in three separate cases (*Maher* v. *Roe, Beal* v. *Doe, Poelker* v. *Doe*) that abortion need not be made available to welfare or Medicaid recipients, made abortions for the *poor* subject to the discretion of individual states. Candidates in national, state, and local campaigns run on ''anti'' or ''pro'' abortion tickets.

Antiabortion activists ask, ''How can abortion be justified?'' And many pro-abortionists have attempted to answer that query. The moral, ethical, theological, and medical responses to this question go well beyond the province of this book. However, we might profitably ask, as Hardin did (1975), a different question: ''How can compulsory pregnancy be justified?'' This question places the issue squarely within the context of sex roles. What are the rights of males over the bodies of females? What are the interests of the state?

If men have the right to enforce pregnancy in their wives, Hardin argues, then ''such compulsion is akin to rape'' (1975:246). Further, it is a form of indentured servitude, because if ''pregnancy is continued to term, it results in parenthood, which is also a kind of servitude, to be continued for the best years of a woman's life'' (1975:248). It is the female whose body is being used for the prenatal period, and the mother who will be held principally responsible for the upbringing of the child. One wonders, if males were the childbearers but still had their positions of greater power, whether abortion would not have been routinely allowed decades ago.

In addition, it can be argued that the state has a vested interest in the preservation of the lives of its female citizens. Making abortions illegal will not prevent them. Women will return to the prelegal forms of abortion—self-inducement and the dangerous knife of the unskilled abortionist. Consequently, it can be argued that the state has an interest in providing abortions in order to preserve the lives of women.

Further, Hardin argues that the society has another vested interest in allowing women to abort. A study of Swedish children who were born to mothers who were refused abortions found that these children received less education, needed more therapy, were arrested more frequently, and bore children sooner (if females) than their matched controls. The result was a vicious cycle of unwanted children producing more unwanted children. Hardin asks, ''How then does society gain by increasing the number of unwanted children?'' (1975:248). Clearly, voluntary parenthood is in the interest of the society, and compulsory pregnancy is not.

Reproductive rights issues also affect men. In terms of abortion, the court has ruled that the woman has sole right to the decision. Some doctors will require the consent of the spouse before they will perform a vasectomy or tubal ligation (sterilization procedures). The reproductive rights of males and females, therefore, continue to be major legal, moral, and sociopolitical issues (also see Chapter 8).

EQUAL RIGHTS AMENDMENT

The proposed federal Equal Rights Amendment states "equal rights under the law shall not be denied or abridged by the United States or any state on account of sex." Such an amendment proposing equal rights for males and females was first introduced by the National Woman's Party (NWP) in 1923. However, judicial and legislative opinion held that "sex-based classification has always been made and—unless prohibited in express terms in the Constitution—is a natural and proper one to make" (judicial decision, *Salt Lake City* v. *Wilson*, 46, Utah, quoted in Freeman, 1975:210). The resolution was introduced in each succeeding congress, but it was not until after the emergence of the Women's Movement that the idea took root. On March 22, 1972, the amendment passed both houses of Congress. As of this writing, 35 states have ratified the federal ERA. On June 30, 1982, lacking the support of three states, the amendment failed; but it has not died: It is yearly reintroduced into the Congress (see Chapter 14 for a further discussion of the ERA).

Opponents of the ERA base their opposition on seemingly inconsistent arguments. First, it is held that the amendment is not needed because women's rights are covered under the equal protection principle in the Fourteenth Amendment. However, courts have been ambivalent in their reliance upon and interpretation of that amendment in sex discrimination cases. Secondly, it is argued that what is needed is not a constitutional amendment but a state-by-state law revision in such areas as divorce, family law, employment, and criminal code. As Rosemary Guning, New York State assemblywoman, commented, "We have just passed a bill requiring both parties in a divorce action to file financial statements. . . . That little piecemeal item took us five years" (quoted in Lear, 1976:115). Given all the piecemeal items in our 50 states, we can see that full legal equality between the sexes would take an interminably long time and be extremely expensive.

Although ratification of the ERA will not eliminate sex discrimination overnight, its existence will not only be a symbolic statement of the mutual dignity of both sexes, but it will also provide the courts with a principle through which the legacy of sex discrimination can be removed.

As it now stands, though, the courts are not without a principle that can eliminate a great deal of sex-based legal discrimination. Beginning with the decision in *Reed* v. *Reed* in 1971, when the courts ruled that choosing males over females to administer estates was "arbitrary," judicial opinion has developed to the point where formal "legal equality between men and women is the general rule" (Erickson, 1979:591–592). In most circumstances, the law cannot discriminate between "similarly situated" women and men solely on the basis of sex. It does not matter whether the consequences of discrimination are benign or only hurt men, they are illegal if men and women are "similarly situated"—such as both equally able to administer an estate, both similarly employed, both widowed, and so on. "In essence, the court has declared war on sex stereotyping by law" (Erickson,

1979:594). The law does provide the court with the machinery to end legal sex discrimination, but to do so requires that the law be "fairly and judiciously applied" (Erickson, 1979:610).

Although this is true, "the equal protection" clause, nevertheless, has failed to ensure sex equity in a number of different cases where the legal argument is that men and women are not "similarly situated." One example of this is the ruling in *Schlesinger* v. *Ballard* (1975) that although a female naval officer had to be "up or out" after 13 years of service, a male officer was "up or out" after three mandatory trials, taking place in less than 13 years, and thus discriminating against men. The court argued that the males and females were not "similarly situated," because females were more restricted in gaining the necessary experience that entitles them to promotion—such as being restricted on their sea duty. Although these restrictions are probably unconstitutional, the court accepted this as a demonstration of the fact that male and female naval officers were not "similarly situated."

In summary, the domestic, criminal, educational, and economic legislation has a tradition of affirming gender stereotypes. Only in the past few years have we seen any substantial alteration in the legal code. Those legal gains, however, have not been systematically implemented by the agencies charged with their enforcement, and powerful interest groups have arisen to turn back the legal clock. We will discuss these forces in more detail in the last chapter. Now it is necessary for us to consider another important source of social control, namely, the medical and mental health system.

□ □ *8* □ □

Medical and Mental Health Systems

One of the major strategies for maintaining cultural values is the repackaging of them as truths that are based on the research of scholars and scientists. As such, they are handed down matter-of-factly as wisdom from generation to generation, taught unquestioningly in the schools, and reiterated with conviction in the mass media. Doubting their veracity labels one "irrational," "ignorant," or "mentally ill."

If scientists and scholars remained sequestered in an ivory tower, their ideas would hardly concern us. However, their ideas do have direct consequences on our lives. Scientists and scholars provide definitions and descriptions of the world, establish the methodologies for apprehending it, and decide which areas of knowledge should be explored, thereby directly affecting the practices of journalists, doctors, social workers, and psychologists—all professional agents of social control and cultural maintenance. These knowledge systems and practices exercise control of the body, the mind, and structured social interactions.

Because the sciences of physics and chemistry have had such a remarkable impact on the material level of our existence, a kind of semisacred quality has been imputed to all of science. However, the findings of the biological, psychological, and social sciences do not have the same high level of reliability as do the physical and chemical sciences. Further, for all sciences, that which is chosen to be studied or not studied is always influenced by the sociohistorical context. Consequently, it behooves us to retain some degree of skepticism toward science and, on the subject of gender, to look for assumptions that may distort scientific findings and clinical practices.

In this chapter I discuss some of the major systems of knowledge in terms of what they have assumed about the sexes, the consequences of these assumptions for the practice of medicine and therapy, and some alternative views and practices. Knowledge is a form of social control that is extensive and relevant to all people's lives. We now turn to a discussion of the body, reproduction, and sexuality.

THE BODY

Our Bodies, Ourselves (Boston Women's Health Book Collective, 1984) is an elegant summary of a very important understanding. Our sense of our bodies—our knowledge about them, the pleasure we derive from them, and the joy or distress we experience when we contemplate them—is the basis upon which we build our self-image.

The cultural preference for males, as we have seen, has its tolling effects upon females. But more inclusively, the cultural definitions of attractiveness, the cultural inclination to limit and distort biological knowledge, and the cultural injunctions regarding sexuality and physical pleasure take their toll on both males and females.

The perpetuation of ideal physical standards, which generally cannot be met, leads to self-doubt and self-denigration. The anguish of the young, middle-aged, and aging regarding how they look is endemic. Women are frequently concerned about their breasts because they are often categorized and labeled on the basis of their cup sizes. Two comments—one from a small-breasted woman and the other from a large-breasted woman—are illustrative:

> . . . Guys will get friendly with me and I'll really like them and then they'll say, "Sorry, your lack of tits just turn me off." Here I am almost 30 and I still can't accept my flat chest. That's why I'm getting silicone transplants.

> . . . When I was in junior high, I was always called a slut because I had big boobs. It was like I had no business looking like I did unless I put out; and they assumed I must put out because I looked that way. . . . I was a virgin till I was 22. And today, it happened again—these guys wouldn't let me pass into the restaurant just going on and on about me. I feel so dirty, so mortified and so guilty—like it is my fault. [The woman was crying in rage and guilt while retelling the episode.]

Although men are not subject to the "sex object" assault as women are, they are subject to both the "sex object" refusal and the "social object" refusal. Despite the changing values that permit young men to look "less manly," they are still subject *internally* (and, on occasion, externally) to doubts about their penis size or shape and doubts about their height or musculature—that is, despite the freeing of the culture, persons still measure themselves and are measured by universal standards that usually cannot be met.

In the case of men, stereotypes about their behavior are based on their body builds. The male mesomorph—the one with a body build predominately of muscle and bone—is associated with socially desirable behavior, whereas his ectomorphic (thin and linear) and endomorphic (predominately fatty-tissued) brothers are stereotypically associated with socially undesirable traits (Lerner, 1969:363). The traits that are assigned to each body type go well beyond those one might reasonably expect to be body related. Mesomorphs, for example, are not only seen as good athletes and soldiers, but are also viewed as leaders, good friends, mentally healthy, and potentially the best fathers and doctors. Ectomorphs are seen as needy of friends and as making poor fathers and doctors, whereas endomorphs are viewed as heavy drinkers, poor soldiers, athletes, fathers, and doctors. In brief, a man's life chances are enhanced or limited based on the culture's interpretation of his body type.

Although children of different body types are probably socialized differently and therefore develop differently, the biological knowledge system has played a role in the perpetuation of the cultural standards upon which this differential socialization is based.

The role of the biological knowledge system in the perpetuation of these stereotypes begins with what appears to be simply an "objective" depiction of the physical characteristics of the "normal" male and the "normal" female (Herschberger, 1948:71). Accordingly, the "normal" male has broad squared shoulders, facial hair, bulging calves, blunt toes, small hips, a heavy brow, and a square jaw, whereas the "normal" female has sloping shoulders, bent arms, conical thighs, wide hips, small feet, a demure nose, and slightly knocked knees. Accompanying the standard biology text are illustrations that clarify the descriptions.

These are presented as the typical, average, normal male and female; however, if we look around us, nobody really looks that way.[1] What is being actually represented is the ideal offspring of the mating of statistical facts and cultural preferences. Unfortunately, these ideals that pass as normal become the standards against which we measure our own physical deviances and "abnormalities." Not only do the billions of dollars spent on breast developers, muscle builders, depilatories, hirsuties, silicone transplants, and cosmetics testify to the tyranny of the ideal, but, more tellingly, so do the fractured self-images that we carry with us when we judge ourselves as inadequate and imperfect.

Additionally, this knowledge system has distorted the facts concerning sexuality and sensuality, has deprived many men and women of pleasure, and has caused them considerable confusion. By withholding information from the public—although perhaps unintentionally—medical and paramedical institutions prevent individuals from understanding their bodies, their feelings, and, hence, themselves.

REPRODUCTION

Although most children learn about human reproduction from older children, the knowledge system regarding human sexual behavior is officially written in the authoritative texts of biologists and sexologists. Although the sex tales that are handed down by the already initiated, older, and wiser child carry a pecking order

---

[1]The concept *normal* has two significant connotations in biology. It can be synonymous with *statistical average*, or *mean*, a statistic highly influenced by extreme scores. If all the characteristics of the human body are measured and separate averages are computed for the male and female, a composite "average" male or female can be drawn. But no one individual male or female will look like that average. Further, the two sets of distribution of male and female scores will have considerable overlap. Put another way, for most characteristics, there will be greater differences *within* the sexes than *between* the sexes. Consequently, the depiction of normalcy is highly misleading.

A second meaning of the concept *normal* in biology is that a particular characteristic is widespread in the population and is important for species survival. In that it cannot be shown that most of the anatomical characteristics are relevant to the survival of the species biologically—and indeed it can be argued that the "normal" traits are a result of *selective mating* due to *cultural* preferences—there is no reason to treat those characteristics as normal.

authority, this authority is simple child's play compared to that which is given to the scientist of human sexual and reproductive behavior. Just as the street knowledge is slanted and only partially true, so is the knowledge that is propagated by the scientist. The conceptual language of reproductive biology, as well as the questions it asks and the questions it does *not* ask, is more than just reminiscent of the cultural stereotypes that are associated with masculinity and femininity: It is an exact replica.

The tone, orientation, and taken-for-granted assumptions of biology are well illustrated in Herschberger's brilliant review of our society's male-oriented view toward reproduction in contrast to a matriarchal society's viewpoint (1948). Selected examples from her work are presented in Table 8.1. In the usual, taken-for-granted account of impregnation, the male sperm and organs are the central concerns. The sperm are characterized as manly little creatures—"single-minded . . . full of charm, resourcefulness, and energy"—who decide to win the egg, "the blushing bride" waiting receptively for the arrival of her suitors (Herschberger, 1948:71). The biological account of the sperm and egg is strikingly similar to the traditional social account of the mating process between men and women. The egg is "feminine"—passive, receptive, helpless, waiting to be conquered—while the sperm is "masculine"—active, independent, daring, and selective.

Of course, the matriarchal accounting is also biased; it aggrandizes the female role and minimizes the male role in the reproductive process. When we read it, perhaps, we find ourselves laughing out loud. However, when we stop to consider how the socially accepted version of reproduction is received without even the smile of irony, we can perhaps more fully recognize how totally ingrained in our own lives the ideological component of the biological knowledge system is.

Just as other activities and practices are socially constructed, so are ways of experiencing reproduction. Pregnancy and birth are accomplished in socially devised ways that are warranted by one's community; and developments in technology, as well as changing social interests, have resulted in dramatic changes in how modern reproduction is practiced.

Upon first examination, reproductive technologies seem to present women with positive advances. They seem to offer women who are labeled infertile the ability to reproduce, and they appear to promise competence in monitoring pregnancy and birth, as well as proficiency in allowing for related medical breakthroughs—such as fetal cell implants (Levine, 1987:62). Still, upon closer examination, another advance is apparent, and that is the further medicalization of women's lives (Raymond, 1984:427). Most women reproduce within a social and medical system that incorporates technology where treatment procedures are managed and regulated by the use of that technology and where the obstetricians—a largely male group—set the norms.

In examining the interactions of science and society in the social construction of childbearing, biologist Ruth Hubbard suggests that reliance on so-called technological improvements gives physicians "authority and control" over how women experience pregnancy (Hubbard, 1984:338). The evidence of this medicalization includes the need for numerous checkups and even a change in the reproductive time-keeping calendar. Barbara Katz Rothman finds that many women no longer

Table 8.1 THE "FACTS OF LIFE" AS USUALLY WRITTEN CONTRASTED WITH A MATRIARCHAL CULTURE PERSPECTIVE*

A patriarchal society writes biology	A matriarchal society writes biology
The simple and elementary fact behind human reproduction is that a fertile female egg awaits impregnation in the fallopian tube, and the active male sperm must find this egg and penetrate it.	The simple and elementary fact behind human reproduction is that the active female egg must obtain a male sperm before it can create life.
The female sex apparatus is a depression to receive the sex cells; the male organ is advanced in order to expel the cells.	The male sex apparatus is a tiny factory that continually manufactures sex cells for the female.
When the male becomes sexually excited by internal stimuli, his sexual mechanism is called into play. There is a spontaneous erection of the penis and the passageways from the testicles are thrown open.	When the female becomes sexually excited by internal stimuli, there is a spontaneous erection of the clitoris and a flow of blood into the fine sensitive tissues of the vagina. This causes a similar erection of the region and of the vulva, while the involuntary musculature of the vagina begins rhythmically to contract.
The sperm has a long way to travel through the vas deferens, through the penis, through the vagina and uterus, and finally into the tiny tube where the female egg is waiting.	The sperm is provided with a continuous enclosed passageway—thus making its conveyance as simple as possible. For the female, there is a remarkable gap—which the egg must traverse alone.
Nature has provided for this purpose an aggressive and active male cell. Each sperm is composed of rich and highly specialized material and is equipped with a fine wriggling tail that gives it the power of self-locomotion.	Because of the central importance in reproduction, the female egg has been provided with a size much greater than that of the male sperm. The female egg is actually visible to the naked eye and is the largest cell in the body. The male "germ" cells are unbelievably small and must be magnified one hundred times to be visible at all.
No less than 225 million cells are emitted from the man's body with each ejaculation.	The male sperm is produced in superfluously great numbers since the survival of any one sperm is improbable. The egg, being more resilient and endowed with solidity, toughness, and endurance, can be produced singly and yet affect reproduction.
When coitus and ejaculation take place, the male sperm—millions in number and each one swimming like a fish—begin their concentrated search for the egg.	At the height of orgasm, the uterus contracts, becomes erect, and prolongs its neck downward, dipping into the seminal fluid that draws the semen up to the vicinity of the egg.
The instant one of the sperm penetrates the receptive egg, the creation of a new human being has occurred.	Sometimes none of the sperm suits the egg. When an egg does select a male sperm, the sperm is required to shed its wisplike tail. Nature seems to be insisting that the sperm sacrifice its independence for the larger destiny of the female egg. For the future, the new human being wholly depends upon the courage and acumen of the egg in establishing a placenta.
Many women say that they do not experience either pleasure or orgasm. . . . And from the point of view of function, it may be said that orgasm for women is a luxury, whereas the satisfactory discharge of the male function of orgasm is indispensable for conception.	If a woman obtains her orgasm before the man obtains his, it is absolutely essential that she sees that he receives one. This is especially true if fertilization is desired . . . but, also, for the humanitarian reason of reducing the congestion of the penis.

*Adapted from Herschberger (1948), with permission of the author.

count off their pregnancies in months. Instead, many women calculate the length of their pregnancy in weeks, as do their physicians (Rothman, 1986:96–98).

Many physicians encourage women to include ultrasound visualization in their routine prenatal care. The real-time ultrasound recording allows women and their technicians to view a live image of the fetus, and numerous women report this is when the fetus becomes "real" to them (Hubbard, 1984:333; Rothman, 1986). Traditionally, women have experienced the fetal "quickening" or movement as evidence of life.

For some women, ultrasound visualization is followed by amniocentesis. The procedure, to determine whether fetal chromosomal abnormalities are present, is recommended for "older" women, although older women are getting younger all the time. Amniocentesis was first prescribed for pregnant women over age 40. In the United States, the procedure is now recommended for pregnant women age 35 and over, and many believe the age for routine amniocentesis will soon be lowered to 32 or 30 (Arditti, et al., 1984).

The fear of chromosomal abnormalities has been instilled in "older" women, so that many would not dream of having a child without the reassurance that most receive from a negative amniocentesis report (Rothman, 1986). Still, amniocentesis carries with it the possibilities of having to consider a second-trimester abortion. As a result, Rothman reports that many women must live with a "tentative pregnancy" (Rothman, 1986).

Many women do not commit themselves to the reality of their pregnancies until after they have received "good news" of the test results, at about 20 weeks of pregnancy. Some women do not announce their pregnancy to anyone or perhaps only to their partners. Many do not wear maternity clothes until after they receive the test results (Rothman, 1986:98–100). As Rothman states, "For women in tentative pregnancies, pregnancies that may be terminated, the stigma of (appearing) fat may be preferable to risking the stigma of late abortion" (1986:99). Still other women do not notice fetal movement until after negative amniocentesis results have been received.

For some women, the pregnancy is medically recognized and made socially real, but the fetus (a medical term) or baby (a lay term) is not. In order to manage their anxiety, these women cannot develop a relationship with the developing fetus. To defend their own psychological well-being, they may not feel the movement of a *baby* until the *fetus* has been declared chromosomally normal (Rothman, 1986:100–107). Obstetric textbooks say movement is felt at 16 to 18 weeks of pregnancy, a few weeks before the time women have amniocentesis performed and then begin the several week wait for results. Some women reported to Rothman not "feeling the baby" until as late as 22 to 23 weeks of gestation. Consider that by 20 weeks, movement is externally visible: The movement that these women do not feel can be observed (Rothman, 1986:107).

Just as women are learning to wait for medical authorization to acknowledge the existence of their "babies," a separation is being made by the medical establishment between the woman and the patient within her. Traditionally, women have been thought of as reproductive bodies, and obstetricians have made references to pregnant women as "maternal environments." Given technological advances, the fetus has become a patient in its own right, and the new specialty of "Fetal Medicine" has evolved to treat this "'fetus *in situ*' (*in situ* is Latin for 'in place' and a relatively common expression in scientific writing)" (Hubbard, 1984:350). So the woman becomes the fetus *in situ*, and new social questions arise. Must a woman submit to "fetal therapy" or surgery against her will? Can a woman be legally responsible for birth defects due to damage that she may have caused the fetus through cigarette smoking or drinking alcohol?

Still other technological advances may lead us even further from our traditional notions about reproduction. Efforts are underway to improve artificial insemination, which, as performed today, is most likely to produce a male child; research continues on the possibilities of clonal reproduction and artificial wombs. All this leaves many wondering whether the time will come when pregnancy as we know it will be considered medically unsound and perhaps even socially irresponsible. Interestingly enough, as our cultural attitudes toward reproduction are changing, our assumptions concerning "normal" sexuality—to which we next turn—have not lost their ubiquitous nature.

SEXUALITY

Persons are socialized sexually in the context of the culture in which they live. Sexologists and biologists themselves are subject to a culture's norms and values. Consequently, before addressing their work, we shall briefly review the process of sexual socialization in this culture.

The process may begin as early as the crib, when anxious parents prevent their infants from exploring their own genitals. Later, many children are specifically told that their genitals must be always covered and never touched—for all practical purposes, viewed as nonexistent. Soon many children learn to associate the words *dirty* and *bad* with their own genitals. Some would contend that this early sex socialization "creates in the child, and subsequently in the adult, an elemental negative attitude toward sexuality" (Johnson, 1968:63).

In regard to such practices as masturbation, it is as though our socialization procedures were masterminded by some evil experimental psychologist. Johnson suggests that if socialization were an experiment, the conditions of it would sound something like this:

> Arrange a most severe punishment for a certain behavior. But then, make the same behavior so rewarding that the experimental animal cannot quite resist it. Then, observe the avoidance, frustration, desperate action, and subsequent anguish of the animal as the punishment built into the experiment is administered (1968:69).

Although children are sexual creatures (capable of deriving pleasure from their genitals), they are socialized to have negative feelings toward their own sexuality. Further, the cultural context in which this socialization occurs is one of intense preoccupation with sexuality—in the media, in advertising, and in adult conversations and humor. Children, therefore, are reared in the "context of a *sex-*

centric society, which is at the same time profoundly anti-sexual'' (Johnson, 1968:64). Such conditions are bound to create sexual problems.

Further, according to the *traditional* sexual code of our society, there are four stages of sexual development. Before puberty, children are assumed to be *nonsexual*. During adolescence, the young are viewed as simply *asexual*—that is, capable of sexual experiences but with that potential remaining dormant until marriage, when they become *sexual*. (Note the heterosexual assumption of the scheme.) In the later years of life, it is assumed that persons return to their original *nonsexual* stage.

This model of sexual development, of course, veers considerably from the actual behavior of people. Prepuberty children experience sexual arousal and often orgasm (although not ejaculation); adolescents frequently act on their sexual potential; and older persons can and often do remain sexually active. Not only are guilt and anxiety consequences of this sexual code, but institutions are designed to enforce it, despite the actual needs of people. Examples are the routine prohibition against sexual liaisons in homes for the aged and sex education courses that stress the reproductive aspects of sexuality.

Although almost all manner of human biology has been subject to scientific study for generations, only recently has the human sexual response been taken into the laboratory. These studies—most notably, those of Masters and Johnson (1966)—have contravened many myths about sexuality that we hold as a culture. Let us review some of the research findings that contradict the culture's teachings.

The society teaches that the male is more sexual than the female. Masters and Johnson find, however, that the female, if anything, is more sexual than the male in that her ability to experience multiple, intensive orgasms within a given time span is greater than the male's. Physiological measurements of the female indicate that each of her orgasms can be as intense as the male's.

The culture has also misperceived the nature of orgasm. Members of society are taught that male and female orgasms are different and that females have two kinds of orgasm—vaginal and clitoral. However, "Orgasm is orgasm" (Johnson, 1968:53). It consists of four stages—excitation, plateau, orgasm, and resolution. The orgasmic process is "not anatomically localized, but rather involves the whole body. . . . The physiological events are the same" whether orgasms are produced by fantasy, masturbation, vibrator, or coitus (Johnson, 1968:50).[2]

Further, as has already been implied, the society teaches that masturbation is dangerous. Many children—probably boys especially—have been told that masturbation leads to pimples or loss of sight, hearing, hands, genitals, and sanity. Not only are these outcomes false, but Masters and Johnson suggest that masturbation is actually useful in helping people to overcome genital fears and in learning what sexually gratifies them.

There are several common folk beliefs about males' sexuality specifically. One is that penis size is related to sexual capacity; another is that impotence is a sign that a man is not masculine. As for the first, there is no relationship between organ size, capability, or satisfaction to the mate (Johnson, 1968:52). As for the latter,

---

[2]This is not to deny the importance of emotional relations; but in this chapter, the concern is not with loving but with the physiology of sex.

impotence is usually the result of excessive fatigue, heavy drinking, and/or over-anxiousness about sexual performance—all of which are characteristically associated with masculine activities.

Finally, there are two particularly disturbing misconceptions about intercourse—namely, that the man should be astride the supine woman and that simultaneous orgasm is the goal to achieve. As for the first, the female astride the male is more likely to lead to maximal female enjoyment; and as to the second, striving for synchronization may actually reduce a couple's pleasure because of the psychological pressure to achieve a particular goal, and because of the restrictive presumption that the female will enjoy only one orgasm per intercourse.

Just what the consequences of the dissemination of these facts have been for sexual relationships is not totally clear. Some women argue that greater knowledge of their own sexuality frees them from dependence upon men for gratification. They see themselves in control of their own sexual needs. In addition, some men report that women's greater knowledge and interest in receiving sexual gratification have threatened their own masculinity. What is the social cost to the patriarchal system of recognizing the legitimacy of homosexuality among men and women? Can men satisfy the "new woman" who is capable of multiple orgasms? Should they try?

Some authors argue that the myth of the sexually passive woman (Koedt, 1976) will persist, despite the facts, because it is in the interest of men to keep women sexually dependent upon them. In other words, the quality of sexual life in general in our culture is a direct representation of the socially defined inequalities between the sexes. Given that our knowledge of sexual response has increased rapidly during the past decade, the question is to what extent have the professionals disseminated this knowledge, and to what extent have they retained the mythology of the culture.

CHILDBIRTH AND LACTATION

Medical research on pregnancy and childbirth argues that the acceptance of "femininity" is associated with uncomplicated maternity. So strong is the ideology that associates "femininity" with "biological mothering," that the researchers not only stretch the meaning of "femininity," they also ignore their actual results (Seneca, 1980).

In medical research, lack of "femininity" may be judged to exist if a woman dislikes any of the following: "menstruation, pregnancy, childbirth, breastfeeding, (hetero) sexual intercourse; their status as wives, husband-servicing work, their husbands; their status as housewives, housework; their status as mothers, childcare work; their children" (Oakley, 1979:619). Moreover, medical research does not bear out the conclusion that rejection of femininity is associated with difficult pregnancies and childbirth. Indeed, the opposite appears to be true: Women who are passive, dependent, emotional, and excitable—all stereotypes associated with femininity—are precisely those who are likely to experience difficulties, probably because childbearing requires strength, independence, and assertiveness (Seneca, 1980).

Not only is the medical research mispresented and misinterpreted, but also the meaning of childbirth and lactation to women as *sexual* experiences is downplayed or denied. The full range of a woman's sexual experience has been discussed very little. The work of Newton (1973) has demonstrated (as many women will attest) that women are "trebly sensuous." Their sexuality includes three major functions: coitus, parturition (labor and birth), and lactation (nursing).

Because nursing is a voluntary act upon which the survival of the species has depended, it is logical for nature to have designed it to be pleasurable. Nursing mothers repeatedly report the sensual pleasure experienced during breastfeeding (Richardson [Walum], 1972); and that pleasure is not just imagined, for certain physiological changes occur during nursing that are comparable to those that occur during orgasm—contraction of the uterus, the erection of the nipples, the stimulation of the breasts, vascular and skin changes, and a raised body temperature. In addition, nursing mothers report a greater interest in sex than nonnursing mothers (Newton, 1973).

Because childbirth has been advertised in our culture as a process that requires expert medical help, it can be shocking for some to discover that it is sexual. And, yet, Newton has demonstrated, by analyzing comments made by *undrugged* mothers and by studying the physiological changes that occur during parturition, that childbirth can be an orgasmic experience. Some women report the experience as the "most incredible orgasm ever."

This is not to argue that medical complications never occur in childbirth, nor is it to suggest that obstetricians have no role to play. Obviously, the course of gestation and delivery is not perfectly predictable. Therefore, it is both fallacious and potentially dangerous (to the physical and psychological health of the mother) to establish natural childbirth as the goal to which all pregnant women must aspire. Rather, what is being argued here is that taken-for-granted assumptions about childbirth limit the kinds of experiences women might have during the birth process.

Coitus, parturition, and breastfeeding all are sexual experiences that are based on neuro-hormonal reflexes; as such, they are affected by the environments in which they take place. If intercourse were on a schedule, limited to so many minutes, and occurred in a semipublic place with the participants partially clothed, it is unlikely that many people in our culture would find it sexually satisfying. Yet, what I've just described is the culturally prescribed way for engaging in nursing. Similarly, if intercourse were to take place in a brightly lit room with both parties drugged, their feet in stirrups, their hands strapped to a table, supervised by a sterile helper who manually or with forceps joins the members, few people would consider the experience as a "joy of ecstasy"; and yet, this is our culturally preferred way of childbirth.

Consequently, even in the most basic of biological functions, the knowledge that is transmitted not only perpetuates dependence, helplessness, and frailty but, incredibly, also robs the woman of experiencing the fullness of her sexuality. By the writ of authority, sexuality is reserved for her experiences with males; her other experiences as a sexual creature are not acknowledged.

MEDICAL PRACTICE

The writings of the biologist and sexologist, in turn, become the content in the textbooks for the applied biologist, the medical doctor, and, in particular, the gynecologist. Notably, there is no medical specialty for male sexual problems; these are handled under the rubric of urology.

With a title and degree, the gynecologist becomes enshrined as the officially legitimate specialist on women, their needs, personalities, and illnesses. Apart from learning what the culture teaches about women, the obstetrician-gynecologist learns from the official guidebook—the gynecology textbook. Scully and Bart report a content analysis of 27 such texts (which incidentally have changed little over the past 125 years, despite the work of Masters and Johnson). According to their analysis, "these texts continually define female sexuality as inferior to male sexuality, insist that 'aggressive' behavior in women is abnormal, and maintain that it is inherent in the female essence to submit to the male" (1972:10–11).

The medical practice biases are seen quite fully when menopause is considered. Menopause is still described as an endocrinological disorder, a "living decay" (Seaman and Seaman, 1977), creating a large market of aging women for medical services. In areas of the country where there is an oversupply of gynecologists, hysterectomy rates are the highest (Gifford-Jones, 1977). Annually, there are over 300,000 such operations performed for questionable reasons. In fact, hysterectomy is *the* most commonly performed major surgery in the United States; 50 percent of all women will have had this surgery by age 65 if the present rates continue (Scully, 1980:141).

Traditionally, the medical profession has enjoyed a *legitimated* monopoly over the health of the population. Medical doctors have controlled entrance into their profession, resisted any external regulation, and reserved the right to define and label diseases, the right to decide which clients and which problems are legitimate, and the right to determine which medical problems deserve research priority. In short, doctors have enjoyed a monopoly over knowledge, diagnosis, service, treatment, prescriptions, and research in health. And this monopoly has been used to perpetuate cultural stereotypes. Not only are women defined as "constipated bipeds with backaches" and doctoring women considered "dirty work" (Bart, 1974), but common phenomena such as menstrual cramps, morning sickness, and lactation difficulties are not considered important enough to deserve research priorities.

ALTERNATIVE VIEWS AND PRACTICES

However, alternative models and practices have been developed and disseminated. Primary among these are theories that concern female sexuality and its implications, along with the institutionalization of paramedical social movements that challenge the traditional monopoly of medicine.

Perhaps one of the most inventive of the theories of female sexuality is that advanced by Sherfey (1966). She asks, "What does it mean in terms of the evolution of humankind and the structure of societies that women are capable of inordinate cyclic sexual capacity . . . leading to the paradoxical state of sexual insatiation in the presence of the utmost sexual satiation'' (1966:229). She hypothesizes that while the aggressive sexual behavior of early primates might have been an important factor in overcoming adaptive barriers that led to the evolution of humankind, it perhaps stood as a major impediment to the rise of civilization, because ''women's uncurtailed continuous hypersexuality would drastically interfere with maternal responsibilities and with the rise of settled agriculture economies'' (1966:229). Consequently, social structures were invented to curtail the female's natural sexual insatiability. She argues that two of the primary structures today—monogamy and deferred sexual activity—although directly contrary to the female's biology, are functional for the survival of the family and hence of the society.

In effect, Sherfey is proposing that civilization is built upon the tethering of the female's sexual nature. To unleash this female sexuality, she suggests, will have consequences well beyond the bedroom, ''the magnitude'' of which ''is difficult to contemplate'' (1966:222).

Less abstract and radical in consequence is the resocialization language that is suggested by Shulman, who argues that although we have been taught that sex organs are used to create babies, ''This is a lie. In our society, only occasionally are those organs used to make babies . . .'' (1972:292).

Further, borrowing from her perceptive analysis, what a difference it would make in the expectations and attitudes of men and women if boys and girls were told something like the following about their sex organs:

> A boy has a penis; a girl has a clitoris. It feels good when the penis is touched, and it feels good when the clitoris is touched. The boy uses his penis for feeling good and making love, for reproduction and for urinating. The girl uses her clitoris for feeling good and making love, her vagina for reproduction, and her urethra for urination (1972:292).

Out of a concern with language and social power, Dale Spender (1985) suggests that the language that names sexuality shapes the reality of how sexual behavior is constructed, and that reality reflects a male perspective. Therefore, male sexual power becomes *virility* and *potency*, but there is no equivalent term for normal female sexual power. The sexual double standard names women who engage in extensive sexual activity *nymphomaniacs*, *ballers*, and *bitches* (Spender, 1985:175).

Male-defined values also surface in names such as *foreplay* in sexual activity. The activities of foreplay include stimulation of the clitoris, and although this can be foreplay for men, it can be experienced as an end—as a means of achieving orgasm—for women. ''Because males have decreed penetration necessary for their own sexual fulfillment, they have been obliged to name other sexual activities as less important—from their own point of view'' (Spender, 1985:178). Similarly, feminists have noted that *penetration* is a male-defined act. From a woman's perspective, the same act can be construed as enclosure, enfoldment, or envelopment. Clearly, language constructs the ''reality'' of the activity.

In a more general context, men's and women's attitudes toward their sexual relationships are culturally learned, and their sexual responses are culturally conditioned. As Ford's and Beach's cross-cultural study of sexual behavior shows, there is a wide variety of sexual activities and symbols (1951). Because sexual response is culturally transmitted, it is capable of being more harmoniously tuned to physiology. In order to effect a change in more than a few persons, however, it is necessary to alter radically the present cultural value structure.

In addition to alternative theories concerning sexuality, such social movements as La Leche League, natural childbirth, and self-help centers have offered alternatives to the traditional practice of medicine. Although these social movements differ ideologically on many points, they share in common the perspective that women have a right to experience their bodies and that these experiences constitute bona fide knowledge that can and should be discussed with others. Through these movements, women have shared "secrets" about their bodies, appropriated the medical knowledge concerning their reproductive biology, and distributed that knowledge along with their own personal experiences to other lay people through books, pamphlets, courses, group meetings, and demonstrations, and thus have challenged the monopoly of the "M.D.-iety" (Thorne, 1974).

For example, La Leche League is an international organization that was founded in 1958 to improve mothering through breastfeeding; it has enrolled over one million women. Although ideologically traditional in most respects, the league has consistently challenged the authority of the doctor in the area of lactation, nutrition, and infant-mother relationships (Marshall and Knafl, 1973; Richardson [Walum], 1972). Because breastfeeding is not common, the folk knowledge that was once routinely passed from mother to daughter has been lost. As the new knowledge-giver, medical doctors know little or nothing about the practical aspects of breastfeeding or its psychological and biological benefits to mother and infant; they too readily assume that any difficulty with the infant can be traced to the mother's milk, and they order a bottled substitute (Richardson [Walum], 1973. La Leche offers nursing mothers an alternative.[3]

More recently, there has been a growth in the self-help movement, a movement that has "seized the technology without the ideology" of medicine and placed it in the hands of laypeople (Bart, 1974). Reitz (1977) suggests, for example, that the only way to dispel myths about menopause that are perpetuated through medical practice is for women to talk to each other, to share their experiences. In the studies of women who report on their own menopausal experiences, only one physical symptom—hot flashes—is commonly experienced; about two-thirds of the women report having them a *couple* of times over the course of a few years (Reitz, 1977)— that is, the actual experience of menopause for many women lacks the negativity and terror that medical practitioners predict for their patients.

More revolutionary, perhaps, is the fact that medical centers have opened where women can learn to diagnose themselves, as well as use the feminist doctors and paramedicals on the center's staff.[4] The oldest of these centers is The Feminist

---

[3]For those interested, write La Leche League International, 9616 Minneapolis Ave., Franklin Park, Illinois 60131.

[4]The *Monthly Extract: An Irregular Periodical* (New Moon Publications, Box 3488, Ridgeway Station, Stamford, Connecticut 06903) is the primary communications medium for the self-help clinics.

Women's Health Center of Los Angeles, accused and acquitted of "practicing medicine without a license."

Although these self-help centers have been primarily developed for and by women, the model could be adopted for males as an alternative or adjunct to traditional medical practice. Although it is falsely argued that men do not need special treatment because nothing is hidden in the recesses of their bodies, consider for a moment the prostate: Where is it? How do you know if something is wrong?

Further, even traditional medicine is coming to realize that the more the patient knows about the cause, course, and symptoms of the disease, as well as about the side effects of the medicine, the more quickly the patient recovers and the less severe the side effects. Thus, by encouraging the patient to become a knowledgeable *advocate*, the practical outcomes for patient and practitioner improve.

In summary, the satisfactory sexual lives of men and women depend upon the knowledge of anatomy and physiology. Further, the application of the culture's ideology by medical personnel limits their ability to help their patients, as well as their patients' ability to help themselves. Perhaps through the new self-help movements, a greater understanding of "our bodies, ourselves" will help us all reach—and enjoy—our potentials.

CLINICAL PSYCHOLOGY AND PSYCHIATRY

From the 1950s onward, the moral and religious categories of good and evil have been increasingly replaced by the psychological categories of mentally healthy and mentally ill. Modern soothsayers are psychiatrists and clinical psychologists—missionaries of Scientific Doctrine from the Temples of Medicine and Academia. Yet with too few exceptions, the psychological theories that are espoused as scientific have not been tested in carefully designed experiments (Weisstein, 1971), nor are they formulated in a way that permits them to be nullified (Tennov, 1976); that is, despite their tone of scientific respectability, most psychological theories are not, in actuality, within the scientific tradition. Nevertheless, despite the lack of reliable scientific evidence, the putative theories of clinical psychology in television, newspapers, magazines, child guidance pamphlets, and classrooms have been presented as truth. Psychoanalytic theories reinforce rigid rules for gender behavior. Let's hear from some major theorists:

Sigmund Freud

Women refuse to accept the fact of being castrated and have the hope of someday obtaining a penis in spite of everything . . . I cannot escape the notion . . . that for women the level of what is ethically normal is different from that of men.

The work of civilization has become more and more men's business . . . What he [the male] employs for cultural purposes he withdraws to a great extent from women and his sexual life; his constant association with men and dependency on his relations with them even estrange him from his duties as husband and father (1930:73).

Esther Harding

[Women's real goal is the] creation of the possibility of psychic and psychologi-cal relation to man . . . It is a significant turning point in [the successful wom-en's] relation to man, when she finds that she can no longer look him frankly in the eyes, for it means that her real feeling which may not be shown openly has begun to stir. . . . (1933, quoted in Chesler, 1972:78).

Erik Erikson

[T]he identity formation of women differ[s] by dint of the fact their somatic design harbors an "inner space" destined to bear the offspring of chosen men and, with it, a biological, psychological, and ethical commitment to take care of human infancy. . . . (1968:266).

Carl Jung

[Female] psychology is founded on the principle of Eros, the great binder and deliverer; while age-old wisdom has ascribed Logos [rationality] to man as his ruling principle (1928, quoted in Chesler, 1972:77).

Joseph Rheingold

[W]oman is nurturance . . . anatomy decrees the life of a woman. . . . When women grow up without the dread of their biological functions and without subversion by feminist doctrines—and therefore enter into motherhood with a sense of fulfillment and altruistic sentiment—we shall attain the goal of a good life and a secure world in which to live (1964:714).

Bruno Bettleheim

Naturally, boys are more ready to fight . . . [but] nature, physiology, and biology go just so far. They have to be encouraged to go in the right direction (1972). . . . It's the mother who creates the predisposition for both boys and girls because naturally she is the one who takes care of the infant. But she should also have entirely different expectations about the future and personalities of the boys and girls (1972).

Notions about the natural differences between men and women—as they are presented by these therapists and subsequently propagated—have been com-monplace, repetitious, and tyrannical. Many of these clinical theories have been influenced by Freud's analyses of psychosexual development, which can be sum-marized simply: Genitalia are destiny. Essentially, women are "breeders and bearers," occasionally generous of the spirit, but more likely "cranky children with uteruses, forever mourning the loss of male organs and male identity" (Chesler, 1972:79). The "masculinity complexes" and neuroses of women are simply spite-ful refusals to accept their naturally passive, morally defective natures. Successful manhood, on the other hand, requires overcoming the Oedipus complex (sexual attachment to the mother) and castration anxieties by sublimating the superior power of the (sadistic) phallus into the creation of civilization (Freud, 1930). Indeed, the theory of psychosexual development seems to be an intellectual reincar-nation of what little boys supposedly believe about girls' "lost penises" and the consequent threat to their own (cf. Horney, 1967).

Critiques of Freudian biological-destiny theories are, at this point in history, almost as popular as the Freudian theories themselves (cf. Millet, 1970; Weisstein, 1971; Cooper, 1970; Szasz, 1970; Strouse, 1974), and the numbers and kinds of therapies have multiplied. Therefore, rather than looking at some particular kind of therapy, we might ask whether there is a sex bias in therapy.

Criticism of the therapeutic enterprise has included critiques of the various categories of mental illness that are listed in the *Diagnostic and Statistical Manual of Mental Disorder (DSM-III)*, the therapist's guide to classification of mental illness. Kaplan (1983a, 1983b), for example, sees the categories, themselves, as reflecting a masculine bias in regard to what behaviors and attitudes are mentally healthy and what ones are mentally ill. Behaviors judged ''crazy'' in a female, she argues, are considered normal in a male. No man, for example, who put his work above his family, did not show his feelings, or put his own interests above the interests of others would be labeled mentally ill. Yet, women are so judged.

Scholars from diverse disciplines for almost two decades (cf. Angrist, 1968; Broverman, et al., 1970; Chesler, 1972; Rickles, 1971; Rawlings and Carter, 1977; Taylor, 1987) have noted this double standard of mental health (also see Chapter 1). Child rearing and procreation are supposed to be central to women, and tangential to men. Women who are sexually promiscuous, unwed mothers, and, paradoxically, sexless or seductive are mentally disordered. Promiscuity and unwed fatherhood are not judged aberrant in males, but sexual passivity and impotence are; that is, the cultural stereotypes are reinterpreted and reinforced in the classification and diagnosis of mental illness.

Women who veer from gender expectations are likely to be labeled ''sick'' and men who veer are likely to be labeled ''criminal.'' If women, however, overly incorporate the female role or men act in female-stereotyped ways, then they are judged mentally ill. The female role, as we have seen, is not highly valued in this culture. If men act out that role by behaving in passive, dependent, timid, or sexually inactive ways, they are considered sick; if they are treated clinically, they are often judged schizophrenic. Paradoxically, women who overly incorporate the female role are judged as exhibiting character disorders—neuroses and psychoses. The major characteristically female symptoms are depression, frigidity, chronic fatigue, and suicide attempts.

Depression is anger turned inward[5]; the female role prohibits aggression toward others. It is safer and more feminine to be depressed than to be physically violent. Frigidity is the final feminine outcome of sexual repression. Chronic fatigue is a way of passively striking back—a technique employed by ''slaves'' (submissive women) against ''masters'' (domineering men) that allows them to ''put their burdens down'' and become even more helpless, frail, and dependent (Szasz, 1961). Female suicides are more frequently attempted than completed. Aggression—even in this most private and desperate act—is difficult for women to effectively express:

> Like female tears, female suicide attempts constitute an essential act of resignation and helplessness. . . . Suicide attempts are the grand rites of "feminin-

---

[5]The anger is usually considered a result of loss. For a perceptive analysis of depression in middle-aged women as a result of ''social role loss,'' see Bart (1975).

ity"—i.e., ideally women are supposed to "lose" in order to "win." Women who *succeed* at suicide are tragically, outwitting . . . their "feminine" role and at the only price possible, their death (Chesler, 1972:49).

For both men and women, then, acting out the devalued female role is to be mentally ill. Ironically, the devaluation of the female role has another kind of negative impact on men. Because men are considered more important, socially, male dysfunctioning is considered a greater loss to the society than is female dysfunctioning. One of the outcomes of this differential evaluation is a greater denial of male dysfunctioning (Chesler, 1972:38–39). Seeking help is not "masculine" (Clancy and Gove, 1974), and males are not encouraged to put themselves in the dependent child-parent relationship found in therapeutic practice (Tennov, 1976). Therefore, men do not usually seek help until late in the disability.

Further, because interpersonal dependency is considered nonmasculine, many difficulties that are experienced by men tend to become submerged in drugs and alcohol. Ironically, the ultimate consequence is severe disability: 75 percent of the hospitalized alcohol addicts and 64 percent of the hospitalized drug addicts are male. As an even more direct and insidious alternative to seeking help, males commit suicide; 70 percent of suicide victims are men. To the end of their "self-taken lives," they remain independent of others as they act out their socially prescribed masculine roles.

Seeking help is consistent with the feminine role; thus, women are more likely to report psychological symptoms and seek psychotherapy than men are (Gomberg and Franks, 1979). In fact, data from psychiatric hospitals and wards, out-patient clinics, and private therapists are all consistent: Women are more likely than men to be treated for mental illness (Gove, 1979). We need to ask, again, whether the treatment that men and women receive is sex biased. Is standard therapy dangerous to women's mental health, as many social scientists have cautioned (cf. Chesler, 1972; Tennov, 1976; Mowbray, et al., 1984)? To test this indictment of the therapeutic enterprise, considerable research has been directed to assessing whether or not therapists treat women differently than they treat men. Two kinds of research strategies have been used. First, researchers have done *analogue* studies. These studies ask the clinician to decide how to treat a fictitious client, whose case has been presented. The gender of the client is the independent variable. The second strategy is a *naturalistic* one in which actual therapy sessions are recorded and analyzed.

An analysis of thirty analogue studies showed that clinicians did not show significant sex bias in how they *said* they would treat their male and female clients, and that sex bias had lessened over time (Smith, 1980). Yet, naturalistic studies consistently find severe sex bias in the treatment of patients, and find that bias has remained fairly constant over time (Sherman, 1980). How are the conflicting sets of data explained? The most likely explanation is that the analogue studies are methodologically at fault: Telling someone how you would behave is not as good a measure of behavior as the actual behavior is. In the case of sex bias in therapy, moreover, therapists over the decade have been aware of the problem; therefore, they are likely to respond in the analogue situation as they know they are expected to respond, namely, without sex bias. It is not what people say they do, it is what they actually do that matters most, and what therapists do—especially older ones, Freudian-oriented ones, and male ones—is to treat females in sex-stereotyped and disempowering ways (Sherman, 1980; Hare-Mustin, 1978).

ALTERNATIVE THERAPIES: THE CASE OF EATING DISORDERS

Because of the problems with traditional therapists and therapy, new forms of therapy have entered the practice of psychotherapy.

These new treatments assume that clients should set their own goals; personal equality between the sexes should be promoted; therapists should be aware of their own values; gender role reversals are not pathological; marriage is not necessarily desirable; anatomical difference theories are indefensible (Rawlings and Carter, 1977:51–52); and gay or lesbian sexual orientations are not pathological.

These new therapies can be divided into two categories: nonsexist and feminist (Fishel, 1979). Although both therapies promote *personal* freedom from gender stereotyping and gender equality, "feminist therapy incorporates the political values and philosophy of feminism from the women's movement in its therapeutic values and strategies while non-sexist therapy does not" (Rawlings and Carter, 1977:50). Thus, feminist therapy is suggested for those who are dissatisfied with the restrictive cultural gender roles and are seeking alternatives. Clinical strategies include such diverse techniques as assertiveness training (Franks, 1979), feminist consciousness-raising groups (Mander and Rush, 1974), vocational and career counseling (Dewey, 1977; Weissman, et al., 1973), and social activism (Adams and Durham, 1977).

An illustration of how feminist therapy approaches clinical issues can be found in its approach to eating disorders. There are two eating disorders of nearly epidemic proportions in the United States today: anorexia nervosa and bulimia. *Anorexia* is characterized by severe self-induced weight loss, a lack of menstruation, and an acute fear of becoming fat. Anorexics starve themselves, but no matter how emaciated they become, they still see themselves as overweight. If left untreated, the person can die. Approximately one percent of females, age 12 to 25, are anorexic (Coleman, et al., 1984). Not all these women are upper-middle-class, white, college-bound women, as had been assumed. Rather, anorexia occurs in women of all social, racial, and economic categories—a fact we will return to shortly.

Bulimia or the "binge-purge" syndrome is characterized by secretive food binges that might last an hour or more. During the "binge," the bulimic might consume a dozen hamburgers, a dozen orders of fries, bags of potato chips, peanuts, candy bars, tacos, and more. The binge continues until it is interrupted by someone, stomach pain, sleep, or until "purging" takes place through induced vomiting or induced defecation. Unlike the anorexic, the bulimic is of normal or near normal weight and has a normal menstrual cycle; she is like the anorexic, though, in her intense fear of being fat. Although death is less likely for the bulimic, the loss of vitamins and minerals, and the destruction of the esophagus, gums, intestinal tract, and rectal muscles are major health threats; and if the bulimia continues, her life is seriously endangered. However, because bulimics look normal and because their behavior usually takes place secretly, it is difficult to get an estimate on their numbers. Estimates of female bulimics in college populations, though, range from five percent (Stangler and Printz, 1980) to 19 percent (Halmi, et al., 1981).

Psychoanalytically oriented therapies have made assumptions about the eating disorders, and these have affected their treatment. Let's look at anorexia. The *family* dynamics that lead to the problem have been analyzed. Anorexics, thus, have been viewed as girls who were afraid to grow up and embrace the female role. They were seen as girls who rejected their femininity or, alternatively, overincorporated the feminine standard of beauty. As discussed earlier, being "too feminine" or "not feminine enough" are the putative explanands of mental illness. Whichever, the girl got that way because of how her mother, primarily, and her father, secondarily, reared her, according to psychoanalytical practice. Treatment of the anorexic, along with the psychodynamic analysis, requires hospitalization during which the patient is force-fed if necessary, given medication, and in some cases, kept away from feminist influences, which are seen as counterproductive to the patient's well-being; the reasoning is that feminist ideology challenges femininity.

Feminist therapy regarding eating disorders, however, takes a different stance. It recognizes that anorexia and bulimia are life-threatening problems that may need medical intervention, but it adds some other dimensions to its treatment. First, it takes the fact that women are much more likely to have an eating disorder than men as a statement about women's lives, generally. Secondly, it considers how cultural norms about appearance affect *all* women: Feminist therapists stress how the social order creates eating disorders in women and they seek remedies that will empower women.

Norms of appearance have a major influence on the life goals and daily behaviors of girls. No woman or girl in this culture seems to be immune to the issue of weight. Nearly every woman has been on a diet at some point in her life; even prepuberty children diet. Women do not think they are thin enough, no matter what they weigh; for example, in 1986—well after the "fitness craze" hit the female population and when presumably some muscles on the bones would be acceptable—Vann (1986) found that approximately 74 percent of women of normal weight thought that they were overweight, and 29 percent of underweight women thought they, too, were overweight. American women are obsessed with their weight because attractiveness is equated with thinness.

Cultural proscriptions emphasize physical appearance as a means by which women can attain success (cf. Brownmiller, 1984). Attractiveness becomes a commodity that can be exchanged for affection, recognition, and especially, love from men. The fear of being fat may reflect a fear of failure to attain success, love, or approval. This fear is perpetuated by the media portrayal of relatively unattainable ideals, and suggests the importance of cultural proscriptions for appearance, self-perception, and mental health.

For women, eating disorders are, thus, a symptom of a larger social-psychological problem that afflicts nearly all women in this society. Anorexia and bulimia are the most extreme cases of this "negative body consciousness," life-threatening indicators of the conflicts and consequences generated by restrictive appearance norms (Shurr, 1983). The cultural imperative for thinness for women encourages attitudes and behaviors that promote eating disorders. Women share knowledge with each other about how to control their weight. Similarly, anorexics are known to exercise together and to share diet tips. Bulimia is sometimes passed down from mother to daughter, from older sister to younger, from friend to friend, as was Jane Fonda's youthful experience with purging.

Feminist therapists, thus, stress the need to alleviate the weight obsession among all women. Education and major cultural change is needed to stop the high incidence of eating disorders among women. Treatment of individual women with eating disorders, moreover, must empower them; it must help them to recognize their own self-worth, and to reject idealized societal norms of female thinness and beauty. One of the ways to raise the self-esteem of these women, feminist therapists argue, is to introduce them to feminism and feminist therapeutic methods, such as involving them in peer-counseling and peer support sessions, assertiveness training, and body-imaging workshops.

In summary, the biological, medical, and clinical sciences and practices are major instruments of social control. They have incorporated the presumptions of the society regarding gender into their teachings and practices; they have not been wholly objective. But, recently, critiques of the biological, medical, and clinical sciences have created alternative ideologies and practices that promise to create more equalitarianism between the genders. Just how unequal the sexes are in terms of power, wealth, and prestige will concern us next.

SECTION

□ 3 □

The Structure of Sex-Based Inequality

In the forthcoming chapters, the institutionalized structure of sex-based inequality—the unequal distribution of power, property, and prestige between males and females—will be examined. The form, ideology, and dynamics of our political and economic institutions lead to the unequal distribution of valued rewards. The impact of this on the intimate relationships between men and women will be analyzed.

In this section, we confront the full exigencies of the external, objective world—the sex-based stratification system. We can (and do) make choices regarding attitudes toward our subjective states. We can (and do) choose to do things that are not prescribed for our sex. Often, however, our choices are difficult to implement. A woman can choose to be a bricklayer, but this choice will not necessarily provide her with the job of bricklayer. A man can choose to be a preschool teacher, but that choice will not necessarily guarantee him the position. The perpetuation of sex-based inequality is not simply a "woman's issue." In short, we have reached a point in our analysis of sex and gender where we must realize that to whatever extent our interpersonal lives might be changed if we choose to act differently, our subjective states are no match for the power of institutions and the interests of those who are already powerful.

□ □ *9* □ □

Sex-Based Stratification

Social stratification is one of sociology's most central concepts. As might be expected, there are many different theories and perspectives to explain it. In what follows, I have attempted to construct a framework that explains the universality of social stratification in general, and sex stratification in particular. In this process, I have not been tied to a particular *school*, but have been influenced by many scholars and researchers. What is offered is a perspective for understanding the social and cultural *roots* of sex-based inequality, as well as for understanding how and why sex-based inequality is perpetuated in modern industrialized societies.

All known societies have stratification systems for the hierarchical arrangement of people. Members of a society are differentiated (categorized) on the basis of such ascribed characteristics as age, sex, race, and on the basis of such achieved characteristics as occupation, salary, and educational level. The higher a person's position in the stratification system, the greater the socially valued rewards that are received.

Depending upon one's placement in the stratification system by virtue of one's age, sex, family, wealth, occupation, education, and so on, a different probability exists concerning whether one will or will not receive the valued goods.

A particularly crucial factor is one's position in the division of labor. Division of labor occurs in all societies. It refers to the fact that no individual supplies all his or her own goods and services. Rather, labor is specialized, and the results of one person's activities are exchanged with those of others. The more valued one's position in the division of labor, the more likely one is to receive rewards; further, if one is highly placed due to family, wealth, and so on, then one is more likely to acquire such a position as an adult.

Social inequality, then, both *results from* and is *perpetuated through* the unequal opportunity to control the extradomestic distribution and exchange of valued goods and services. If one receives scarce goods, one is in a better position to control their further distribution. Therefore, the stratification system has a kind of built-in feedback process, such that those who are more highly situated are more likely to control the distribution of scarce goods, which in turn reinforces and heightens their dominance.

Although almost anything can constitute a valued good, it must be something that is *publicly exchanged* and *socially scarce*. Valued goods can be classified under three major headings: *power*, or the probability that one's will will be done; *property*, or material or monetary compensation; and *prestige*, or respect and honor. These three—power, property, and prestige—are closely and reciprocally linked. These will be discussed more fully in Chapter 10. They are conferred at the societal level rather than at the familial or individual levels. This is not to deny that a person may have domestic power and privileges by exchanging services and goods within the home. However, it is only when these are exchanged extradomestically that there is a public, social conferral of prestige and power. Stratification systems grow up around public exchanges, not domestic ones (Tumin, 1967).

In that power, prestige, and property are valued prizes in a society, it makes a great deal of difference to both the individual and the society *how* these are distributed (Tumin, 1967). Consequently, all societies have norms for governing the distribution system—rules whose most salient feature is that they reflect the interests of those who are already in positions of power, even if the cost to the entire society is great. Regardless of one's position in the stratification system, adherence to the rules is usually forthcoming. This testifies not only to the strength of the established norms but also to the power of the ruling group to enforce those norms.

Socially structured inequality is a fundamental feature of social life. Individuals are socialized to know their place, to accept the legitimacy of their role options and the rewards attached to their performance, and to recognize the rights and obligations that they have as members of a particular group. Social order is partially maintained, then, by individuals accepting the options society offers them. In the United States, for example, we learn that it is or is not an option to be a nurse or a doctor, and that it is legitimate, moral, and just, after all for a doctor to receive more power, prestige, and property than a nurse.

At the individual level, then, the induction into the stratification system begins at an early age and is inextricably woven into the socialization process. However, conformity and acceptance are ensured by the ability of those who are more powerful to constrain the less powerful. They are able to do this because they control the distribution of the scarce goods and services. Such control means that they have the right to make the rules regarding the distribution, and the right to enforce those decisions through negative sanctions and violence. Just as there is a strong and overarching tendency for systems to perpetuate themselves, however, they inevitably are also subject to change. This change may be due to alterations in the technological base, recognition by the subordinate groups that their place in the system is unjust, purposeful redistribution efforts by ascending power groups, or some interplay of these. In any case, to effect such change requires wresting control of the distribution of scarce goods and services.

BIOGENETIC AND BIOCULTURAL THEORIES: AN OVERVIEW

It is within the context of universal social stratification that sex-based inequality occurs. Most researchers and theorists, regardless of their ideological stance on issues of sex equality, agree that male dominance is a fundamental and universal feature of social life. Sociologist Janet Chafetz (1984) notes that sex stratification exists in degrees with one variable and one constant component. What varies is the extent of female disadvantage, while the constant is that females have never been more advantaged than males in any known society.

Over the past decade, researchers have struggled to understand why sex-based stratification is so ubiquitous. Basically, the explanations fall into one of two schools of thought: the biogenetic and the biocultural.

Recently, the *biogenetic* school—biological deterministic thinking—has gained a strong and ascending grasp on the consciousness of many (well-meaning) people, including some feminists (cf. Alpert, 1972; Rossi, 1984). Consequently, I will spend some time addressing biogenetic arguments and evidence, for I am firmly convinced that although biology is a necessary condition for social life, it is not a sufficient *explanation* for that life. Rather, I subscribe to the biocultural view: Social and cultural life is explainable by social and cultural factors—it cannot and should not be reduced to the biological level. Doing so not only distorts reality and limits knowledge, but, logically, also roots social change in biology—a notion that is not only radically conservative but on the face of it patently false.

Biogenetic explanations—explanations for the origin of the social in the biological—are based on the idea that social behavior is biologically caused and genetically based. Humans are the way they are because of their genetic inheritance. Consequently, biogeneticists argue that the *behaviors* of men and women are rooted in the sexual determination that is found in all species from ants to felines to deer to our fellow primates.

In its more traditional form, the biogenetic argument states that we cannot change what is biologically given, evolutionarily necessary. We must not even try, for to do so might create evolutionary armageddon for our species or, at best, would be a waste of time and energy. "We can't fool 'Mother Nature.'" The biogeneticists argue that sex inequality, then, and the natural superiority of the male are both inevitable and necessary for the survival of the species.

In its feminist version, however, the argument is different. Elizabeth Gould Davis, for example, proposes that "In nature, the female is the all important pillar that supports life, the male merely the ornament, the afterthought, the expendable sexual adjunct. . . . In Nature's plan the male is but a 'glorified gonad.' The female is the species" (1971:329). The female is naturally superior to the male and only by *returning* to that species imperative can we hope to prevent the inevitable cataclysmic destruction that male social superiority is creating, states Davis.

Whether the biogenetic proponent argues the natural superiority of the male or the natural superiority of the female, evidence to support the position is drawn from three distinct but overlapping areas of knowledge.

First, biogeneticists argue that males and females differ physically and hormonally. Males have higher levels of androgens, the "aggressivity" hormone, whereas females have a monthly hormonal cycle. On the average, males are taller and heavier. Their skeletal structure and musculature are adapted to tasks that require sudden bursts of energy and strength. On the other hand, the female's skeletal, anatomical, and hormonal systems are not adapted to those tasks but, rather, to her biological functions in childbearing and lactation. Because of these innate biogenetic differences between males and females, it is argued, a natural division of labor occurs.

In the traditionalist version, the biological suitability of the male for hunting and fighting, for providing and protecting, confers on him greater social power and prestige. He will always—and rightly so, goes the argument—be dominant over women. In a feminist version, the fundamental "female principle," the *capacity* to bear and nurture children, gives women superior psychological qualities (Alpert, 1972:92)—such as empathy, nurturance, courage, strength, intuition, and integrity (Davis, 1971:333–334).

Second, some sociobiologists argue that as a species of primates we have inherited a gene pool that includes certain social behaviors; for example, in the highly publicized tome, *Sociobiology: The New Synthesis* (1975), E. O. Wilson argues that aggressive dominance systems, are where males generally dominant over females, who care for the young, are universal evolutionary-based traits. From these basic traits, Wilson contends, naturally flow a hierarchical social structure; a sexual division of labor, economics, and trade; deception and hypocrisy; territoriality; a lust for war; and a hatred of strangers. Alice Rossi, a well-known feminist scholar, adds that social policy should, therefore, take into account women's biological suitability for child rearing (1984).

In a more extreme and less sophisticated version, some feminist biological determinists argue:

> the male is a biological accident, the Y (male) gene is an incomplete X (female) gene. . . . In other words, the male is an incomplete female, a walking abortion, aborted at the gene stage. To be male is to be deficient, emotionally limited; maleness is a deficiency disease and males are emotional cripples (Solanis, 1970:514–515).

The primary evolutionary principle, accordingly, is the female one and rests in the "maternal instinct." "Motherhood . . . is imprinted in the genes of every woman" (Alpert, 1972:92). Therefore, it is the female who is wholly allied with the primal force.

Third, there is the argument that as a human species we are tied to the early forms of social organization because they are part of our evolution. For the traditionalist, those early forms of social life are viewed as the arena in which the male's aggressive instincts wrought civilization. In the feminist version, a *matriarchy*—a society dominated by women—is postulated to have existed in which peace, sisterhood, community, and love reigned. Returning to the matriarchy, they argue, will restore love and peace.

Let us look, now, in more detail at each of these three primary sets of evidence—the physiological, primate research, and early human evolution—upon which biological deterministic thinking and the presumed inevitability of sexual stratification is based.

PHYSIOLOGY AND GENDER

Chromosomal, hormonal, and even anatomical sex can be overridden by social factors, as Chapter 1 has made clear. What is crucial in a child's gender identity formation is being labeled male or female. However, since the argument persists that physiological differences between males and females *cause* gender differences, we will look at some of those arguments.

Males do tend to be taller and heavier than females; however, if those size differences were really as important as their traditional proponents assert, then we would expect them to be even greater. The seven percent height advantage, on the average, that males enjoy over females seems rather minimal. And, if size differences were really important, we would not expect the size and height curves of male and female populations to overlap, as they do, such that some women tower over some men. In any case, since no one would seriously argue that the tallest, strongest, fastest, and heaviest man should naturally be the leader of other *men*— that the decathlon winner ought to be our president—then why is the equally absurd but parallel argument made that because the male is larger than a female, he is naturally *her* superior?

Further, although there is no doubt that men cannot bear or nurse children, it does not logically follow that bearing children creates biological inferiority, as some biological determinists insist; nor does it follow that the bearers are superior, as others contend. In fact, no conclusion regarding inferiority or superiority logically follows.

The fact that women bear children does not mean that they must (or should) rear them. Indeed, so much anthropological evidence has been amassed over the years that demonstrates the variability in cultural patterns of child rearing, that it seems rather archaic to argue that child rearing is a woman's duty/prerogative/birthright. What is expected of a "good mother" in the United States, for example, would be expected of a "good father" among the Marquesan (Leibowitz, 1978: 118); and neither Marquesan nor American would judge the society members, who routinely abandon their children (Turnbull, 1972), as "good" mothers or fathers.

Let us turn, however, to those mysterious hormones. Despite popular belief, both sexes have a hormonal cycle[1] and possess identical hormones. They differ quantitatively rather than qualitatively. Moreover, the quantitative differences have been misrepresented and exaggerated; the similarities have been minimized.

Sex hormones (estrogen, progesterone, androgen, and testosterone) are produced by the sex glands (ovaries in females, testicles in males) and by the adrenal cortex—a gland that is located above the kidneys in both males and females. Development as a male or female requires the activity of the sex glands *and* the

---

[1]The male testosterone secretion cycle averages 20 to 22 days; the female menstrual cycle averages 28 days.

adrenal cortex. Consequently, it is misleading to refer to androgen and testosterone as the "male sex hormones" and estrogen and progesterone as the "female sex hormones," for males and females have all these sex hormones, although in different proportions. Ironically, the symbolic epitome of virility—the stallion—excretes more estrogen than any other living creature—including the pregnant mare (Briscoe, 1978:39).

Progesterone is the hormone that is accused of making women pre-menstrually irrational, tense, and touchy, and, therefore, unsuitable for public office or executive power. Males, however, have progesterone in their bloodstreams in amounts similar to those in women in the preovulation stage of their menstrual cycles. Therefore, following the premise of the hormonal determinant theorists, one could argue that postmenopausal women—women who have their ovaries removed, and women on the birth control pill (which prevents ovarian release of progesterone)—are equal to men since they "share the same amounts of the chemical demon," progesterone (Briscoe, 1978:43).

Androgen is the hormone linked to aggressivity. The claim is made that the higher the androgen level, the greater the aggressivity. Males, as the name of the hormone implies, have higher levels of androgen; therefore, the argument contends, they are better suited for combat, leadership, and executive roles than women are. What is the evidence that supports the link between androgen and aggressivity?

Most of the androgen research has been on animals. It is always intellectually dangerous to generalize from animals to humans, since, to paraphrase Stuart Chase, the proper study of humankind is humankind. Nevertheless, let us look at that animal research. In a typical experiment, a male rat will be experimentally injected with androgen. Following the injections, the experimenter notes that fighting behavior increases. Inject a female rat with androgen and her fighting behavior increases, too. To clinch the argument, castrate newborn rats; record the decrease in their fighting behavior. The experiments appear convincing: androgen does seem to be causally linked to aggression. However, as the neurophysicist Bleir points out, "Would most nonspecialists know . . . that when *estrogen* is injected . . . fighting behaviors may be increased in males and females?" (1978:160). And do most nonspecialists know that in rats, as in humans, androgens are converted into estrogens within the cells, including the brain cells? Antiandrogen drugs will not block the effects, but antiestrogen drugs will. What now becomes of the so-called "androgen effect"? Is it not an "estrogen effect"?

High levels of androgens may be linked with aggressivity. However, it is quite plausible that social situations that require aggression stimulate the secretion of androgen, rather than the other way around. In a study of rhesus monkeys, for example, the researchers reported that the testosterone secretion was directly related to the kind of social situation in which the monkeys were placed. In those situations that demanded "deference" by the monkeys, their androgen secretion increased (Leibowitz, 1978:107).

Indeed, social factors may play a major role both in the production of hormones and in the *production of aggressivity*. Researchers have consistently noted, for example, that boys by age 2 act more aggressively than girls do. Since differences in hormone secretion between the sexes, however, does not occur until puberty, differing androgen levels cannot be used to explain the behavioral differences of such young children. Rather, social factors that encourage aggressive behavior in boys and that discourage it in girls are at work. Perhaps the most telling "antihormonal" argument, however, is that in general, human beings respond to the social situation in which they are placed. If a person who is experimentally injected with an "aggressivity" hormone is placed in a peaceful environment, she/he will be peaceful and sociable; that is, for humans, social environments can and do override hormonal stimulation.

Finally, despite the wishful thinking of biological determinists of either traditional or feminist learnings, there is no known causal relationship between sex hormone levels and other traits, such as intelligence, intuition, and creativity (Briscoe, 1978:44).

In summary, although males and females differ in the proportions of hormones they secrete, both secrete all the sex hormones. Although the effect of hormones on human behavior is still being researched, one of the consistent findings is that the social setting in which humans (and other animals) interact affects hormone secretion levels and the effects of those hormones on behavior.

PRIMATE RESEARCH

Some biogeneticists propound the idea that physical and behavioral differences between the sexes originated in our prehistory as primates. Although the reasoning appears circular, some have argued that the physical differences between the sexes are "outward manifestations of fundamental behavior differences between the sexes" (Leibowitz, 1978:25); that is, "form follows function."

One version of this argument holds that the physical size of the male leads to his natural superiority over women. He is naturally both the aggressor and the protector; it is a species imperative. However, if that were true, we would expect that in the 170 or so species of primates, *sexual dimorphism*—two distinct *forms* in the same species such that the males and females differ in both primary and secondary sexual characteristics—would be universal. Rather, among our primate relatives, there are species—such as the tiny golden marmoset—in which males and females are of equal size; species—such as the baboon—in which some females are larger than some males; as well as species—such as the gorilla—in which the male bulk dwarfs the female. In brief, universal size differences that favor the male do not exist among the primates.

Not only are physical size differences not universal, there is also no universal behavior by sex across the species. Consider the gibbon. Male and female are virtually visually indistinguishable (to humans, anyway). Behaviorally, both males and females equally care for and groom the young, equally engage in aggressive displays and defense, and equally maintain food supplies (Leibowitz, 1978:72–74). Or consider the orangutan. Although the physical size differences are great, the females take care of themselves and their young for years without the protection and support of the larger males. The males remain essentially loners; they range over a large area, but do not compete with each other for dominance over the females (Leibowitz, 1978:74–76).

In addition, there are the gorillas, who are closer to our own species, which may explain their bad press. They live in troops of adults, juveniles, and infants. The large silver-back male engages in defensive chest-thumping and posturing and generally directs troop movements; contrary to common belief, his greater size does not give him any sexual advantage over the smaller (black-back) males. Sometimes, troops are even led by old females (Blumberg, 1978:4). Moreover, despite the size of the gorilla, they are gentle creatures (Schaller, 1963). In 2000 hours of observation, the ethologist, Fossey, saw fewer than five minutes of aggressive behavior—and that was bluff (referred to in Blumberg, 1978:4). In the species closest to our own—the chimpanzees—the female is the sexual initiator; the dominance hierarchy is loose; and the dominant chimp is not necessarily the largest one—and not necessarily *a male* (Leibowitz, 1978:79–82).

Obviously, physical differences between the sexes among our primate relatives do not lead to universal behavioral differences between the sexes. Big male primates, for example, are not necessarily sexually favored, leaders, combatants, defenders, or breadwinners. If we want to extrapolate to the social roles of humans from primate evidence, then we would have to argue that the primate "destiny" is one of social diversity.

Recently, based on the emerging sociobiological literature, a more sophisticated argument about our link to the primates has been proffered. The sociobiologists argue that behavior that is adaptive and that has a genetic component is selected in evolution in order to maximize the probability of passing the adaptive trait on to offspring. Looked for are traits (behaviors) that exist in both nonhuman and human populations, for then, they argue, a case can be made that natural selection has operated in the evolution of the trait (behavior).

However, with the exception of reproduction and lactation, as we have seen, there are no universal sexual dimorphisms among the species of primates. Even more relevant, though, is that sex differences not only vary between the species but *within* a species (Lowe, 1978:122). Hamadras baboons, for example, show little male dominance in forest settings, but considerable display of such in open plains (Lowe, 1978:122). Rhesus monkeys who dwell in temples have an entirely different social organization—size of troop, relationships between the members, responses to outsiders—from rhesus monkeys who reside in forests; that is the *environment* in which the primates find themselves affects their social organization and social behaviors (Leibowitz, 1978:70). Members of the same species adapt and modify their behavior significantly to suit their environment.

Since biological differences in reproduction and lactation are universal, however, let us examine the research on the parenting behaviors of primates. Do female primates have a "maternal instinct"?

Laboratory studies with rhesus monkeys that were begun about 15 years ago by Harlow and his associates have raised serious doubts about such an instinct. These researchers found that monkeys that were raised in isolation with wire surrogate mothers were social misfits, unwilling to mate, and that the females, when grown to motherhood, mistreated and rejected their infants; that is, if an instinct to mate and mother existed, social factors extinguished it. Moreover, Mitchel and his associates (discussed in Leibowitz, 1978:109–114) found that when infants were placed with male rhesus monkeys, the males "mothered" the infants; that is, "maternal" behavior can be learned.[2] Laboratory studies with primates, therefore, are showing that even in species that are sexually dimorphic, there is considerable malleability in parenting behavior.

In natural settings, however, we see how diverse parenting behavior is within and between primate species. In many more primate species than commonly recognized, the males care for the young. In some species, the male spends more time than the female caring for the young—carrying them around and grooming them—and returns them to their (presumed) mother only for nursing (Leibowitz, 1978: 114–116).

In summary, primatologists (cf. Goodall, 1968; Lancaster, 1975; Schaller, 1963) and anthropologists (cf. Leavitt, 1975; Leibowitz, 1978; Tanner and Zihlman, 1976) have clearly shown through observation and experimentation that there is "no single pattern of aggressivity, dominance, troop defense, sexual dimorphism, territoriality, competition or any other social behavior that exists across or even within primates species" (Bleier, 1978:162). If any argument is to be made based on the evolution of our species, it must be that our adaptation and survival have depended upon our ability to *modify* our behavior to suit our environment; that is, as a species, we share with the primates the potential for behavioral malleability.

HUMAN SOCIAL EVOLUTION

Some evolutionary deterministic thinkers argue that sexual inequality is a natural outgrowth of our unique *human* evolutionary experience. They argue that the social arrangements of early societies were necessary for human survival and that these have been genetically passed on.

One of the theorists from this school, Lionel Tiger (1969) argues that during the hunting-gathering period of human history, males who bonded together for hunting and defense had a survival advantage over those who did not. Species survival, according to Tiger, did not require female bonding or female leadership potential but, rather, females who could be emotionally adaptable to the needs of children. Male bonding—"the particular relationship between two or more males such that they react differently to members of their bonding unit as compared to individuals outside it"—Tiger argues (1969:27), creates strong emotional ties and satisfaction that cannot be met by women or by men outside the bond. Consequently, men carefully choose work partners and build barriers to exclude women from male preserves. The sex division of labor is a natural outgrowth of male bonding since "it is unnatural for women to engage in defense (and) politics . . ."

[2]The males interacted differently with the infants than the mothers did; for example, they roughhoused more, threatened the threatener (rather than removing the infant as mothers did), and remained attached to the juvenile for a longer period of time than did the mother. The researchers concluded that the male rhesus monkeys could learn parenting behaviors, but that "fathering" was different than "mothering." However, Leibowitz (1978:113) points out that their conclusion may be erroneous. Because the researchers matched *nonnursing* males with *nursing* females, feeding the young, for example, may replace the roughhousing activity or may inhibit it; and being the food source may encourage a mother to want her growing youngster to be independent of her.

(Tiger, 1969:112); and since such engagement is detrimental to the survival of the species, men must periodically expel women who have entered male terrains.

Related to Tiger's theory are several others (cf. Ardrey, 1966; Morris, 1967; Tiger and Fox, 1971) that view early human social organization as adapting to the innate aggression in the human male. These theories endow the human male with instincts for aggression, dominance, competition, and territory (man is a hunter, "a killer") and argue that these traits are necessary for the survival of the human species. Females are not so endowed; they are "the passive carriers of genes selected through the male action" (Lowe, 1978:123). As Kephart so aptly comments:

> Since only males hunt, and the psychology of the species was set by hunting, we are forced to conclude that females are scarcely human, that is, do not have built in the basic psychology of the species; to kill and hunt and ultimately to kill others of the same species (1970:5, cited in Slocum, 1975:38).

In one broad sweep, the theory excludes females from evolutionary destiny, accents one aspect of human behavior (aggression) to the exclusion of all other human traits, and derives culture from the male's desire to hunt and kill (Slocum, 1975:38).

Evidence of prehistoric and contemporary hunting-gathering societies, however, challenges these "Man, the Hunter" theories of social evolution. In reality, these societies should be called "gathering-hunting" to reflect the fact that gathering preceded hunting chronologically and exceeded it in dietary importance (Blumberg, 1978:6). Between 60 and 80 percent of the food in these societies was supplied through gathering; food was universally *collectively shared* (Blumberg, 1978:7). Both males and females gathered food, but since in more advanced societies (those with projectile weapons), men did the hunting (Leibowitz, 1978:18), the primary food supplier was "Woman, the Gatherer" (Slocum, 1975). Thus, women did not have to trade sexual favors for food supplies, as is sometimes posited. Finally, these societies were quite leisurely, with a work week averaging perhaps 12 to 19 hours (Blumberg, 1978:9). In one day's work, an individual could provide for five others—including, of course, the old and the young, who were provided for despite their economic dependence.

Hunting-gathering societies, then, are primarily gathering societies, which are socially organized to share the fruits of individual and collective labor, and which are characteristically leisurely. Within those basic parameters, then, what is the evidence for male bonding, male territoriality, male aggression, and male domination?

Based on data on contemporary hunting-gathering societies, male bonding is not different from female bonding; rather, the evidence suggests that all members are *loosely* bound to the *group*. Territory in hunting-gathering societies is only very loosely defined, and the group's resources "are almost never denied to visiting groups. In fact, evidence indicates that sharing of territory seems to *increase* with scarcity—whether we are examining Eskimo, Bushman or Australian Aborigines" (Blumberg, 1978:9–10). Support for a territorial imperative appears virtually absent.

As to aggression, the three primary contemporary examples of hunting-gathering societies (!Kung (bushmen), Mbuti (pygmies), and Tasaday) are all societies characterized by peace, gentleness, and cooperativeness (Blumberg, 1978: 10). In the Mbuti society, for example, if a disagreement should arise, the disputants simply part ways; perhaps one will simply join another group. Violence is not resorted to (Turnbull, 1961); or, as among the !Kung, where any form of aggressive posturing or behavior is negatively sanctioned, physical punishment of the young and physical aggression between adults do not occur (Draper, 1975:91).

Finally, as to male dominance, leadership, and privilege, contemporary hunting-gathering societies appear to be extremely egalitarian. Prestige is based on personal accomplishment and, in the simplest groups, is not associated with special privilege. Male dominance, however, does seem to exist, although the extent and depth of it vary considerably. We shall, therefore, return to this question of male dominance shortly.

In summary, then, hunting-gathering peoples are characterizable as primarily gatherers, rather than hunters; as relatively peaceful and equalitarian; as only loosely territorial; and as socially organized around *sharing*, rather than killing. Therefore, if early human social organizational forms are carried in the genes, and if those forms are necessary for human survival as has been argued by the traditional biogeneticists, then what is necessary if we are to survive is a return to our "species imperative"—the imperative of sharing. If *we* must remain true to our "instincts," then males must be made to embrace their hereditary destiny as gentle and peaceable creatures.

If this is so, does that mean that the feminists who postulate an ancient matriarchy are correct? Is our social evolution rooted in a matriarchal social organization—a social life in which . . . "every virtue, every nobler aspect of existence . . . the principle of love, of union, of peace . . . of universal freedom and equality" (Bachofen, 1976:79–81) reigned because women were in charge and the "female principle" dominated?

After reviewing the relevant arguments and literature, Friedl, a well-known anthropologist (and feminist), concludes that there is no archaeological or anthropological evidence to support the contention that a matriarchy once existed (1975:4). Further, when we turn to contemporary hunting-gathering societies, what we find, as has already been discussed, is a diversity of social organizational patterns, often with greater male dominance. Moreover, despite the male dominance, these societies are generally peaceable, friendly, and egalitarian; that is, although hunting-gathering societies do not meet the model that is proposed by traditional determinists, they do not fit the model of the matriarchists either. We can only conclude, then, that the idea of the matriarchy is a utopian vision—an archetypal metaphor.

The persistence of biogenetic arguments continues despite an enormous amount of contradictory evidence. The research that has been done along these lines has been criticized by feminists because of its implications and due to the flaws in its assumptions and methods that have resulted from its male bias. Others have contested such research simply on the grounds that it represents poor science. Perhaps it is as Fausto-Sterling (1985) has said—one's acceptance of such research depends on the standard of proof that is demanded by one's own ideology. For feminists, a high standard of proof is required of biogenetic research on sex differences because of the implications of the findings of such research. For those who approve of the current structuring of relationships between the sexes and the status of women socially, a lower standard of proof may be acceptable.

Fausto-Sterling is equally critical of biogenetic research in support of sex differences from a masculinist and an ostensibly feminist perspective. To her, the flaws in assumptions and methods are much the same, and with both, the implications are questionable and potentially disturbing. One of the examples she cites has to do with animal research that is generalized to human male sexual aggression. Sociobiologist David Barash (1977, cited in Fausto-Sterling) conducted observations of the mating behavior of mallard ducks. One of the conclusions of his study was that lone male ducks often *rape* mated female ducks. Fausto-Sterling points out that the common dictionary definition of rape stresses forcing a *woman* to have sex against her *will*, and says: "When scientists apply the word to fruit flies, bedbugs, ducks, or monkeys, the common definition expands to include all living beings . . . and the idea of will drops out . . ." (Fausto-Sterling, 1985:160). What then are we to infer from these findings? Do these duck behaviors, even if accurately described (setting aside questions about labeling and interpretation), really offer insight into human male sexual violence? The fact that this research was later reported in *Playboy* speaks to the issue of the implications of such studies.

The work of physician Katharina Dalton (1964, cited in Fausto-Sterling) is presented as an example of biogenetic research with similar flaws that is sometimes embraced by feminists. Dalton's work on premenstrual syndrome has been used as a basis for the defense of women who have been accused of violent acts that were committed under the influence of "raging hormones," and is not far removed from hormonal theories of male aggression. Fausto-Sterling suggests that standards of proof should also be consistent—one should not require a high standard of proof when research findings are viewed negatively and a low standard when they support one's own views.

BIOCULTURAL APPROACH

Rejecting the biogenetic approach, bioculturalists argue that sexual inequality exists due to a complex interplay of biological, technical, and sociological factors. The degree of male dominance, *cross-culturally*, and the sexual division of labor vary among societies; and in some societies, women do perform major public roles. In short, the diversity of cultural adaptations to biological differences is so great that biological deterministic arguments are not sufficient explanations. Thus, bioculturalists ask: "What are the social arrangements between the sexes in this *particular* society?"; or, more theoretically, "How is this society organized such that males and females have differential access to the distribution of scarce goods and services?"

One means of answering such questions has been to examine the conditions under which male dominance is produced historically and cross-culturally. Anthropologist Peggy Sanday (1981) cautions against overemphasizing the extent of male dominance. In her theory, male dominance is a relatively late historical development that is influenced by environmental and cultural factors. Furthermore, "real" male dominance (where males dominate in theory and practice) must be differentiated from societies where women hold some forms of secular power. Extreme male dominance occurs frequently in situations of social stress (such as where there is cultural disruption, or threats from outside forces) where the sexes are already physically and conceptually separate.

Rae Lesser Blumberg (1984) proposes a different set of factors to account for male dominance. First, female power is greater where women's work is viewed as indispensable. This is the case where women produce most of the diet (as in hunting and gathering societies), where they control the technical expertise for their work (as in some horticultural societies), where women work in female groups without male supervision, and where there is a shortage of male labor (as occurred in the United States during World War II). Second, female power is greater in certain kinship configurations—namely where female to female inheritance and matrilocality (where residence is established with the family of the woman) are to be found. Finally, female power bears a relationship to larger stratification systems. Female power is greater in societies that are organized on a community basis and where there is also little stratification of other types.

Joan Huber and Glenna Spitze (1983) provide a theory that accounts for the origins of sex stratification, as well as its current-day manifestations. The two propositions of their theory are that power and prestige accrue to those who control the extradomestic distribution of valued goods; and that this will be determined by the manner in which society's subsistence technology permits women to combine pregnancy and lactation with valued work. Utilizing insights that are drawn in part from Lenski and Friedl, they demonstrate the manner in which recent demographic changes have affected these two determinants of female power and how they have altered patterns of sex stratification in contemporary industrialized societies.

According to their theory, during the nineteenth century, a decline in mortality and a rise in the educational level of women resulted in a decline in fertility. This decline freed women to enter the paid labor force in increasing numbers, as they were needed. The theory thus uses the same propositions to explain patterns of sex stratification in modern societies as would apply in simpler societies. The fertility decline that began in the nineteenth century meant that women could more easily combine a job or career with motherhood; the fact of participation in the labor market increased the economic power of women. Female status improved as women came to increasingly produce and distribute, rather than merely consume, valued goods. They see full social equality as hinging on the division of household labor—a factor that may still impede equal labor force participation on the part of women.

Friedl (1975) had earlier attempted to explain sexual inequality in foraging (hunting and gathering) and horticultural (cultivating by hand or hoe) societies. These are the earliest and most developmentally primitive forms of subsistence technology. In these societies, the level of technology plays a major role in how inequality is structured. Although in both these societal forms, males are dominant, the reasons for their so being depends upon the subsistence level.

In hunting and gathering societies, meat (protein) is scarce, and men have a monopoly on hunting and fishing. However, contrary to common opinion, men are the hunters not because they are physically stronger or more agile, nor are women excluded from this role because they cannot wander far from the campsite (in fact, they do). Rather, it is primarily because hunting and carrying burdens are incompatible activities. Women not only carry fetuses *in utero*, upsetting their balance in the later months, but they also carry nursing infants. Compatible with the toting of babies is the bearing of other burdens—plants, roots, seeds—and other children. Therefore, although women supply the major source of subsistence in these foraging societies, they do not provide the most valued goods—meat. Further, because these societies are universally governed by a "generosity" norm—one should share scarce resources—the meat is publicly distributed. In that men are the providers, they have greater control over meat distribution and, therewith, greater dominance. (For a more complete discussion, see Friedl, 1975.)

In horticultural societies, although women usually participate in the actual farming, it is not the growing of food that is the scarce good; rather, it is the acquisition and clearing of new land, after the old has gone fallow. Men are assigned these tasks because new land is usually at territorial boundaries, where warfare is more likely. It is not because men are physically more able, however, that they are allocated these tasks; rather, Friedl argues, it is because males are less necessary for the survival of the society; females, due to their role in reproduction, cannot be assigned high-risk tasks. Consequently, men are more likely to be involved in alliances and exchanges of valued goods with others and will more frequently acquire the rights to their distribution. (For a more complete discussion, see Friedl, 1975).

In agricultural (Boserup, 1970), industrializing, industrialized, and postindustrial economies (Galbraith, 1973; Huber, 1976a), males continue to be more likely to acquire the rights over the distribution of scarce goods. In societies where money rather than protein or land is exchanged, for example, males are encouraged to work outside the home and are given more opportunities than women to acquire positions that are highly monetarily compensated (see Chapter 10). The system is structured in such a way that the extradomestic advantages that are gained by men can be used to purchase the domestic services of women (see Chapter 12). Ironically, Western intervention and assistance to developing nations has often undermined traditional positions of power held by women and increased the extent of male dominance in these societies (Scott, 1984). Male dominance persists. Is it inevitable?

Is Male Dominance Inevitable?

If one assumes, as the biogeneticists do, that male dominance is the result of heredity and species survival, then it is, obviously, inevitable. Any attempts to alter it will prove either impossible or destructive for the individual, the society, and, ultimately, the species. Indeed, some would argue that the changes that have been wrought already are damaging.

However, if one assumes that dominance is a result of the interplay among culture, biology, and technology, then it *may* not be inevitable. Indeed, from this perspective, much of the current feminist agony and social unrest is a result of trying to limit the options according to some predetermined notion of biological suitedness.

The dominance of males *appears* inevitable and immutable for many reasons. One of the primary ones is that in industrialized societies, ideology has a significant impact on the distribution system (Lenski, 1966). The ideology that has supported the sex-based stratification system in all industrialized societies—capitalist and communist, democratic and authoritarian—is that of patriarchalism, a belief that men are naturally superior to women and are entitled to greater power and prestige.

Why this ideology arose is difficult to say, although its underlying theme— the devaluation of women's work—is present throughout the world (Friedl, 1975). However, it is common for groups to propagate beliefs that aggrandize themselves, and it is equally common for the subordinated group to accept the dominant group's definitions. Further, it is a stance that meshes well with the demands of industrializing and industrialized nations. The important point, however, is that significant support for sex inequality in contemporary nations rests on a set of *ideas. Ideas are always culturally produced and are, therefore, always subject to social revision.*

If, however, we are to refute the idea of the inevitability of male dominance, we must address the one indisputable difference between the sexes: No man can bear a child. As we have seen in earlier societal forms, women's lesser access to the control of extradomestic resources is directly related to her biological role in reproduction. However, "Technology permits humans to transcend biology—people can fly although no one was born with wings" (Huber, 1976a:2). That is, although women have wombs, the technological level of industrialized societies is such that either sex could be assigned to the role of child rearer.

Consequently, the argument to be developed is that male dominance is not inevitable, but that it will be sustained and perpetuated until two related social changes are accomplished. These are that males and females be accorded equal access to the control and distribution of scarce goods and services; and that males and females be given equal responsibility for child rearing. We have reached a point in our technological development where these social changes can feasibly occur, although ideology and opportunity structure have not kept pace with technology.

We have reached this point of technological development for two primary reasons: the rapid and long-term decline in fertility rates and the widespread bottle feeding of infants (Huber, 1976). The fall in fertility has been a persistent pattern over the past 200 years in all industrialized societies. A major reason for the decline in fertility is that children have become economic liabilities to families. Currently, governments and individuals see a low fertility rate as desirable, and there are indications that this will continue (Huber, 1976a). Therefore, the average woman in industrialized nations will be pregnant for only about two years of her entire life.

The importance of the widespread adoption of bottle feeding during the twentieth century cannot be overemphasized. No longer is an infant's survival dependent upon a lactating mother. Consequently, the childbearing function is technologically separable from the child-rearing function. Indeed, the average infant in the United States is not breastfed; for those who are, best estimates are that three weeks is the median duration.

Since the average woman is involved in childbearing for only a few months of her life, and because the average woman is also working outside the home, and because the average baby is bottle fed, on what grounds can the assignment of domestic tasks to women be socially justified? Such a division of labor made sense for our ancestors—the foragers and horticulturists. After all, fertility control was difficult then, and childbearing and child rearing were necessarily intertwined. This particular division of labor, however, is no longer functionally necessary in industrialized societies.

The allocation of domestic tasks to women and extradomestic tasks to men is the primary reason why men have achieved greater dominance, and since it is no longer technologically necessary to retain this division of labor, male dominance is not immutable. It is retained, however, both through the ideology that states "Women's place is in the home" and through social structures that prevent men and women from sharing child-rearing/bread winning tasks. Speculatively, Huber (1976a) suggests that if the decline in fertility continues, greater sex equality may result: Inducing women to have children may require reallocating the primary responsibility for their care.

Large-scale social trends would seem to lend credence to a projected continuing decline in the birthrate: The proportion of singles is growing; the age at first marriage is increasing; the rate of remarriage is decreasing; the length of time between marriage and first child is increasing; and the divorce rate is burgeoning. Further, since one of the primary factors in reducing fertility is viewing children as liabilities, Huber postulates that we are reaching a point not only where the couple views children as economic liabilities, but also where women view them as *personal liabilities*. Because women are still expected to raise the children, women are likely to weigh more seriously the gains of motherhood against the costs. If the low birthrate among educated and occupationally successful women is any indication, as more women aspire educationally and occupationally, we can expect more to choose to have few or no children.

If the fertility rates continue to dip, falling below the rate necessary for population replacement, Huber speculates that governments will intervene with policies and programs that will redistribute the responsibility for child care. When the state has a vested interest in having more children, it may provide the necessary incentive: free day care to all. By releasing women from the primary child care duties, a redistribution of domestic responsibilities will occur. The result will be greater equality. However, it seems unlikely that it will happen soon. Maintaining the outmoded and dysfunctional system is in the interest of those who already have power and prestige.

Sex-based stratification, then, is universal but not inevitable. The particular shape and form such inequality takes depends upon the society in which it exists. Now, let us look at its shape in modern societies, and modernizing and modernized societies generally, and at the United States specifically.

□ □ *10* □ □

Inequalities of Power, Property, and Prestige

Every society makes decisions about how it will reward its members; that is, every society is stratified. In addition, every society has the same set of rewards that it might proffer: These are power, property, and prestige. The greater one's access to and control over the distribution of goods outside the family, the greater are one's social rewards—the greater one's power, the more one's wealth, and the higher one's prestige.

Sociologists have been studying how one's gender affects one's receipt of valued social goods. They find that men and women end up with different amounts of power, property, and prestige. Let's look at how inequalities in power, property, and prestige in the contemporary United States is accomplished.

POWER

Power—the probability of having one's will done despite opposition—is a complex phenomenon. Some of the more visible means of power are economic power, political power, and even sheer physical power. A less visible but still critical basis for power may be interpersonal power. (The perceived importance of this type of power may be seen in the popularity of assertiveness-training courses and books for women.)

The result of a male monopoly over one or more of these power arenas depends in large part on the significance of that type of power for social subsistence. In contemporary industrialized societies, for example, the slight advantage held by males in physical size and strength has little bearing on actual social power, because society does not depend on these traits for daily survival. Rather, as discussed in Chapter 9, power comes to those who control the distribution of goods outside the family. In the United States, this power rests in persons who hold key decision-making positions in corporations, labor, universities, foundations, the mass media, government, and political parties, and in those who control great wealth—or the *establishment*.

When the system by which values, goods, and services are distributed to members of the society remains unchallenged, the probability is high that the interests of the establishment are those that will be served. Only when *interest groups* become politically active in relationship to particular issues does the potential for impact on decision making on those issues shift away from the dominant group. This political activity may take the form of a social movement or of a coalition between diverse pressure groups. Without such political activity, however, the system will *de facto* profit those who are in positions to make decisions that are in their own interests.

In the United States the feminist movement has agitated for equal rights for women for nearly a century and a half. Some of the fruits of that labor include the extension of suffrage to women via the nineteenth Amendment to the Constitution in 1920; passage of the Equal Pay Act in 1963; approval of Title VII of the Civil Rights Act of 1964, which prohibits sex discrimination in employment; and passage of Title IX of the Higher Education Act of 1972, which prohibits sex segregation in education. These along with other legislative reforms are evidence that women have joined together as an effective interest group with both political access to and influence over legislation (Klein, 1984). Women's rights organizations are recognized as representing legitimate interests, and they have won some major gains (see Chapter 14).

Despite such evidence of the gains that have been won by the movement, it has had its failures—most notably, the failure to ratify the Equal Rights Amendment. Even though Congress had overwhelmingly endorsed the amendment in 1972, and even though a majority of Americans favored its passage, when the deadline for ratification came in 1982, the pro-ERA forces were still three states short. The organization and funding of anti-ERA interest groups held sway (see Chapter 14), along with a conservative executive, legislative, and judicial stance.

But there is more to politics than trying to sway legislation. One can participate as a voter, or as an elected or appointed official. How do males and females compare in these arenas?

Government

An institution that obviously must be considered when discussing differential power in the representation of males and females is the government. Although it is simplistic to assume that a man will represent the interests of men and that a woman will represent the interests of women, it is a place to begin. As the black political force has recognized, there is greater likelihood of a black representing black interests than a white, and the likelihood of those interests being met increases with the number of black representatives. What, then, is the differential access to the legitimated power of the government office? We will first consider elected positions and then turn to the appointed ones.

No woman has ever held either of the top two executive positions—the presidency and vice-presidency—although Geraldine Ferraro, the 1984 Democratic vice-presidential candidate, made such an idea seem probable and not just some feminist dream. Both the U.S. Senate and the House of Representatives have historically been overwhelmingly male. In the One Hundredth Congress (1987–1988), women comprised two percent of the Senate seats (2 out of 100) and 5.3 percent of the House seats (23 out of 413). Table 10.1 shows the total number of women members of both houses in the federal government from 1947 to 1988.

The representation is small; growth is slow; and the process of entry may be altering, particularly in the House. Before 1949, congresswomen entered via the right of widow's succession: "If power is thrust upon a woman by her husband's death, she may accept it without blame" (Lynn, 1975:376). Although female senators are still more likely to be appointed than elected to their first term, new women representatives are more likely to run on their own professional and political merit (Lynn, 1975:378). However, simply being elected to the halls of Congress does not insure the representative an active role in legislating. Influencing budgets, initiating legislation, taking part in investigative functions, and responding to the particular needs of one's constituency all depend upon one's seniority, committee assignments, and access to the informal communication network (Amundsen, 1971:69).

Longevity in office is one of the primary ways in which a representative moves along in the power hierarchy of the Congress. As one 67-year-old male freshman representative remarked upon his choosing not to run again for office, "Nobody listens to what you have to say until you have been there 10 or 12 years. . . . There are only about 40 out of the 435 members who call the shots. They're the committee chairmen and ranking members" (quoted in Amundsen, 1971:69).

Table 10.1   WOMEN MEMBERS OF CONGRESS: 1947–1988

Congress	Year	Senate	House
80th	1947–1948	0	8
81st	1949–1950	1	9
82nd	1951–1952	1	10
83rd	1953–1954	2	11
84th	1955–1956	1	16
85th	1957–1958	1	15
86th	1959–1960	1	16
87th	1961–1962	2	17
88th	1963–1964	2	11
89th	1965–1966	2	10
90th	1967–1968	1	11
91st	1969–1970	1	10
92nd	1971–1972	1	12
93rd	1973–1974	0	16
94th	1975–1976	0	19
95th	1977–1978	0	18
96th	1979–1980	1	16
97th	1981–1982	2	19
98th	1983–1984	2	21
99th	1985–1986	2	21
100th	1987–1988	2	23

It is not until his or her fifth term in the House of Representatives, that a member of Congress might expect to have influence (Lynn, 1975:378). From 1918 to 1973, only 17 women held their seats in the House for the minimum five terms (Lynn, 1975:378). In the One Hundredth Congress, only six female representatives had retained their seats for five terms or more. The major exception in the Senate was Margaret Chase Smith, who served nearly a quarter of a century. (She entered politics by running for the House seat that her husband vacated due to serious illness.)

Committee assignments and leadership positions are further avenues to power within the Congress. No woman has held the important leadership positions, such as majority leader, Speaker of the House, or party whip. Further, not all committees have equal power and importance. Women are assigned to low-prestige and uninfluential committees, making their participation unequal to that of males.

The third path to successful influence in Congress is through the informal social network. As is true of most important policy making in business, much of the important work of government takes place on the golf course, the steam room table, and the men's clubs. These informal settings not only provide safe contexts for negotiating problems, they also provide environments in which personal allegiances and friendships can be built. The importance of these informal contexts in developing friendships has led at least one male administrative aid to contend, "No woman can quite make it. So much of the power is built [in the male-only preserves]. I doubt that the best or most able women can ever get to the inner circle, where there is complete acceptance" (quoted in Lynn, 1975:379).

Decision making in government goes on not only at the legislative and executive levels but also in a wide variety of bureaus, the functioning arms of the government. Emanating from these bureaus are policies, practices, and programs that encompass the entire dictionary of our social life, from atoms to zoos. Individuals in positions to make decisions at this level either have been appointed to or have worked their way up through civil service. The question is: Do males and females have differential access to these positions? Let us look at the highest level appointments.

The president's cabinet has access to the president and, presumably, the power to influence decisions at the executive level. Few women have ever held cabinet rank. Two cabinet level positions in the Reagan administration have been held by women—the positions of secretary of transportation and secretary of health and human services, although HHS Secretary, Margaret Heckler, was later pressured to resign. The appointment of Sandra Day O'Conner by President Reagan in 1981 placed the first woman justice on the Supreme Court in its history. Ambassadors and ministers to foreign states have been predominately male, as has been the hierarchy of civil employees who work for the federal government.

Voting Behavior

The lack of female representation in the government at all levels and in all branches is not the result of lack of female participation in politics at the level of voting. In fact, as Jaquette comments, the differential voting *turnout* of men and women is so slight as to bring forth a studied "ho hum" from political scientists (1974); nor can it be explained by differential engagement at the campaign level. The women volunteers—in their canvassing, phoning, typing, and mailing—are the real armies of the night; they provide the free labor upon which campaigns depend.

Until quite recently, moreover, women and men voted the same way on candidates and issues. However, in the 1980 elections, the phenomenon that had been expected and feared by some with the granting of the vote to women in 1920 finally materialized. A *gender gap*, whereby voting behavior and positions on political issues is differentiated by sex, became apparent. In that presidential election year 54 percent of the men voted for Reagan, while only 46 percent of the women did. This was the largest difference between the electoral choices of men and women since such statistics have been kept (Abzug, 1984:90). Since that year, such statistics have become a standard component of political analyses in the United States, and evidence of such a gap persists (Baxter and Lansing, 1983:180).

In the 1982 elections, women voted the Democratic ticket in 33 of 44 U.S. Senate and gubernatorial races, provided the winning margin in three of the gubernatorial races, and were responsible for some landslide victories among candidates regarded as pro women's rights (Abzug, 1984:1, 2). Public opinion polls demonstrate that the gender gap applies to issues, as well; for example, women have been more critical of the economic policies of President Reagan than have men, are more favorable toward peace initiatives and disapproving of the arms race, and are more favorable toward environmental protection initiatives (Abzug: 1984:120, 121).

Concern over the potential impact of the gender gap became so great among Republicans prior to the 1982 election (since the gender gap had thus far been more favorable toward Democratic candidates and party platforms) that one official, in responding to a question about how the election might be changed to benefit his party, proposed (jokingly, we assume) repeal of the Nineteenth Amendment (Baxter and Lansing, 1983:179).

The gender gap, although apparent in the 1984 presidential election, as well, was not great enough to result in the defeat of Ronald Reagan (males, 62 percent for Reagan; females, 54 percent). Thus, while there are indications that the political power of women is increasing slightly in the United States in the form of interest group voting, political participation, and representation, the impact of such changes has thus far been limited.

What about other forms of power, however, such as control over the valued good of property in the United States today? We turn, now, and examine economic indicators of equality.

PROPERTY

Property, or material or monetary compensation, is closely tied to political power in that politically powerful people tend to be wealthy and vice versa. In fact, economic power often translates into political power. In this section, we will look first at how wealth and political power are interconnected, and then at the distribution of wealth and earnings by sex in American society.

Wealth is a power resource if its owner controls its investment. Despite the common myth that women control the wealth, in fact, men earn, own, and control most of the wealth in this country. Fifty-eight percent of stock shares are owned by institutions whose boards of trustees and brokers are almost exclusively male. Individually, women own approximately 18 percent of privately held stock shares; men own approximately 24 percent. In terms of privately held real estate holdings, only 39 percent belong to women, despite the fact of female longevity. Approximately 60 percent of persons with financial assets over $60,000 are male.

These statistics are probably quite liberal estimates of the wealth of women, because it is common for men to place holdings in the names of their wives, daughters, or mothers for tax purposes. Women are neither wealthier than men, nor are they situated to use their wealth as a power resource.

Rather, it can be argued that the control of the wealth in this country rests in the hands of a very small elite—approximately one percent of the population that is composed of owners and managers of the megaconglomerates. Members of this elite own 25 to 30 percent of privately held wealth in America and 60 to 70 percent of all privately held corporate wealth. Further, the amount of wealth held by these people has been increasing and there is a remarkable continuity in the families that hold wealth.

Our nation's "upper crust" belongs to interlinking social, financial, and governmental networks. They attend the same prep schools and universities, revel at the same men's clubs and resort-retreats, and marry into each other's families; that is, not only do these persons share common financial interests, they are also socially and familially bound to one another.

The policy decisions of this elite are discussed informally in boardrooms and social clubs, and consensus is reached in their major policy-setting organizations, which themselves are "directed by the same men who manage major corporations and financed by corporation and foundation monies" (Domhoff, 1974:93).

In turn, these decisions affect our government through a number of channels. First, many of the members of these corporate organizations serve in high-level government offices, commissions, and committees. Second, "hired experts intimately identified with these organizations serve as government advisors" (Domhoff, 1974:98). Third, these organizations provide experts for testimony at congressional committees and for advising those committees. Fourth, many members of these corporate organizations are large contributors to campaigns and have, therefore, easy access to politicians.

The relationship of corporate executives and politicians is developed through informal modes of interaction, and these modes are exclusively male. One of the settings for the development of this social cohesion, which Domhoff has closely studied, are exclusive retreats—The Bohemian Grove, Rancheros Visitadores, Round Up—that "women are strictly forbidden to enter" (1974:24).

The weight of the evidence seems quite clear that the corporate economy is effectively controlled by a few megacompanies—banks, insurance corporations, and conglomerates.

Activities at these retreats, such as boozing, high jinks, calf roping, cross-country horseback caravans, stag movies, the Bulls' Balls Lunch (donated yearly by a cattle baron following the castration of his herd) liken the retreats to a transplanted "college fraternity system" or "an overgrown boyscout camp" (Domhoff, 1974: 23). But apart from the stereotypically masculine orientation of the fun and games, these retreats provide a context of intimacy wherein the corporate rich cement their social bonds with governmental officials, university chancellors, and presidents of television networks.

Within these encampments, policies are suggested, proposals are made, and appointments are discussed. Women are conspicuous in their absence. They are not presidents of financial institutions, members of boards of directors, high-placed corporate lawyers, nor are they in any other way situated to control the wealth of this country.

Without inherited wealth, the route to property—for men and women—is through participation in the labor force. People work for wages to acquire goods; money is the reward for one's toil. Presumably, the more valuable one's work, the more one will be rewarded—the greater will be one's salary. But to get the reward in the first place, you have to be in the labor market: You have to work outside the home for pay.

Since the turn of the century, women in American society have steadily increased their representation in the labor force. In 1900, 20 percent of all women were in the labor market, and they comprised 18 percent of all wage earners. By 1940, those numbers had grown to 28 percent and 25 percent, respectively. During the World War II years, female labor force participation grew faster than before, and in 1945 nearly 36 percent of all women were employed, and they comprised just over 29 percent of all workers. In the years following the war, this rate of participation dropped sharply as women were forced out of their wartime jobs; it was ten years before female representation in the labor market reached the 1945 levels (Blau, 1984:301–302).

The growth of female participation in the labor force has occurred primarily since 1940, with sequential waves of women from various backgrounds—immigrant, young black, older married, and, most recently, young married women, many with preschool children. The demographic characteristics of employed women have become increasingly similar to the characteristics of the entire population in terms of race, ethnicity, education, age, and marital and family status (Blau, 1975:218–219); that is, "it is becoming more difficult to consider working women as in some sense an unrepresentative or atypical group" (Blau, 1975:219). It is not atypical for a woman to be employed outside the home, nor is the gainfully employed woman typically different in demographic characteristics than the full-time homemaker.

In the 1980s, the participation of women in the labor market has approached that of men. In 1984, 63 percent of women between the ages of 18 and 64 were employed and they constituted 43 percent of the total labor force (Reskin and Hartman, 1986:1). One might reasonably expect, with this evidence of increasing labor market activity on the part of women, that female wages as a consequence would expand relative to those of males, but this has not been the case. In fact, the median earnings of women have declined relative to those of men. In 1955, the median earnings for year-round, full-time female employees was 64 percent of those of males; in 1981, the percentage had fallen to 59 percent (Blau, 1984:308).

Table 10.2   MEDIAN INCOME BY YEARS OF EDUCATION AND GENDER FOR YEAR-ROUND, FULL-TIME WORKERS OVER 25 YEARS OLD (1984)

	Median income		Women's earnings
Years of school	Women	Men	for male dollar
Elementary			
8 years	10,421	16,112	.64
High School			
1–3 years	12,134	20,067	.60
4 years	14,733	24,000	.61
College			
1–3 years	17,114	26,302	.65
4+ years	22,089	28,089	.62

Source: Cynthia M. Tauber and Victor Valdisera. *Women in the American Economy.* Current Population Reports (1986) Special Series P-23, No. 146. U.S. Department of Commerce, Bureau of the Census.

As Table 10.2 demonstrates, these wage discrepancies are not the result of differences in the educational attainment of women and men, as the wage inequities are consistent within each educational grouping by sex.

The discrepancies are not the result of differences in general occupational category, as Table 10.3 makes clear. In fact, as the table indicates, education and job responsibility do not reduce the discrepancy between men's and women's incomes. Indeed, when education, occupation, years of experience, and other relevant variables are taken into account, men's salaries are still higher than women's.

There is also evidence that race stratification and sex stratification interact. While the income gap between white males and females has increased since 1955, the gap between black males and females has decreased. Although black women remain at the bottom of the hierarchy of income, recently, there has been an increasing convergence between the wages of black women and white women (U.S. Bureau of the Census, 1984:21).

What then is the explanation for the extreme income discrepancies between women and men? Possibilities include direct wage discrimination, disruptions in female employment patterns, and occupational segregation by sex. Direct wage discrimination, where females are paid lower wages than men for the same work, can still be found and is evidenced by the number of suits that have been taken to court, some of which are still pending. Disruptions in female employment patterns as an explanation cannot be dismissed—either as women have a generally shorter tenure at their jobs due to their late group entry into the labor market, or due to time out because of pregnancy, homemaking, and child-rearing responsibilities. These work disruptions, however, do not uniformly affect all women, and such disruptions are becoming less frequent due to lower fertility rates and increased use of child care services. We have seen, though, that the wage discrepancies between women and men are not abating as we would expect them to if women's erratic job histories were a primary causal factor of unequal pay. Rather, after controlling for many other factors, researchers find that the most powerful explanation is *occupa-*

Table 10.3   MEDIAN EARNINGS BY OCCUPATION OF LONGEST JOB HELD AND SEX: 1985

(Year-Round, Full-Time Employment)

Major occupation	Male	Female	Ratio: women's earnings to men's
Executive, administrative and managers	$33,536	$20,565	.61
Professional	$32,812	$21,781	.66
Technical and related support	$26,266	$18,177	.69
Sales	$25,445	$12,682	.50
Clerical and administrative support	$22,997	$15,157	.66
Craft and repair	$23,269	$15,093	.65
Machine operators, assemblers	$20,786	$12,232	.59
Service workers	$16,824	$ 9,204	.61

Source: United States Department of Commerce, Bureau of the Census, *Statistical Abstract of the United States (1987).* No. 681: 403.

tional segregation by sex. This factor affects the life chances of more women on a continuing basis than any other factor: Men and women have different occupations; the occupations that men have provide greater rewards than the occupations women have. Occupations are *sex typed*. Those that are sex typed female are devalued.

Table 10.4 gives some examples of the sex segregation in occupations. Males dominate in some categories, females in others. The categories that men dominate—such as dentists—are better paid than the categories that women dominate—such as nurses. Moreover, men are spread out among a greater number of occupations. Fully one-fourth of the employed women, though, are concentrated in only five occupations—secretary, bookkeeper, elementary-school teacher, waitress, and retail salesclerk (Blau, 1984:307). None of these occupations are noted for their financial remuneration.

The occupational placement of black females is especially skewed. Although 66 percent of white women are white-collar workers, only 52 percent of black women are so situated (U.S. Department of Labor, 1983). While a high proportion of the white women are teachers, registered nurses, and secretaries, a high proportion of the black women are key punchers and file clerks—positions that are poorly paid. In addition, while approximately only 18 percent of white women are service workers, nearly 30 percent of black women are; over 5 percent of the employed black women work as domestics in private homes (U.S. Department of Labor, 1983). Although this rate of employ as a domestic is high, it has been steadily declining, and black women are increasingly being employed in clerical positions. Yet, it is still true that "gender allocates black women to sex-typed occupations while their race separates them from white women within the female-intensive occupations" (Douglas, 1980:61). Overall, black women are relegated to the lowest-paid and lowest-status jobs.

Table 10.4 PERSONS EMPLOYED IN SELECTED OCCUPATIONS, PERCENTAGE FEMALE, 1981

Occupation	Percentage female
Secretaries	99.1
Child-care workers, except private household	95.5
Bank tellers	93.5
Telephone operators	92.9
Registered nurses, dietitians, and therapists	92.6
Waiters	89.3
Billing clerks	88.2
Cashiers	86.2
File clerks	83.8
Elementary school teachers	83.6
Librarians, archivists, and curators	82.8
Sales clerks, retail trade	71.2
Social and recreation workers	62.4
Secondary school teachers	51.3
Real-estate agents and brokers	49.8
Writers, artists, and entertainers	39.8
Bank officers and financial managers	37.5
College and university teachers	35.2
Computer specialists	27.1
Sales managers	26.5
Life and physical scientists	21.9
Stock and bond sales agents	17.0
Post-office mail carriers	15.7
Lawyers and judges	14.1
Physicians, medical and osteopathic	13.7
Precision machine operatives	12.8
Police and detectives	5.7
Dentists	4.6
Engineers	4.4
Truck drivers	2.7
Construction laborers, including carpenters' helpers	2.2
Carpenters	1.9
Electricians	1.6
Automobile mechanics	0.6
Plumbers and pipe fitters	0.4

Source: United States Bureau of the Census, *Statistical Abstract of the United States, 1982–83.* Washington, D.C.: U.S. Government Printing Office, 1982:388–390.

Simply looking at the large occupation categories—such as *teacher* and *salesperson*—conceals more about sex segregation than it reveals. Within job classifications, there are male sex-typed and female sex-typed positions. Sales is a good example. Men are more likely to hold the higher-paying corporate and commission sales positions, while women are more likely to be retail salesclerks, often working for minimum wage. Even within retail sales, women will be selling clothing, notions, and linens, and will be working for an hourly wage, whereas men will be selling dishwashers, riding mowers, computers, and furniture, and will be working for a commission on high-ticket items. In many stores, shoes are commission items—and their departments are heavily male staffed. Perfumes and cosmetics are one of the few female-dominated sales areas that are sold on a commission basis, although the percentage is lower than for appliances or shoes, and, interestingly, more males are entering the sales fray. (More information of sex segregation will concern us in the following chapter.)

In terms of earnings, then, women do not fare as well as men do. No matter how earnings differences are computed (or explained), the differences are not erased. Part-time women workers make about 47 percent of what part-time male workers make; and, a woman with a college degree can expect to make about the same income as a man who has dropped out of high school. What is the reason? She will work as a nurse or a teacher, and he as a union worker or a skilled craftsman.

There is another indicator, however, of where the economics of sex is clear—namely, poverty. The sex ratio differences of living in poverty are so great that a phrase has been coined to describe the situation: "the feminization of poverty" (Pearce, 1979).

Currently in the United States, two poor adults out of three are women. Among the aged population, two and a half times as many women live in poverty as men do. Fully one-half of all elderly black women are officially poor (Scott, 1984:19).

Hilda Scott defines the feminization of poverty as the complex of forces keeping women in an economically precarious situation (1984:3). In her estimation, the forces that maintain this situation include the assignment of primary responsibility for child rearing to women and its effects following divorce, and the limits on women's income and economic mobility that result from occupational segregation, sex discrimination, and sexual harassment (1984:23). A key feature of her analysis of women's poverty is the amount of unpaid work that is done by women. Such work—including child-rearing and homemaking responsibilities—lessens women's economic mobility in a variety of ways. For women who devote their full time to this type of work, it may increase their economic dependence on men and actually work to their disadvantage should they later decide to enter the labor market. For those women who perform these tasks while working outside the home for pay, the double duty of balancing both sets of responsibilities may impede advancement in the labor market or make it impossible to function effectively in both settings.

Finally, let us turn to sex inequities in the control over the valued good of prestige and its relationship to access to power and property.

PRESTIGE

Prestige is commonly used to denote the respect or esteem that is accorded an individual or a social category of persons. It is highly congruent with power and property in that individuals with a great deal of these valued attributes typically will carry a great deal of prestige, as well. Prestige is linked with social status in that a status, or a defined position in the social structure, is frequently thought of in terms of ranking from higher to lower. Statuses are of two types: An achieved status is one that is acquired through individual effort, while an ascribed status is one that is determined by birth, or that is automatically assigned on a systematic basis by others. While all women theoretically have the ability to influence, affect, or determine their achieved statuses, no one can control their sex assignment at birth. It is to the ascribed sex status of being a female in our society that we will now turn.

Much of this book has already served as an exploration of female status. The existence of sexist language, the extent of violence against women, and the nature of religious and clinical ideologies about women are all indicators of women's shared and devalued status as females. These indicators may be denied or ignored, but there is no getting around the fact that women are treated similarly as women. Edwin Shurr examines the consequences of such sex stereotyping in his book *Labeling Women Deviant* (1983). He sees the status, female, as categorically constituting a master status, whereas the status, male, does not. A master status is one of such significance that it becomes the primary identity of the individual. All other statuses held by the individual are defined by the master status: "Individual women are perceived of and reacted to at least initially, and often primarily, in terms of their femaleness" (Shurr, 1983:25).

Schurr argues further that to be female in our society is by definition to be deviant and part of a devalued status group in four ways. First, due to their lower position in the stratification system, there is a tendency for women to be evaluated unfavorably as a group and for this placement to be explained as resulting from inherently female characteristics. Second is the widespread objectification of women as a group that occurs when women are treated as nonpersons or as interchangeable objects. Third is the extensive devaluation of women in cultural symbolism, such as in common language usage and the mass media. Finally, a further indication of the low value placed on femaleness is the special relationship women have with definitions of deviance—including the failure of society to condemn many male offenses against women and the double standard of deviance that is applied to males and females (Shurr, 1983:35–36).

One indicator of the master status aspect of femaleness is what Shurr refers to as the "hyphenization phenomenon": the tendency of others to note instances when the achieved statuses of particular women are incongruent with the stereotypical features of the ascribed sex status, female (Shurr, 1983:25). This phenomenon occurs every time a woman's sex is noted along with some other status as in "woman-doctor," "female-lawyer," "woman-athlete," or the typically disparaging label, "woman-driver." These remarks are also indications of status inconsistency; it would be unusual to hear labels such as "woman-nurse" or "female-secretary." (Status inconsistency will be explored more fully in Chapter 11.)

The low-prestige level of women can be seen clearly in the occupational sphere. Not only is there sex segregation in the labor market—but also in the job categories in which women predominate; they are among the lowest in occupational prestige. A further indication of the low-prestige level of women's work is that a great deal of the work that women do—primarily in the home—is unpaid labor. This work may be highly valued within a woman's family and by homemakers themselves, although it may actually count for nothing should such a woman later attempt to enter the labor market.

In Chapter 9, we explored the notion of sex stratification and examined theories that account for its existence. In this chapter, we looked at sex stratification more closely, by looking at differential male and female control over the valued goods of power, property, and prestige. We found these to be closely linked, and found that female control over their distribution was severely limited despite some indications of improvement in women's status. In Chapter 11, we will further explore these themes by focusing our lens on the world of work.

11

The Work World:
Organization and Process

The hallmark of an industrialized society is its intense and widespread division of labor. With the advent of the factory system, goods that were usually produced in the home were produced outside. Workers in factories were assigned increasingly narrow and specialized tasks. As the population grew, the specialization of labor increased, leading to a more efficient output of goods and to greater profits for the industrialists. The economy shifted from agriculture to one of manufacturing to—in advanced industrial nations—a service industry.

Paralleling the changes in the production of goods was a change in the manner in which the production was administrated. The administrative form that developed was that of the *bureaucracy*—a hierarchical structure that is designed to manage large-scale undertakings through the coordination of the work of many individuals who are unequal in their positions in the division of labor (Weber, 1946; Coser and Rosenberg, 1976:353). The bureaucratic structure, therefore, is based upon specialization of labor within an organization in which both the *lines* and *levels* of authority are formally structured. Today, the corporate bureaucracy dominates the American economy. The corporation is a system jointly owned by many shareholders, but *control* rests in the board of directors and its high-level managerial staff.

During industrialization, due to increased specialization and hierarchism, the surplus of scarce goods increased. This meant there were more of the valued goods to distribute and more *levels* of decision making. As a result, *social mobility*—moving from one position in the hierarchy to another—became possible. In societies with service economies, the probability of such mobility is great, because service occupations are expanding and confer more rewards than blue-collar jobs.

Specialization of labor and bureaucratic structure have contributed to the economic growth of nations; however, they have also created groups of workers who could be categorized on the basis of their specialization and their position in the hierarchy and who could aspire to move up. Simpler and closed classification systems—such as ''peasant/lord''—were replaced by more complex and open ones. In relation to complexity, for example, in the United States, the classification scheme that is used by the Department of Labor (in descending order of prestige) is professional, technical; managers, officials, proprietors; clerical workers; sales workers, craftsmen, foremen; operatives; nonfarm laborers; service workers (e.g., household help). In terms of openness, individuals could not only move from one category to another (e.g., from sales to managerial) but could advance within a given category (e.g., from lawyer to Supreme Court Justice). One's occupation became, and continues to be, an excellent indicator of one's power, wealth, social prestige, life chances, and life-style. The "better" the occupation, the greater the opportunity to control the distribution of scarce goods and services.

The everyday accomplishment of work is a socially structured activity that takes place in the context of a culture. It is at the social-interactional level—in the offices, factories, universities, and stores—where the assumptions of the culture that concern gender differences are enacted. Consequently, we would be highly remiss if we did not address the organization and processes of the workaday world—the practices and rituals that are retaining walls of sexual inequality. Despite the work setting, level of training, and prestige of an occupation, the same basic rules and practices apply. We will discover that ironically, the same processes and structures that serve to systematically exclude women systematically produce a sense of failure in men.

STATUS INCONSISTENCY

We have already seen how the work world is divided up so that women and men are sex segregated, and so that women are clustered in low-paying jobs and rewarded less than men when they do advance. Earlier, we discussed how the socialization process encourages males and females to have different occupational expectations. We also saw that the prestige level of women's work is less than that of men's. Now, we need to know how job differentiation is structured and preserved through the everyday operations of work organizations.

Let us first of all examine the assumption that men's work and women's work are different. Whether a job is viewed as masculine or feminine is often quite independent of the work skills that the job actually requires; for example, in the United States, medicine is seen as a profession that requires such masculine attributes as intelligence and assurance. In the Soviet Union, on the other hand, medicine is defined as a career that requires such feminine-defined traits as nurturance, service orientation, and humaneness. In the United States, 13 percent of the doctors are female, whereas in the Soviet Union, 2 percent are women (Seager and Olson, 1986). The Soviet Union and the United States share the same sex stereotypes, but define the occupation in terms of different skills. Further, however, I would hypothesize that the social valuation of the physician is higher in the United States than in the Soviet Union and that the social organization of medicine in the United States, in effect, establishes medical care as a scarce service.

In the United States, if women enter a predominately male occupation, they tend to be slotted into those positions that have the least prestige; for example, women in medicine tend to be in three low-status specialties: pediatrics, psychiatry, and public health; woman lawyers are disproportionately in the fields of domestic and public defense law. It is generally true, throughout the occupational world, that the higher the position, the fewer the women.

On the other hand, men who enter predominately female occupations tend to be upwardly mobile; for example, in the predominately female professions of nursing, teaching, and library science, a higher proportion of males moves into administrative roles than females.

Sociologists have paid considerable attention to the phenomenon of *status inconsistency*, or the fact that a person may hold different statuses that are inconsistent from the perspective of the culture. Examples are the Christian Science professor of medicine, the Jewish John Birch Society member, the black male domestic worker, the female judge, and so on. Meeting someone of the ''wrong'' sex (or for that matter of the wrong age, race, ethnic background, or class) for an occupation causes dissonance. The result is that students with a male professor of nursing, for example, tend to be distracted by the fact that he is male; or, rather than assessing the worth of a female attorney's defense, the jury focuses on her femaleness. Although ''sex—female'' is irrelevant to the skills that are required to manage a board meeting, tar a roof, teach a class in physics, admonish a jury, or minister to a parishioner, each of these occupational roles is sex typed as male. Consequently, coworkers and others reduce their discomfort of dealing with a woman in these positions by focusing on the fact of her femaleness. In short, they make *sex salient*—when it is objectively irrelevant. Sex saliency frequency places a woman in a double bind (''damned if she does, damned if she doesn't''), as the following statement from a female steelworker illustrates:

> At first, everytime I started to do something, they said, "Come here. Let me show you how." Then they would do it and you wouldn't get the experience, so gradually at first I let them show me how and then I'd say let me try it first and if I have trouble, I'll let you help me. You are under so much pressure. If you walk out of the shanty and you are carrying this heavy bucket, the other workers come along and say, how come you let her carry all that? You should be carrying that for her. But if you let them help you, someone else says, see that, you're doing all her work (Fonow, 1977:43).

Persons who have status inconsistency tend to think of themselves in terms of their highest status and expect others to do the same. However, because people have a vested interest in elevating their own self-images, many unconsciously want to see others in terms of their lowest status (Lenski, 1966:86)—a kind of one-upmanship. The effect is one of ''considerable stress for many persons of inconsistent status''; such persons find social interaction outside of their background area ''somewhat less rewarding than does the average person'' (Lenski, 1966:87).

The question then becomes: How is it that sex becomes salient in the organization of work? In what follows, we will look at two sets of factors that contribute to this process. First, we will examine the structural features of sex segregation in the workplace and the hierarchical organization of most work environments. Then, we will turn to the organization of relationships in the labor market by examining the sponsor-protégé system, the occurrence of sexual harassment, and socioemotional bonding.

SEX SEGREGATION

In Chapter 10, sex segregation in occupations was identified as a key factor in maintaining wage discrepancies between women and men and in reducing the mobility of women in the labor market. Reskin (1984) identifies three varieties of sex segregation in work. First, an ideology of separate spheres—the notion that work within the home is most appropriately done by women and work in the public sector by men—creates a physical separation between many male and female workers. This ideology of separate spheres most clearly applies to housework, whether done by homemakers for their families or domestic workers for pay. Second is the visible segregation of the labor market by sex, with some occupational categories being dominated by females or males. Third is the functional separation of work by sex within occupational categories or workplaces, which has the further effect of creating an institutionalized social distance between female and male coworkers (Reskin, 1984:2).

In an attempt to determine just how great occupational segregation was, Gross (1968) devised an "index of occupational segregation." The index was constructed to measure the proportion of women who would have to change jobs in a given year in order for the occupational placement of men and women to be equalized. His conclusions were threefold. First, the amount of occupational segregation had remained fairly constant—the difference between the high- and low-integration scores was only four percentage points. Second, the magnitude of the segregation was large. In order for occupational integration to be a fact, approximately two-thirds of the female labor force would have had to change jobs in any given census year. And third, sex segregation was more severe than racial segregation. Whereas the index for sex segregation was 68.4 percent, the index for racial segregation was 46.8 percent. (Although Gross has not reported a separate index for black females, we can surmise that that index was higher than either of those reported.) Gross concluded that women's entry into the labor force has been accomplished through the expansion of those occupations that were already female, the creation of new female jobs (e.g., keypuncher), or "through females taking over previously male occupations" (1968:202). Oppenheimer (1973) concurs with this analysis, arguing that the great influx of women into the labor force is a result of the demands of industry for "women workers to fulfill 'women's jobs' "—service industries and clerical positions.

This is known as the "pink collar" ghetto (Howe, 1977). Research confirms that sex segregation is an institutionalized practice of considerable magnitude within the occupational structure (cf. Blaxall and Reagan, 1976; Lloyd, 1975; Oppenheimer, 1973; Blau, 1976; Almquist, 1976; Kanter, 1977; Hartman, 1979). Although there are indications that the degree of sex segregation in employment eased in the 1970s, its magnitude is still so high that over 60 percent of the labor force would have to change jobs before sex segregation would disappear (Blau, in Reskin, 1984:118).

Labor analysts and feminist theoreticians have focused, recently, on the reasons for and impact of occupational sex segregation. Four major theoretical models have been developed: status attainment; dual market; Marxist; and Marxist-feminist. Each shall be briefly discussed (for a more complete analysis and critique of these models, see Acker, 1980 and Sokoloff, 1979).

The *status attainment* model, a descendant of the economist's human capital theory, looks at what individuals bring to the marketplace—that is, occupational aspirations, education, values, attitudes, and experiences—and assesses which variables affect the attainment of high status. It assumes that men and women compete in the *same* job market; the extent to which women lose is attributed to factors that make women less desirable as employees, that is, marital status, number of children, previous work experience, and so on. Once those factors are controlled, the model argues, lesser achievement by women in the marketplace can be attributed to discrimination. Thus, the model assumes a "rational" marketplace ("We would hire women, if they were qualified") and latently "blames the victim" ("If she really cared about her work, she would . . ."; "She obviously is happy to have any job"; "She's not very motivated"); it does not address capitalism or patriarchy as cultural ideologies with structural consequences—the differential placement of men and women (Sokoloff, 1980).

Unlike the status attainment model, the *dual market* model argues that there are two distinct labor markets: one for men—the primary or core market—and one for women—the secondary or periphery market. This model maintains that even if the "supply" characteristics of women were changed, unless the market structure were changed, women would see little relief (Acker, 1980). As the economy is now, women are slotted into the less desirable secondary labor market, which is characterized by lower wages, fewer fringe benefits, less chance of promotion, higher turnover rates, and more nonunion control. This dual market model views socialization as an accommodation to limited job opportunity, rather than as a cause of it. However, it assumes that the dual market can be altered without destroying capitalism (Acker, 1980).

The *Marxist* model also assumes a dual labor market; however, this model sees the dual market as a tool of monopolistic capitalism (big business) that is used to divide the working class (including men against women) and to inhibit its attempts to organize. Women become a ready pool of expandable and expendable workers, placed in seasonal slots and in newly developing sections of the economy (Sokoloff, 1980). This secondary pool of workers lends greater stability to the primary sector and greater profits to the capitalists. The inferior status of women in the labor market is thus understood as a special feature of the capitalistic oppression of the masses. Women's positions will be improved accordingly, the Marxists argue, when capitalism is overthrown.

Marxist feminism, unlike the three models thus far discussed, attempts to link women's domestic labor—nonsalaried work—to the class structure and job segregation. Women not only reproduce the next generation of laborers, but they also provide domestic services (cooking, cleaning, child rearing) to men in the work force. Both the capitalists and the male working-class members, therefore, benefit from this social arrangement, according to Hartman (1976)—a leading proponent of

Marxist-feminist thought. Occupational sex segregation, she argues, is the primary way in which the superiority of men over women is maintained in a capitalistic society. Women are slotted into low-paying jobs, which keep them dependent on men and marriage. Married women perform domestic chores for their husbands. Thus, men benefit from both higher wages and the domestic division of labor. This domestic division of labor, in turn, weakens women's positions in the labor market and increases the capitalists' profits because women are a class of easily exploitable laborers. The Marxist-feminist model, then, does not blame the victim, the dual market, or capitalism. Rather, it attempts to explain the interactions of patriarchy and capitalism in the perpetuation of sex stratification—the unique rights to distribute scarce resources and the unequal receipt of such resources.

Depending on the theoretical view one has regarding the social basis for sex segregation in the labor market, different remedial actions are proposed. People who hold the status attainment explanatory model have proposed that the problem rests in women: They must be changed so that they are more marketable commodities in a male-dominated labor force. Included in this approach are training seminars where women can learn aggressive male tactics of competition for the business world, a concern with the "packaging" of female employees as in "dress for success" manuals and courses, and efforts at directing young girls into coursework and activities that will help them develop skills that are valued more highly in the labor market. This type of redirection of workers has yet to demonstrate its effectiveness in altering the sex composition of the labor market, though, possibly because it does not address the devaluation of the kinds of work that have been traditionally done by women.

A second approach is consistent with the dual market model, and it involves efforts at reapportioning the supply of workers into each labor market. The idea is that once enough women enter the core labor market, the situation in the periphery market will improve (due to the elimination of the oversupply of workers for these jobs) and more men will seek employment there, thus eliminating severe occupational segregation by sex with its resultant consequences for women. Some programs have made limited inroads into this sort of occupational movement by training women in some of the skilled blue-collar trades that are represented in the core market.

A new approach to dealing with the economic inequality that arises from sex segregation is to accept, for the time being, the fact of sex segregation, but then to reevaluate the pay scale for the female sex-typed jobs. What proponents of this remediation are proposing is that work be looked at in terms of *comparable worth* (cf. Steinberg, 1980). Does the work that is done by a secretary require as much skill and have as much value as that which is done by a maintenance worker? If so, the two salaries should be comparable (Remick, 1984:ix–x). Once economic rewards have become comparable, the proponents of this approach argue, sex segregation in occupations will tend to atrophy. This proposal, thus, also recognizes the dual market as a fact of economic life, but proposes alleviating its consequences in the short term, and its very existence, in the long run, through comparable worth salaries. Support for this type of pay equity is growing, and there are networks of activists who are lobbying at national, state, and local levels. At this time, the city of San Jose, California, and the state of Washington have enacted comparable worth legislation. Opponents argue, among other things, that the cost of this remediation would be staggering (Hutner, 1986:208).

HIERARCHICAL NETWORKS

With the exception of pure entrepreneurial enterprise, work in modern industrial countries is carried on in organizations. These organizations are internally hierarchically structured. Whether business, army, university, hospital, factory, or road crew, the practical way of knowing who is where is to look at order giving and order taking (Collins, 1975:62; Richardson [Walum], 1975). The higher a person's position in an organization, the more orders that are given and the fewer orders that are received. Giving orders has profound effects on both the order giver and the order taker. The behavior, deportment, and litany of the order giver reflect his or her position of power and prestige. And the order taker "accepts one thing . . . to put up with standing before someone who is giving orders and with deferring to him at least for the moment" (Collins, 1975:63).

Receiving deference enhances a person's ability to use power successfully, but to receive deference a person must be perceived of as worthy. According to Goffman (1967), receiving deference is primarily a function of a person's bearing, demeanor, and deportment—carrying oneself as a person who expects to be obeyed. It is through that presentation of self that others are convinced that authority rests within that person.

Further, where one fits in the organizational hierarchy determines to a great extent the amount and diversity of one's personal contacts. The more persons one knows, the more alliances and exchanges in which one can engage. People can be asked to deliver support based on previous negotiations. The fewer personal contacts, the fewer the potential exchanges and the less the power. The structure of work when it is viewed as a hierarchy of power-relations helps explain why and how women are excluded from management (order-giving) positions throughout the occupational hierarchy. Dominance is a trait associated with males: neither men nor women want to take orders from a woman. Women, consequently, are more likely to be professors than deans, lawyers than judges, doctors than chiefs, and line workers than foremen.

Understanding the power structure is the key to survival and success in any organization (Kanter, 1977). In large bureaucracies, understanding the "politics" at work is a way of surviving by making the "large, incomprehensible, and unmanageable" organization smaller, more human and familiar; it is also a way of succeeding by commanding if not a "lion's share of scarce resources, at least some share, a sphere of autonomy and a right to call on some resources" (Kanter, 1977:165). Those persons who appear to have entré to the "inner circle," who "look like" they will command a share of the organization's resources, and who "look like" they will distribute those resources to their subordinates are considered "effective leaders" (Kanter, 1977:169). Since males have greater access to power *because* they are men, they are preferred as bosses by both men and women; that is, the preference for a male boss is a preference for a *powerful* boss (Kanter, 1979: 169). Women, because they are women, are viewed as powerless and to be avoided.

Successful domination also depends on carrying off one's authority through verbal and nonverbal communications. As we have already seen (Chapter 2), women are taught to communicate submissiveness. Few women have learned to style themselves as persons not to be questioned. This probably is especially true for order giving to men. And even those women who have learned to act authoritatively still have a flaw—their sex—that continually affects the reactions of others to them (cf. Macke and Richardson, 1980). Put another way, others respond to their lower status (female) rather than to their higher status (manager). In addition, by being removed from communication networks, women become increasingly submissive, subservient, and alienated from the goals of the company. Whatever commitment they may have had to career success is undermined by these structural features of work.

Several concrete examples will illustrate how these features are manifested in work situations. Michael Korda's *Male Chauvinism: How It Works* is particularly informative. He reports, for example, the reaction of a 50ish man to a 30ish woman— both famous lawyers. "When the man came in he smiled, turned to me [Korda] and said, 'Listen, you should have told me she was a great looking chick. . . .'" (1973:47). Rather than recognizing her professional status, he responded to her sex status. Imagine for a moment what would become of the male lawyer's bearing if the woman had said, "Hey, why didn't you tell me he was so well hung?" (Korda, 1973:47).

Publishing houses are notorious for their in-house power relations; for example, Time-Life was charged with 75 sex discrimination complaints. One of the items focused on the practice of the magazines of hiring college-educated women as researchers (nonwriting jobs) at 40 to 60 percent of the salaries that were paid to equivalently educated men who were hired as writers. Employed in nonwriting positions, they were ordered by the writers to perform such nonprofessional tasks as preparing coffee and making plane reservations (Korda, 1973). As the percentage of women increases in publishing, public relations, and in the advertising and communications industry, what is arising is another women's ghetto, recently referred to as "the velvet ghetto" (Cline, 1986).

Women are treated in terms of their sex status within the organization of work and are, thereby, denied the authority to which their positions might entitle them; but, in addition, they are excluded from the network of communications and, therefore, access to the power base within the organization. The informal processes by which this occurs will concern us later, but we need to note here two kinds of formalized processes. The first formal process is the propensity of organizations to use architectural barriers to split males and females (Richardson [Walum], 1975). Factories may separate male and female assembly lines. Korda reports corporate offices where female executives are placed in one corridor, male executives in another. Once the women are placed together in corporate purdah, each individual woman becomes invisible and can be treated as a member of the group *women* (Korda, 1973:129–130). Soon, their status as executives can be ignored, and their functions within the organization can be limited and managed (Korda, 1973:129–130).

The second major formal process is to encourage women to specialize in some small area of the corporate or research enterprise. With expertise in a minor area, their network communication lacks diversity. I would hypothesize further that the specialty probably is one that is neither highly valued nor likely to lead to control over others in the organization.

Similarly, the typical organizational structure has direct consequences for the careers of men. Many men—due to ethnic or social-class backgrounds—are not seen as having management potential by their supervisors. But many men who are not high in the hierarchy, nevertheless, carry around images of masculinity that require occupational success. The full impact of this structure on men will concern us shortly. However, we should note that those men who do succeed tend to perpetuate the same organizational structure through which they advanced. They do that through the recruitment and socialization of new members.

SPONSOR-PROTÉGÉ SYSTEM

The saying "It is not what you know, but whom you know" finds some credibility in the second major feature of the social organization of work: the sponsor-protégé (master-apprentice) system. "Entry to the upper echelons of many professions is commonly gained through the protégé system" (Epstein, 1970:55), as is entry to top administrative posts, skilled trades, and so on. For most elite professions and skilled trades, the sponsorship system is formalized; in others, such as in the corporate world, it is more informal, with the success of the sponsor determining the career of the junior.

The system is used to select candidates who are suitable for the skills of the trade. For many jobs, such as corporate law and neurosurgery, the necessary skills can be learned only on the job. Only by being accepted into the field can one learn the trade secrets (Becker and Strauss, 1956). Entering the field, however, requires convincing the gatekeepers that one is already similar to, or is able to learn to be like, those already in the occupation. The more prestigious the speciality, the heftier the security guards, for greater care must be exercised in protecting its secrets.

Further, because sponsors probably already have greater authority and greater commitment to the organization's goals, protégés are those who will ensure a continuity of leadership. The probability of such continuity is greater if the apprentice fits in well with the occupational peer group. Consequently, both internal desire for corporate immortality and external pressure from colleagues lead masters to recruit apprentices whose statuses are consistent with those of the occupation's membership.

The sponsorship system, therefore, functions within organizations to maximize in-group solidarity by minimizing the amount of dissonance and intragroup conflict. In addition, it functions to maintain the practices of the organization (profession, trade, etc.) by offering positions to those who are most likely to concur with those practices. In effect, the smooth transition of leadership ensures both the longevity of the sponsor's memory (research, power, etc.), and the maintenance of the organization's practices. Both the personal needs of retiring elites and the needs of the organization to maintain itself *as is* are favored through the practice of sponsorship. Consequently, there is a considerable amount of personal and communal interest regarding new recruits.

To the extent that the master-apprentice system functions to maintain an organization's practices, so does it function to limit women's economic rewards. Women are less likely than men to be acceptable as protégés due to their sex status. The status, female, is seen to be inconsistent with the status of neurosurgeon, bricklayer, and Provost. In the skilled-craft unions, women were explicitly barred. As late as 1942, seven of the American Federation of Labor unions officially excluded women, although women were employed in the industries that were covered by these unions. The most extreme example was in the constitution of the International Moulder's Union, which stated that "any member, active or honorary, who devoted his time in whole or in part to the instruction of female help in the foundry or in any branch of the trade shall be expelled from the union" (Henry, 1923:100, quoted in Falk, 1975:256). In effect, wherever occupations are sex typed as male, women are seen as not belonging and, therefore, as ineligible recruits.

Without building long-term and stable alliances with peers—subordinates and superordinates—one's chances of success in an organization are reduced. One way alliances are built is through the sponsor-protégé system (Kanter, 1977:181–182). A "good" sponsor fights for and promotes the protégé; enables the protégé to bypass formal procedures, signaling to peers and subordinates that the protégé is "well-connected"; allows the sponsor's resources to "halo" the protégé (Kanter, 1977:181–182); and teaches the protégé the workings of the informal system (Henning and Jardin, 1976). Because women are less likely to have access to other avenues of knowledge and power, most researchers (cf. Cook, 1980; Kanter, 1977; Henning and Jardin, 1976) agree that having a sponsor is especially important for a woman; at the same time, however, women are less likely to be sponsored than men are.

Beliefs about women affect any given woman's chances of being sponsored. One of these beliefs has to do with succession—handing over the reins (tools, methods, power, etc.) to one's chosen follower. In her study of professions, Epstein, for example, noted that, although a professional may even prefer a female assistant to a male, "he cannot identify her (as he might a male assistant) as someone who will eventually be his successor" (1970:170). In the trade labor unions, rigid apprentice rules have been established, requiring sponsorship by craft members and, in some cases, requiring that the apprentice be a son or nephew of the union member.

The belief that women will not be good successors rests on assumptions about their psychological and biological natures; for example, women's commitment to the company is questioned because employers believe her family will come first. Korda reports the threat of dependence on a good secretary is great enough ("What if she leaves me, what will I do?"), but it is clearly trivial compared to the threat of a groomed junior executive on maternity leave.

Further difficulties exist in the potential consequences that close relations between a male sponsor and a female apprentice might have on their personal lives; for example, the wife of a sponsor might be suspicious of the relationship; similarly, the pressures on the female worker, if a mother, are great in terms of role strains and familial obligations.

Finally, even when a woman is able to enter a career through sponsorship, she is less likely to be promoted along a career path. This is so primarily because it is assumed that women are not dependent, psychologically or financially, upon their careers. Consequently, male sponsors feel less responsibility toward them. This is quite common in academia; for example, one academic woman reported asking her dean why two men whose vitas were less strong than hers were promoted and she was held back. His response was, "You have a house and a husband here. You're not in a hurry." Three years later, when she was divorced, the same dean commented, "Now, you're promotable." The classic case, however, involves the academic history of Ruth Benedict, the famous anthropologist. Frank Boas, who was her mentor at the Department of Anthropology at Columbia, recognized the value of her research but, nevertheless, regarded her as Mrs. Stanley Benedict. He considered her as "someone whose talents he must find work and a little money for, someone on whom he could not make extreme demands and for whom he need not be responsible." Only when she separated from her husband was she given the position of assistant professor (Bernard, 1964:105–106).

Men, more than women, are expected to fulfill the American dream of occupational success. However, their background can limit their mobility as much as sex stereotyping can limit women's; for example, one of the most striking and consistent findings in stratification literature is the extent to which high-prestige occupations are passed on from father to son. The son of a bricklayer who wishes to be a surgeon has little chance for such upward mobility; the son of the factory hand who wishes to be a typesetter similarly has little chance for such upward advancement. Sponsors aid persons with whom they feel an identity and a closeness. Ethnicity, race, and family background all effect the possibility of being sponsored.

Women are viewed as inappropriate for sponsoring for certain positions, as are certain men. To understand more completely why this is, we need to look in more depth at the culture of occupations—at the practices that create a "consciousness of kind." To do so, we turn to the question of socioemotional bonding as an important element in the social organization of work.

SOCIOEMOTIONAL BONDING

Because work is a network of interpersonal relationships, we would be highly remiss to view those relationships as only task-related interactions. Rather, where there are people, there are socioemotional bonds. Work is a social activity wherein persons who are similar to each other come to spend increasingly more time together—at work and at leisure; they develop affective bonds—that is, the organization of work is built upon socioemotional relationships between workers, and these work-originated relationships often develop into after-hours friendships. In turn, these provide further bases for work-related alliances. The relevance of the socioemotional character of work, therefore, concerns both the internal dynamics of the organization and the external life of the workers. The theoretical dichotomy of work and pleasure does not reflect the actual social life of persons. Work life and extrawork life are intricately related.

The kinds of socioemotional bonding that occur in work settings are to a great extent determined by those who are in positions of dominance. Persons with power not only establish the instrumentalities of work, but they also determine what kinds of emotional rituals and social climate will prevail. Hierarchies within organizations are visible in terms of those who create emotional ritual, those who follow, and those who are excluded (Collins, 1975:61).

Parallel to the role of ritual in religious institutions, the organization of work depends upon ritual exchanges that create a sense of emotional solidarity in the community of believers (organizationally committed persons). By partaking in the rituals through personal proximity, shared focus on an object, and coordination of activities, one's identity as a participant in the community is confirmed (Collins, 1975:58). The creation of the emotional solidarity that is based on the participation in the ritual activities of the organization provides the worker with a sense of belonging, just as exclusion confirms one's sense of alienation.

In addition to these consequences for individual workers, control of the production of emotional solidarity has the consequence of perpetrating the organizational power of the order givers, because it provides a very important vehicle for inculcating the work's culture. Through socioemotional bonding, alliances are formed and intragroup struggles are defined as relevant or irrelevant. By establishing preferred emotional rituals, an ideal way of being is offered to others to emulate. If they lack the necessary resources to imitate the ideal, due to personal or positional traits, their exclusion from the network becomes a reality, and, most importantly, their exclusion is perceived as *legitimate* by both themselves and the order givers.

In the professions, this bonding is referred to as the "colleague system"; in the trades, as the "buddy system"; and in business, as the "old boy" system. To succeed, one must be able to participate in the socioemotional rituals both within and outside the work setting—the greater the participation, the greater the commitment and potential for exchanges and alliances; the greater the exclusion from the rituals, the greater the alienation, the less the potential for alliances, and the less the chance for upward mobility.

The alliance networks are male preserves, and a major obstacle to mixed-sex alliances is that men do not trust women (Lorber, 1979). Because men do not trust women, they exclude them from informal work groups where the "true requirements" of the job are shared (Lorber, 1979:373). Exclusion from such insider knowledge may result in a loss of promotion in the professions, but in many blue-collar jobs, it also may result in injury, as is demonstrated by the following incident that was reported by a female steelworker whose (male) coworkers highly resisted her presence in the plant.

> While I was working on the lids (coke ovens) I was told to move 100 lb. lead boxes. I wanted to prove that I could do it. That all women could do it. After the third lift, I ripped open my intestines and had to be rushed to the hospital. It took surgery and a three-month recovery period. What I didn't know at the time was

that no man would have lifted that much weight. They would have asked for a helper or simply refused (Fonow, 1977:142).

Fasteau (1975) speculates that many men in low-prestige blue-collar occupations have traditionally derived a sense of satisfaction from knowing that they were doing a "man-sized" job. "Where work is less rewarding, the aura of masculinity created by keeping women out is even more important: If holding a job as a steelworker proves nothing else, it at least proves that you are a man" (1975:51).

This structural feature of socioemotional bonding in the world of work has other consequences on the participation of women in occupations that are sex-typed male. It has consequences for two primary and related reasons. First, most socioemotional bonding is built upon the status, male, and its associated attributes, life-styles, and preferred activities. The shared status, male, provides a set of rituals that are culturally defined as masculine—swearing, backslapping, handshaking, girl watching, and so on. The rituals are used to transform the occupational class into a male status group. The occupation itself becomes associated with its masculine rituals; that is, these particular socioemotional rituals, although in fact irrelevant to job performance, are seen as part of the job requirements. Second, participation in off-hours socializing is often requisite to career advancement. Some of these nonwork settings are such masculine preserves as the steam room, the golf course, the men's club, the local tavern.

These two factors—masculine rituals within male occupations and the dependence upon the buddy system outside the job—create not only structural barriers to women's advancement but also psychological barriers. If success requires emulation of the male model with its attendant ulcers, heart attacks, power tripping, workaholic mentality, women must ask themselves. "Is it worth it? Are the extra hours that are spent socializing with my colleagues worth the time I lose with my husband/lover/children?" And one must ask about the man who has his ulcers and heart attacks and still has not succeeded. Do the structural arrangements of work bring more satisfaction to him, or even to those who do succeed, than dissatisfaction?

Recently, women have been responding to these realities of male-dominated workplaces by establishing not an "old girls' network" but a "new women's network"—a "feminist underground." Professional and high ranking women are meeting informally, establishing support networks, aiding each other's careers—and the careers of their protégés. Such networks are being built locally and nationally to counter the "old buddy system."

Even if networking is extremely successful, the fact remains that male occupations have been steeped in male ritual for decades; for example, the male social bonding of union members has a long history. In the early 1800s, the first trade unions were formed as an outgrowth of men's social clubs. They met in local saloons and were adamantly male. With the advent of the twentieth-century labor movement, the earlier traditions were perpetuated and persist into the present (Falk, 1975:225). However, we should not ignore the consequences that our cultural beliefs about sexuality may have for male bonding in occupations. Because the culture teaches that women are (should be) either sex objects or virgin mothers and that men should be sexually potent, we might wonder whether these beliefs contribute to the development of masculine rituals within male occupations, and if so, how.

On the face of it, the sexual images of women and of men, which men are socialized to hold, are potentially anxiety producing. If a woman is a sex object and a male is to perform, involvement with her exposes him to the potential humiliation of sexual failure. If she is a mother-virgin figure, then she holds the power to withdraw love and nurturance. If any particular woman represents all women, as Korda argues, then men need a place where they can escape from their own fears—a male heaven. Male occupations, then, provide the safe harbor for which men are looking. To ensure the safety of the port, masculine rituals are emphasized. Construction workers who whistle at passing women, male junior executives who discuss sex at the water fountain, and professors who compare notes on coeds in effect are performing for each other without the concrete threat of failure.

The extent to which these speculations are true must await research. However, we should not discount the importance of sexuality in the dynamics of work organizations. Sex in the office (or on the campus) is not new. The pattern of male bosses (professors) having temporary sexual liaisons with female employees (students), for example, is apparently quite common (but see, Mackinnon, 1979; Farley, 1978; Fonow, 1977). But the work arrangements that are now contemplated (and in some work settings accomplished) of males and females as colleagues present still another set of issues. As is well known from psychological research, the greater the interaction between equals, the more they like each other. Because our society increasingly condones sexual activity between persons who like each other, the probability of such sexual exchanges will increase (Richardson, 1986). ''When sexual relations are a possibility, the comfortable intimacy of colleague relations is disrupted by threat of seduction, pursuits, rivalries, jealousies, and the private intimacy of the couple'' (Lorber, 1979:376).

The dynamics of socioemotional bonding are structurally and sociopsychologically complex, then, and one of the outcomes is to make it difficult for women to gain full acceptance in male-sex-typed occupations. However, it also has the consequence of permitting men to view any woman in their work sphere in terms of their sex status, female. One of the outcomes of this is the widespread occurrence of sexual harassment at work.

Sexual harassment exists when a physical or verbal sexual overture is made (the victim's sex status is made salient over other statuses) that is not desired by the victim, and that is experienced implicitly or explicitly as a threat to a woman's job or her work performance (Martin, 1984:55). Quid pro quo harassment is a coercive action whereby a woman is forced to comply sexually or else lose some occupational benefit (Mackinnon, 1979). A cosmetologist, for example, may be coerced into having a sexual relationship with the beauty shop's owner as the basis for her continued employment. The power differences are clear, and the consequences are obvious.

Less immediately obvious and much more prevalent, though, than direct coercion, are innuendos, comments, pinches, and pats that are made routinely in the work environment, making sex salient and the work environment uncomfortable for women. A male supervisor, for example, may comment ''in jest'' that no woman has advanced who hasn't worked ''under him.'' Women who hear this feel intimidated; and even such everyday comments about how a woman looks (''What great legs you have!'' ''What's a good-looking girl like you doing trying to compete with a man?''), can constitute harassment because they make sex salient. Although coercion to engage in sex is not present, discomfort and intimidation are.

Studies have established that sexual harassment is not rare: In fact, just the opposite is true. Of the recent studies on the incidence of sexual harassment that were reported in Martin (1984), most documented that from 30 to 50 percent of the female employees who were surveyed had directly experienced some form of sexual harassment at work, with much higher numbers reporting knowledge of such behaviors (1984:56, 57). The options for dealing with such harassment are limited and for the most part not encouraging. Women may adopt an informal approach— possibly by asking the abuser to stop or by ignoring the behavior; they may leave their job or seek a transfer; they may take legal action against the abuser; or they may acquiesce. None of these strategies has produced especially good results in getting the abuse to stop, probably because of the low power and prestige of women workers generally. Martin reports one study that found that among those women who took formal action, over 40 percent had a negative outcome, where the action either had no effect or where it actually seemed to make things worse. The same study documented a link between high job turnover rates and absenteeism rates among female employees and sexual harassment (1984:63).

In summary, then, we have seen how the structural features of the workplace—its sex segregation and hierarchial arrangement, as well as the organization of relationships between workers and employers in the sponsor-protégé system, and socioemotional bonding, including its derivative, sexual harassment—reinforce gender inequity in the social organization of work. Success at work is difficult for women to achieve because of this special organization of work.

Moreover, the social organization of work has degrading effects on most men. Men have been socialized to expect to work outside the home, to find fulfillment in their jobs, to achieve occupationally, and to find their basic sense of identity in their employment. In addition, they are expected to be autonomous, independent, and capable of decision making. In the eyes of the society and most men, themselves, a man's worth is measured by his occupational success.

WORK LIVES OF MEN

The way in which work is socially organized makes it difficult for men to live up to the expectations that they have been taught to have for themselves. Most work takes place in bureaucracies and factories. With roughly only 20 percent of the working population of the United States self-employed, most men are in the positions of order takers at work.

For the 50 percent who are blue-collar workers, alienation from work is becoming increasingly severe, in that blue-collar work is in the process ''of losing its once distinct and always precious ability to affirm manhood'' (Shostak, 1976: 100). Craft jobs still retain a sense of control, responsibility, and initiative; but, for the vast majority of blue-collar workers, work consists of simple assembly line tasks, supervised as though the workers were children. And, indeed, in some plants the subdivision of labor has placed young boys and women on the same lines with the older men, depriving them of even the pretense that their work is "man's work." The mechanization of work further tends to blur the distinctions between one's own work and that of the machine. "Blue-collarites, in short, may find the meaning of work as often as not a negation rather than an affirmation of a basic sense of worthiness. . . ." (Shostak, 1976:101). As the meaninglessness of the work increases, commitment to it seems to grow less (Shostak, 1976). Consequently, most men are alienated from the work that is supposed to provide them with a sense of self-identity.

Three dimensions of the alienation of the male worker are particularly salient. First, he is *powerless* because he has little or no control over the results of his labor and because he is subject to the demands of "the machine or the front office brass" (Brenton, 1976:93). Second, he may experience a sense of *meaninglessness* "because all he knows are his specialized little tasks, which he can't relate to the various other departments, to the organization as a whole" (Brenton, 1976:93). He is simply a cog in the bureaucratic or factory machinery, replaceable by another cog when broken or worn-out. Third, he may experience *isolation*, spawned from the understandable difficulty of identifying with the firm or its goals (Brenton, 1976:93).

Few men can find the fulfillment or self-esteem that they have been socialized to expect to gain through their occupations. Few have the autonomy to make decisions. Most jobs do not contribute to a sense of autonomy, require one's best efforts, or provide a sense of accomplishment for one's unique service. Further, few jobs can be viewed as worthwhile ways to spend one's life. "Thus for the great ego investment a man makes in his job, the great emphasis he places on it in terms of his masculinity, the work he does, generally speaking, will not reward him commensurately" (Brenton, 1976:94).

Because work itself is unlikely to provide intrinsic rewards for most men, the only rewards possible are power, prestige, wealth. Men, therefore, frequently measure manhood by a position in the organizational hierarchy, by the respect a job commands in the community, by the size of the paycheck, and by family life-style; that is, work is viewed as a means to gain extrinsic rewards, which confirm for men their masculinity. Unfortunately, a man's wife and children also tend to view him in this way. Just as he is useful to his firm, he is useful to his family. "Utility," however, does not lead to deep and intimate relationships, as we will discuss in Chapter 12.

Occupations in all societies are differentially evaluated. Some have higher prestige than others. In a society such as ours, where competition is a virtue and "the best man wins," a man's prestige is a function of the particular career that he pursues. With over 50 percent of the working male population in blue-collar industries, prestige is automatically denied. Because a hierarchical prestige system, by definition, limits the number of valued positions, the cards are stacked to produce a mass of "losers." Manual laborers are at the bottom of the hierarchy (Shostak, 1976:98). "Blue-collarites begin and end the work day with the knowledge that their employ could hardly have less status [prestige]" (Shostak, 1976:98). Even blue-collarites who enjoy their work hold back on their positive estimation of themselves because their work is not middle-class (Brenton, 1967:95).

Nor can blue-collar workers expect upward mobility: *downward* mobility is more frequently the case. As they reach age 40, "most blue-collar workers are frozen at the top salary they will ever reach. After this age they face job loss [due to injury or illness] and job demotion due to an inability to perform adequately with younger men" [Stoll, 1974:147]. Although they have ambiguous feelings about white-collar work, "in the last analysis, many would rather have their sons follow the white-collarite into a technical, professional, administrative or even clerical post than follow the 'old man' into the plant" (Shostak, 1976:104).

Even for those men who have ostensibly made it—those who have achieved a modicum of prestige—the problem is not settled, for prestige is a particularly unstable commodity in the work world. "Once achieved, it has to be maintained, leaving the man who banks on it at the mercy of all kinds of competitive pressure and changing circumstances" (Brenton, 1976:95). Part of the process of maintaining it is to hold others back; another part is to enhance one's own position. This means successful men cannot rest on their laurels. Continuation of the infighting, jockeying for positions, expending of energy to enhance one's position, and picking off those who might rise above one, become daily preoccupations. As the novel *Something Happened*, by Joseph Heller (1974), makes clear, fear is a compelling emotion in high-prestige persons in bureaucratic organizations, as they struggle to enhance their own position and power.

Although moving women into positions that are now held by men might help many women financially, it by itself will not alter the deleterious effects of the social organization of work. Why is work structured in such a way as to exclude women and dehumanize men? Who benefits? In whose interest is it to perpetuate this particular structure of work? We now turn to some answers to these questions.

WHO BENEFITS?

The social organization of work takes shape in the context of the American culture. It is not isolated from the values of that culture or its other institutions—particularly, the family. Therefore, it is not surprising that such values as achievement, competition, individual success, and male superiority are represented as they are in organizational structures. The traditional structure of the family (male breadwinner, female housekeeper and supplementary breadwinner) meshes with the structure of work. (The full extent of this relationship of work and home is the concern of Chapter 12.) Evolving since the Industrial Revolution, the pattern of work organization has been consistent with the culture's values. But why has this pattern been perpetuated?

The corporate economy requires three primary classes of workers: dependable cogs, executive decision makers, and a temporary reserve labor force. The perpetuation of a class of persons who view themselves as required to work to support their families and/or to fulfill their role expectations, provides industry with its first two classes of workers; the perpetuation of a class of workers who view themselves as supplementary breadwinners provides industry with part of its third category of workers.

Men who have executive aspirations are willing to spend from 70 to 90 hours a week to advance their careers. Their advancement, however, is dependent on what profits they bring to the company. Their success may bring personal gratification, but for the company it brings greater financial dividends. The most substantial portion of these financial benefits does not go directly to the executive but to the owners of the corporation.

Most men, however, fulfill coglike positions in bureaucracies and factories. Increased financial gains depend upon the increased output that mechanization ensures the owners. The routine and monotonous labor of these men, while systematically destroying their sense of human dignity, systematically increases the wealth of the business elite.

The categorization of many women in the third pool of workers—the reserve labor force—provides considerable financial benefits to employers. The use of women as temporary workers—whether as full-time or part-time employees, whether in the canning factory at harvest time, or as salesclerks at Christmas, or in the university as visiting lecturers—is one of the most profitable arrangements available to employers in contemporary times.

Hiring women as temporary help is economically profitable for the institution. Not only do temporaries receive lower wages, they are also not entitled to fringe benefits—retirement, health plans, sick leave, vacation pay, and so on. Maintaining a skeleton staff of full-time workers and supplementing them seasonally with temporary help, according to economist Joan Jordan, has become a common industrial pattern (Jordan, 1969). Incidentally, the local unions have supported this industrial pattern. Temporary help are expected to pay union dues, but, if their positions are lost within 90 days, they are not considered union members and, therefore, are not entitled to support during their layoffs.

The profits from withholding fringe benefits, however, are slight compared to the extra profits that are derived from paying women lower salaries than men for the same work. In 1950, Hutchins estimated that 23 percent of the profits of manufacturing companies ($5.4 billion) was the result of paying women less money than men for similar work (1952:9). Because wage differentials for men and women have remained fairly constant since that research, we can estimate that a similar proportion of the profits is still based on differential wage scales. When we review the differential salaries of the male and female workers at each occupational category and subcategory (see Chapter 10), we can see that the personal cost of lower wages for women amounts to a considerable gain for institutions.

Further, occupational segregation serves to maintain lower wages for women and, most importantly, to prevent a restructuring of occupations; for example, the manufacturing industries tend to be of two kinds: the labor-intensive and the automated. The labor-intensive industries (e.g., textiles) have a greater need to control wages than do the automated ones (e.g., chemicals) because higher labor costs in the former industries reduce the profits and potentially destroy the ability of the industry to compete with foreign exports. As might be predicted, the less automated the industry, the greater the proportion of female workers, because they are paid less. This pattern of extra profits applies wherever females constitute the majority of the employees. The female-sex-typed professions of nursing and teaching are the lowest paid professions. Service workers, who are predominately women, barely earn subsistence incomes.

Institutional sexism is not only a problem for women, but is also intricately tied to the demands that are made upon men. Viewing women as supplementary breadwinners necessitates that men view their work as primary in their lives. In addition, it has a direct financial impact on men, because they are closely related by marriage and kinship to particular women. It would economically benefit individual men to have female family members whose economic contributions can lessen their own toil. Although a man profits by having a domestic laborer, his wife, and although he may profit psychologically by feeling superior to her, those gains underscore how brutalizing and dehumanizing work is for many men, and how its organization has consequences for the home lives of people.

By continuing to structure the occupational system so that women are not likely to control the distribution and exchange of scarce goods and services, and so that most men will not achieve those rights, the already powerful continue to remain so, and the lives of men and women *at home* are circumscribed and limited. We turn now to a more thorough examination of the linkages between home and work.

□ □ *12* □ □

The Linkages Between Home and Work

The self-contained worlds that we live in as single adults with or without children, as wives or husbands, as mothers or fathers, or as cohabitors, are not insulated from the institutional arrangements of our society. Rather, it is when we address ourselves to private lives that we can perhaps see most clearly how culture, socialization, and the institutions that socially control adults are integrally intermeshed.

The social institution of the family in its various forms is probably universal. "No society has ever existed without some kind of social arrangement that may be labeled kinship or familial" (Scanzoni and Scanzoni, 1976:4). Most sociologists would argue that the family is the major institution upon which the rest of the society depends; and there is every indication that "family patterns of some sort will continue to exist in all modern and developing societies" (Scanzoni and Scanzoni, 1976:4).

Marriage is not isolatable or separable from the other social institutions. At the structural level, the ideology, legal system, and opportunity structure that support and perpetuate the assignment of domestic responsibilities to women are some of the primary ways through which sex inequality is maintained.

In our society, the family form is becoming so varied that scholars are rethinking their ideas about the family (Thorne, 1982). The traditional notion of a family that is composed of an employed father and a homebody mother who takes care of the children now constitutes less than 10 percent of American families. Most prevalent is the dual-provider home, with a husband and wife who both work outside the home. Two other quickly growing family forms are the child-free home and the single-parent home; this is due primarily to marital dissolution (Mortimer and London, 1984). Approximately 20 percent of all children currently live with a single parent (Mortimer and London, 1984); and by age 18, nearly 60 percent of all children will have been in single-parent homes for a portion of their childhood (Glick, 1984).

Divorce has altered the family in other ways, too, because divorced people remarry. Twenty percent of all American homes include a previously divorced spouse; a third of these include two previously divorced spouses. As a result, approximately two-thirds of the children who grow up in America will have a step-sibling and/or a half-sibling; one-sixth will have both (Huber and Spitze, in press). Add to these new family forms, the high rate of cohabitation for heterosexual and gay and lesbian couples—many of whom have children living in the home—and there is no doubt that the family form has become increasingly differentiated and complex.

The linkages between home and work are many, complex, and variable depending on the family form and the particular demands of the occupation. To explore all these linkages is a major and consuming research agenda, as witnessed by the wealth of excellent literature that has appeared on this topic during the past decade (cf. Fox and Hesse-Biber, 1984; Voyandoff, 1984; Kahn-Hut, et al., 1982; England and Farkas, 1986; Gerson, 1985). In general, though, scholars recognize an interactive effect between home and work.

Because work provides money and social status for the family, it sets the standard of living; and, because without the work income the family is put under considerable strain, adjustments to work demands are made, even at the cost of the emotional well-being of the family members. In addition, work influences the attitudes, feelings, and behavior of family members. People do not live one life on the job and another one at home. One's employment has an impact on one's behavior at home; for example, a husband who is powerless at work may exert dominance over his wife and children; or an employed wife may exert more rights on the spending of the family income than does a wife who is not employed outside the home.

Family also affects work; for example, the next generation of workers is socialized through the family (Mortimer and London, 1984). In families where both the mother and father work outside the home, the children are being socialized toward greater gender equality. Teenagers who have mothers who are employed outside the home have more equalitarian attitudes than those whose mothers are solely homemakers (Hoffman, 1980). As families alter in structure, the conditions under which employees are willing to work changes, and this can influence the structure of work. An example of this change in work structure is the ''flex-time'' alternative in federal government, which permits parents to adjust their workday to their children's school day.

However, whatever the particular configurations between home and work, one general principle has remained throughout human history: Power and privilege go to those who have greater access to and control over the extradomestic distribution of scarce goods and services. The ideology of the culture and the structure of work are such that today greater access to and control over scarce goods still go to the male. This greater power has consequences for the distribution of power within the home. Let us look at how this works in a marital relationship.

The marital relationship is important to look at because 93 percent of the population does get married at some point—even if much of those lives are spent as singles. (Nonmarital relationships will be discussed at length in Chapter 13.) We will want to look at how the greater power and privilege that accrue to males in the workplace have consequences for the relationships between husbands and wives. Do greater rights to extradomestic goods and services contribute to power imbalances within the home?

MARRIAGE

Power, or the probability that one's will will be done, is greater if one controls the distribution of scarce goods and services. Historically, in the United States, when women entered into marriage, they legally surrendered many rights, such as the right to inherit property, to make a will, to control their property or salaries. If children were born, the husband was granted full authority over their education, religious upbringing, and their guardianship. In consonance with the religious belief system, a man was deemed master of his home and property, which included his wife, children, and slaves.

More recently, the laws and social customs that surround the institution of marriage have altered, providing women greater access to their inheritances, wages, children, and husbands. Sex inequality, however, as should be clear from the first section of this book, is partially sustained through the socialization process. Women are still expected to find their *greatest* fulfillment within the roles of housewife and mother. The personality traits that are attributed to them are those that are consistent with servicing roles within the home. Men, on the other hand, are expected to find their identities in the occupational sphere; the skills they are expected to master are those that are compatible with occupational success. Consequently, the two partners are differentially socialized toward marriage as an institution.

In effect, "the principle of least interest" is operable here. In all human exchanges, economic or romantic, the person who has the least interest in the continuation of the relationship has the greater power, because he or she can more easily withdraw from or terminate the exchange. Males are socialized to have "least interest" in marriage. Working-class women especially feel that getting and staying married is an economic necessity rather than an option (Ferree, 1975). Consequently, at the social-psychological level, women are socialized to be less powerful in marriage than men: the greater their perceived need for marriage, the greater their psychological powerlessness. Adult control mechanisms such as religion, law, and the sciences reinforce this early socialization. Whether by religious creed, legal doctrine, or scientific findings, the man is the head of the house.

These major processes of socialization and adult social control, then, have direct impact on the social-psychological power relationships within a marriage. In addition to these, the structure of the political and economic system has a direct impact. We have already seen how barriers to women's occupational success are erected and maintained, and the consequences of those barriers: the higher the position, the fewer the women. Now we need to turn the question around: Does a man's greater occupational success lead to greater power within his marriage? The answer appears to be "yes."

A man's place in the stratification system does have consequences for the balance of power *within* the marriage; in general, the higher the occupational status of the husband, the greater his marital power; the greater the discrepancy between the husband's and wife's income, the greater his power; and the higher the husband's overall social status (based on occupation, income, education, and ethnic background), the greater his marital power (Gillespie, 1971).

Although these are general conclusions, there are interesting differences between the social classes. White-collar husbands have more power in their marriages than blue-collar husbands. This is not surprising, given the society's preference for professional rather than manual achievements. Nor is it surprising that there is a direct association between income and amount of power.

In middle-class families where the husband is the sole provider, women and children are expected to make no demands that might interfere with the husband's work. "He takes preference as a *professional*, not as a family head or as a male; nevertheless, the precedence is his" (Goode, 1963:21). In effect, the doctrine of equality has little impact on the distribution of marital power (Goode, 1963:21). The wife provides domestic labor and support for his career—including doing clerical tasks, entertaining business associates, and being an emotional sounding board for him. Papanek (1973) referred to this pattern as the "two-person career"; although only the husband is employed, the wife is a necessary adjunct to his career, a career she becomes invested in due to the expected soaring income (Grieff and Munter, 1980).

In blue-collar families where only the husband is employed outside the home, traditional sex role norms are strong, and there is a barrier between a husband's activities and a wife's activities, both inside and outside the home. One of the primary ones is the exclusion of the wife from his work world (Mortimer and London, 1984). Unlike the absorption of the wife of a professional man into his career, the blue-collar wife may not even know how to reach her husband, and she probably cannot describe his work because *he* has decided that home and work are to be separated: home, being the woman's sphere, and work, being the man's. Although he may have less overall power in his marriage because his occupational status is a devalued one, nevertheless, he has the power to enforce the traditional sex role division of labor, a division that we shall soon see disempowers the wife even more.

Moreover, even though the blue-collar husband may claim that work and home are separate, his feelings about his work have consequences for his family (Farrell and Rosenberg, 1981). His alienation and depletion at work cause him to seek "personal space" at home, thereby distancing himself from his wife and children (Piotrkowski, 1978). In addition, the nature of his work—being supervised and/or doing dull, repetitive tasks—affects how he disciplines his children. Children are expected to conform and be obedient—the same behaviors that are necessary at work. Because of frustration that is born of lack of work autonomy, he is more likely to physically punish his errant children (Mortimer and London, 1984). What is important here is that he is given the right to determine these family dynamics, even if they are costly to his wife and children.

Given that a husband's power in a marriage is related to his extradomestic power, it is reasonable to ask whether a wife can increase her marital power by increasing her extradomestic power. Both anthropological (Friedl, 1975) and sociological evidence indicate that she can. Reviewing the research that concerns the effect of wives' labor force, educational, and organizational experiences, Gillespie concludes that these have an impact on the distribution of marital power (1971:452). Wives working outside the home, regardless of class, have more power than those who do not; the longer their labor force participation, the greater their power.

Dual-provider families are becoming the most prevalent family form. Forty-nine percent of all married women are in the labor force, as are 52 percent of the mothers of children under 18; and the fastest rate of growth of maternal employment is for women with preschool children (Mortimer and London, 1984). One-fourth of all total family income is based on the wife's economic contribution.

Yet, in only 5 percent of the homes are household tasks equitably shared (*Christian Science Monitor*, 1980). Seventy-five percent of women who are employed outside the home still do the majority of housework (Ross, 1986). In one study, the Berks and Berheide found that women with full-time jobs outside the home still devoted almost a quarter of each day to housework, and that in most families women still do 80 to 90 percent of the housework (*Christian Science Monitor*, 1980). It is not the husbands who pick up the slack; it is the children. Husbands of employed women spend only an average of 15 minutes more a *week* on household chores than husbands of homemakers (Mortimer and London, 1984). Study after study up to the present report the same general finding: There has been little change in the division of domestic labor. Women have two jobs—home and work. The male retains his prerogative to resist household labor (Goode, 1982), and retains his power to bargain for household tasks (Hiller and Philliber, 1986).

One of the primary reasons that the male is able to have power over the domestic division of labor is that his work is still considered the primary one; her work, the supplementary one. Women are expected to disrupt their work for the needs of the family, whereas men are allowed to disrupt their families because of work demands (Pleck, 1977).

In the early stages of the marriage, the wife is frequently working and the power is not as unequally balanced as it is when children arrive. During the time following the birth of the first child through the preschool years, the husband's power is the greatest. Because it is common for a woman to stop working during these years, she tends to become highly dependent economically, socially, and emotionally upon her husband. His world is expanding while hers contracts. Despite the fact that women are contributing full-time work in the home during the early years of their children's lives (Chase Manhattan Bank estimates 99.6 hours per week), this work is so little valued socially that in reality her power within the family diminishes to meet the social worth that is attributed to her role. Indeed, the greatest equality is registered in the older, retired couple—a situation where the husband takes on more of the domestic labor. However, even here, he tends to take on such jobs as vacuuming and grocery shopping, not planning or tidying.

Domestic labor does not bring one power and prestige in the stratification system; it also lessens one's power within the home. If a wife is to gain more power in a marriage, she must have access to external resources (Ross, 1976). Paid labor force participation, a superior education, and a greater organizational involvement than her husband will increase her power position. "Equality of resources leaves the power in the hands of the husbands" (Gillespie, 1971:457).

Despite the intentions of husbands—who may indeed want equal partner-ships—equalitarian marriages will remain mythic ideals until women have had for a long time the same access to the control of the distribution of valued goods as men enjoy, and, therewith, men are equally engaged in the domestic labor. Until then, the likelihood of any couple achieving an equalitarian bond remains slim. No matter the goodwill or intentions of the partners, the institutional arrangements reach down into the living rooms of couples and affect the context of their intimate lives.

Although it is unquestionably true that males, regardless of their sex role attitudes, do profit in their marriages by dint of their social status, occupation, and income, it would be inaccurate to discount the costs to them. One of the costs is the continued expectation that they achieve occupationally—whether they want to or not. A loss of job, demotion, retirement, or employment in a less socially valued occupation, affects the self-esteem and longevity of the male. If his position as "head of house" is dependent on his external statuses, then loss of one often means that he loses on all fronts—home and work. In turn, these family dynamics have some negative consequences for men's work.

Although a wife is contributing to the support of the home, her contributions have not substantially lessened the economic burden that is felt by the husband, because the wife's work tends to be viewed as secondary. Despite the actual needs of the family for her economic contribution, both the husband and wife are still likely to discount her contribution; because they do, it has real consequences for the man, who continues to feel economically burdened.

Nearly half of all male workers are in the manual trades—factory work, construction industries, and semiskilled crafts. The fact that their labor is physical rather than mental, hazardous rather than safe, supervised rather than supervisory, means that, although certain elements of their work life are "masculine," on balance, they do not meet the culture's standards for male success. Rather than leaving their home and entering a world in which they are in control, they perform monotonous, routine, and unimportant tasks. There are few intrinsic or extrinsic rewards. With little autonomy and dignity arising from their work lives, the belief that they are the economic strength of the family is an important rationale to hold on to.

White-collar workers have a similar need to validate their work. According to Filene (1976:398), two-fifths of these workers report that they would prefer a different job. Home life and the symbols of affluence become important to these men as justifications for their employment. In the upper-middle classes, there is an especially insidious pattern—such that the more successful the male is occupa-tionally, the greater the conflict and dissatisfaction within his marriage. If men choose to try to fulfill the culture's expectations for occupational success, they spend a greater proportion of their time on their career and participating in commu-nity organizations. This leaves less time for enjoying their home and for sharing life with their families. In addition, the attitudes that men develop in the pursuit of occupational success (e.g., individualism, competitiveness, aggressiveness) are particularly unsuited for developing and sustaining intimate relationships (Dizard, 1972:196–198).

The poignancy of this trap is illustrated by the results of a survey of business and corporate executives. Four-fifths of them reported that "their attitudes toward achievement and success were changing: They located their basic aspirations not in the companies that employed them, but in their families and private lives" (Filene, 1976:393). However, although they stated such changing beliefs, "The tug of man-work expectations [is] hard to resist" (Filene, 1976:393). When it comes down to the nitty-gritty of risking the economic and psychological security that serious commitment to a career offers men in exchange for spending more time at home, few men are prepared to do so.

Ironically, then, the interconnectedness of home and work seems to ensure that most men will lose in at least one of these spheres, and many in both. The more occupational success they attain, the more difficult it is for them to find time for home-oriented activities. If they are not occupationally successful, they experience doubt about themselves—doubt that is carried home with them. The economy has ensured its labor force of highly committed professionals and executives and dependable laborers. Perpetuating the present ideology and structure of work, with greater importance placed on occupational success than interpersonal pleasures, irretrievably places most men in a "no win, no way out" situation. The full implications of this, however, can be understood only in the context of the division of labor that is based on the allocation of child care responsibilities.

CHILD CARE

Sex inequality in all industrialized societies is sustained by assigning the child-rearing role to women and the economic-provider role to men. This social arrangement meshes well with the demands of industry. Moreover, this pattern is the basis for "most of the sex-role divisions and of their consequences in modern society" (Grønseth, 1972:175). Without a major restructuring of this division of labor, "it will be impossible to achieve an end to other destructive sex-role divisions" (Grønseth, 1972:175).

This sex role division probably originated in the biological differences between men and women: Only women bear and nurse children. However, it is technologically no longer necessary to assign women the child-rearing role. Due to the bottle feeding of infants, it is feasible to allocate primary child care responsibilities to the father, the mother, both parents, the extended family, or child care centers. The division of labor by sex in modern societies is a matter of societal *choice* and, therefore, is subject to alteration (Huber, 1983). The ideology that still supports a sex-based division of labor is so persistent and deep that it is almost unconscious. Consider for a moment why fathers are not asked, "Well, if you don't want to stay home and raise the children, why did you have them?", or why mothers are not asked, "Have you made economic provisions for your child in the event of your death?"

Even our language reinforces these ideas about child rearing; for example, the expression "maternal care" is used generically to refer to the child-rearing activity.

The use of the feminine generic is not accidental. Consider the connotative difference between the following two sentences:

1. The baby was fathered by X.
2. The baby was mothered by X.

The first sentence implies biological paternity; the second, tender loving care (example drawn from Polatnick, 1975:204).

Further, the language blurs the two meanings of *nurturant*. The first meaning is simply to provide food or nourishment; the second is to promote the development of another through education, training, rearing, and so on. Through language blurring, the physical ability to lactate is enlarged to incorporate the second meaning of nurturance and therewith the responsibility for rearing children. Through an even greater semantic leap, women are then held responsible for nurturing (feeding, taking care of, etc.) the entire family.

In addition to the language that identifies women with child rearing, biological arguments are widely proffered. The argument states that because women bear children, they have the physiological and emotional capacity to rear them. And, in a companion belief, it is assumed that men are sociopsychologically and physiologically unsuited to such an endeavor.

But we might equally as "logically" argue that males should be responsible for child rearing because women cannot force men to have intercourse through which the sperm is supplied and because women fulfill their obligation by providing prenatal nurturance. Because this logic is obviously spurious, why is it so difficult to recognize the equally spurious nature of the argument that is based on female biology? It does not follow that the impregnator or the bearer should ipso facto be responsible for the raising of the child.

Chodorow has argued that "mothering," although not biologically innate, is socially constituted in order to "reproduce" women as mothers. She proposes that because women *do* the mothering, they "produce daughters with mothering capacities and the desire to mother" (1978:7). Boys have neither the capacity nor the desire to mother built into their personalities. This is so, Chodorow contends, because daughters and sons are *related* to differently by their mothers.

According to Chodorow, "adequate personalities" for interpersonal relationships are formed through "good enough" experiences as an infant with one's primary caretaker. "Good enough" experiences arise when the caretaker empathizes with the infant, and views the infant as an extension of the self. "Good enough" parenting is more likely to be experienced by a daughter than by a son. This is so, according to Chodorow, because a mother strongly identifies with her daughter and views the baby girl as an extension of herself; a son, on the other hand, is perceived as "the other," implacably different and distinct, perhaps even an erotic object. The boy is thus deprived of the kind of parenting that is necessary to create the capacity for parenting in him; pulling back further from his mother, identifying with the male world, he becomes emotionally deficient and psychologically inept at emphathizing relationships.

Not only does the boy lack the capacity to mother, he also lacks the desire to do so, according to Chodorow's theory. A woman wants to mother in order to recreate the mother-infant symbiosis that she experienced when an infant herself. Being a mother allows her to return to the primary emotional experience of her life—the unity she experienced with her own mother. Heterosexual experiences will not substitute, because men (as noted earlier) are relationally incapacitated. Only a child (a daughter?) can fulfill the woman mothered by a woman. Men, not having experienced this primitive sense of unity with a parent, thus lack the desire to retrieve the experience through being a parent. Intergenerationally, then, women reproduce women with the capacity and desire to mother, and produce men who fit into the public nonpersonal sphere.

If Chodorow is correct, then, clearly, child care arrangements will not change in this society; women will continue to want to mother and to be skilled at it. Indeed, if she is correct, the child-rearing pattern should not change, unless we want a generation of children who are reared by emotionally incapacitated and psychologically shrunken men. Yet, she offers as the solution "equality" in child rearing—a solution that strikes me as requiring *itself* as a solution before the solution can be had.

As interesting as Chodorow's analysis of "the reproduction of mothering" is, her theory leaves much unexplained—such as the "deviant" male who *does* nurture, the diversity of mothering cross-culturally, and the universal preference for sons (even among mothers). Her theory is inadequate, because the domestic division of labor cannot be understood without constant and concomitant attention to the extradomestic division of labor. Forces that are external to the family create and sustain the assignment of "mothering" to women.

Because there is no biological basis for the sex-based division of labor nor any compelling social need at this point in history to perpetuate it, we must conclude that continuing to assign child rearing to women and child supporting to males is a societal choice. Who profits from assigning child rearing to women?

Persons with greater power can enforce their decisions more readily than those who are relatively powerless. The structure of sex inequality is such that males as a group have more power than females. Consequently, they are in the position to both make and enforce decisions. One of these decisions has been to continue to assign child rearing to women. "Men as a group don't rear children because they don't *want* to rear them" (Polatnick, 1975:213). If they did want to, they could and would. Rather, "it is to men's advantage that women are assigned child-rearing responsibility, and it is in men's interest to keep things that way . . ." (Polatnick, 1975:213).

This is so because the child carer loses power both domestically and extradomestically. There are several reasons for this. First, in terms of society's values, child caring is not a high-prestige occupation. In fact it has low status, is vacationless, pensionless, isolated, full-time on-call, and financially uncompensated. Although child rearing may be a superior activity to many of those available in the labor market, it is not viewed as real work because it is outside the market economy.

Second, full-time child rearing limits what else one can do. It especially diminishes one's ability to pursue a professional career. The 70 or so hours that are required for a high-level business or professional career are not available to the full-time child rearer, nor are the 50 hours for middle-management success. Even if one does not have professional aspirations, the exigencies of child raising are such that the one who is charged with that responsibility has virtually no private time or space. The child's needs and desires are ever-present and unpredictable.

Moreover, the spouse who takes care of the children forfeits bargaining power within the marital union. Once a formal or informal pact has been made that allocates child rearing to the wife, she becomes even more disadvantaged in future negotiations. Most telling in all of this is that the power to make the decision as to who will raise the children does not reside in the hands of the person who almost invariably has the task—the mother. For most women today, the choice is to have children and be their primary caretakers or not to have them at all.

In a particularly compounding way, sex typing the occupation child rearer as "women's work" ensures that it will continue to have low prestige. Insidiously, it signals that the culture does not value its children as highly as it does its economic growth, despite the folklore to the contrary. If one universal pattern does exist cross-culturally, it is that the work deemed most important is assigned to men (Friedl, 1975).

As further evidence of the society's disregard for child rearing—and therefore for children—neither government, business, nor labor has shown any interest in rewarding women who have raised children or in altering work so that men can take a fuller part in their children's lives. If we value motherhood, why aren't there programs with medical care, advanced education, occupational hiring preference, early retirement, and loan benefits for women who have served their countries in the capacity of mothers?

Men, as a class, then, gain certain power advantages from assigning child rearing to women. However, for many individual men, the losses far outweigh the gains. Some individual men suffer losses because they may be unexpectedly cast into the role of child rearer; others are denied the right to fulfill that role; and still others feel the cost of the emotional estrangement from their children. Men who want to rear their children but who are denied that role, lose.

It is likely that many of these men will lose a great deal and have their future lives controlled in great measure. To the extent that divorced men are deeply concerned that their children's financial and emotional disruptions be minimized, they are less likely to risk incurring the displeasure of their ex-wives. Such divorced men, further, are probably the ones who are most desirous of limiting the time and commitment they have to their careers in order to have more time with their children; unfortunately, however, they are also the ones who are least likely to be able to diminish their work time, because two households are more expensive than one. Consequently, it is a likely hypothesis that those divorced men who care the most about their children are the ones who lose the most as individuals, because of the advantages gained by men as a class.

There is another category of fathers who do not benefit. These are the men who at some point in their lives question the value of how they have lived and sense an acute loss of something no longer attainable: a reciprocal emotional bond with their children.

Even though the present sex role division of labor costs many men, it, nevertheless, benefits men as a group. The primary assignment of child rearing to women perpetuates sex inequality. By perpetuating the sexual division of labor, the economy is provided with a family structure that is subordinated to the demands of the occupational structure.

Given the changing economy, is it likely that the allocation of child care responsibilities is likely to change? Huber and Spitze (in press) argue that, historically, child care has adjusted to women's work, rather than the other way around; for example, during World War II, when women's labor was needed in the war industry, on-site day-care centers were routinely provided. As women workers become increasingly necessary to the economy, and as the emotional, economic, and time costs of children to women accelerate, women are limiting their fertility. The benefits of children, and especially large numbers of them, are few to the postindustrial family (Huber and Spitze, in press). The single child who is born late in a woman's reproductive life is becoming a common childbearing choice for the professional woman. Some predict (e.g., Huber, 1976b) that the population will decline to such an extent that strong external inducements will have to be offered to women in the future to get them to reproduce. One of those inducements might be relieving them of the primary responsibilities for child rearing.

SINGLE PARENTING

Largely due to the high divorce rate, but also due to mothers who never married and widowhood, the single-parent family has become the second most prevalent family form in America. Currently one-fourth of American homes—nearly 16 million— are headed by single parents. About 90 percent of these single-parent homes are headed by women, 10 percent by men. Since 1970, the rate of increase has almost doubled (U.S. Department of Commerce, 1985). By 1990, demographers predict that nearly 16 million children will live in single-parent homes, and that 60 percent of all children will spend some part of their childhood with a solo parent (Glick, 1984). At any given time, 25 percent to 30 percent of American children are now living in a single-parent family (Shorr and Moen, 1984).

Despite these social changes, the single-parent family is still regarded as ''deviant,'' ''broken,'' and ''unstable.'' Although the historical trend toward single parenthood has been clear, the public's attitude has not kept pace, nor have the institutional accommodations to it. One of the reasons for this has been that the society has viewed single parenthood as a transitory status, and, therefore, not in need of institutional response. Yet, divorced mothers over age 30 are increasingly tending to remain single (Richardson, 1985). A recent five-year longitudinal study of divorced women, for example, found that fewer than 20 percent of them had remarried (Shorr and Moen, 1984).

A more trenchant cultural reason, however, is that single parenthood has been viewed as somehow immoral. Either the children were born ''illegitimately'' or else the woman ''failed'' at keeping her marriage together. In either case, she was seen as bringing her problems onto herself. The solution, if there was one, was for the government to provide welfare for the children or for the husband to provide child support. Consequently, the society has come to believe that single mothers are financially cared for either by the government or by the children's fathers. As to the actual support that is provided to single mothers, two thirds of them never receive welfare (Shorr and Moen, 1984). Only 60 percent of the mothers are awarded child support payments, and the majority of the husbands default on their obligations. Moreover, the court-ordered support is inadequate, in any case (Weitzman, 1985). Repeatedly, it is found that men financially profit by divorce, and women and children financially lose (Weitzman, 1985).

The central problem, then, that faces mother-headed homes is an *economic* one: About one-third of these homes are below the poverty level; the average mother-headed home is barely above poverty level. The primary reason for the economic problem is the ideology of the two-parent traditional family with its sex role division of labor, and its consequences for the structure of gainful employment. The economy still treats women as secondary wage earners, as supplementary income bringers to a two-parent family. Women are marginally employed in low-income, sex-typed occupations. Although job inequity affects all women, it especially affects single mothers.

The linkages between home and work affect single mothers in other ways, as well. Without another adult to count on and with limited economic resources, the single mother is subject to extreme role overload. Having to manage work and home means dealing with school appointments, doctor appointments, and repair and utilities people during her work hours; or, alternatively, hiring child care services, further reducing her income, and reducing her time spent with her children. She is bound to feel exhausted, anxious, and depressed. Indeed, two-thirds of single mothers report those feelings at some point (Shorr and Moen, 1984). Her most compelling feeling, though, is a sense of isolation (Shorr and Moen, 1984).

Compounding these feelings are feelings of guilt and fears that she is not adequately mothering her children, who, she worries, will become juvenile delinquents. Although the evidence is to the contrary, it does not allay her fears and guilts, probably because the knowledge, for one thing, is not distributed widely in the press, and, for another thing, because she, too, holds the societal belief in the preferability of the two-parent family.

Research shows that the presence or absence of a parent in and of itself "makes little difference in the adequacy of childrearing" (Shorr and Moen, 1984). Indeed, a longitudinal study showed that there was more delinquency in unhappy two-parent homes than in single-parent ones. Divorce is probably better for children than living in a conflict-ridden home (Shorr and Moen, 1984). Moreover, the difficulties that befall children in mother-headed homes are traceable to their *economic* conditions, rather than to the conditions of their parenting, which once again points the sociological finger to gender inequity in the marketplace.

We can also see the effect of traditional ideas about the division of labor by sex when we look at father-headed single-parent homes. This family form is growing more quickly than female-headed homes—an increase of 180 percent since 1970 (Grieff, 1985:3). Approximately one million children are in father-only homes (Grieff, 1985:3).

As a group, single fathers make about twice as much money as single mothers (Shorr and Moen, 1984), thus reflecting an economic system that favors males. The more money the father makes, the easier he finds being the custodial parent (Grieff, 1985:151), because money allows him to hire housekeepers and child care. More troublesome for these single fathers, though, is managing to adjust their career orientation to the demands of child rearing, on the one hand, and that of feeling competent as parents, on the other.

Men usually enter the workplace assuming that their careers will have primacy in their lives, and that their wives will be primarily responsible for the children. Some single fathers find that they have to adjust their career goals downward. This readjustment requires the father to rethink his sense of worth and identity—a task that is always difficult to accomplish. If he reduces his commitment to work, refusing, for example, to work overtime or to travel because of the demands of child rearing, his supervisor may decide that he lacks sufficient career commitment to advance in the company; he may be categorized with the "other mothers" at his place of work. The lack of fit between being a single parent and a worker, then, affects single fathers, too.

But single fathers are, also, affected by their lack of socialization toward and comfortableness in doing domestic work, including child care. One of the primary problems that single fathers report is feeling inadequate in the role; for example, one man, whose wife left him with their 8-year-old son, wrote:

> I began to wonder if I had ever really known how to be a warm nurturant parent. I know how to be a firm but fair authority figure. I knew how to have fun . . . in a playful way. And I knew how to push him [his son] to explore and test his mind, strength, and agility. But that was no longer enough . . . I felt inadequate (Boren, 1976:427).

Men who are active in child care and domestic responsibilities before their divorce, have the least problem in their roles as single fathers (Grieff, 1985:150). Once they have taken on the parenting role, single fathers, in general, find it brings them feelings of success and satisfaction (Shorr and Moen, 1984). With few role models to guide them, though, and little cultural support, the single father must be a family pioneer (Grieff, 1985:162–165). His active involvement in child rearing can have a major impact upon the familial and work structures, changing the linkages so that work is more accommodating to the emergent single-parent family form, and making life easier for parents and children.

Home and work, then, regardless of the family form, are not independent. The consequences of being socialized into the male or female gender in combination with social structure that assigns the primary responsibility for economic functions to the male, and the primary responsibility for domestic functions to the female affects all men, women, and children.

SECTION

□ 4 □

Social and Political Change

Socialization, social control of adults, and political, economic, and domestic institutions converge to produce and sustain a social and cultural world that differentially values males and females. These combined forces are strong and steady.

Yet, in a democratic and fairly open society such as ours that places an emphasis on social change through both individual consciousness and through social movement activity, the potentials for change at the individual and structural levels are many. In this section, we look at this change process.

First, we examine how individuals are trying to create alternative life arrangements to fulfill their needs. We look at singles, single parents, heterosexual couples, lesbian and gay couples, and we consider some of the particular issues that confront people living those lives—including the impact of children and dual locations on those relationships. The lens is turned to see how gender affects lives.

We, also, look at how social movements affect change in the society. As legitimate forms of social action in a democratic society, they have the power to change the economic, social, and intimate lives of people. We look at the modern Women's Movement and at its links with black interests and the Men's Movement. The role of blacks within the Women's and Men's Movement is explored, as well as the effect of antifeminism and ''passive feminism'' on continuing social change. Finally, we look at whether the movement is in touch with today's younger generation as we explore the future of feminism.

□ □ *13* □ □

Changing Intimate Relationships

The maintenance of sex-based inequality does not depend entirely on the socialization process that teaches it, the institutional arrangements that foster it, or the ideology that legitimizes it. In the final analysis, it is not institutions or ideas that act—it is you and I. Through the daily and often unconscious acceptance of and compliance with the norms of the society, we create intimate and public environments that perpetuate sex inequality.

Intimate relationships do not take place in a social or cultural vacuum. Rather, the processes by which personal lives are constructed are invariably linked to overarching social institutions and cultural ideologies. Although individuals may view themselves as separated from the controlling institutions, it is very likely that the very structures they stand in opposition to are repeated within their "alternative" relationships.

This is so because people carry with them, consciously and nonconsciously, the definitions and expectations of their society. Despite their intentions to the contrary, they judge and evaluate themselves against the norms and values of the dominant society. Most simply stated, ideas have consequences—even when they are rejected. Persons intellectually freed from sex stereotypes may nevertheless find themselves emotionally torn, guilty, and ashamed for acting in ways that are contrary to society's dicta. Like anticommunist crusaders, who are dialectically tied to that which they oppose—communism—persons rejecting traditionality may find themselves, nevertheless, measuring themselves against it.

In the past decade, though, social movement and economic and demographic changes have created a cultural climate that makes possible alternatives in intimate lives. Strong support to forge new lives is available. What successes have people had? Have they been able to find ways to live less sexist lives and to achieve more growth in their personal and career arenas?

In what follows, I will be looking at how normative definitions continue to limit and structure the potentials for personal growth and pleasure. Although there

207

are many ways to organize and categorize alternatives, I will discuss singlehood and coupledness, based *primarily,* but not exclusively, on research with heterosexually oriented people. Following that, I will discuss changes within lesbian and gay male relationships. The term *gay* will be reserved for male homosexuals.

BEING SINGLE

Marriage has been held as an ideal that everyone could attain if only they wanted to and tried hard enough (Duberman, 1977). To not marry meant you were possibly homosexual and/or Oedipally fixated, and certainly immature and aberrant, if you were a male, and hopelessly unattractive, if you were a female. "Failure" to marry reflected one's personal and social shortcomings (Kuhn, 1955).

The culture's normative preference for marriage has also been reflected in the lack of social-scientific research on singles. What little research had been done focused on singlehood as a stage on the way to marriage. Recently, however, and partially as a result of the Women's Movement, the Gay Rights Movement, and other human rights movements, singlehood is being viewed by both singles and scholars (cf. Stein, 1981; Richardson, 1979, 1985; Cargan, 1982) as a voluntary life choice—a status possibly even preferable to marriage or a paramarital relationship. In the past, the high rate of singlehood among educated women was attributed to their lack of "femininity," their undesirability to men. More recently, sociologists have begun to view it differently. They suggest these women are choosing not to marry. For educated and occupationally successful women, the costs of marriage may exceed the rewards. By remaining single, they have a better chance to retain their autonomy, to move geographically, to spend their income as they please, and to commit energies to their career without the constraints of marriage. Increasingly, both males and females are expressing a belief that singlehood is an agreeable state. Fewer singles see themselves as misfits or "leftovers." Many have found that marriage is no longer necessary "to find emotional support, sex, or an active social life" (Stein, 1976:420). In addition, as acceptance of lesbian and gay male rights increases, there is less need for homosexuals to choose to marry in order to hide their sexual orientation.

Singlehood is becoming an increasingly common status. Thirty-four percent of American men over 18 and 40 percent of American women over 18 are not married (Guttentag and Secord, 1983). Individuals are less likely to get married than they were 15 years ago and more likely to marry later, delay remarriage, or not remarry at all. Both men and women spend a sizeable portion of their adult lives unmarried.

Approximately one in every three adults is unmarried. Obviously, a group this large must be extremely heterogenous with respect to race, ethnicity, age, social class, sexual preference, desire to marry, desire to be in a "lasting" relationship, previous marital status, parental status, living arrangements, and so on. Nevertheless, singles as a class are discriminated against.

Unattached persons, especially women, are seen as a threat to couples and are excluded from many social occasions (Richardson, 1985). In work and other settings, singlehood may threaten colleagues' spouses. In one work organization, for example, a highly influential male member and his wife kept a list of his divorced colleagues taped to their refrigerator. This list was entitled: People Not Welcome Here. Job discrimination also exists. In one survey, for example, it was found that although 80 percent of the management of major corporations stated that their executives need not be married, only two percent of those executives were single.

Because the culture does not value singlehood, the unmarried are subject to misrepresentation by the mass media and commercial exploitation (Stein, 1976). Entrepreneurs sell singles everything from weekends to workshops, from sweat-shirts to perfumes, from computer dating services to vibrators. The singles bars that exist in all major, and not so major, cities are one form of exploitation. Although individuals may go to these bars to find companionship, affection, excitement, and social acceptance, for the most part, the singles bar enhances one's loneliness and alienation. It does this partly because it is structured to facilitate heterosexual pairing through the accentuation of sex stereotyping. Superficial elements such as clothes and looks are the basis for pairing; one's same-sex friends are useful as "props" or supports, but they are less important in this setting than is the possibility of finding a partner. Although there is greater freedom for women and men to break out of their roles, in the typical singles bar today men are still the initiators. Women are still uncomfortable with making the first overture, so they wait to be chosen: this always puts women at a power disadvantage.

However, with the epidemic of sexually transmitted diseases—such as her-pes, which may affect childbearing, and acquired-immune deficiency syndrome or AIDS, which is fatal—accepting sexual companionship with strangers has become an ominous proposition. One of the unanticipated outcomes of the (justifiable) fears regarding "safe sex" may well be greater equality between the sexes, because sexuality will be less linked to institutions—such as the singles bar—that are built upon sex role stereotypes that degrade the feminine. Males and females will both be more interested in knowing more about their intended partner before they risk a sexual union.

Given that over one-third of American adults are single (never married or divorced) and millions of them will be single for the rest of their lives, what are some of the ways in which this large and diverse group is attempting to construct lives that, from their perspective, provide them with greater pleasure and success?

Marriage is no longer necessary for men to get sex, or for women to get economic support. People can, and do, choose relationships that emphasize free-dom and compatibility; they can and do create relationships that need not be hetero-sexual, permanent, or exclusive. Let us look at persons who *embrace* the single life, meaning those who do not want to live with another adult in a sexual and economic liaison.

These voluntary singles view singlehood as a desirable status, at least at this point in their lives. After an initial phase of casual sex and/or frantic searching for a permanent partner, these voluntary single persons positively value their single friends, their life, and their support network.

Stein (1976) suggests that choosing singlehood results from a set of "pushes" and "pulls." Pushes are negative experiences that are associated with being "cou-pled," whereas pulls are *attractions* to singlehood. Voluntary singles report several factors that push them away from a coupled relationship. First, the permanent relationship was seen as an obstacle to personal growth, because the individuals became ingrown and dependent upon each other for fulfilling needs; few ideas from outside the couple infiltrated their world. Second, being coupled created a sense of isolation and loneliness, caused separation from old friends, and placed limitations on new friendships. Only *mutually* acceptable friends were "friends." If one's partner was an emotionally distant type, the loneliness was especially acute. Third, permanent relationships were seen as restricting advancement and mobility and requiring too much compromise and accommodation.

On the other hand, individuals were "pulled" toward singlehood by seeing it as a state that permitted greater freedom and growth potential and greater economic and social independence. Women, especially, see the single state as preferable because they can follow their own careers, excel at them, and not have to make their lives in any way secondary to a man's. Men, on the other hand, value the single state for the loosely structured life that it permits. Not being held responsible to fulfill certain roles—such as father, husband, breadwinner—the men report pleasure in trying on different roles—clown, playboy, and friend—and in being totally self-motivated, responsible only to themselves. Thus, it would seem that males and females get different rewards from the single state, and those rewards are tied to the reciprocal costs of marriage and quasi-marriages for men and women. Women get greater *freedom to* pursue careers and to tend to their own personal needs; men get greater *freedom from* responsibilities for others.

Single Woman/Married Man

Single women who are fulfilling their careers unencumbered by an exclusive or permanent relationship may find themselves turning to married men to fulfill intimate needs. Indeed, with a conservative estimate that 50 percent of married men have extramarital sex, Richardson (1985) estimates that about one-third of single women will at some point have a relationship with a married man. No longer is a liaison with a married man a deviation from the norm: It has become a major social trend. This is due to major demographic, social, and cultural factors.

Demographically, there is a shortage of men—particularly for educated women over the age of 30—because men still tend to choose women who are younger and less well-educated than they are. With a high divorce rate, the shortage is exacerbated because the ex-husband marries a young woman, creating a burgeoning population of divorced women. Socially, women's lives are such that they are frequently in transition from one role to another: They are students, newly divorced, newly employed, and so on. They see a liaison with a married man as temporary, and therefore as fitting in with their own transitory statuses. And culturally, although they see themselves as capable and empowered persons, they still hold the major cultural imperative for women: Command the love of a man.

To research these liaisons from the perspective of the single woman, Richardson conducted in-depth interviews with single women who had been or currently were involved in long-term (1 to 17 years) intimate relationships with a married man (1985). The styles that were used by the women to manage relationships could be arrayed along a *power* continuum (Richardson, 1979, 1980). At one end were the women who were nearly powerless in the relationship, totally submissive, and subordinated to their lover's (emotional, social, occupational, and familial) needs. Such women spent much of their time and energy waiting for him (to call, to come, to leave his wife) and were grateful for any indication that he cared (a Valentine's Day card, an unexpected phone call, a promise). These submissive-style women are, obviously, not forging an alternative life-style free of sex-based inequality; rather, they seem to epitomize "femininity"—passively waiting for a man. At the other end of the power-continuum were the women who adopted a dominance-management style. At the time that their affairs were initiated, these women were highly dedicated to pursuing or advancing goals that they considered incompatible with marriage. What they were seeking were intellectual, financial, or low-level emotional involvements that would not interfere with their major current life goals. Consequently, these women acted within their relationships with considerable independence, assertiveness, and dominance; for example, if the affair began to interfere with their other goals—of if the man escalated his commitment by leaving his wife—the dominant-style woman would terminate the relationship.

These dominant-style women are finding a way to have intimate relationships without the traditional rules or roles. However, there is some question as to whether they are not simply substituting the pitfalls of "masculinity" for the pitfalls of "femininity." In the interviews, these women frequently would wonder, for example, if they would ever have a permanent and deeply intimate relationship—or whether they would always allow their career goals to overrule their emotional needs.

Despite the power imbalances in these relationships, many single women describe their relationships with married men as "total," "emotionally pure," "uniquely intimate"; and many describe their married lovers as "compassionate and exciting," "like no man ever known before," "every woman's dream." Rather than dismissing these laudations as romantic fantasies or thought disorders, we might ask if there are ways in which the man's marital status might, in fact, be structurally conducive to relationships and behaviors that many single women label *ideal*.

One of the primary realities about relationships between single women and married men is that they are secret. The felt need for secrecy is rooted in *his* marital status. Consequently, activities that sustain the relationship are carried on in private. The world out there—the normative social structure with its roles and rules, expectations and obligations—can be laid aside as the couple construct a world in here, a world freer of social constraint and cultural definition. The pair, alone together, can construct the relationship, its boundaries, and its focus. Secrecy, therefore, leads to privacy, and privacy to greater autonomy. In addition, because the couple at this stage do not view their liaison as even potentially permanent, to share with each other is viewed as fundamentally safe. The lovers are more willing to take personal *risks* in the context of a *safe* relationship. The partners experience freedom to safely share secrets about the self and to experience a kind of intimacy that is based on self-disclosures.

However, because the relationship is nonnormative, freedom can lead to anomie. Rites are created through which the partners prove their existence as a relationship with a structure and a history. These rites—such as keeping a scrap-book—in turn, become new *mutual* secrets that cannot be shared with others. To protect their secrets, strategies are devised. These strategies intensify the feeling of intimacy by reducing the woman's contact with others and/or by increasing her dependence upon her married lover.

By withdrawing from social life, for example, the single woman is unlikely to even meet other men, much less establish ties with them. Opportunities for a new liaison are virtually eliminated. In addition, she is less likely to reveal her secret to friends and family in order to avoid the risk of condemnation or, perhaps worse, the demand that she "come to her senses." Further, since the risk of revealing her secret is increased should she share anything of importance about her life, the kind of interaction she has with her friends and family tends to become more distant and matter-of-fact. That is, she no longer trusts herself to discuss anything in her life, for fear that she will reveal everything. Hence, what support network she had developed before her entanglement atrophies. As she withdraws further into social and emotional semi-isolation, the one person who does remain in her life is her married lover; he does, in fact, therefore, become her "whole life."

The double standard plays a major role in the constitution of relationships between single women and married men. Whereas secrecy gives the married man *control* over both relationships, it also protects the woman's "reputation." Al-though it is the male who is breaking the monogamy norm, it is the single woman who, should his transgression be known, will be subject to such epitaphs as "other woman," "home wrecker," "husband stealer," and/or to accusations that her career success is attributable to "whom she knows—in the biblical sense—not what she knows." Few women are immune to the potential impact, should their relationship be revealed. Secrecy, therefore, allows the male to have and control both of his worlds and protects the woman from social denigration. However, her reputation needs protecting only because she lives in a society in which the double standard circumscribes her life. And that circumscription can lead to the woman's total withdrawal from her usual routines and social support networks and to the construction of lies and fantasies. In that respect, she may have a stronger link than she recognizes with her married lover's "other" woman, his wife.

Parenthood Without Marriage

Due to changing cultural norms, social needs, and technologies, it is now possible to separate having a child from being married. Just as the decades of the sixties separated sex from love, and the seventies separated love from marriage, the eighties are separating marriage from reproduction. Through adoption, single men and women are becoming parents by *choice*; through the use of surrogate mothers, single men can become biological and social fathers; and through artificial insem-ination, as well as regular intercourse, single *adult* women are becoming mothers by choice. Indeed, the fastest growing rate of births out of wedlock are for women ages 30 to 34.

Unlike the poverty-stricken, black, teenage "unwed mother" that the social-policy pundits have focused on, the "new unwed mother" is a professional or career woman in her thirties who is unwilling to give up the idea of *family* just because she has not found a suitable man to marry. Some of these women, including lesbian women, propose that marriage is undesirable, anyway, and they have purposefully chosen to avoid it, but not to avoid motherhood. They are *adult* women, "single mothers by choice"—the name, not so coincidentally, of a support group network for these single women that exists in many cities.

These *adult* single mothers by choice are potentially creating a new family form—a form in which children are being voluntarily reared in an economically stable home without a father present. Most of the deleterious effects on children who are reared by solo mothers, which are described in the research literature, can probably be ascribed to economic hardship, rather than to the absence of the father per se (Kamerman, 1980).

Since these single-mother homes are more affluent, the effects of poverty can be removed. Moreover, some literature is now proposing that the absent father may have positive consequences on the children (Fox and Inazu, 1982). In father-absent homes, female children are less likely to be sexually molested or abused, and both male and female children are more likely to reject sex role stereotypes about women. Seeing their own mother fulfilling a career and taking care of the home may well affect their attitudes toward and expectations for women.

Similarly, men who are adopting children (either through the courts or through surrogate mothers) and rearing them without wives are providing new models for children. Men are being presented as people for whom parenthood is so important that they voluntarily assume the tasks of parenthood; men are being modeled as persons who can be simultaneously capable of taking care of the economic and emotional needs of children.

Separating reproduction and child rearing from marriage might in the not so distant future be one of the most radical ways in which intimate lives are altered. To fulfill their needs for *family* without marriage, men and women may end up drawing upon their own internal resources to become more complete and androgynous persons, and may offer that model to their young.

BEING HETEROSEXUALLY COUPLED

Most people at some point in their adult lives spend time as a member of a couple. Most people either get married or, increasingly, simply live together. Nonmarital cohabitation is becoming so commonly accepted that "in time to come a majority of persons will experience this lifestyle at some point in their life cycle" (Macklin, 1978:1). At this point, four percent of the adult population are in live-in relationships; 28 percent of these homes include children. Cohabitors tend to be under 35, but there is a sizable minority of older, urban, and black couples who live together (Huber and Spitze, in press). Currently, the socioeconomic characteristics of cohabitors is converging with that of married couples, so much so that Spanier (1983) suggests living together no longer be viewed as an alternative life-style.

For some persons, living together provides a sense of emotional security and predictability without the full constraints of marriage. However, living together may not be structurally much different than marriage. Individuals easily fall into prescribed roles. Despite the claims of cohabitants that they are freer of sex stereotyping and that they are "androgynous," available data suggest that the division of labor between cohabitants follows the traditional sex-linked pattern (Macklin, 1978). Young cohabitants are about as equalitarian as young marrieds (Macklin, 1978). Socialization and role scripting serve to retain conventional behavior despite the apparent nontraditionalism of the relationship; for example, recent research on a large sample of cohabitors finds that the more successful the women, the more problems the relationship has (Blumstein and Schwartz, 1983). As to whether marriage "changes" the relationship between the cohabitants, what little available data there is seems to be equivocable. One might expect that, because marriage is a legally and socially sanctioned state, the rights and responsibilities of being married would impinge upon the couple. Macklin (1978) summarizes the research by hypothesizing that marriage will increase commitment, increase ease of interaction with relatives, and increase the probability of traditional sex-typed behaviors, possessiveness, and dependence. However, "both married and unmarried couples are likely" to act conventionally unless they "contract against this and make a determined effort to maintain the provisions of the contract" (Macklin, 1978:8).

Married Couples

If persons choose to marry, the question becomes: What factors are associated with the development of equalitarian marriages? Because those factors are probably many and complexly interrelated and because they undoubtedly include the psychological and biological, as well as the sociological, I shall not attempt anything approaching a complete inventory. Rather, I shall discuss a few of the sociological factors that seem especially pertinent.

Although only two states require a woman to take her husband's name upon marriage, most women do so. This probably has ramifications for the spouses' marital and extramarital interactions, as well as for their careers. To assume the man's name, to submerge one's personal identity linguistically (to become Mrs. John Doe), cannot help but set the stage for the couple to be seen by themselves and others as "Mr. Couple." Breaking with convention by retaining separate names by hyphenating them probably indicates the partners' intention to build a marriage that is satisfying to them rather than one that conforms to the social norms.

The consequences of breaking with traditions are probably positive for the wife's career. By continuing to work under her maiden name, colleagues and employers are probably more likely to consider her a career-committed person. Further, whatever recognition that she has received under one name may not be easily transferred to a new one—and if she changes her name each time she marries in the course of a lifetime, she may acquire three or four different ones. (Changing names is particularly dysfunctional in cosmopolitan careers such as academia, writing, show business.) The consequences for the male's career may not necessarily be detrimental; for example, one vice-president of a large business firm commented,

"*Because* my wife has not taken my name, my associates see her as an interesting person to get to know. . . . Unexpectedly, she has helped rather than hurt my career." Clearly, research on marriages in which the wife does not adopt the husband's name is needed.

Another factor is the relationship each member of the couple has to the occupational system. I would hypothesize that equality is more easily achieved if each spouse has a similar relationship to the economy: Either both work or neither does; and, if both are employed, then the occupational statuses and income should be similar.

However, I would argue that similar relations to the workplace, although probably a facilitating condition, is not a sufficient one. In addition, equality is more likely to be achieved if the couple's careers are viewed as equally important. However, because the tendency is to favor the husband's career (Epstein, 1971; Rapoport and Rapoport, 1978), and because the political and economic structures also favor men, achieving an egalitarian marriage may require placing the woman's career before the man's. His marital state and her marital state will be differentially rewarded. Men who are married make more money than single men, whereas married women make less than single women, controlling, in all instances, other variables (Parcel, et al., 1986). To treat each career as equally important, then, may require implementing decisions that are *preferential* to the wife.

Closely intertwined with the relationship to work is the couple's allocation of domestic responsibilities. If the wife continues to be held responsible (through her own or her husband's expectations) for the routine cooking, shopping, and cleaning, as well as for decision making in these areas, then the marriage will perpetuate an imbalance of power. Not only are those duties time- and energy-consuming, but their performance lessens one's domestic power. What is needed is a division of labor in which both partners are responsible for domestic decision making and task performance.

Although balancing career opportunities and domestic responsibilities may lead to greater equality, it will not necessarily maximize the emotional interchange between the couples nor will it sustain an equalitarian marriage. Indeed, Blumstein and Schwartz (1983) report that married couples have more problems finding time for each other than gay or lesbian couples do, partly because gender socialization has created different leisure time interests in the husbands and wives. Dizard (1972) reports that emotional closeness is more easily achieved if both partners *decrease* their emphasis on occupational achievement. Job-sharing (Arkin and Dobrofsky, 1978) and part-time employment for both partners (Grønseth, 1978) create more equitable and emotionally tolerable conditions. When both are primarily committed to occupational success, concerns about getting ahead may dominate the relationship. Miller concurs, stating, "Egalitarian relationships cannot survive if people are not somewhat equally involved with each other and if the major commitment is to things outside the relationship which inevitably intrude on it" (1976:380).

Most people enter marriage and careers at approximately the same time in their lives. For couples committed to equality, the compounding strains of a new marriage and new job may be difficult to surmount. Speculatively, I would hypothesize that equality is more likely to be achieved by delaying marriage until both partners are firmly entrenched in their professions, or until they have reduced their desire to achieve in that sphere.

Perhaps the factor that most impedes equality, however, is the addition of a child. Although folklore about parenthood contends that child rearing is fun, that children are sweet and cute (there are no bad children, only bad parents), that the sacrifices are worth it (LeMasters, 1976), and that children bring a couple closer together, there is little or no evidence to support any of these beliefs.

In fact, children have a strong and often negative impact on the marital relationship. Children take an incredible amount of time, energy, money, and emotion; they radically alter a couple's life. The addition of children "makes even a low-level decent relationship [between the parents], let alone, an equalitarian one, difficult" (Miller, 1976:380). The negative impact of children on marriage is a consistent finding over the past 30 years, and holds across sex, race, and religion (Huber and Spitze, in press). Stepchildren make a remarriage especially difficult, and are the major factors in dissatisfaction in second marriages (Booth, et al., 1985).

If the husband is expected to have a high degree of participation in child rearing, then he may feel resentment as Miller reports he did. Child rearing, he stated, "seemed to interfere terribly with the work I desperately wanted to achieve. . . . To make matters worse I did not know of other work-oriented husbands who were as involved as I was with their children" (1976:376–377). Although Miller saw himself intruded upon by the demands of his children and the expectations of his wife, he notes that his disruptions were considerably less than those his physician-wife experienced. Despite his "good intentions," his marriage became a "typically upper-middle-class collegial, pseudo-egalitarian American one." Although he "helped his wife," he recognized

> that is not the same thing as direct and primary responsibility for planning and managing a household and meeting the day-to-day needs of children. . . . The more crucial issue, I now think, is not the specific omissions or commissions, but the atmosphere I create. . . . In the long run I have undoubtedly lost more . . . but the long run is hard to consider when today's saved and protected time helps meet a deadline (Miller, 1976:378–379).

Having children, then, can have a serious negative impact on couples. Childlessness, on the other hand, can have "benign effects on marriage" (Bernard, 1976). Voluntarily childless women report being more satisfied with leisure time activities, division of household chores, and career decisions than women with children; and childless husbands are more likely to support their wives' careers and share domestic responsibilities (Houseknecht, 1979). Contrary to all clichés, childless marriages that do survive are happier than marriages with children (Bernard, 1976:323). Childlessness releases both parents from the prescriptive sex roles of father-breadwinner/mother-child rearer.

For those who choose to marry and have children, it is probably true "the fewer, the better." Delaying the birth or adoption of the children—until both individuals are more certain with regard to their own self-images and goals, until the financial burdens that children bring can be minimized, and until both are established in their professional lives—probably diminishes the negative impact of children.

Dual-Location Couples

"If a tree falls in the forest, and there is no one to hear it, does it make a noise? Does a relationship exist if you don't spend time in it?" (Gross, 1980). How is it possible, people want to know, to create satisfying, long-lasting intimate relationships *and* to succeed in a career? It is not surprising, then, that considerable research has been generated over this past decade on "dual-career" marriages—marriages in which, supposedly, both partners are strongly committed to career advancement (cf. Rapoport and Rapoport, 1971, 1976, and 1978; Epstein, 1971; Holmstrom, 1972; Poloma, 1972; Poloma and Garland, 1971). This research, however, repeatedly bears out that in "dual-career" marriages, the *husband's* career is primary, the wife's career, secondary. Although the domestic division of labor may be altered in these homes so that domestic tasks are more equitably shared between the couple, the *right* of the husband's career primacy is usually retained. In most of the emergent dual-career marriages, the problem of primacy of relationship versus primacy of career has been resolved in a traditional way: The wife is responsible for the relationship; the husband is the primary breadwinner.

However, some couples have been attempting to truly structure relationships in which neither husband's nor wife's career is primary. Holding that view, they have found themselves increasingly having to choose *between* living together and career advantages. No longer can a couple count on finding two "good" jobs in the same city, or expect that career advancement will not require geographical mobility; thus, couples who are committed to egalitarian relationships are finding that the time and space they share may be weekend catch-me-ups, holidays, and long-distance phone calls (Kirschner and Richardson [Walum], 1978). It is important to look at how these couples manage, not because they are living apart, but because their experiences point to the ways in which truly egalitarian relationships might be created. I shall report the findings from that research, first, and then its applicability to paramarital relationships.

Certain occupations (e.g., executives, salespersons, and politicians) and certain social conditions (e.g., immigration and war) have long been associated with marriage partners residing in two different locations. Historically, the pattern has been for the male to leave the family for an extended period of time. Despite their absence from their wives and families, the soldier, the salesman, and the politician define themselves as a *member* of the family. Male-determined two-location families, thus, are not unusual, though they have not been studied (Kirschner and Richardson [Walum], 1978).

Today, however, a new pattern is emerging; the female-determined dual-location couple (family) (Kirschner and Richardson [Walum], 1978). Living apart as a way to maximize the *career* potentials of *both* partners is not chosen lightly nor heartily endorsed; rather it is a living arrangement that one at best puts up with

(Gross, 1983), and copes with only because the couple believes that the separation is necessary/fair and that it will be temporary (Kirschner and Richardson [Walum], 1978).

The strains and rewards of dual-location marriages are many. The separation obviously affords the individual greater freedom and time to pursue career objectives (Kirschner and Richardson [Walum], 1978; Gross, 1983). Concomitantly, guilt and resentment, and guilt about the resentment, emerge to cloud the objective advantages of living separately (Gross, 1983). This emotionally debilitating overlay arises because the partners, regardless of their commitment to an equalitarian marriage and regardless of their intellectual acceptance of each other's careers, take traditional marital roles as their vantage point in evaluating their life-style. "For all their conscious rejection of them," traditional roles "are still the only model of a marital relationship upon which they can draw" (Gross, 1983). They view traditional marriage as the norm, and experience dissonance, despite themselves, for not having the "right" kind of marriage. Enthusiastic as they are about being the kind of people who care about each other's careers and who can manage the two-location relationship, their very pride in this accomplishment, as Gross (1983) so correctly points out, underscores how vivid and pervasive are traditional marital roles and norms in their evaluations of their life-style. Thus, wives report missing the *emotional intimacy* and protection they expect from a husband in a marriage. Husbands, on the other hand, do not report missing the emotional intimacy, but feel guilty about not being able to protect their wives emotionally (Gross, 1983).

The other kinds of strains that emerge for commuter marriages are tied to the longevity of the relationship and the existence of children (Gross, 1983; Kirschner and Richardson [Walum], 1978). Gross' (1983) analysis of these strains is worth reporting.

A young wife feels "special" and advantaged by having her career needs accepted and attended to by her husband; this creates guilt, however, in that she knows that her husband has become disadvantaged by having an absent wife. "Her sense of advantage is mitigated and undermined by the attendant guilt, leaving her with a burdensome, perplexing sense of somehow wronging him" (Gross, 1983). The young husband, correlatively, has a "sense of loss." He does not miss a scullery-maid or a private cook: He did not marry a woman to serve his meals and dote upon him. What he does miss is "a wife willing to acknowledge his 'inherent' right" to career *supremacy*. "Of course her career 'counts' . . . It's just not *as* important as his" (Gross, 1983). He is resentful and bereft: She has been "given" to, and he "taken" from. He then feels guilty, for although he intellectually subscribes to equalitarianism, he realizes he also wants her to be subordinate like a "wife should."

Career ascendancy struggles are increased in these young couples because they are young. Their careers are new and they have yet to prove themselves. Extra pressure to succeed in order to justify their unorthodox living arrangement is experienced, especially by the woman (Kirschner and Richardson [Walum], 1978); because they are young, their marriages are fairly new. They have yet to prove to themselves that their commitment can survive the stress of a dual-location living arrangement, and have yet to have constructed a history, a backlog of shared experiences that objectify the existence and permanence of the relationship.

The *power* struggle over career/marriage ascendancy looms large for young couples—larger, in fact, than the problems of the dual-location arrangement per se (Gross, 1983). Living in two places is simply the objectification of the troublesome reality that the couple is creating. As one wife commented, "Am I an emotional freak? Why is my career as important to me as my marriage?" (quoted in Gross, 1983).

Older couples are not as subject to this career/marriage ascendancy struggle, partly because, typically, the male has already established his career; the dual-location arrangement is defined as "righting a previous wrong," or "correcting an imbalance," or "giving the wife a chance to fulfill herself" (Gross, 1983). With a longer marital history behind them, moreover, they know there has been a permanence and they know what pressures their marital relationship can sustain (Kirschner and Richardson [Walum], 1978). Sources of strain appear to arise primarily over the redistribution of child care responsibilities, especially if the children live with the father. Husbands express resentment over the *existence* of chores, chauffeuring, P.T.A.'s, and bedtime rituals that are created by the children's existence; wives express guilt over shirking maternal obligations and question whether their husbands are sufficiently nurturing surrogate mothers. For older couples who have no children, the strains primarily revolve around the added expenses, the time/distance factors, and fears of growing "too far" apart (Kirschner and Richardson [Walum], 1978).

Dual-location marriages, therefore, are under different stresses and strains depending upon the longevity of the relationship, the existence of children, and the career cycle of the husband and wife. As a solution to the problem of creating both meaningful intimate lives and meaningful careers, commuter marriages seem to work best the longer the couple is married, the greater the freedom from child care responsibilities, and the greater the career settledness of one of the partners (Gross, 1983; Kirschner and Richardson [Walum], 1979).

It is difficult to determine whether long-distance relationships between unmarried people would have fewer or more structural difficulties than those between married people. Normatively, it is not considered all that unusual for persons in a *relationship* to reside in different cities, particularly if that separation is seen as a precursor to, or, "trial separation" before, marriage. However, if the couple is not marriage-oriented and if they adopt the definition of a relationship as a face-to-face one, then without the added legal and social constraints that marriage creates, these commuting couples may find it very difficult to sustain their relationship. Clearly, research on this topic is needed.

LESBIAN ALTERNATIVES

Throughout most of history, lesbians have lived quietly and invisibly. They have passed as heterosexuals in marriages of convenience, sometimes wed to gay men. They have lived with a female "friend" and have grown into presumed spinsterhood. They have lowered their career aspirations to protect their secret. Some have lived a life without love, withdrawing from friends and family, and hiding their affectional preference, perhaps even from themselves.

Little social-scientific research had been directed to lesbian experiences, primarily because of the androcentric bias that holds that love between women, like other spheres of women's lives, is dull, worthless, and uninspiring. However, feminist scholars have begun to fill in our knowledge (cf., Ponse, 1978; Tanner, 1978; Lewis, 1979; Wolf, 1979), and recently a unique study that contrasts cohabitating heterosexuals, lesbians, and gays on domestic, sexual, and economic issues has been completed (Blumstein and Schwartz, 1983). In keeping with the understanding that men and women may inhabit distinct cultural worlds, feminist scholars have analyzed lesbianism as a variation of *female* sexuality rather than as a variation of gay sexuality. The research has focused on lesbian identity, relationships, and community, and has asked about female-typed values such as emotionality, nurturance, and empathy as sources for the lesbian experience, rather than about the etiology and sex practices of lesbians (Taylor, 1980).

In the 1960s, lesbians found themselves treated as second-class citizens by the men in the Gay Liberation Front, and as deviants by the straight women in the Women's Liberation Movement. From those experiences, a lesbian-feminist consciousness was shaped, which has had major impact on the lives of all lesbians— radical and moderate, "closeted" and "out" (Fleener, 1977). Nearly all lesbians see that impact favorably, as making their lives easier. Over the past quarter of a century, the world has changed dramatically for the American lesbian. "No longer is the word *lesbian* unmentionable. . . . No longer need she be quite so isolated as she was twenty, ten or even five years ago" (Lewis, 1979:154). In contemporary society, her lesbian identity can be shaped in the context of feminism rather than in the context of a lesbian underground or in a context of male homosexuality.

In the 1950s, lesbian couples tended to model themselves after heterosexual ones. In the bar culture, women had to be either a *butch* (male role) or a *femme* (female role); there were no other options. Butches epitomized "masculinity" and were responsible for the femme, fought with other butches, roughhoused, and were entitled to "butches night out" (Davis and Michelson, 1980). Femmes were "feminine" in speech, clothing, expectations, and affectations. Role relationships were sex role stereotyped and rigidly adhered to, almost as though these lesbians were announcing to each other: "Yes, we love women, but we love each other the way normal people do. We haven't rejected the male and female *role* division. We're not nuts and we're not revolutionaries."

Although the bar was a place where lesbians met and socialized, more important was the friendship network, or what women referred to as "our real family" (Lewis, 1979:59). Most lesbian experiences took place in this secret subculture. Women who trusted each other implicitly and who depended upon each other for emotional and other support formed extended families, each family linked to others so that link by link across the country an underground "lesbian nation" was formed. Unlike patriarchal families, however, these tended to be nonauthoritarian and nonhierarchical.

As with any family, secrets were to be kept inside the family. Highly taboo was breaking the code of silence to outsiders about the affectional bonds between family members. Because families were linked together, sexual indiscretions were hard to hide; however, because family members needed each other and because the network was a quasi-kinship one, indiscretions were tolerated. At the termination of relationships, the kinship bond remained. Indeed, lesbians frequently held a personal ethic that one should remain friends with former lovers (Lewis, 1979:62).

Some of these subcultural characteristics continue into the present. The lesbian community continues to be organized around a network of friends—an extended family who help each other emotionally, financially, and in other ways—and these families continue to be linked to one another. In some of these families, incest taboos have arisen (Quintinalles, 1980), and the friendship norms persist. But, unlike the older community in hiding, lesbian feminists have "come out"—if not always to their parents or their employers, increasingly to straight friends, gay men, and in political and cultural activism. Also unlike their older sisters who depended on the bar culture to meet and socialize with other lesbians, lesbians today have access to over 1000 organizations and clubs for lesbian women, 100 lesbian-feminist bookstores, and over 50 magazines and newsletters, as well as coffee-houses, retreats, vacation resorts, and communities in which lesbians can openly express their affections without fear of insult or abuse.

Lesbian feminists are refusing to kowtow to the request of the patriarchal order—that they stay out of the way, hidden in the closet. They are coming out and attempting to find alternatives *within* the lesbian life-style that will enhance their lives.

In any widespread social movement, radical viewpoints emerge; in the case of lesbianism, some radical lesbian feminists have proposed that the lesbian life-style must be expunged of all derivatives of patriarchy. Two of these cultural appendages are monogamy and romantic love. Monogamy, they argue, was devised to protect the inheritance rights of men's sons, is unnecessary, and oppresses the personal growth of women; romantic love, they contend, is based on the captor/captive syndrome and is dangerous, materialistic, and manipulative. "Instead of love, coupledness and monogamy, the desired attributes for the radical lesbian feminist were sisterhood, comradeship, and class loyalty" (Lewis, 1979:170–171). To love women as women loved men was judged as counterrevolutionary as loving a man.

Accordingly, one's personal life is a political statement, radical lesbian feminists maintain. There are Politically Correct (P.C.) and Politically Incorrect (P.I.) statements—and lives (Bunch, 1975). In the 1970s and early 1980s, Politically Correct were multiple relationships, with no one relationship considered primary. Multiple involvements, it was argued, make a woman the top priority in her own life and radicalize her to assert and to nurture herself, rather than to defer to and nurture others. Celibacy was also Politically Correct. Also coming out of the closet were women who called themselves "political lesbians"—women who rejected ties to men, emotionally identified with females, but equivocated on their sexual desire for women (Cassell, 1977:77).

Although multiple relationships and sexual abstinence may work for some women at some time in their lives, on the balance, it seems that the ideology and the pressure to be Politically Correct create more grief than growth; further, it is based, unwittingly, on sexist assumptions. This radical lesbian feminist rhetoric is perpetuating some of the very institutions that it wishes to dispel. Moreover, to the extent that the ideology is held as the *only* Politically Correct one, we are faced with what Lewis calls "latter-day lesbian fascism" (1979:178).

First, their rhetoric assumes that monogamy between males and females is the *same* experience as monogamy between women. Yet, everything we are learning about gender suggests that one cannot take the experiences of men, or of women *with* men, and generalize them to women, or women *with* women. Women and men inhabit different gender worlds, and they enact gender differently, depending upon the sex of the other participants. We have much to learn about how monogamy works between women; we need to learn that before it is rejected for spurious reasons. Indeed, the very little we do know about lesbian monogamous relationships suggests that women in such relationships are more self-accepting, have fewer sexual problems, and report greater happiness than nonmonogamous lesbians (Bell and Weinberg, 1978).

Second, what has been appropriated and commended as Politically Correct— that is, the idea of multiple relationships—is simply the new left *male* idea of what constitutes liberation (Evans, 1979). There is nothing inherently feminist about that ideal. One of the outcomes of this ideological stance "is the coldness of instant, anonymous sexuality," which is similar to the male model, especially the stereotypical gay male's model, of quick sex. Women who want more than casual sex, or a one-night stand—women who want affection, nurturance, and emotional contact— will quite likely be hurt and dejected by this "meat rack" mentality (Lewis, 1979:178). As one woman commented, "They proclaim they're real feminists, but what I see is a bunch of women taking up the same values that have oppressed women for centuries, except now we're busy oppressing each other" (Lewis, 1979:197); that is, they are replicating some of the very forms of dehumanized and distancing sexuality that they abhor in male-female relationships.

Not only are stereotypically male attitudes toward sexuality being enacted, but female stereotypical ones are, as well. A lack of interest in sex is commonly attributed to women, and the radical lesbian feminist rhetoric makes it Politically Correct to be sexually abstinent. One cannot help but wonder about the doubts of self-worth and attractiveness that must be generated in a sexual lesbian woman who has the misfortune to love a political one. The inadvertent creation of feelings of inadequacy in the "bed gay" by the "head gay" is apparently Politically Correct. Such ideological extremism and orthodoxy demand and justify the sacrifice of the rights and pleasure of the individual to the goals of the group.

Despite the rhetoric, or perhaps because of some of the deleterious fallout from it, most lesbians have not changed their minds regarding their relational preferences: Most hold as an ideal the long-term, monogamous commitment (Lewis, 1979; Bell and Weinberg, 1978).

In terms of financial and domestic division of labor and in the social-emotional arenas, lesbian couples tend to look like the Scanzonis' (1976) flexible "nurturing-caretaking" type of marriage (Tanner, 1978; Blumstein and Schwartz, 1983). This kind of relationship is typically companionship-oriented, child-free, and flexible in role assignments. Lesbian couples, typically, are freer of role restrictions and behaviors than are heterosexual ones (Tanner, 1978). The patriarchal axiom that assigns tasks by sex can be dismissed by lesbians. They can create their own rules and roles, unbound by a sex-based division of labor (Tanner, 1978). However, although two women may be freed from male-female imbalances, they may find themselves enacting sex stereotypes that are prescribed for women. Some of these may help and others may hinder the development of a truly alternative life-style; for example, to the extent that "tidiness" and "whose kitchen is it anyway" becomes issues, or to the extent that withholding sex is used as a weapon or as a way of maintaining distance and autonomy (Lewis, 1979), these women will be reproducing in their man-free environment behaviors suitable for manipulating oppressors, not for creating equalitarianism. On the other hand, if they build their relationships on such female-attributed values as friendship, familial ties, community immersion, and mutual emotional caretaking—all values held by lesbians— then they can create nurturing relationships relatively free of the dominant patriarchal institutions. Lesbians are in the vanguard of social change in terms of women's roles (Blumstein and Schwartz, 1983:329). They are trying to solve the problem of independence and interdependence without resorting to traditional female roles, or without adopting traditional male ones.

The creation of alternatives is a possibility available to the lesbian single, couple, and community for several reasons. First, the lesbian cultural tradition of mutual support and trust is so strong that members see each other as family. The values of that family include nonauthoritarianism and egalitarianism, empathy, nurturance, and emotional involvement. Second, there is greater support among straights for the legal rights of lesbians to exist, to love, to work. Third, there is a growing source of knowledge and literature about their present and their history (cf. Cook, 1979; Smith-Rosenberg, 1975; Sahli, 1979; Rupp, 1980). Available to them is "a proud affirmation of women's right to love other women," supported by "activist communities" that are feminist in principle and striving to be egalitarian in practice (Taylor, 1980:225).

GAY MALE ALTERNATIVES

Not until the late nineteenth century did the social *categories* of homosexual and heterosexual emerge in Europe and America, which, of course, is not to say that homosexual and heterosexual practices did not exist before that time. However, before the 1890s, society apparently felt no great pressure to divide persons into categories based on their sexual orientation, and to label, ostracize, and persecute one category—homosexuals (Pedgug, 1979; Weeks, 1979). At the peak of this persecution and prosecution, persons who were accused of being homosexual lost civil rights and were incarcerated as criminals. Through the activities of the Gay Rights Movement, greater public acceptance and more legal rights have been accorded homosexuals, although full human rights are far from having been achieved (Bell and Weinberg, 1978).

Like the lesbian community, the gay male community is a "loosely knit extended series of overlapping networks of friends" (Hooker, 1967:180). The networks vary. Some are tightly closed cliques of "married" gays and/or singles, including heterosexually married men, whereas others are more loosely organized. Similar to the lesbian community, which is organized around female-based values, the gay community is organized around male-based values. Isolated from the heterosexual world, the gay man finds support and social acceptance within the gay community and develops a "deep emotional involvement with his group, tending toward a ready acceptance of its norms and dictates, and subjection to its behavior patterns" (Leznoff and Westley, 1977:187). Depending upon the gay community in which the male immerses himself, he may be socialized into a supermacho society, or alternatively, a fairly nonsexist one. His social and psychological dependency upon the community for support, however, will intensify his identification with the culture of that community.

The culture that dominated the male gay world from the sixties through the mid-eighties was a highly androcentric one, in many ways a macho one similar to and in some respects more extreme than the straight male society from which it has derived. Accentuated in that gay male culture, as in its parallel straight male culture, was sex—sexual exploits, sexual experiences, and sexual competition. Anonymous sex, instant sex, and multiple sex partners were normative.

Gay descriptions of sexual experiences were physically explicit, expressed in macho slang, and frequently degraded the speaker, the person being spoken about, and sexuality. Prestige is allocated to the physically attractive and sexually potent; youth is revered. Therefore, hostility and sexual rivalry were created and sustained within the macho gay community—just as they are in the straight male culture.

Flowing from this accentuation on sex is another supermacho cultural element—namely, rigidifying "masculinity" versus "femininity." "Femininity" is publicly displayed in the exaggerated mimicry of the female's language patterns, body postures, and movements. The female model chosen to be imitated is not the strong and assertive one but the "gossipy, backbiting bitch." Institutionalized is the practice of "drag"—dressing and making oneself up to pass as a woman. Drag queens, drag shows, and drag parties are common—even among men who are active in the Gay Rights Movement. Although some view dressing in drag as a "challenge to the patriarchal definition of maleness," it is accomplished through identifying with the "most oppressive aspects of femininity; that of being nothing but a bubble-headed sex object, helpless, overemotional, playing up to their opposite—real (butch) men" (Dappletree, quoted in Holland, 1978). Even if a man claims to dress in drag for political reasons (challenging definitions of masculinity), most feminist criticism would argue that drag is a "blatant mockery of women, as genuine a manifestation of misogyny as the straight male practice of sexual harassment" (Lindsey, quoted in Holland, 1978:400). Not only does the male in drag mock women, he also mocks his own femininity.

If the drag queen is one kind of exaggeration with macho gay culture, the macho man is another. Representing "total manhood," he may sport a Mohawk haircut, tattoos, a leather motorcycle jacket, or cowboy boots. His walk and posture show off his muscle-building body. Speech, demeanor, and style—all are out of a James Dean movie.

Similarly to the "butch" and "femme" roles that were played in lesbian culture in earlier periods, gay men have replicated the sexist assumptions of heterosexual couples. A particular gay couple may, therefore, assign one member the "wife" role and the other the "husband" role. The "wife" has been expected to run errands, be sexually receptive, take care of domestic needs, and to accept being put down in front of friends.

Frequently, the "wife" will be younger, less powerful, more physically attractive, and dependent upon the "husband" for financial support. One partner "fully embodies and expresses the cultural norm of male sexuality and male supremacist values and behaviors," whereas the other enacts a lack of virility (Stoltenberg, 1978:93); that is, some gay couples adopted heterosexual role models and created worlds that are based on masculinist principles. This is probably so for several reasons.

First, because men are severely sanctioned for adopting behaviors that are stereotypically associated with women, they may come to see such behaviors as *extremely* different from the ones that are assigned to men. They may, therefore, exaggerate the actual behavior and adopt their *idea* of it, rather than its actuality. Second, gay men are *men*. They have been raised in the same culture as straight men, and they have learned the same masculine assumptions. Gay men, like other groups of men—the American Legion, Bulls' Balls retreats, the Friday night bowling club—accentuate male-associated values, such as anonymous sex, competition, violence, and misogyny. And third, the Feminist Movement and the Men's Movement have not had the same impact on gay men as they have had on lesbians and straight men.

However, the macho gay world is not the only one that is available to gay men. Some men have "come out" through men's support groups that are concerned with eradicating sex stereotypes—including the stereotypes that are demeaning and disabling to men, and to gay men in particular. Rather than coming out as "queens" or "macho men," they are simply coming out as themselves. These men are trying to reshape their personal lives to fit more consistently with their political ideas about equality and freedom from gender rigidities.

Although these men were few in number a decade ago, their numbers, by all appearances, seem to be growing. First, because it is more acceptable to be gay, today, there are more places where these men can meet each other than in the gay bars. Gay dating services, gay support groups, and gay activists leagues are some such examples. Secondly, due to the AIDS epidemic, not only have gay men been altering their sexual practices, they have been rethinking how they are structuring their lives. One of the unexpected outcomes of AIDS has been the social mobilization of gay men and lesbians; through the social movement and social support organizations, gay men have been finding new resources for designing alternate lifestyles, and they are associating with lesbians who embody alternative life and relationship values.

Given that gay men are attempting to create long-lasting and egalitarian relationships in much greater numbers than before, what kinds of hurdles will they have to face? According to Blumstein and Schwartz's (1983) monumental study that contrasts gay men, lesbians, and heterosexual married and cohabitating couples, gay men currently have the hardest time achieving both equality and autonomy in their relationships.

On a day to day basis, Blumstein and Schwartz find that the gay male relationship is hard to sustain precisely because they are men and have incorporated male values; for example, it is hard for gay couples to move into an interdependent relationship (1983:110). Dominance and submission are difficult modes to overcome because each person feels that he should carry his own weight. If one makes more money than the other, for example, he feels he has the right to dominate; the one who makes less feels inferior as a male. Moreover, as men, they tend to be competitive over their work: The greater success of one threatens the other. Sexually, they compete for the right to initiate and determine the course of the encounter. In addition, because they have fewer skills for relationship building than women, they have fewer resources for mending the relationship when it has problems.

The overarching reason, then, that gay men are having more trouble establishing personally satisfying and long-lasting relationships is because to do so requires them to liberate themselves from the male culture. The historian of homosexuality, Jeffrey Weeks, has argued that until gay men become feminists, they will be exploited and exploitative (1979). Feminism that is incorporated into gay culture and that is lived by gay couples would create a "sexual politics" between men that is independent of sex-stereotyped role divisions and masculinist values that detract from the construction of truly intimate and trusting relationships between equals.

In general, then, cultural definitions persist and continually affect the kinds of relationships people can create. Regardless of affectional orientation, singles are subject to normative expectations. Their status is exploitable and exploited. Couples, whether married or unmarried, heterosexual or homosexual, are similarly subject to expectations. Despite the very best intentions of persons, and despite particular community and social support, normative standards persist and are carried into one's relationships.

For those who want a more egalitarian and meaningful life together, considerable energy, time, and strength must be devoted to finding a path that takes them where they want to go. All too frequently, "individual attempts to resolve the dilemmas posed by competition and hierarchy, in combination with the subordination of women, have failed to sustain meaningful lives" for the persons involved (Dizard, 1972:200).

The commitment and energy to change one's everyday life, therefore, can only take us so far. As long as our lives are constituted within a political, economic, and social structure that is sex stratified, our personal lives will be tainted and constrained. Only when the social and political institutions are changed, and cultural stereotypes and sexist ideological underpinnings are erased, might we find it possible to establish truly equalitarian intimate relationships. Inseparable—yesterday, today, and tomorrow—are the personal and the political. We look now at social movements whose goals are political and social change.

□ □ *14* □ □

Social Movements

If unchallenged, the political system will represent the interests of the governing elite. Socialization, social-control mechanisms, and powerful institutions, in a kind of synchronized dance, ensure the reproduction of the kinds of people who are needed to keep the dance going, night and day, day and night. If there was no way to question the goodness/pleasure/values of the dance, it would persist unchallenged and unchanged. However, a political system such as ours is designed not only to perpetuate elites but also to allow the interests of less well-placed persons to have an impact on the political arena. This impact is accomplished through *legitimate* "antisystem" activities, such as boycotts, strikes, mass demonstrations, and social movements. Indeed, it is a primary function of the disenchanted groups within a democracy "to hold a democratic system to its own pretensions" (Lowi, 1971:56).

Social movements are a part of the democratic political process—a necessary part in that they tend to restrict the oligarchic tendencies of the system by presenting alternative ideologies. Successful movements can change laws, provide for their implementation, and organize their membership to receive greater benefits (Freeman, 1975:2).

At the psychological level, involvement in movement activities tends to transform one's self-image. Part of this self-redefinition involves the recognition that what one previously thought of as personal problems are in fact experienced by many others. Sharing private realities counters social myths and helps politicize the problems; that is, perceiving personal problems as public issues leads to the need to influence public policy. "If such private recognitions are translated into public demands . . . the movement enters the political arena" (Freeman, 1975:5); if not, personal growth may occur, but the political institutions will remain unchanged.

Not all social movements enter the political arena, and not all that do are successful in achieving their goals. Increasingly, researchers are attempting to understand the structural conditions that lead to a movement's success. Because the

227

study of social movements is a complex one that contains many competing theories, I will limit this discussion simply to the conditions under which movements are likely to emerge, grow, and succeed.

Social movements emerge slowly, and usually painfully, when two preconditions exist: "a long period of discrimination and oppression coupled with a short period of progress that generates rising expectations in a particular substrata" (Baldridge, 1975:207). It is not the absolute hardships of oppression alone, but also the perceived relative deprivation—the gap between rising expectations and reality—that are prerequisite conditions for the emergence of a social movement. Although blacks have suffered long-term and absolute oppression in this country, for example, it was only after they compared their position to that of whites that the Black Power Movement arose.

However, in order for conditions to lead to the emergence of a social movement, there is a need to recruit and link together members. One effective way of accomplishing this is to locate an existing communications network that connects the potential recruits—one that is "co-optable to the new ideas of the incipient movement" (Freeman, 1975:48). This is most likely to occur if the persons who are linked in the network have similar backgrounds, experiences, and social status. If such a network does not exist, more energy must be expanded on initial organizing activities.

Further, for the movement to emerge, a precipitant is necessary. The precipitant may take the form of a crisis—an event (such as the refusal to serve blacks in a restaurant) that symbolizes the general discontent. Or the precipitant may be the formation of an organization that both disseminates the new ideology and provides an association with which the disenchanted can identify. "If a co-optable communications network is already established, a crisis is all that is necessary to galvanize it. If the network is organizationally rudimentary then an organizing cadre of one or more persons is necessary" (Freeman, 1975:49).

At this point, the movement is ready to flourish or flounder. If it is to grow, a movement organization must develop leadership that is able to perform both administrative and ideological functions. Leaders must be able to recruit members and inspire them to provide the movement with resources such as time, money, energy, contacts, and skills (Freeman, 1978). Enough structure must be provided to ensure the utilization of these resources, but enough "looseness" must also be permitted so that members will develop through interaction a loyalty to each other and a dedication to the movement.

Ideologically, the intellectual leaders must specify the goals and strategies of the movement, its enemies, and its utopian vision so that the "feelings, hopes, frustrations, and dreams" of its members are translated into action (Baldridge, 1975:319). Movement organizations that try to be everything to everyone are pushed into stating vague goals and strategies; consequently, although a social movement should draw upon a broadly based membership, each movement organization must develop its own strategy, style, and focus in order to mobilize membership. Social movements thrive when movement organizations are heterogeneous, with each organization having a unique and distinctive identity and style.

Success is largely determined by the movement's ability to mobilize resources, as well as the responses of other groups and agents of social control. Those who are in positions of power can respond in different ways: coopt the movement, grant the demands, or suppress the activities. Few movements are successful in having their demands fulfilled; even fewer see their goals enshrined as social policy and law. In addition, there is an irony here—if the movement does indeed succeed, it must die.

The social movement is a legitimate path that is open to the discontented, male and female alike. It has been the route chosen by women who are interested in altering institutionalized sexism. More recently, it has been tried by men who are similarly interested in liberating themselves from cultural and institutional restraints. Let us look at these social movements.

FEMINIST SOCIAL MOVEMENT

In 1776, Abigail Adams, the wife of John, firebrand of liberty and revolutionary thought, commended her husband that in shaping the constitution of the new republic he should "remember the ladies." She wrote:

> In the new code of laws which I suppose it will be necessary for you to make, I desire you would remember the ladies and be more generous and favorable to them than your ancestors. Do not put such unlimited power into the hands of the husbands. Remember, all men would be tyrants if they could. If particular care and attention is not paid to the ladies, we are determined to foment a rebellion, and will not hold ourselves bound by any laws, in which we have no voice or representation (Adams, quoted in Ruth, 1980:149–150).

Her husband told her to be patient, that there were more important issues than "women's rights."

Less than 75 years later, the energies of women were directed toward the freeing of slaves and enfranchisement. Commitment to human rights, however, did not extend to rights for women, and under the new constitutional amendments, protections and privileges were extended only to black males. Women, it was argued, were too "special" and "too vulnerable and weak" to be allowed the vote. The convenient lie of the pedestalled women is immortalized in the words of exslave Sojourner Truth, in 1851. Standing nearly six feet tall, head erect, and "eyes piercing the upper air like one in a dream" (quoted in Papachristow, 1976: 36), she addressed an Ohio Rights Conference in 1851:

> Dat man ober dar say dat womin needs to be helped into carriages, and lifted ober ditches, and to hab de best place everywhar. Nobody eber helps me into carriages, or ober mud-puddles, or gibs me any best place. . . . And a'n't I a woman? Look at me! Look at my arm! . . . I have ploughed, and planted, and gathered into barns, and no man could head me! And a'n't I a woman? . . . I have borne thirteen children, and seen 'em mos' all sold off to slavery, and when I cried out with my mother's grief, none but Jesus heard me! And a'n't I a woman?

In the 1920s, women finally won the right to vote. With that success, some women retired from social-movement activity. Others, however, such as Alice Paul, organized the Congressional Union and the National Women's Party. In 1923, they introduced into Congress the Equal Rights Amendment, and lobbied for its passage that year, and each succeeding year. Still others formed organizations such as the League of Women Voters, the Women's International League for Peace and Freedom, and the National Council of Women.

In the following 30 or so years, although women's movement activity appeared dormant, the Equal Rights Amendment and other women's rights issues were kept alive by these women's organizations (Rupp and Taylor, 1980). Although these organizations were elite-sustained social-movement organizations that were composed of only a few members, they kept ideas of women's equality alive "during the doldrums"—the late 1940s through the early 1960s—and provided resources for the transition, during the 1960s, into a mass-based social movement (Rupp and Taylor, 1987). Scholars emphasize that there is an historical continuity to the movement. As Rupp and Taylor (1986) argue, "Since at least the 1840's, the women's movement, although not always in the same form or with the same vigor, has raised a challenge to sexual inequality in America."

The 1960s witnessed a flourish of political activism—the Civil Rights Movement, student protests, and mass demonstrations for peace. The political activity of the 1960s sensitized many women to their second-class citizenship and led some to seek redress through political activity. There is some disagreement among scholars concerning the membership bases of the Women's Liberation Movement (cf. Cassell, 1977; Deckard, 1979; Freeman, 1978; and Taylor's review, 1979), although there is agreement that the membership was heterogenous and was drawn from at *least* two bases. First, there were older, college-educated women who were cast into the domestic and/or supplementary breadwinner role(s). If employed, they were receiving fewer monetary benefits and fewer chances for promotions than their husbands, male college friends, or male colleagues were. Second, there were younger women, who were then enrolled in college and/or immersed in the university street community. This street community of "flower children" touted such general values as "love," "sensitivity," "peace," "doing your own thing," "letting it all hang out," as well as more specific ones, such as ending the Vietnam War, decriminalizing marijuana, and racially integrating schools. In any case, three major structural preconditions for the resurgence of a mass-based women's movement existed—namely; greater education of women; greater rates of employment outside the home; and declining fertility (Klein, 1984).

The two social bases—older, professionally trained women and younger "hip" college students—created and built, as one might expect, different forms and styles of movement organizations. The organizations that they developed reflected their perception of the kind, amount, and source of their own relative deprivation. The older women moved toward a *moderate* ideology and organizational structure, whereas the younger women had a more *radical* vision.

The moderate branch of the movement was most prominently associated with the National Organization for Women (NOW), although other organizations such as the Women's Equity Action League (WEAL), Federally Employed Women (FEW), and the National Women's Political Caucus (NWPC) are also part of this branch. A major force for NOW's formation began in 1961, when President Kennedy established the first Commission on the Status of Women. The report of that commission in 1963 documented extensive legal and economic discrimination against women and proposed that commissions be established at the state government level. These commissions were composed of talented, politically active women. Their research not only supported the conclusions of the federal report, but also convinced other women that the situation required redress. Further, the existence of the official reports raised expectations that corrective action would be taken at the state and federal levels. The women who served on these commissions exchanged communiqués and reports and attended national meetings, thereby forming "an embryonic communications network among people with similar concerns" (Freeman, 1975:53).

Two important events occurred during this period. First was the publication of Betty Friedan's *The Feminine Mystique* in 1963. The book described the "problem that has no name"—the malaise, frustration, and boredom of the middle-class, middle-aged woman. Unpredictably and almost immediately, it became a bestseller. The second event concerned Title VII of the Civil Rights Act of 1964. In what was referred to as "ladies day" in the House of Representatives, Representative Howard Smith (D., Va.) introduced an amendment to include "sex" in Title VII, thereby making discrimination in employment illegal. The amendment, ironically, was introduced in order to defeat the bill in its entirety by splitting the liberal vote. The debate had a circuslike atmosphere and was an occasion of much laughter. However, through the determined activity on the part of its supporters, including Representative Martha Griffiths (D., Mich.), the amendment passed, only to have it described as a "fluke . . . conceived out of wedlock" by the executive director of the agency that was charged with its enforcement, the Equal Employment Opportunity Commission (quoted in Freeman, 1975:54). Subsequently, Representative Martha Griffiths attacked the agency on the House floor for its disrespect and ridicule of the law (Freeman, 1975:54).

The Citizen's Advisory Committee on the Status of Women rejected the resolution from nondelegates that the EEOC "be urged to treat sex discrimination as seriously as race discrimination" (Freeman, 1975:55). On June 30, 1966, 28 women, including Betty Friedan, decided the time had come to try to bring women into full participation in American society; thus, the National Organization for Women was founded.

NOW was conceived of as a kind of NAACP for women, with a general focus on economic and legal equality. It was (and is) a top-down, hierarchically structured organization with a formal constitution, officers, boards of directors, and so on. The initiators of the organization were drawn from women who had served on the state commissions and their friends, disgruntled employees of EEOC, and a Betty Friedan contingent. These women had few skills in organizing masses of people, but considerable expertise in using the media. "They could create the appearance of activity but did not know how to organize the substance of it. As a result, NOW often gave the impression of being much larger than it was" (Freeman, 1975:56).

NOW's goals were clearly within the mainstream of the American value system and thereby provided an organization with which women could identity.

Their initial goals were specified as a Bill of Rights and were adopted at the first NOW national conference in 1967. These were: an equal rights constitutional amendment; to enforce the law banning sex discrimination in employment; maternity leave rights in employment and in social security benefits; tax deduction for home and child care expenses for working parents; child day-care centers; equal and nonsegregated education; equal job training opportunities and allowances for women in poverty; and the right of women to control their reproductive lives.

Meanwhile, the more radical branch of the movement drew from women who had worked in other movements that were concerned with civil rights, peace, or socialism. Despite these latter movements' ideology of freedom and participatory democracy, their women members were cast into the traditional roles of serving men coffee, sex, food, and typed copy. Further, these movement organizations refused to consider the issues of women as relevant; for example, in December, 1965 (*after* the passage of the Civil Rights Act), the question of women's liberation was laughed off the floor at the Students for a Democratic Society's (SDS) convention. The requests of SDS women to place a resolution in the organization's newsletter, *The New Left Notes*, were honored by "decorating the page . . . with a freehand drawing of a girl in a baby doll dress holding a picket sign and petulantly declaring, we want our rights and want them now" (Freeman, 1975:58).

At the 1967 National Conference on New Politics in Chicago, although women succeeded in gaining the last place on the agenda, the chairperson refused to recognize them. Irate women rushed to the podium demanding an explanation. The chairperson "just patted one of the women on the head and told her, 'Cool down, little girl, we have more important things to talk about than women's problems.' The 'little girl' was Shulamith Firestone, future author of *The Dialectic of Sex* (1971) and she did not cool down" (Freeman, 1975:60). These incidents repeated themselves throughout the radical community.

Soon, women began to form caucuses and to use the underground press to communicate with each other. Spontaneously and independently of each other, at least five women's liberation groups formed in 1967 and 1968. Although these women lacked the resources and desire to form a national organization, they were skilled at local organization and at using the existing structure of the underground press. This branch was originally referred to as Women's Liberation. Structurally, it was composed of many small autonomous groups linked together by the feminist press and friendship networks. The groups were characterized by the exclusion of males, shared tasks, lack of formal leadership, and an emphasis on participation. The value system and organization structure are a direct consequence of the concerns of the radical community for participatory democracy.

Let us look more closely at these two branches of the movement—the moderate and the more radical—in terms of conditions necessary for a successful social movement. First, the two branches had available to them social bases from which membership could be drawn. The membership bases were different, but probably both had experienced long-term discrimination and recent rising expectations relative to significant reference groups. Both branches had preexisting communications networks: the older women through the states commissions on the status of women; the younger, through the radical community. Further, these networks were cooptable in that they linked together like-minded people. The older branch was highly sensitized to the unjust treatment of women, due to their own involvement in research on the status of women. The radical women shared an ideology of liberation for oppressed people. The sexist behavior and attitudes of their male counterparts highlighted their own exploitation. Both groups were confronted with crises. The older branch was spurred on by the refusal of EEOC to enforce the sex provision and by the nonchalant attitude toward it from federal officials. For the younger branch, the crises were frequent, each one serving to further symbolize the discontent and to focus it on the need for change. Given these conditions, the need for organizing the discontented into social movement organizations was requisite. In the older branch, organizers were virtually absent, which its slow growth of members evidence. In the younger branch, organizers were the major reason for the rapid growth and spread of the Women's Liberation Movement.

Lesbian feminists, a group oppressed in this society both for their sex and their sexual orientation were attracted early to the women's movement and helped forge its goals and strategies. Since they did not rely on men to financially support them, they especially felt the effects of discriminatory employment practices. Many lesbians hid their sexual identity in the early stage of the movement for fear their "aberration" would hurt the cause of feminism, since it was commonly believed within the movement that any taint of "lesbianism" would undercut the broad base needed to legitimize the movement's goals. By the late 1960s, however, lesbian feminists were "coming out" to their sisters and to the media; they insisted that a movement dedicated to the liberation of women could not ignore the double oppression experienced by lesbians. By 1970, the issue of lesbianism could not be contained: Rita Mae Brown formed a group, the Radicalesbians; at the second Congress to Unite Women, 20 lesbians wearing "Lavender Menace"[1] T-shirts took over the hall; Kate Millett announced her bisexuality; Ti-Grace Atkinson spoke to older lesbian groups; the Women's Strike Coalition marched in New York with all its members—lesbians and straights—wearing lavender arm bands. They handed out a New York NOW leaflet that read, in part:

> It is not one woman's sexual preference that is under attack—it is the freedom of *all women* to openly state values that fundamentally challenge the basic structure of patriarchy. If they succeed in scaring us with words like "dyke" or "Lesbian" or "bisexual," they'll have won AGAIN. They'll have divided us, AGAIN. . . . They can call us all Lesbians until such time as there is no stigma attached to women loving women.

Not all NOW locals were supportive; lesbians and lesbian supporters were purged from some local NOW chapters. Only after an extensive controversy and a bitter debate did the National NOW Convention in 1971 recognize its own culpability and resolved:

> That a woman's right to her own person includes the right to define and express her own sexuality and to choose her own life-style [and] that NOW acknowledges the oppression of lesbians as a legitimate concern of feminism.

---

[1]Lavender is a color composed of pink and blue—the color associated with homosexuality; and Betty Friedan had called lesbians the "lavender menace," a menace to the women's movement.

By 1970, the women's movement exploded in the media. Major stories appeared about it in the newsmagazines, magazines, telecasts, and prime-time specials. More members joined the existent organizations, and, more importantly, more organizations that drew upon different social bases were formed. Virtually no social category of women or social institution was left untouched. Within religious institutions, many activist groups formed—the National Coalition of American Nuns, the Women's Board of the Methodist Church, Church Women United of the National Council of Churches, the Unitarian-Universalist Women's Federation, to name a few. Professional women organized associations and caucuses within practically all professions and academic disciplines, which are united under the Federation of Organizations for Professional Women. Within government and politics, organizations such as Federally Employed Women (FEW) and the National Women's Political Caucus emerged. Labor women organized the Coalition of Labor Union Women (CLUW).

Throughout the 1970s, the numbers of women's activist groups proliferated, and NOW became an umbrella organization, clearing house, and media "spokes-organization" for the movement. During this period, moreover, NOW became increasingly radicalized, although not without considerable embittered fighting and "trashing" (Ryan, 1986). By 1977, with the NOW membership numbering 60,000, their convention adopted such planks as the recruitment of minority members; recognition of the interrelatedness of oppressions that are based on race, sex, ethnicity, class, and sexual orientation; and the use of more militant tactics to achieve goals (Rupp and Taylor, 1986).

During this same period, however, also with considerable infighting over "ideological purity" (Ryan, 1986), the radical branch of the movement became increasingly *issue*-oriented and focused on women's health, pornography, reproductive freedom, and women's culture, rather than on the transformation of the whole society. What was happening was a convergence between the two branches of the movement, with the older women becoming more radical in principle and in practice, and the younger branch taking on what might be thought of as reform activities, such as doing rape prevention workshops, opening shelters for battered women, and producing women's theater and concerts (Rupp and Taylor, 1986).

Thus, since the late 1970s, as Rupp and Taylor (1986) point out, the women's movement has become both more radical and more institutionalized. Women have been radicalized through reading feminist literature and seeing feminist culture, through the extensive network of feminist education (Klein, 1984), through participation in women's issues organizations, and through having their consciousnesses raised by personal experience—such as job discrimination, divorce, rape, and so on. Similarly, the feminist ideology has grown more comprehensive and wide-ranging (Taylor, 1983). "Feminism in the 1980's is transformational politics, a comprehensive ideology that addresses nearly every issue in the world" from nuclear proliferation to pollution to colonialism to poverty (Rupp and Taylor, 1986). Feminist thought now links diverse political and economic issues—all issues that affect the quality of life and potentiality of death for all the world's citizens.

Alongside this radicalization of the movement as a whole, there has been increasing institutionalization of its organizations and its goals. NOW, for example, is a sought-after political ally, an active "interest group" in democratic politics. Rape prevention groups, which grew out of the radical arm of the movement, are now supported by federal and state grants; the feminist analysis of rape as violence, and not sex, has widespread acceptance in classrooms and the media. Shelters for battered women are publicly supported, in some states through a "marriage tax" (!) (Rupp and Taylor, 1986).

Because there is no single organization or single spokesperson for the movement, though, the original decentralization is still operative and there continues to be diversity within the movement—divergence and differences, despite the convergences. Ferree and Hess (1985) have examined the divergence with a means-ends schema along the individual versus the community dimension. Is the *means* to social change the transformation of the individual or sociopolitical change? Is the *end* of feminist activity the freedom of the individual from social restraint or a transformed social and political world? (Ferree and Hess, 1985:41–42). Based on an analysis of these means-ends questions, Ferree and Marx develop a four-point typology of feminist activists: career feminists, radical feminists, liberal feminists, and socialist feminists. The typology, they propose, does not reflect "better or worse" feminists, but differences in "styles and strategies" that are appropriate at certain times and in certain circumstances (1985:42). Indeed, at different times in her life, the same woman may find herself at different points on the typology.

Career feminists see the means to liberation as coming through their own personal empowerment; and the end is to have greater freedom to pursue their own directions within the male world. For many, it means fighting for employment rights and opportunities, and networking with other women. *Radical feminists* are, also, concerned with individual transformation, but their reason is to create new communities that provide visions of sociopolitical alternatives outside the male world. Lesbian feminism and cultural feminism are variants of radical feminism.

In contrast to the focus on the individual as the change agent, *liberal feminists* focus on changing the sociopolitical world in order to make it more just and equitable for the individual. It is through changing social policy, laws, and the division of domestic labor, that liberal feminists see the possibility of changing the individual's life. Like the liberal feminists, *socialist feminists* see the means to social change as coming through the alteration of social structure, but they reject the idea of individualism as a goal. They see that belief as a harmful one that separates people and creates hierarchal arrangements between them. Capitalism is seen as creating competition between people; and both capitalism and patriarchy are impugned as distorting and limiting human potential. Socialist feminists envision a community as an end that develops the potential of all human beings.

Each of these kinds of feminist activity has accomplished different goals during the resurgence of the Women's Movement, and they illustrate the diversity and scope of the movement (Ferree and Hess, 1985:141–166). Career feminism has moved toward the sexual desegregation of the labor force, the involvement of women's issues in union negotiations, the uncovering of sexual harassment at work, and in the building of networks of women. Radical feminism has redefined "acceptable" female looks and presentation of self, created new language and concepts to "name" the oppression and to free one's thinking from male models of thought,

created new art and cultural forms of expression, redefined spirituality, and produced viable all-female communities. Liberal feminism has changed sex-discriminatory state and federal laws and policies, introduced affirmative action policies,
and established networks of women who are concerned with policy changes. Socialist feminism has introduced such new ideas as the "feminization of poverty"
(Pearce, 1979), "comparable worth" as the gauge for salaries, wages for domestic
labor, and sex, class, and race (as interrelated) systems of oppression.

ANTIFEMINISM

Any social movement that endures and is successful, spawns a backlash. The
women's movement has been no exception. During the 1970s, the New Right, a
highly organized countersocial movement engaged in antifeminist activism. Beginning as a coalition of groups that were opposed to abortion, busing, and the ERA,
the New Right has widened its goals to include a broad range of familial, institutional, economic, and foreign-policy issues (Rupp and Taylor, 1986). Their program calls for a return to an "idealized past," a time when America's military
strength was the envy of all and its governmental apparatus was small and non-
regulatory of individual's lives, a time when Protestant prayers were allowed in the
schools and sex education was not, and a time when the family hierarchy was clear:
Children obeyed parents, and wives obeyed husbands. Families remained intact.
Women did not work outside the home. What is desired is a return to masculinist
values—including "displays of strength, control over others, willingness to use
violence, and competitive success—all of which are rejected by the new feminism"
(Ferree and Hess, 1985).

Who are the women in the antifeminist movement? They tend to be disproportionately older, married homemakers, who are white, middle-class, religiously
fundamental, and politically conservative (Taylor, 1983; Ferree and Hess, 1985).
They have come to know each other through membership in churches and in such
organizations as Stop-ERA, Right To Life, antischool busing groups, private-
school tax-credit groups, and so on (Taylor, 1983). They oppose black civil rights,
see poverty as a personal failing (Smith and Kluegel, 1984), and worry about sex in
society (Ferree and Hess, 1985). Some believe that if women advance, men will
lose (Spitze and Huber, 1982). Others think that equality means women will have to
go into combat (Stiehm, 1982). They see feminists as antifamily, antihomemaker,
and as selfish narcissists (Klatch, 1986).

Ironically, antifeminist women are responding to many of the same issues that
concern feminist women; only their solutions are different. Antifeminist women are
probably more distrustful of men than feminist women, for example (Ferree and
Hess, 1985). Marabel Morgan, for example, is the author of *The Total Woman*,
which preys on women's fears that their husbands will leave them for younger and
sexier women; the underlying assumption is that men—and especially one's husband—cannot be trusted to be economically responsible or emotionally true.
Schlafly used this fear to forge a defense for conservative values. "Women who
fear the consequences of their inevitable failure to attain perfect femininity feel
perpetually vulnerable," and that vulnerability can be used to mobilize them to

"oppose changes" that create competition between husbands and wives or that puts husbands into close contact with other women (Ferree and Hess, 1985:135).

The antiabortion issue, in addition to being a moral and religious one, is consistent with the antifeminist distrust of men. Believing that men are irresponsible impregnators, they suspect that abortion gives yet another benefit to the male—a right to have his fun and not to pay for it, to refuse marriage and paternity, and to abrogate his duty to care financially for women and children. Their antidivorce stance, and especially the proposal for punitive alimony for guilty husbands, further underscores this antimale stance.

Some argue that the conservative movement is using the antifeminist stance as a springboard for returning the country to patriarchal and militaristic positions (Petchesky, 1981). The feminist movement is being blamed for most of society's woes: rising divorce, abortion, and teenage pregnancy rates; unemployment among white men; decline of Christian morality; increase in homosexuality, which, in turn, has brought the AIDS epidemic to America; a weakened dollar; slower economic growth; and a weak military posture (Rupp and Taylor, 1986). By denying women abortions, by limiting access to birth control information and products, by reducing welfare, and by turning back sex discrimination and affirmative action legislation, antifeminism policies will make women and their children financially dependent upon men, who will no longer have to compete with them or contend with their feminist values. Viewed in this way, antifeminism is more than a backlash; it is a method for "preserving domination that extends far beyond the family" (Ferree and Hess, 1985:136).

PASSIVE FEMINISM

The gains of the feminist movement have been many, and a high percentage of women endorses specific goals of the movement, such as "equal pay for equal work," reproductive rights, help for battered and displaced women, and more male involvement in child care (Ferree and Hess, 1985). They vote for women candidates, work for women supervisors, take courses from women professors, take advice from women counselors, and listen to females comment on the news. Many have the salaries and positions at work that they do, and the division of labor at home that they do, because of the political and social actions of feminists. Consistent patterns are emerging: Women, regardless of social class, educational level, or employment, have similar attitudes toward gender equality, and those attitudes have changed in a feminist direction (Schneider, 1987). A majority, now, for example, blame sex discrimination and not themselves for low salaries (Ferree and Hess, 1985). Yet, only a minority of women identify themselves as feminists (Ferree and Hess, 1985).

Why do so few women identify with the women's movement? Why do women so commonly say, "I'm not a feminist, but . . . ." One of the reasons rests in women's ideas of what "feminists" are. Women see the identity, feminist, as a stigmatized identity (Schneider, 1986). Feminists, they believe, deviate from gender norms in significant ways. First, women see feminists as presenting a self that is "unfeminine," aggressive, hostile, tough, and unattractive. If you're a feminist, the fear is that you will have to "give up" your beauty and your manners. Second, feminists are viewed as antimarriage and motherhood, which for older women translates into "antifamily," and for younger women, "antimale." If you're a feminist, the fear is that it will "pose insurmountable obstacles to involvement with men" (Schneider, 1986:15). Third, feminists are seen as lesbians. If you're a feminist, the fear is that you will have to advocate lesbianism. Finally, feminists are seen as women who want to beat men at their own game. If you're a feminist, the fear is you'll have to be an "ultraachiever" and/or enter male occupations, such as truck driving and combat soldiery.

The category, feminist, therefore, is a stigmatized one because women are making judgments based on the "taken-for-granted normative culture concerning womanhood" (Schneider, 1986:23). Societal norms have been so deeply internalized, that women still see deviance from them as undesirable and threatening. Women, young and old, are afraid that identification with feminism will make change in their lives necessary. The hardest changes and the most radical ones would be within the private domain.

Since, however, there is a considerable diversity among feminists in regard to their personal appearance, their marital and motherhood statuses, their sexuality, and their occupational achievement and choice, what is needed to confront the stigmatized label, feminist, is for this diversity to be publicized through the media and through personal interaction with women who accept feminist goals but do not identify with the label. As Schneider proposes (1986:26), "This means transforming the disclaimer 'I am not a feminist but' to 'I am a feminist and here's what it means to me.'"

RACE AND GENDER

In America, there are four race/sex groups: black men; black women; white men; and white women. Traditionally, all members of this society have been socialized to believe that white malehood is the superior status and that, as their legitimate birthright, white males should receive the greatest power, prestige, and opportunity. Socialization, however, is never complete, perfect, or omnipotent. Although the norms and values of the society are formally inculcated into its members, compliance is not always forthcoming. The more people perceive these norms as unfair, the less likely they are to comply. Because the demands made on subordinates are great and the rewards few, individuals located low in the social hierarchy have more reason to question the legitimacy of the norms that govern their lives.

Noncompliance within each of the four groups becomes even more predictable when we examine the gap between society's values and their own, and society's images of them and their images of themselves. A black girl, for example, may be taught by society that black women are irresponsible and lazy, yet she may experience the black women around her as competent, hardworking, and highly motivated; or she may learn that women are to be protected and pampered, yet, vicariously she may experience her own mother's exploitation.

In order to function, it is psychologically necessary to make sense out of the inconsistencies of the experiential world and the formal dictums of the society

(Festinger, 1957). One way to make sense out of the dissonance and to reduce the contradictions is to strive toward changing the norms of the system—the rules of the game. That striving to change the norms persists in our society. The major subordinate groups—black men, black women, and white women—have challenged definitions of themselves as weak, dependent, and worthless. They are trying to reduce their dependence and increase their power. Unless the total amount of power in the society can be increased, those with less power have to improve their positions by lessening the power of those groups above them in the hierarchy.

Because the power relationships between blacks and whites and between men and women in this society have been imbalanced, there is a complex pattern of power relationships between the four gender/race groups—white males, white females, black males, and black females (Franklin and Richardson [Walum], 1972). White males have historically and contemporaneously enjoyed the greatest power and prestige. The distribution of power among the subordinate groups is largely controlled by the values, ideology, and policies of the superordinate group. Being "white" in the eyes of the dominant group is superior to being "black," and, consequently, white women have enjoyed greater power than either black men or black women.

The distribution of power between black women and black men is a more complex problem. Objectively, black men have had greater access to educational and employment opportunities (Jackson, 1971:3–41). In terms of occupational placement and income, black men fare much better than black women do. Black men, in fact, have greater rights to distribute key resources than do black females. Black females, however, are generally perceived as being more powerful. This is for several reasons. First, white policies have been such that, historically and even currently, black females are defined as more powerful than black men. In the words of Thomas and Znaniecki, "If you define a situation as real, it is real in its consequences" (1918:76). The consequences have been the perpetuation of the belief that black women are dominant in black society—the "myth of black matriarchy." By defining reality in this way, black women have gained an unsought psychological advantage. It is profitable for the white male group to define black males as powerless, thereby lessening threats to their own masculinity. It is even more profitable to produce discord in the black community by favoring the black female; and it is most profitable if the black male, then, diverts his rage away from the white community toward the black female.

Second, more social-psychological power accrues to the black female than to the black male as a result of relative deprivation (Runciman, 1966). The black male, like all individuals in this society, has been taught that the ideal role model is the white male. Although he makes more money than the black woman, the black male is not measuring his performance in relation to the black woman, but to the white male. Compared to the white male's status, the black male experiences a sense of very real deprivation. The psychological response is to see himself as even less powerful than he is, which leads to "a self-fulfilling prophecy."

Consequently, the power hierarchy might most profitably be viewed as two separate hierarchies. There is an objective one, which places groups in descending order as follows: white males, white females, black males, and black females; but there is also a subjective or social-psychological one, which orders the groups as follows: white males, white females, black females, and black males.

In that the white female's positions on both the objective and subjective power hierarchies are consistent, she can increase her power by lessening her dependence upon the white male and by increasing her own power resources. Consequently, she has fought for access to educational and employment opportunities to reduce her financial dependence and has engaged in consciousness-raising activities to lessen her psychological dependence. In addition, she has developed alternative sources of gratification, such as sisterhood and career involvement, and she has sought access to decision-making positions. Some white men have aided this process either through involvement in the Men's Movement or through using their positions within organizations.

However, because the objective and subjective power hierarchies are not consistent in regard to blacks, the question is: Where has the political energy of blacks been directed? Major energy has been along the objective power hierarchy. Blacks have struggled to lessen their dependence upon the white structure through such techniques as black separatism and black capitalism, and they have worked to increase their access to key decision-making positions within the white structure. However, black males have played a predominant role in the Black Liberation Movement, and part of their energies have been directed toward lessening the perceived psychological advantage of the black female.

Lessening the power of the white male, then, has been an object of white women, black men, and black women. In addition, however, black men have been seeking to increase their psychological power within the black community and to reduce the advantages of black women in the white power structure.

BLACK WOMEN AND THE FEMINIST MOVEMENT

Why, then, when one of the outcomes of black liberation is to lessen her power and one of the outcomes of women's liberation is to increase her power, do so few black women elect to join the Women's Movement? Of course, there is no singular prototype black woman. Consequently, there are various reasons for not joining the Women's Movement, depending on socialization, perception of reality, and goals. In what follows, I offer five major reasons why black women refrain from involvement. These are based on students' journals, reading, and discussion. It is understood that not all black women will share the same reasons, but I believe this to be a fairly complete accounting of the important factors.

1. *White women's racism.* The membership and leadership of the Women's Movement are composed of white, educated, privileged women. Although ideologically they favor egalitarianism—between races and classes, as well as between the sexes—their behavior and feelings are frequently inconsistent with their intellectual precepts. White women are, after all, *white*; their feminism has not prevented them from acquiring the society's racist attitudes. Being black is less valued in this society than being white. If blacks numerically dominate or control an organization (institution, business, school), the cultural assumption is that the organization is less prestigious, less well run, and less desirable than its white counterpart. For some

women, entering the feminist movement is possible only if the members of the movement meet other standards—such as highly educated, business or professional, heterosexually married, Christian, white, and so on. For others, white liberalism takes over, and their discomfort with black women is demonstrated by expecting any particular black woman to speak for all black women ("Tell us, what do *black* women want?"). Black women who join to the Women's Movement, therefore, are confronted with white women's conscious and nonconscious racism.

2. *Race is a more salient variable than sex.* Despite the claim by Shirley Chisholm that she has experienced more discrimination as a woman than as a black (Chisholm, 1970:43), this is not the common perception of black women. As one black woman recorded in her journal, "As a woman, I am *suppressed*. But as a *Black* woman, I am *oppressed*. What can the [Women's Movement] do for me as a Black?"

The black woman's experience is qualitatively different from the white woman's experience. The impact of blackness is omnipresent, and totally structures the life chances of black women. Consequently, although the power of black women is diminished in the Black Movement, progress toward increased power in the society is more readily realized through black identity. One student wrote, for example:

> The view of black women and men in a very real struggle, for survival on the physical level, makes it necessary to lay to rest the myth that the black woman needs to join the Women's Liberation Movement. . . . The black man and woman can work together against the system.

Thus, black women perceive more at stake due to their blackness than due to their femaleness.

3. *Black male and black female relationships.* Just as the black experience is different from the white experience, the relationships between the sexes in the black substructure have been different from those in the white substructure. As one black woman stated, "We don't join women's lib because we're already liberated." Or, as Toni Morrison writes, "In a way, black women have known something of the freedom white women are now beginning to crave. But oddly, freedom is only sweet when it is won. When it is forced it is called responsibility" (Morrison, 1971:64). Stated another way, these women are saying that they have had a psychological advantage within the black power structure. This arrangement, which has been foisted upon them by the policies of the white substructure, has led to intolerable relationships between black men and black women. The black woman, by being defined by the white culture as more competent and responsible than the black man, has acquired an increasing lack of respect for black males (Morrison, 1971: 64). Black males, in turn, vent their rage on black women, seeing them as Geraldinesque enemies or "cobras" (Cleaver, 1968). The problem for black women is not to gain more power but to come to terms with the black male, to restructure new role relationships with him. Further, the restructuring between the sexes in the black community is, as one student puts it, "a family concern . . . and outsiders [white women] aren't invited."

4. *Attitudes toward white women*. Attitudes toward white women that are held by black women are decisively important in their reticence to join the movement. I will discuss two of the most crucial attitudes—namely, *distrust* and *distaste*. White women are, first and foremost, white; although they may not have been the ideological presenters of racism in this country, they have been ideological supporters. Why should they be trusted? Many black women believe that if they did join white women's caucuses, they would simply be used by them. Second, many black women have a distaste for white women. This distaste comes from two different sources. On the one hand, they have been taught that white women are the standard of beauty and behavior against which they are to be measured. Association with these images of femininity taught long ago serves to court in the black women feelings of worthlessness, ugliness, and inappropriateness—and in their offspring, rage. Black women in pure sanity voluntarily choose not to associate with persons who make them feel put-down or angry. On the other hand, black women have a distaste for white women because they don't respect them. Toni Morrison writes:

> Black women have found it impossible to respect white women. . . . Black women have no abiding admiration for white women as competent, complete people. Whether vying with them for the few professional slots available to women in general, or moving their dirt from one place to another, they regarded them as willful children, pretty children, mean children, ugly children, but never as real adults. . . . They were totally dependent on marriage or male support (1971:64).

To align with white women, then, is to align with a group that is neither trustworthy nor desirable. To feel sisterhood is difficult, insane, or impossible.

5. *Opposition to goals*. Opposition to the goals of Women's Liberation comes from at least three very different directions. First, some black women, as alluded to earlier, see the goals of the movement as completely irrelevant in their life experiences. Getting into medical school, getting a seat on the stock exchange, or getting lunch at the Men's Grill are not very pressing problems compared to getting medical services, getting a job, and getting food for the table. ''Escaping motherhood'' is not relevant compared to how to successfully *be* a mother (Morrison, 1971).

Second, there is opposition to the women's movement on the grounds that if it does succeed, it will only push black political goals further behind. The success of the Women's Movement means greater competition for scarce rewards, such as employment. Whites being white will reward white women with the positions. Further, the persons who will profit by the Women's Movement will not even be the radical women who spearheaded it, but rather the latecomers, the more traditional women. These traditional women, once they are vested with power, will continue the policies of the white men. In this struggle, neither the black nor the radical women will win; instead, the fruits of their struggle will go to continue the power imbalance.

Third, black women, like white women, have been socialized by the dominant culture, which declares that ''woman's place is in the home.'' Many black women are seeking what white women are turning their backs on. Some black women choose it for politicized reasons, like ''preventing genocide'' or ''getting behind her man.'' However, many choose it for glamorized American ideological reasons; for example, one black student wrote the following:

> To the White Women in this Class: The way you talk here, you seem to want what I've had all along. Well, you can have it. As for me, I'm going to marry a black brother, stay home, raise flowers and children and read recipes. You don't know what you're giving up . . . and what you're going to get isn't worth it.

The American ideal of pampered womanhood, for some black women, is the preferable goal—not liberation *from* the home, but liberation *to* the home.

These reasons for not joining the movement are clearly interwoven, and when the weave is examined, it looks like a proper fabric for shrouding Women's Liberation. The black woman, regardless of her ideological viewpoint, sees little to gain in direct or indirect advantages by participation in the Women's Movement and potentially a great deal to lose. It should not be surprising then that there are so few black women in the Women's Movement.

Although few black women have joined the Women's Liberation Movement, the Women's Movement has had an impact on black women and can play a role with Black Liberation. As discussed earlier, one of the chief problems within the Black Liberation struggle is the role relationship between black males and black females. The black power struggle has been directed not only to increasing black power within the white system but also to increasing the power of black males in the black community. One of the outcomes, as Linda LaRue suggests, is that:

> The Black Liberation Movement has created a politicized, unliberated copy of white womanhood. Black women who participated in the struggle have failed to realize for the most part the unique contradiction between their professed renunciation of capitalist competition and their acceptance of sexual colonialism (1970:61).

Consequently, LaRue argues, black women who are ashamed of their strength and competency seek to suppress it, adopt white notions of femininity, compete fiercely for black males, and rationalize the adoption of traditional domestic roles by politicizing them. In redressing the imbalance of power within the black community, then, black women have been politicized to imitate white women's roles—roles that white women have been casting aside.

Black intellectuals have diminished the importance of sexism for fear that raising the issue would lead to greater divisiveness between black men and black women. According to Stone (1979), however, a feminist consciousness would reduce internecine conflict in several ways. First, it would help black men to recognize how the sexist structure of work-home relationships contributes to their unemployment and absence from the home; second, eliminating sexism would encourage the development of individual talents; and third, it would reduce the anxieties of being ''masculine'' or ''feminine'' enough, thereby strengthening the interpersonal bonds.

Feminism, therefore, has a contribution to make to black male/female relationships. Black men and black women need not adopt worn-out white role relationships, nor retain worn-out white policy-based role relationships. Unlike the dynamics within the white power structure, where the white male is both dominant and threatened by the white woman's moves toward equality, the black woman is not threatened by the black man's increasing ability and competency. She welcomes it. Therefore, they are in a unique position to move toward an equality of respect, responsibility, and companionship.

The Feminist Movement, then, serves to keep alive the notion that other roles are possible, that the traditional white role relationship is faulty, and that persons can uniquely define and redefine themselves.

Should black women, today, become active in the Feminist Movement, it will not be for the first time in American history that black women's voices have been raised in protest. Although the history of the black women's struggle for freedom from both sexism and racism has been ignored, recent work by black feminist women have made that history visible (cf. Davis, 1983; Hooks, 1981). Nineteenth-century black women were active participants in the struggle against racism and sexism. "The harshness of her lot in a racist, sexist world and her concern for the plight of others led her to join the feminist struggle" (Hooks, 1981:193).

Over a hundred years ago, at the First Convention on Women's Rights in 1841 in Akron, Ohio, a white man spoke in opposition to equal rights for women, because they were physically delicate and physically inferior to men. Sojourner Truth, an exslave, took the podium in defense of women (see p. 229). Sojourner Truth's recognition of her oppression as a woman and as a black was shared by many other black women of the time (Hooks, 1981). Indeed, "Nineteenth Century black women were more aware of sexist oppression than any other female group in American society has ever been" (Hooks, 1981:161). Their status in society not only oppressed them, it prevented them from taking part in organized collective action. The nineteenth-century women's rights movements were racist—not one black woman was included in the Seneca Falls Conference on women's rights, for example (Davis, 1983:57); and women's clubs were totally racially segregated. This does not mean, however, that black women did not work for gender equality; for example, Mary Church Terrell, a president of the National Association of Colored Women, passionately worked for black rights and women's rights (Hooks, 1981). In 1892, Anna Julia Cooper wrote that the black woman is "confronted by the woman question and a race problem" and that her status is one that represents all the crossed "forces which makes for our civilization" (quoted in Hooks, 1981:166).

Black feminist activism went hand in hand with the articulation of the double oppression. Having been denied full participation in the white woman's rights movement, Josephine St. Pierre Ruffin organized the First National Conference of Colored Women in 1895. She told the assembled body that black women had particular problems to confront, such as how to raise children in a racist society and how to improve their own lot, physically and educationally. She also said:

We want, we ask the active interest of our men, and, too, we are not drawing the color line; we are women, American women, as intensely interested in all that pertains to us as such as all other American women; . . . we are only coming to the front, willing to join any others in the same work and cordially inviting and welcoming any others to join us (quoted in Hooks, 1981:164).

Black women worked for women's rights in the suffrage movement, but found that winning the vote had little impact on their lives. White women voted as their husbands did, and the National Women's Party worked for the interests of elite white women (Hooks, 1981; Davis, 1983). Black activists felt betrayed. While white feminists were rejoicing about winning the vote, a system of racial segregation was being instituted in America, and it was being ignored by those white feminists. Black women turned their attention to the civil rights struggle. From 1920 to 1960, black female leaders turned their back on sex equality for fear that appearing "feminist" would hurt the cause of black liberation (Hooks, 1981). Black women became depoliticized throughout the 1950s, and were socialized as white women were to some idealized version of femininity. When the women's movement reemerged, black women were suspicious and remained outside of it for all the reasons that have previously been discussed.

Today, the great majority of black women remain outside the Feminist Movement because they fear feminism. "They have stood in place so long they are afraid to move. They fear change" (Hooks, 1981:195). Fearful of losing what little gains they have made, they do not confront feminists on their racism, or black men on their sexism, or white men on their racism and sexism. Some black women, however, have joined the ranks of active feminism and have rekindled the spirit of their nineteenth-century foremothers. As Hooks states, "We, black, [feminist] women . . . are clearing the path for our sisters. We hope that as they see us reach our goal—no longer victimized, no longer unrecognized, no longer afraid—they will take courage and follow" (1981:196).

MEN'S MOVEMENT

When the Women's Liberation Movement was reaching its crescendo in the press during 1970–1971, a new movement began to emerge on college campuses: the Men's Liberation Movement. According to its scant chronology (Pleck, 1973), predominantly white, middle-class males met together initially in reaction to alterations of their lives or psyches, due to their involvements with newly emergent feminists. One such Chicago group, Men Against Cool (MAC), stated, "[We] are a group of guys who, almost to the man, have come together out of confrontations with women over the nature of our sexism" (1970). The Berkeley Men's Center, issued a manifesto that included the following statements:

We, as men, want to take back our full humanity. . . . We no longer want to feel the need to perform sexually, socially, or in any way to live up to an imposed male role, from a traditional American society or a "counterculture."

We want to relate to both women and men in more human ways—with warmth, sensitivity, emotion, and honesty. . . . We want to be equal with women and end destructive competitive relationships between men.

We are oppressed by conditioning which . . . serves to create a mutual dependence of male (abstract, aggressive, strong, unemotional) and female (nurturing, passive, weak, emotional) roles.

We believe that this half-humanization will only change when our competitive, male dominated, individualistic society becomes cooperative, based on sharing of resources and skills. We want to use our creative energy to serve our common needs and not to make profits for our employers (n.d.).

Although some of the spokespersons for the Men's Movement focus on the need for institutional change, the groups themselves adopted the model of the younger branch of the Women's Liberation Movement—small, autonomous, and, theoretically, leaderless. Their ideology closely paralleled the radical feminist model—social change was to come through changing individuals.

Through the next decade and a half, the Men's Movement became increasingly institutionalized and centralized. Conventions on "Men" and Men's Studies programs began to appear at universities. On January 1, 1984, the first "Men's Studies Newsletter"—a mimeographed four-pager that listed books, announcements, and courses—was published by a fledgling organization, The National Organization for Men. Less than eighteen months later, the organization was ready to publish a more substantial journal and to change its name to The National Organization for Changing Men—a name that more fully reflected its goals and purposes.

NOCM does not claim that men are oppressed *as men* in the same way that women and minorities are oppressed, but it insists they have problems that are brought on by the male role. These problems include spending too much time at work to the neglect of personal relationships; acting aggressively rather than in nurturant ways; avoiding anything that appears feminine; competing with men rather than being friends. NOCM believes that "men can help ourselves and other men diversify beyond the limiting boundaries of the 'macho training' we have all received" (National Organization for Changing Men, n.d.). Moreover, they acknowledge an intellectual and emotional debt to feminism, and express their desire to work to change the larger patriarchal society—a society that negatively affects men, too. Their statement of purpose says:

The social structure of our society is closely connected to other ways in which some men have power over others: rich over poor, white over black, old over young, etc. NOCM members recognize the injustice of all such forms of oppression, and see them as historically connected to the ancient patriarchal pattern whereby a few powerful men obtain power over other men, women, children, and the environment. We believe that struggle against sexism is closely related to other struggles against oppression.

Seeing the advantages that accrue to certain men in a patriarchal system and the links between all forms of oppression, NOCM has set itself a broad agenda. It is concerned with the aspects of the male role that impoverish men; the oppression of women in all its guises; and oppressions that arise from homophobia, classism, and racism. As they have become institutionalized, their programmatic goals and analysis have become more diverse, paralleling the varieties of feminism that are found in the Women's Movement.

Membership in NOCM, like most feminist organizations, is largely composed of white men, although women are welcome in the organization. Contrary to popular belief, most of the men in NOCM are not gay men, who tend to gravitate to gay activist groups, but men who are primarily concerned with building their relationships with women and children (Ferree and Hess, 1985). Also contrary to some men's interpretations, the organization is not a backlash organization.

Recently, NOCM has been addressing issues of its own racism and the special problems that are experienced by black men, in general, and by black men in a white man's movement, in particular (Franklin and Mosmiller, eds., 1986). Tony Bell, NOCM's Liaison to Concerns of Ethnic Men of Color, analyzes some of the problems of men of color and proposes some alternative strategies for the recruitment of minority members (1986). The few men of color in the organization have been assigned the task of "minority recruiter." White men become absolved of the responsibility of recruiting minority members, and men of color become race task specialists; they become the "expert" on race-defined issues, which are segregated from the general issues that all men face as *men*.

Without denying that men of color have particular problems that are based on race, Bell proposes that the best way to recruit minority members is to disseminate policy statements on issues that are of concern to black men as men—issues such as fatherhood, work, and war—through the media. Within the organization, moreover, the black man should not have to be the "confronter" on racism issues; white men can take on that role.

What success might be expected from the Men's Movement becoming a mass-based social movement? Is there a potential social base? In that women are inconsistently socialized, it is easier, once the myths are exposed, to organize the discontented and relatively deprived around political, and social issues. The complexity of the demands of the Women's Movement, further, allows various people to plug into it at different times; for example, the goals of equality of opportunity and the right to be rewarded for achievements are within the mainstream of the American value system.

But parallel supportive arguments cannot be made for the Men's Movement. White males are consistently socialized to view themselves as valuable and to achieve within the system. Their privileged position within the system does not give them the structural advantage of challenging their own treatment as unfair. Most of the goals of the Men's Movement are not easily politicized. Although one of these goals—men's relationship to their work—has a great potential for politicizing—particularly in times of economic uncertainty—the Men's Movement has not treated it as a public issue that is capable of alteration through political action.

The Men's Movement is also hindered by major social-psychological obstacles within the male population. Women who feel comfortable and protected are not likely to join the Women's Movement. Analogously, most men, even if they don't feel they "have it made," are living in a society where to admit disillusion is to suggest that there is something wrong with them—as men. This is a difficult mindset for a social-movement organization to overcome.

Perhaps the most important barrier to the Men's Movement, however, is the fundamental dilemma that any antipower group faces. Farrell has articulated this dilemma well: "On the one hand they are attempting to obtain enough power to stop a system (capitalism) which only recognizes power from its tendencies toward power aggregation. However, in the process of gaining this power, they are faced with the prospect of individuals in the new system becoming power hungry themselves" (1975:172–173).

The Men's Movement—striving as it does to wrest its members from the tyranny of power and competition—faces this dilemma. How can it engage in the political sphere without reinforcing the power in the psychology of its adherents?

THE FUTURE OF THE FEMINIST MOVEMENT

The diversity of the Women's Movement has provided it with a particular strength. The radical branch had skills in organizing at the local level and in providing feminist analyses, while the moderate branch had been prodded by these analyses to implement change at the governmental level. In effect, a symbiotic relationship between the two branches developed. The symbiosis has led to an irony: The more conservative branch became more radical, whereas the more radical branch became more reformist in activity (e.g., establishing local self-help clinics, women's media centers, rap groups, and cooperative garages).

Before the development of the Women's Movement, there was virtually no national policy on women. Since the emergence of the movement, however, a national policy has been created to favor legal equality of rights and protection for men and women. Much legislation has passed, including the Credit Bill, which prohibits discrimination in loan eligibility based on sex or marital status; Title VII of the Civil Rights Act, which prohibits discrimination in employment based on sex; Title IX of the Education Amendments Act; which withholds federal financial assistance to any educational program that discriminates by sex; equal rights legislation within some states; the legalization of abortion; the revision of the income tax laws; the displaced homemaker act; and state provisions for abused women.

Much of this legislation has been a direct result of the ability of the Women's Movement to mobilize its constituency into effective political participation through demonstrations, letters, lobbies, and so on. What is particularly remarkable about these achievements is the speed with which the notoriously slow legislative apparatus has moved.

The first step toward social change—legislation—has been accomplished for some of the goals of the movement. More equal rights laws than ever before are on the books at both the federal and state levels. As such, a legal-moral climate is provided for them, and legal recourse for redress is open.

There has, also, been a major change in the society's consciousness about women, men, and their relationships to each other at work and at home. New words—such as *sexism, male chauvinism,* and *androgyny*—have entered daily discourse. New institutions—such as programs for displaced homemakers, shelters for battered women, and rape crisis centers—have arisen. Women are clergy, judges, truck drivers, diplomats, fire fighters—all occupations denied to them less than 20 years ago. Indeed, the accomplishments of the Feminist Movement have been so great that young men and women are increasingly unlikely to recognize the role that feminist action played in achieving the gender equality that they are experiencing. Young women may feel that the older feminists are "old-fashioned" and "out of touch" with the lives of "today's woman"—a woman who has expanding opportunities at work, and a more equal relationship at home.

There is no question that women in the 1980s face different problems and have different choices than the women in the 1960s did. Due in great measure to the success of the Feminist Movement, few women view job discrimination as justifiable; few want to be full-time homemakers; few think of violence against women as acceptable; and most expect their husbands to share in domestic responsibilities (Ferree and Hess, 1985). ". . . the sense of changeless repression, of constant pressure for women to become kitchen-bound domestic servants that animated young feminists" in the 1960s is not the experience of young women, "who blithely expect to 'have it all' " (Ferree and Hess, 1985:181).

Does this mean that feminism cannot successfully address the problems of younger women? What do the life experiences of the 1980s woman portend for the future of feminism? Ferree and Hess (1985) suggest three different possibilities. One possibility is that because this generation has grown up with a feminist consciousness, its expectations will be high. When they meet up with the inevitable obstacles to their occupational success, and when their youth and sexual desirability begin to wane, they will become active feminists. A second possibility is that this generation will not find feminism personally relevant. If this is so, then the older feminist's task is to try to reach these women, and teach them about other women's lives, including the history of feminism. Third, because generations change, older feminists have to consider that the feminist agenda for this generation has to change. This generation, like the one before it, will have to speak for itself; "feminism is not simply a form of received wisdom" (Ferree and Hess, 1985:182). If this happens, the direction that the movement takes will change, reflecting the interests of this generation. Rather than simply being disciples in an existing feminist movement, these younger women can set their own goals within their movement (Ferree and Hess, 1985).

Each generation inherits a different world, changed and altered by the generations that preceded it. Social-movement activity, as a result, has a generational component. Rossi (1982) proposes that the Woman's Movement has a two-step, two-generation process. The first generation recognizes the injustices and inequities of sexual stratification, and struggles to achieve social change. The second generation inherits those changes, and lives within that new world, testing its boundaries, experiencing its freedom as well as its constraints. The third generation takes freedom for granted, but feels the restraints intensely, thus becoming a first generation, striving to accomplish sociopolitical change. Structural changes have to become a part of women's daily lives and consciousnesses, though, before women can make demands for further change. The changes have to be assimilated as life experiences before women can articulate what else needs to change in the society: The second generation is the assimilation generation.

Today, while the younger generation is testing the limits of its world, the

Women's Movement is being kept alive by the older cadre of feminists (Schneider, 1986)—just as feminism was kept alive after women's suffrage by a small cadre of older women (Rupp and Taylor, 1987). If the women who come of age in the 1980s opt not to be feminist activists, that will not mean that feminism has died. Rather, they are the midwives to the next generation—a generation that will have a striking affinity with their ''feminist grandmothers.''

References

Abbott, Sidney, and Love, Barbara. *Sappho Was a Right-on Woman*. New York: Stein and Day, 1973.

Abrahams, Roger. "Joking: the training of the man of words in talking broad." Pp. 215–240 in Thomas Kochman (ed.), *Rappin' and Stylin' Out: Communication in Urban Black America*. Albuquerque, NM: The University of New Mexico Press, 1972.

———. "Negotiating respect: patterns of presentation among black women." Mimeographed. Austin: University of Texas, n.d. Abbreviated version in *Journal of American Folklore* 88 (1975): 58–80.

Abzug, Bella, and Kelber, Mim. *Gender Gap*. Boston: Houghton Mifflin, 1984.

Acker, Joan R. "Women and stratification: a review of recent literature." *Contemporary Sociology* 9 (1980): 25–35.

Adams, C. F. (ed.). *Familiar Letters of John Adams and His Wife Abigail Adams*. New York, 1876. Quoted in Sheila Ruth, *Issues in Feminism: A First Course in Women's Studies*. Boston: Houghton Mifflin, 1960.

Adams, Harold J., and Durham, Leona. "A dialectical base for an activist approach to counseling." Pp. 111–128 in E. Rawlings and D. Carter (eds.), *Psychotherapy for Women: Treatment Toward Equality*. Springfield, IL: Charles C. Thomas, 1977.

Adamsky, Cathryn. "Changes in pronounal usage in a classroom situation." *Psychology of Women Quarterly* 5 (1981): 773–779.

Adler, Freda. *Sisters in Crime: The Rise of the New Female Criminal*. New York: McGraw-Hill, 1975.

Almquist, Elizabeth M. "The income losses of working black women: product of racial and sexual discrimination." Paper presented at American Sociological Association, New York, August, 1976.

———. *Minorities, Gender and Work*. Lexington, MA, Lexington Books, 1979.

Almquist, Elizabeth, and Angrist, Shirley. "Role model influences of college women's career interests." Pp. 301–323 in Athena Theodore (ed.), *The Professional Woman*. Cambridge, MA: Schenkman Publishing, 1971.

Alpert, Jane. "Mother's right." *Ms.*, August 1972: 90ff.

Altman, I., and Nelson, P. A. "The ecology of home environments." Technical Report,

Project No. 0–0502, U.S. Department of Health, Education and Welfare, Office of Education, Washington, D.C., January, 1972.

Alwin, Duane F. ''From obedience to autonomy: changes in traits desired in children, 1924–1978.'' Paper presented to the American Sociological Association Meetings. New York: 1986.

American Association of University Professors. ''Table: Percentage of faculty members with tenure status, by category, affiliation, academic rank, and gender, 1985–86.'' Washington, D.C.: American Association of University Professors, 1986.

Amir, Nebachem. *Patterns of Forcible Rape*. Chicago: University of Chicago Press, 1971.

Amudsen, Kirsten. *A New Look at the Silenced Majority: Women and American Democracy*. Englewood Cliffs, NJ: Prentice-Hall, 1977.

———. *The Silenced Majority*. New York: Prentice-Hall, 1971.

Angrist, Shirley; Dinitz, Simon; Lefton, Mark; and Pasamanick, Benjamin. *Women After Treatment*. New York: Appleton-Century-Crofts, 1968.

Anonymous. ''The evolution of a suffragette, 1912.'' *RAT* 18 (1971): 14.

Anonymous. *3500 Names for Baby*. New York: Dell, 1969.

Arditti, Rita; Klein, Renate Duelli; and Minden, Shelleky (eds.), *Test-Tube Women: What Future for Motherhood?*. London: Pandora Press, 1984.

Ardrey, Robert. *The Territorial Imperative*. New York: Atheneum Publishers, 1966.

Arkin, B., and Dobrofsky, L. ''Job sharing.'' In Rhona Rapoport and Robert N. Rapoport (eds.), *Working Couples*. New York: Harper & Row, 1978.

Armstrong, Christopher F. ''The education of Christian gentlemen: British and American boarding schools and the perpetuation of class authority.'' Unpublished paper presented at the North Central Sociological Association Meetings, Dayton, Ohio, 1980.

Atkin, Charles K. ''Effects of television advertising on children. Report #2: Second Year Experimental Evidence. Final Report.'' East Lansing: Michigan State University, College of Communication Arts, 1975.

Bachofen, Johann Jacob. *Myth, Religion and Mother Right*. Princeton, NJ: Princeton University Press, 1976.

Baker, Sally Hillsman. ''Women in blue-collar and service occupations.'' Pp. 339–376 in Ann H. Stromberg and Shirley Harkess (eds.), *Women Working: Theories and Facts in Perspective*. Palo Alto, CA: Mayfield Publishing Company, 1978.

Baldridge, J. Victor. *Sociology: A Critical Approach to Power, Conflict and Change*. New York: Wiley, 1975.

Balswick, Jack, and Peek, Charles. ''The inexpressive male: a tragedy of American society.'' *The Family Coordinator* 20 (1971): 363–368.

Bandura, Albert, and Walters, Richard H. *Social Learning and Personality Development*. New York: Holt, Rinehart and Winston, 1964.

Banner, Lois W. *American Beauty*. Chicago: The University of Chicago Press, 1983.

Barash, David. ''Sociobiology of rape in mallards: responses of the mated male.'' *Science* 197 (1977): 788.

———. *Sociobiology and Behavior*. New York: Elsevier, 1977.

Bart, Pauline. ''Women's self-help: a new medical concept.'' Presented at the North Central Sociological Association Meetings, Windsor, Canada, 1974.

———. ''The loneliness of the long-distance mother.'' Pp. 156–170 in Jo Freeman (ed.), *Women: A Feminist Perspective*. Palo Alto, CA: Mayfield, 1975.

Baxter, James C. ''Interpersonal spacing in natural settings.'' *Sociometry* 33 (1970): 444–456.

Baxter, Sandra, and Lansing, Marjorie. *Women and Politics*. Ann Arbor, MI: University of Michigan Press, 1983.

Beard, Mary. *Woman as Force in History*. New York: Collier, 1971.

Beatty, John. "Sex, role, and sex role." Pp. 43–52 in Judith Orasanu; Miriam K. Slater; and Lenore Loeb Adler (eds.). *Language, Sex and Gender. Does La Difference Make a Difference?* New York: New York Academy of Sciences Annals, 1979.

Becker, Howard. *Sociological Work: Method and Substance*. Chicago: Aldine, 1970.

Becker, Howard, and Strauss, Anselm. "Careers, personality and adult socialization." *American Journal of Sociology* 62 (1956): 253–263.

Bell, Alan P., and Weinberg, Martin S. *Homosexualities: A Study of the Diversity Among Men and Women*. New York: Simon and Schuster, 1978.

Bell, Tony. "Black men in the white men's movement." *Changing Men: Issues in Gender, Sex, and Politics* 17 (1986): 11–12 passim.

Bem, Sandra. "Psychology looks at sex roles: where have all the androgynous people gone?" Paper presented at University of California-Los Angeles Symposium on Women, May 1972.

Bem, Sandra, and Bem, Daryl. "Does sex-biased job advertising 'aid and abet' sex discrimination?" *Journal of Applied Social Psychology* 3 (1973): 6–18.

Bem, Sandra; Martyna, Wendy; and Watson, Carol. "Sex-typing and androgyny: further explorations of the expressive domain." *Journal of Personality and Social Psychology* 34 (1976): 1016–1023.

Benbow, C., and Benbow, Stanley J. "Sex differences in mathematical reasoning ability: fact or artifact?" *Science* 210 (1980): 1262–1264.

———. "Sex differences in mathematical reasoning ability: more facts." *Science* 213 (1983): 1029–1031.

Bendix, John. "Linguistic models as political symbols: gender and the generic 'he' in English." Pp. 23–42 in Judith Orasanu; Miriam Slater; and Lenore Loeb Adler (eds.), *Language, Sex and Gender: Does La Difference Make a Difference?* New York: New York Academy of Sciences Annals, 1979.

Benokraitis, Nijole V., and Feagin, Joe R. *Modern Sexism: Blatant, Subtle and Covert Discrimination*. Englewood Cliffs, NJ: Prentice-Hall, 1986.

Benston, Margaret. "The political economy of women's liberation." *Monthly Review* XXI (1969): 13–27.

Bentzen, Frances. "Sex ratios in learning and behavior disorders." *National Elementary Principal* 46 (1966): 13–17.

Berger, John. *Ways of Seeing*. London: Penguin Books, 1972.

Berger, Peter, and Luckman, Thomas. *The Social Construction of Reality*. New York: Anchor Books, 1967.

Berkeley Men's Center. "The Berkeley Men's Center Manifesto." Mimeographed. Berkeley, CA: n.d.

Bernabei, Rita. "Can you tell me how to get to Sesame Street?" Mimeographed. Columbus, OH: Ohio State University, 1974.

Bernard, Jessie. *Academic Women*. University Park, PA: The Pennsylvania State University Press, 1964.

———. "The benign effects of childlessness." Pp. 322–352 in Judy Blankenship (ed.), *Scenes from Life: Family, Marriage and Intimacy*. Boston: Little, Brown and Co., 1976.

Bernstein, Barton E. "Legal problems of cohabitation." *Family Coordinator* 26 (1977): 361–366.

Best, Raphaela. *We've Got All the Scars*. Bloomington, IN: Indiana University Press, 1985.

Bettelheim, Bruno. "Dialogue with mothers: what makes boys masculine. *Ladies Home Journal*, September 1972: pp. 41–42.

Bienen, Leigh; Ostriker, Alicia; and Ostriker, J. P. "Sex discrimination in the universities." Pp. 370–377 in Nona Glazer (ed.), *Women in a Man-Made World: A Socioeconomic Handbook*. Chicago: Rand McNally Publishers, 1977.

Bird, Phyllis. "Images of women in the old testament." Pp. 41–88 in Rosemary Reuther (ed.), *Religion and Sexism: Images of Women in the Jewish and Christian Traditions*. New York: Simon and Schuster, 1974.

Birdwhistell, Ray L. *Kinesics and Context: Essays on Body Motion Communication*. Philadelphia: University of Pennsylvania Press, 1970.

Blau, Francine D. "Women in the labor force: an overview." Pp. 211–226 in Jo Freeman (ed.), *Women: A Feminist Perspective*, 1st ed. Palo Alto, CA: Mayfield, 1976.

———. "Economists' approaches to sex segregation in the labor market: an appraisal." *Signs* 1 (1976): 181–199.

———. "Women in the labor force: an overview." Pp. 297–315 in Jo Freeman (ed.), *Women: A Feminist Perspective*. Palo Alto, CA: Mayfield Publishing, 1984.

Blaxall, Martha, and Reagan, Barbara. *Women and the workplace: the implications of occupational segregation*. *Signs* 1 (1976): Supplement.

Bleier, Ruth. "Bias in biological and human sciences: some comments." *Signs* 4 (1978): 159–163.

———. "Occupational segregation and labor market discrimination." In Barbara Reskin (ed.), *Sex Segregation in the Workplace: Trends, Explanations, Remedies*. Washington, D.C.: National Academy Press, 1984.

Blood, Robert O., and Wolfe, Donald M. *Husbands and Wives: The Dynamics of Married Living*. New York: The Free Press, 1960.

Blotnick, Srully. "Dangerous times for middle-managers." *Savvy*, May, 1986.

Blumberg, Rae Lesser. *Stratification: Socioeconomic and Sexual Inequality*. Dubuque, IA: Wm. C. Brown, 1978.

———. "A general theory of sex stratification." In Randall Collins (ed.), *Sociological Theory* San Francisco: Jossey-Bass, 1984.

Blumstein, Philip, and Schwartz, Pepper. *American Couples: Money, Work, Sex*. New York: William Morrow, 1983.

Bodine, Ann. "Androcentrism in prescriptive grammar: singular 'they,' sex-indefinite 'he' and 'he' or 'she'." *Language in Society* 4 (1975): 129–146.

Booth, Alan; Johnson, David; White, Lynn; and Edwards, John. "Predicting divorce and permanent separation." *Journal of Family Issues* 6 (1985): 337–346.

Boren, Jerry. "The single father." Pp. 423–434 in Judy Blankenship (ed.), *Scenes from Life: Family, Marriage and Intimacy*. Boston: Little, Brown and Co., 1976.

Boserup, Ester. *Women's Role in Economic Development*. London: Allen & Unwin, 1970.

Boskind-Lodahl, M. "Cinderella's stepsisters: a feminist perspective on anorexia nervosa and bulimia." *Signs* 2 (1976): 120–146.

Boston Women's Health Book Collective. *Our Bodies, Ourselves*. New York: Simon and Schuster, 1984.

Boswell, Sally L. "Study on women's career choice and academic achievement." *Association for Women in Mathematics Newsletter* 9 (1979): 14–15.

Brabant, Sarah. "Sex role stereotyping in the sunday comics." *Sex Roles* 2 (1976): 331–337.

Braverman, Harry. *Labor and Monopoly Capital: The Degradation of Work in the Twentieth Century*. New York: Monthly Review Press, 1974.

Brend, Ruth M. "Male-female intonation patterns in American English." Pp. 84–87 in

Barrie Thorne and Nancy Henley (eds.), *Language and Sex: Difference and Dominance*. Rowley, MA: Newbury Press, 1975.

Brenton, Myron. "The breadwinner." Pp. 92–98 in Deborah David and Robert Brannon (eds.), *The Forty-Nine Per Cent Majority: The Male Sex Role*. Reading, MA: Addison-Wesley Publishing Co., 1976.

Briscoe, Anne M. "Hormones and Gender." Pp. 31–50 in Ethel Tobach and Betty Rosoff (eds.), *Genes and Gender*. New York: Gordian Press, 1978.

Brisset, Dennis, and Lewis, Lionel. "Guidelines for marital sex: an analysis of fifteen popular marriage manuals." *The Family Coordinator* 19 (1970): 41–48.

Brody, Leslie. "Gender differences in emotional development: a review of theories and research." *Journal of Personality* 53 (1985): 102–149.

Broverman, I. K.; Vogel, S. R.; Broverman, D.; Clarkson, F.; and Rosenkrantz, P. S. "Sex role stereotypes and clinical judgments of mental health." *Journal of Consulting and Clinical Psychology* 34 (1970): 1–7.

Brown, Barbara; Freedman, Ann; Katz, Harriet; and Price, Alice. *Women's Rights and the Law: The Impact of the ERA on State Laws*. New York: Praeger, 1977.

Brown, Claude. "The language of soul." Pp. 134–139 in Thomas Kochman (ed.), *Rappin' and Stylin' Out: Communication in Urban Black America*. Urbana, IL: University of Illinois Press, 1972.

Brown, H. Rap. "Street talk," Pp. 205–208 in Thomas Kochman (ed.), *Rappin' and Stylin' Out: Communication in Urban Black America*. Urbana, IL: The University of Illinois Press, 1972.

Brown, Penelope. "Women and politeness: a new perspective on language and society." *Reviews in Anthropology* 3 (1976): 239–249.

Brown, Rita Mae. "Queen for a day: a stranger in paradise." Pp. 69–77 in Karla Jay and Allen Young (eds.), *Lavender Culture*. New York: Jove/HBJ Books, 1978

Brown, Roger. *Social Psychology*. Glencoe, IL: The Free Press, 1965.

Browning, Ruth, "Women in religion." Presented to Sex Roles Seminar, Department of Sociology. Columbus: The Ohio State University, 1974.

Brownmiller, Susan. *Against Our Will: Men, Women and Rape*. New York: Simon and Schuster, 1975.

———. *Femininity*. New York: Linden Press, 1984.

Bruner, Jerome. *Toward a Theory of Instruction*. Cambridge, MA: Belknap Press, 1966.

Bunch, Charlotte. "Lesbians in revolt." Pp. 29–38 in Nancy Myron and Charlotte Bunch (eds.), *Lesbianism and the Women's Movement*. Oakland, CA: Diana Press, 1975.

Burton, Sydney G.; Calanico, James; and McSevery, Dennis R. "Effects of preschool television watching on 1st grade children." *Journal of Communication* 29 (1979): 164–170.

Calderone, Mary S. *Release from Sexual Tensions*. New York: Random House, 1960.

Califia, Patricia. *Sapphistry: The Book of Lesbian Sexuality*. Tallahassee, FL: Naiad Press, 1983.

Cameron, Paul. "Frequency and kinds of words in various social settings or what the hell's going on?" Pp. 31–37 in Marcello Truzzi (ed.), *Sociology for Pleasure*. Englewood Cliffs, NJ: Prentice-Hall, 1974.

Cantor, Joanne R. "What is funny to whom: the role of gender." *Journal of Communication* 26 (1976): 164–172.

Cantor, Muriel G. "Where are the women in public broadcasting." Pp. 78–89 in Gaye Tuchman; Arlene Kaplan Daniels; and James Benet (eds.), *Hearth and Home: Images of Women in the Mass Media*. New York: Oxford University Press, 1978.

Cargan, Leonard. *Singles: Myths and Realities*. Beverly Hills, CA: Sage, 1982.

Carroll, Bernice A. "Introduction." Pp. ix–xiii in Bernice Carroll (ed.), *Liberating Women's History*. Chicago: University of Chicago Press, 1976.

Carroll, Jackson W.; Hargrove, Barbara; and Lummis, Adair T. *Women of the Cloth: A New Opportunity for the Churches*. New York: Harper & Row, 1983.

Cassell, Joan. *A Group Called Women: Sisterhood and Symbolism in the Women's Movement*. New York: David McKay, 1977.

Caucus for Women in Statistics. "Factors related to young women's math achievement." *Association for Women in Mathematics Newsletter* 9 (1979): 3–4.

Chafetz, Janet Saltzman. *Sex and Advantage: A Comparative Macro-Structural Theory of Sex Stratification*. Totowa, NJ: Rowman and Allanheld, 1984.

Cheek, F. "A serendipitous finding: sex role and schizophrenia." *Journal of Abnormal and Social Psychology* 69 (1964): 392–400.

Cheles-Miller, Pamela. "Reactions to marital roles in commercials." *Journal of Advertising Research* 15 (1975): 45–49.

Cherry, L., and Lewis, M. "Differential socialization of boys and girls: implications for sex differences in language development." In C. Snow and N. Waterson (eds.), *Development of Communication: Social and Pragmatic Factors in Language Acquisition*. New York: John Wiley, 1977.

Chesler, Phylis. *Women and Madness*. New York: Doubleday, 1972.

Child, Irwin; Potter, Elmer; and Levine, Estelle. "Children's textbooks and personality development: an exploration in the social psychology of education." Pp. 292–305 in Morris L. Haimonitz and Natalie Reader Haimonitz (eds.), *Human Development: Selected Readings*. New York: Thomas Y. Crowell, 1960.

Chisholm, Shirley. "Racism and anti-feminism." *The Black Scholar* 43 (1970): 40–45.

Chodorow, Nancy. *The Reproduction of Mothering: Psychoanalysis and the Sociology of Gender*. Berkeley, CA: University of California Press, 1978.

———. "Being a woman, becoming a man: gender role socialization and the sexual division of labor." Santa Cruz, CA: University of California, unpublished manuscript, 1980.

Christ, Carol P., and Plaskow, Judith (eds.). *Womanspirit Rising: A Feminist Reader in Religion*. San Francisco: Harper & Row, 1979.

Christian Science Monitor. "How couples divide the housework." August 22, 1980.

Cicourel, Aaron, and Kitsuse, John. "A note on the use of official statistics." *Social Problems* 11 (1963): 131–139.

Clancy, K., and Gove, W. "Sex differences in mental illness: an analysis of response bias in self reports." *American Journal of Sociology* 8 (1974): 205–216.

Cleaver, Eldridge. *Soul on Ice*. New York: McGraw-Hill, 1968.

Cline, Carolyn Garrett, et al. *The Velvet Ghetto: The Impact of Increasing Percentage of Women in Public Relations and Business Communication*. San Francisco: ABC Foundation, 1986.

Coleman, J.; Butcher, J.; and Carson, R. *Abnormal Psychology and Modern Life*. Glenview, IL: Scott Foresman, 1984.

Collins, Randall. *Conflict Sociology: Toward an Explanatory Science*. New York: Academic Press, 1975.

Comfort, Alex (ed.). *More Joy of Sex: Lovemaking Companion to the Joy of Sex*. New York: Simon and Schuster, 1974.

Compaigne, Benjamin M. "The magazine industry: developing the special interest audience." *Journal of Communication* 30 (1980): 98–103.

Condry, John, and Condry, Sandra. "Sex differences: a study in the eye of the beholder." *Child Development* 47 (1976): 812–819.

Congressional Record. February 24, 1972 (Dr. Peter Breggins).

Constantin, Edmond, and Kenneth, Craig. "Women as politicians: the social background, personality, and political careers of female party leaders." *Journal of Social Issues* 28 (1972): 217–236.

Cook, Beverly Blair. "The Burger court and women's rights 1971–1977." Pp. 47–83 in Winifred Hepperle and Laura Crites (eds.), *Women in the Courts*. Williamsburg, VA: National Center for State Courts, 1978.

——. "Women judges: The end of tokenism." Pp. 84–105 in Winifred Hepperle and Laura Crites (eds.), *Women in the Courts*. Williamsburg, VA: National Center for State Courts, 1978.

Cook, Blanch W. "The historical denial of lesbianism." *Radical History Review* 20 (1979): 60–65.

Cook, Judith. "Bridging the gap: relationships among business and professional women." Paper presented at the North Central Sociological Meetings, Dayton, Ohio, May 1–3, 1980.

Cooley, Charles Horton. *Human Nature and the Social Order*. New York: Charles Scribner's Sons, 1902.

——. *Social Organization: A Study of the Larger Mind*. New York: Charles Scribner's Sons, 1909.

Cooper, David. *The Death of the Family*. New York: Pantheon, 1970.

Cordes, C. "Tent tilt: boys outscore girls on both parts of the SAT." American Psychological Association *Monitor* (June 1986): 30–31.

Coser, Lewis A., and Rosenberg, Bernard. *Sociological Theory: A Book of Readings*. New York: Macmillan, 1976.

Cowan, Margic, and Stewart, Barbara. "A methodological study of sex stereotypes." *Sex Roles* 3 (1977): 205–216.

Cull, John G., and Hardy, Richard E. "Language meaning (gender shaping) among blind and sighted students." *The Journal of Psychology* 83 (1973): 333–334.

Dalton, Katharina. *The Premenstrual Syndrome*. London: William Heinemann Medical Books, 1984.

Daly, Mary. "After the death of God the father." Mimeographed. Pittsburgh: Know, Inc., n.d.

——. "Women and the Catholic church." Pp. 124–138 in Robin Morgan (ed.), *Sisterhood is Powerful*. New York: Random House, 1970.

——. *Beyond God the Father*. Boston: Beacon Press, 1973.

Darland, M. G.; Dawkins, S. M.; Lovasich, J. L.; Scott, E. L.; Sherman, M. E.; and Whipple, J. L. "Application of multivariate regression studies of salary differences between men and women faculty." Paper presented to American Statistical Association Annual Meetings, 1973.

Davies, Margery. "Woman's place is at the typewriter: the feminization of the clerical labor force." Pp. 248–266 in Zillah R. Eisenstein (ed.), *Capitalist Patriarchy and the Case for Socialist Feminism*. New York: Monthly Review Press, 1979.

Davis, Angela Y. *Women, Race and Class*. New York: Vintage Books, 1983.

Davis, Elizabeth Gould. *The First Sex*. Baltimore, MD: Penguin Books, 1971.

Davis, Madeline, and Michelson, Avra. "Aspects of the Buffalo lesbian community in the fifties" (Buffalo Oral History Project). Presented to the National Women's Studies Association Meetings, Bloomington, IN: May 1980.

Deaux, K. "From individual differences to social categories: analysis of a decade's research on gender." *American Psychologist* 39 (1983): 105–116.

Deaux, K., and Lewis, L. "Structure of gender stereotypes: interrelationships between components and gender label." *Journal of Personality and Social Psychology* 46 (1984): 991–1004.

Deckard, Barbara. *The Women's Movement*, 2d ed. New York: Harper & Row, 1979.

DeFrain, John D. "Sexism in parenting manuals." *The Family Coordinator* 26 (1977): 245–251.

Department of Health, Education and Welfare. *Salaries, Tenure and Fringe Benefits of Full-Time Instructional Faculty in Institutions of Higher Education*. Washington, D.C.: Government Printing Office, 1977.

DeStefano, Johanna S. "A study of developing perceptions of referents in selected English generic terms." Mimeographed. Columbus: The Ohio State University, 1975.

———. Personal communication. Columbus: The Ohio State University, 1976.

Deutscher, Irwin. *Married Life in Middle Years*. Kansas City: Community Studies, 1959.

Dewey, Cindy Rice. "Vocational counseling with women: a nonsexist technique." Pp. 207–220 in Edna I. Rawlings and Dianne K. Carter (eds.), *Psychotherapy for Women: Treatment Toward Equality*. Springfield, IL: Charles C. Thomas, 1977.

Diamond, Timothy. Personal communication, July 10, 1976.

———. *On the Social Structure of Imagery: The Case of Gender*. Unpublished Ph.D. dissertation. Columbus: Department of Sociology, Ohio State University, 1977.

Distler, L.; May, P.; and Tuma, H. "Anxiety and ego strength as predictors of responses to treatment in schizophrenic patients." *Journal of Consulting Psychology* 28 (1964): 170–177.

Dizard, Jan E. "The price of success." Pp. 192–201 in Louise Kapp Howe (ed.), *The Future of the Family*. New York: Simon and Schuster, 1972.

Doherty, E. "Are differential discharge criteria used for men and women psychiatric inpatients?" *Journal of Health and Social Behavior* 19 (1978): 107–116.

Domhoff, G. William. *Who Rules America?* Englewood Cliffs, NJ: Prentice-Hall, 1967.

———. *The Bohemian Grove and Other Retreats*. New York: Harper & Row, 1974.

———. "The women's page as a window on the ruling class." Pp. 161–175 in Gaye Tuchman; Arlene Kaplan Daniels; and James Benet (eds.), *Hearth and Home: Images of Women in the Mass Media*. New York: Oxford University Press, 1978.

Dornbusch, Sanford. "To try or not to try." *Stanford Magazine* 2 (1974): 50–54.

Douglas, Priscilla Harriet. "Black working women: factors affecting labor market experience." Wellesley, MA: Wellesley College Center for Research on Women, March 1980.

Draper, Patricia. "!Kung women: contrasts in sexual egalitarianism in foraging and sedentary contexts." Pp. 77–109 in Rayna R. Reiter (ed.), *Toward an Anthropology of Women*. New York: Monthly Review Press, 1975.

Duberman, Lucile. *The Reconstituted Family*. Chicago: Nelson-Hall, 1975.

———. *Marriage and Other Alternatives*. New York: Praeger, 1977.

Dunning, R. "Discrimination: women in sports." Unpublished manuscript, F 35 North Campus Way, Davis, CA: 1972.

Durkheim, Emile. *Suicide*. Glencoe, IL: The Free Press, 1951.

Dweck, Carol S.; Davidson, William; Nelson, Sharon; and Enna, Bradly. "Sex differences in learned helplessness: II. The contingencies of evaluative feedback in the classroom and III. An experimental analysis." *Developmental Psychology* 14 (1978): 268–276.

Eagly, A. "Gender and social influence: a social psychological analysis." *American Psychologist* 38 (1983): 971–981.

Eckhardt, Kenneth. "Deviance, visibility, and legal action: the duty to support." *Social Problems* 15 (1968): 470–477.

Edelsky, Carole. "Who's Got the Floor?" *Language in Society* 10 (1981): 383–421.

Ehrenreich, Barbara. *The Hearts of Men: American Dreams and the Flight from Commitment* New York: Doubleday, 1983.

———. "Social Welfare: The Attack from the Right." Lecture, College of Social Work, Ohio State University, October 22, 1986.

Eichenlaub, John E. *New Approaches to Sex in Marriage*. New York: Dell, 1967.

Eichler, Margrit. *The Double Standard: A Feminist Critique of the Social Sciences*. New York: St. Martin's Press, 1980.

Eisenberg, Sue, and Miklow, Patricia. "The assaulted wife: catch 22 revised." *Women's Rights Law Reporter* 3 (1977): 138–161.

Ekstrom, R. "Myth: Girls usually are higher achievers than boys on verbal tests and in subjects that require verbal skills, while boys tend to do better than girls on mathematical tests and in math related courses." Paper presented at the Annual Research on Women in Education Conference, Boston, 1985.

Ellsworth, P. C.; Carlsmith, J. M.; and Henson, A. "The stare as a stimulus to fight in human subjects: a series of field experiments." *Journal of Personality and Social Psychology* IV (1972): 302–311.

England, Paula, and Farkas, George. *Households, Employment, and Gender: A Social, Economic, and Demographic View*. New York: Aldine, 1986.

Epstein, Cynthia Fuchs. *Women's Place: Options and Limits on a Professional Career*. Berkeley, CA: University of California Press, 1970.

———. "Law partners and marital partners: strains and solutions in the dual career family enterprise." *Human Relations* 24 (1971): 549–563.

———. "Positive effects of the multiple negative; explaining the success of black professional women." Pp. 150–173 in Joan Huber (ed.), *Changing Women in a Changing Society*. Chicago: The University of Chicago Press, 1973.

———. "The women's movement and the women's pages." Pp. 216–221 in Gaye Tuchman; Arlene Kaplan Daniels; and James Benet (eds.), *Hearth and Home: Images of Women in the Media*. New York: Oxford University Press, 1978.

Erickson, S. Nancy. "Equality between the sexes in the 1980s." *Cleveland State Law Review* 28 (1979): 591–610.

Erikson, Erik. *Identity, Youth and Crisis*. New York: Norton, 1968.

Ernest, John. "Mathematics and Sex." *American Mathematical Monthly* 83 (1976): 595–614.

Etzioni, Amitai. "Sex control, science and society." *Science* 16 (1968): 1007–1010.

Evans, Sara. *Personal Politics*. New York: Alfred A. Knopf, 1979.

Ewen, Stuart. *Captain of Consciousness: Advertising and the Social Roots of the Consumer Culture*. New York: McGraw-Hill, 1976.

Eyesenck, H. J. *The Effects of Psychotherapy*. New York: International Science Press, 1955.

Falk, Gail. "Sex discrimination in the trade unions: legal resources." Pp. 254–276 in Jo Freeman (ed.), *Women: A Feminist Perspective*. Palo Alto, CA: Mayfield, 1975.

Farley, Lin. *Sexual Shakedown: The Sexual Harassment of Women on the Job*. New York: Warner Books, 1978.

Farmer, H. S., and Bohn, M. J. "Home career conflict reduction and the level of career interest in women." *Journal of Counseling Psychology* 17 (1970): 228–232.

Farrell, M. P., and Rosenberg, S. *Men at Midlife*. Boston: Auburn House, 1981.

Farrell, Warren T. *The Liberated Man, Beyond Masculinity: Freeing Men and Their Relationships with Women*. New York: Random House, 1974.

————. "Women's and men's liberation groups: political power within the system and outside the system." Pp. 171–201 in Jane Jacquette (ed.), *Women in Politics*. New York: Wiley, 1975.

Fasteau, Marc Feigen. *The Male Machine*. New York: Dell, 1975.

Fausto-Sterling, Anne. *Myths of Gender*. New York: Basic Books, 1985.

Federbush, Marcia. *Let Them Aspire*, 3d ed. (with addenda). Pittsburgh: Know Inc., 1973.

Felshin, Jan. *The American Woman in Sport*. Reading, MA: Addison-Wesley, 1974.

Fennema, Elizabeth, and Sherman, Julia. "Sex related differences in mathematics achievement: spatial visualization and affective factors." *American Educational Research Journal* 14 (1977): 51–71.

Fernberger, S. "Persistence of stereotypes concerning sex differences." *Journal of Abnormal and Social Psychology* 43 (1948): 97–101.

Ferree, Myra Marx. "Working class jobs: housework and paid work as sources of satisfaction." *Social Problems* 23 (1975): 431–441.

Ferree, Myra Marx, and Hess, Beth B. *Controversy and Coalition: The New Feminist Movement*. Boston: Twayne 1985.

Festinger, Leon. *The Theory of Cognitive Dissonance*. New York: Harper & Row, 1957.

Fields, Rona M. *Public Education: Training for Sexism*. Philadelphia: Know Inc., n.d.

Filene, Peter. "Him/her/self." Pp. 389–410 in Judy Blankenship (ed.), *Scenes from Life: Family, Marriage and Intimacy*. Boston: Little, Brown and Co., 1976.

Firestone, Shulamith. *The Dialectic of Sex*. New York: William Morrow, 1971.

Fishel, Anne. "What is a feminist therapist and how to find one." *Ms.*, June 1979: 79–82.

Fishman, Pamela. "Interaction: the work women do." Pp. 89–102 in Barrie Thorne; Cheris Kramarae; and Nancy Henley (eds.), *Language, Gender, and Society*. Rowley, PA: Newbury House, 1983.

Fiske, Shirley. "Pigskin review: an American initiation." Pp. 241–258 in Marie Hart (ed.), *Sport in the Sociocultural Process*. Dubuque, IA: Willaim C. Brown, 1972.

Fleener, Marilyn G. "The lesbian lifestyle." Paper presented to Western Social Science Association, April 1977 and referred to in Sasha Gregory Lewis, *Sunday's Women: A Report on Lesbian Life Today*. Boston: Beacon Press, 1979.

Flemming, J. B. *Stopping Wife Abuse*. Garden City, NY: Anchor Books, 1979.

Folb, Edith. "A comparative study of urban black argot." Occasional Papers in Linguistics, No 1. University of California at Los Angeles. March, 1972.

Fonow, Mary Margaret. *Women in Steel: A Case Study of the Participation of Women in a Trade Union*. Unpublished Ph.D. Dissertation. Columbus: Department of Sociology, Ohio State University, 1977.

Ford, Clellar S., and Beach, Frank A. *Patterns of Sexual Behavior*. New York: Harper & Row, 1951.

Fox, Greer Litton, and Inazu, Judith. "Influence of mother's marital history on mother-daughter relationship in black and white households." *Journal of Marriage and the Family* 44 (1982): 143–144.

Fox, Lynn H. *Facilitating the Development of Mathematical Talent in Young Women*. Unpublished Ph.D. Dissertation. Baltimore, MD: Johns Hopkins, 1974.

————. "The effects of sex role socialization on mathematics participation and achievement." *Women and Mathematics: Research Perspectives for Change*. Washington D.C.: National Institute of Education, Papers in Education and Work, No. 7, 1977.

Fox, Mary Frank, and Hesse-Biber, Sharlene. *Women at Work*. Palo Alto, CA: Mayfield, 1984.

Franklin, Clyde, and Mosmiller, Tom (eds.). Special Edition on "Black Masculinity." *Changing Men: Issues in Gender, Sex, and Politics* 17 (1986).

Franklin, Clyde W., Jr., and [Walum], Laurel Richardson. "Toward a paradigm of substructural relations: an application to sex and race in the United States." *Phylon* 33 (1972): 242–253.

Franks, Violet. "Gender and psychotherapy." Pp. 453–485 in Edith S. Gomberg and Violet Franks (eds.), *Gender and Disordered Behavior: Sex Differences in Psychotherapy.* New York: Brunner-Mazel, 1979.

Franzwa, Helen. "Working women in fact and fiction." *Journal of Communication* 24 (1974): 104–109.

Frazier, Nancy, and Sadker, Myra. *Sexism in School and Society.* New York: Harper & Row, 1973.

Freeman, Jo. *The Politics of Women's Liberation: A Case Study of an Emerging Social Movement and It's Relation to the Policy Process.* New York: David McKay, 1975.

———. "Crises and conflicts in social movement organizations." *Chrysalis* 2 (1978): 43–51.

Freud, Sigmund. *Civilization and Its Discontents.* London: Hogarth Press, 1930.

Friedan, Betty. *The Feminine Mystique.* New York: Dell, 1963.

Friedl, Ernestine. *Women and Men: An Anthropologist's View.* New York: Holt, Rinehart and Winston, 1975.

Friedman, Leslie J. *Sex Role Stereotyping in the Mass Media: An Annotated Bibliography.* New York: Garland Publishing, 1977.

Gagnon, John. "Physical strength, once of significance." Pp. 169–178 in Deborah S. David and Robert Brannon (eds.), *The Forty-Nine Percent Majority: The Male Sex Role.* Reading, MA: Addison-Wesley, 1976.

Galbraith, John Kenneth. *Economics and the Public Purpose.* Boston: Houghton Mifflin, 1973.

Garcia-Zamor, M. A. "Child awareness of sex-role distinctions in language use." Paper presented to the Linguistic Society of America Meetings, December 1973.

Garfinkel, Harold. *Studies in Ethnomethodology.* Englewood Cliffs, NJ: Prentice-Hall, 1967.

Garland, Neal T. "The better half? the male in the dual professional family." Pp. 199–215 in Constantina Safilios-Rothschild (ed.), *Toward a Sociology of Women.* Lexington, MA: Xerox Publishing Co., 1972.

Gates, Margaret J. "Occupational segregation and the law." Pp. 220–242 in Martha Blaxall and Barbara Reagan (eds.), *Women and the Workplace.* Chicago: University of Chicago Press, 1976.

Gerbner, George, and Gross, Larry. "Living with television: the violence profile." *Journal of Communication* 26 (1976): 173–199.

Gerbner, George, et al. "The demonstration of power: violence profile No. 10." *Journal of Communication* 29 (1979): 177–196.

Gerson, Kathleen. *Hard Choices: How Women Decide about Work, Career, and Motherhood.* Berkeley, CA: University of California, 1985.

Gerstel, Naomi R. "Commuter marriage: constraints on spouses." Paper presented at the Annual Meetings of the American Sociological Association, San Francisco, September 6–10, 1978.

Gifford-Jones W. *What Every Woman Should Know About Hysterectomy.* New York: Funk and Wagnalls, 1977.

Gillespie, Dair L. "Who has the power? the marital struggle." *Journal of Marriage and the Family* 33 (1971): 445–458.

Gilligan, Carol. *In a Different Voice: Psychological Theory and Women's Development.* Cambridge, MA: Harvard University Press, 1983.

Ginsberg, Ruth Bader, "Women, men and the constitution: key supreme court rulings." Pp. 21–46 in Winifred Hepperle and Laura Crites (eds.), *Women in the Courts*. Williamsburg, VA: National Center for State Courts, 1978.

Glazer-Malbin, Nona. "The captive couple: the burden of gender roles in marriage." Pp. 127–141 in Don H. Zimmerman and D. Lawrence Wieder (eds.), *Social Problems in Contemporary Society*. New York: Praeger, 1976.

Glazer, Nona. "Overworking the working woman: the double day in a mass-magazine." *Women's Studies International Quarterly* 3 (1980): 79–93.

Glenn, Evelyn Nakano, and Feldberg, Roslyn L. "Degraded and deskilled: the proletarianization of clerical work." *Social Problems* 25 (1977): 52–64.

Glick, P. C. "Marriage, divorce and living arrangements." *Journal of Family Issues* 5 (1984): 7–26.

Goffman, Erving. *The Presentation of Self in Everyday Life*. Garden City, NY: Doubleday, Inc., 1959.

———. *Asylums*. New York: Anchor, 1961.

———. *Interaction Ritual*. New York: Anchor, 1967, pp. 47–95.

———. *Gender Advertisements*. New York: Harper Colophon, 1976.

Goldberg, Phillip. "Are women prejudiced against women?" *Transaction*, (5) 5 (1968): 28–30.

Goldberg, Steven. *The Inevitability of Patriarchy*. New York: William Morrow, 1973.

Goldenberg, Naomi Ruth. *Changing of the Gods, Feminism and the End of Traditional Religions*. Boston: Beacon Press, 1979.

———. *The End of God: Important Directions for a Feminist Critique of Religion in the Works of Sigmund Freud and Carl Jung*. Ottawa, Ontario: University of Ottawa Press, 1982.

Goldman, Noreen; Westoff, Charles; and Hammerslough, Charles. "Demography of the marriage market in the United States." *Population Index* (1) 50 (1984): 5–25.

Gomberg, Edith S., and Franks, Violet (eds.), *Gender and Disordered Behavior: Sex Differences in Psychotherapy*. New York: Brunner-Mazel, 1979.

Goodall, Jane. "The behavior of free living chimpanzees in the Gombe Stream Reserve." *Animal Behavior Monographs* 1 (1968): 161–311.

Goode, William H. *World Revolution and Family Patterns*. New York: The Free Press, 1963.

Goode, William J. "Why men resist." Pp. 131–147 in Barrie Thorne (ed.), *Rethinking the Family: Some Feminist Questions*. New York: Longman, 1982.

Gordon, Michael, and Shankweiler, Penelope. "Different equals less: female sexuality in recent marriage manuals." *Journal of Marriage and the Family* 33 (1971): 459–466.

Gordon, Nancy M.; Morton, Thomas E.; and Braden, Ina C. "Faculty salaries: is there discrimination by sex, race and discipline?" *American Economic Review* 64 (1974): 419–427.

Gove, Walter, R. "Sex differences in the epidemiology of mental disorder: evidence and explanations." Pp. 23–68 in Edith S. Gomberg and Violet Franks (eds.), *Gender and Disordered Behavior: Sex Differences in Psychotherapy*. New York: Brunner-Mazel, 1979.

Grahame, Alma. "The making of a non-sexist dictionary." *Ms.*, December 1973: 12–14, 16.

Grauerholz, Elizabeth, and Pescosolido, Bernice. "Gender representation in children's literature: 1900–1984." Paper presented to the American Sociological Association Meetings, San Antonio, Texas, 1985.

Greenberg, S. "Educational equity in early education environments." Pp. 457–469 in Susan

Klein (ed.), *Handbook for Achieving Sex Equity Through Education.* Baltimore, MD: Johns Hopkins University Press, 1985.

Greeley, Andrew M., and Durkin, Mary G. *Angry Catholic Women.* Chicago: Thomas More Press, 1984.

Greiff, Geoffrey L. *Single Fathers.* Lexington, MA: D. C. Heath, 1985.

Grieff, B. S., and Munter, P. K. *Tradeoffs: Executive, Family, and Organizational Life.* New York: Mentor, 1980.

Griffin, Susan. "Rape: the all-American crime." Andover, MA: Warner Modular Publications, Inc., 1973.

Griffiths, M. Recommendation of the Commission on the Homemaker to the National Commission on the Observance of International Women's Year. 1976.

Gringold, Judith. "One of these days—pow right in the kisser." *Ms.*, August 1976: 51–52, 94.

Grønseth, Erick. "The breadwinner trap." Pp. 175–191 in Louise Kapp Howe (ed.), *The Future of the Family.* New York: Simon and Schuster, 1972.

———. "Work sharing." In Rhona Rapoport and Robert N. Rapoport (eds.), *Working Couples.* New York: Harper & Row, 1978.

Gross, Edward. "Plus ca change . . . ? the sexual structure of occupations over time." *Social Problems* 16 (1968):198–208.

Gross, Harriet Engel. "Couples who live apart: time/place disjunctions and their consequences." Pp. 402–408 in Laurel Richardson and Verta Taylor (eds.), *Feminist Frontiers: Rethinking Sex, Gender, and Society.* New York: Random House, 1983.

Grunden, Rickie Sue. "Toward a theory of feminine movement and the acquisition of sports skills." Unpublished paper. Columbus: The Ohio State University, 1973.

Gundry, Patricia. *Woman Be Free.* Grand Rapids, MI: Zondervan Publishing House, 1977.

Guttentag, Marcia, and Secord, Paul R. *The Sex Ratio Question.* Beverly Hills, CA: Sage, 1983.

Haas, Adelaide. "The acquisition of genderlect." Pp. 101–114 in Judith Orasanu; Miriam K. Slater; and Lenore Loeb Adler (eds.), *Language, Sex and Gender: Does La Difference Make A Difference?* New York: New York Academy of Sciences Annals, 1979.

Hafter, Daryl M. "An overview of women's history." Pp. 1–27 in Richmond-Abbott (ed.), *The American Women: Her Past, Her Present, Her Future.* New York: Holt, Rinehart and Winston, 1979.

Hall, Edward T. *The Silent Language.* Garden City, NJ: Doubleday, 1959.

———. *The Hidden Dimension.* New York: Doubleday, 1966.

Hall, Robert E. *Sex and Marriage.* New York: Planned Parenthood, 1965.

Hall, Roberta, and Sandler, Bernice. *The Classroom Climate: A Chilly One for Women?.* Washington, D.C.: Association of American Colleges, 1982.

Halmi, K. A.; Falk, J. R.; and Schwartz, E. "Binge-eating and vomiting: a survey of a college population." *Psychological Medicine* 11 (1981): 697–706.

Hamilton, N., and Henley, N. "Detrimental consequences of the generic masculine usage." Paper presented to the Western Psychological Association Meetings, Sacramento, California, 1982.

Hardin, Garrett. "Abortion—or compulsory pregnancy." Pp. 242–254 in Kenneth C. W. Kammeyer (ed.), *Confronting the Issues: Sex Roles, Marriage and the Family.* Boston: Allyn and Bacon, Inc., 1975.

Harding, Esther. *The Way of All Women.* New York: Longmans, Green, 1933.

Hare-Mustin, R. "A feminist approach to family therapy." *Family Process* 17 (1978): 181–194.

Harkness, Georgia. *Women in Church and Society: A Historical and Theological Inquiry*. New York: Abingdon Press, 1972.

Harris, Ann Sutherland. "The second sex in academe," *American Association of University Professors Bulletin* 56 (1970): 283–295.

Hartley, Ruth E. "Sex-role pressures and the socialization of the male child." Pp. 7–13 in Joseph Pleck and Jack Sawyer (eds.), *Men and Masculinity*. Englewood Cliffs, NJ: Prentice-Hall, 1974.

Hartman, Heidi. "Capitalism, patriarchy and job segregation by sex." Pp. 206–247 in Zillah R. Eisenstein (ed.), *Capitalist Patriarchy and the Case for Socialist Feminism*. New York: Monthly Review Press, 1979.

Hatfield, Elaine, and Sprecher, Susan. *Mirror, Mirror . . . : The Importance of Looks in Everyday Life*. Albany, NY: State University Press, 1986.

Heidensohn, Frances. "The deviance of women; a critique and an enquiry." *British Journal of Sociology* 19 (1968): 160–175.

Heller, Joseph. *Something Happened*. New York: Alfred A. Knopf, 1974.

Helson, Ravenna. "Women mathematicians and the creative personality." Pp. 210–202 in Judith Badwick (ed.), *Readings on the Psychology of Women*. New York: Harper & Row, 1972.

Henley, Nancy. "Power, sex and non-verbal communication." *Berkeley Journal of Sociology* 18 (1973): 1–26.

———. *Body Politics: Sex and Nonverbal Communication*. Englewood Cliffs, NJ: Prentice-Hall, 1977.

Henley, Nancy; Hamilton, Mykol; and Thorne, Barrie. "Womanspeak and manspeak: sex differences in communication, verbal and nonverbal." Pp. 168–185 in Alice G. Sargent (ed.), *Beyond Sex Roles*, 2d ed. St. Paul, MN: West Publishing, 1985.

Henning, Margaret, and Jardin, Anne. *The Managerial Woman*. New York: Pocket Books, 1976.

Henry, Alice. *Women and the Labor Movement*. New York: George H. Duran, 1923.

Herschberger, Ruth. *Adam's Rib*. New York: Harper & Row, 1948.

Hiller, Dana, and Philliber, William. "Role expectations and perceptions of partner's role expectations in contemporary marriage." *Social Problems* 33 (1986): 20–32.

Hochschild, Arlie Russell. "Attending to, codifying and managing feelings: sex differences in love." Paper presented at the American Sociological Association Meetings, San Francisco, 1975.

———. *The Managed Heart: Commercialization of Human Feeling*. Berkeley, CA: University of California, 1983.

Hoffman, L. W. "Changes in family roles, socialization and sex differences." *American Psychologist* 32 (1977): 644–657.

———. "Effects of maternal employment on children." Pp. 140–148 in C. D. Hayes (ed.), *Work, Family and Community*. Washington, D.C.: National Academy of Sciences, 1980.

Hogan, C. L. "From here to equality: Title IX." *Women Sports* 4 (1977).

Hole, Judith, and Levine, Ellen. *The Rebirth of Feminism*. New York: Quadrangle Books, 1971.

Holland, David. "The politics of dress." Pp. 396–404 in Karla Jay and Allen Young (eds.), *Lavender Culture*. New York: Jove/HBJ Books, 1978.

Holmstrom, Lynda Lytle. *The Two-Career Family*. Cambridge, MA: Schenkman Publishing Co., 1972.

Holmstrom, Lynda Lytle, and Burgess, Ann Wolbert. "Rape: the victim and the criminal justice system." Paper presented at the First International Symposium on Victimology, Jerusalem, September 2–6, 1974.

———. *The Victim of Rape: Institutional Reactions*. New York: John Wesley and Sons, 1978.

Hooker, Evelyn. "The homosexual community." Pp. 167–184 in John H. Gagnon and William Simon (eds.), *Sexual Deviance*. New York: Harper & Row, 1967.

Hooks, Bell. *Ain't I a Woman: Black Women and Feminism*. Boston, MA: South End Press, 1981.

Horner, Martina. "Toward an understanding of achievement related conflicts in women." *Journal of Social Issues* 28 (1972): 157–175.

Horney, Karen. *Feminine Psychology*. New York: Norton and Company, 1967.

Houseknecht, Sharon. "Childlessness and marital adjustment. *Journal of Marriage and the Family* 41 (1979): 259–265.

Howe, Louise Kapp. *Pink Collar Workers: Inside the World of Women's Work*. New York: Avon, 1977.

Hubbard, Ruth. "Personal courage is not enough: some hazards of childbearing in the 1980s." Pp. 131–155 in Rita Arditti, et al. (eds.), *Test Tube Women: What Future for Motherhood?*. London: Pandora Press, 1984.

Huber, Joan. "Toward a socio-technological theory of the women's movement." *Social Problems* 23 (1976a): 311–388.

———. "The future of parenthood: implications of declining fertility." Paper presented at Pioneers for Century III, Cincinnati, Ohio: April 24, 1976b.

———. Personal communication, April 15, 1976.

Huber, Joan, and Spitze, Glenna. *Sex Stratification: Children, Housework, and Jobs*. New York: Academic Press, 1983.

Huber, Joan, and Spitze, Glenna. "Trends in family sociology." In Ronald Burt and Neil Smelser (eds.), *Handbook of Sociology*. Beverly Hills, CA: Sage, *In press*.

Hudnell, Terese Connerton, and Dunham, Jan Michele. "Rape: a study of attitudes." Unpublished paper. Columbus: The Ohio State University, 1974.

Hutchins, Grace. *Women Who Work*. New York: International Publishers, 1952.

Hutner, Frances C. *Equal Pay for Comparable Worth: The Working Woman's Issue of the Eighties*. New York: Praeger, 1986.

Hyde, Janet. "The perspective from psychology: nonverbal maintenance of inequality." Paper presented at the Fifth Annual GLCA Women's Studies Conference, Rochester, Ind., November 2–4, 1979.

Iritani, Bonita, and West, Candace. "The women behind the man: a study of masculine precedence in the ordering of gender terms." Paper presented to the American Sociological Association Meetings, 1983.

Jacklin, C.; Heupers, M.; Mischell, H.; and Jacobs, C. "As the twig is bent: sex role stereotyping in early readers." Unpublished paper. Department of Psychology, Stanford University, Palo Alto, CA, 1972.

Jackson, Jacqueline I. "But where are the men?" *Black Scholar* 3 (1971), no. 4: 30–41.

Jackson, Phil, and Lahaderne, Henriette. "Inequalities of teacher-pupil contacts." Pp. 123–234 in Melvin Silberman (ed.), *The Experience of Schooling*. New York: Holt, Rinehart and Winston, 1971.

Jacoby, S. "49 million singles can't all be right." *The New York Times Magazine*, February 17, 1974: 41–49.

Jaquette, Jane S. "Introduction: women in American politics." Pp. xiii–xxxiii in Jane S. Jaquette (ed.), *Women in Politics*. New York: Wiley Interscience, 1974.

Jennings, Kent, and Norman, Thomas. "Men and women in party elites: social roles and political resources." *Midwest Journal of Political Science* 12 (1968): 469–492.

Joffee, Carole. "As the twig is bent." Pp. 91–109 in Judith Stacey; Susan Bereaud; and Joan Daniels (eds.), *And Jill Came Tumbling After: Sexism in American Education*. New York: Dell, 1974.

Johansson, Sheila Ryan. " 'Herstory' as history: a new field or another fad?" Pp. 400–430 in Bernice A. Carroll (ed.), *Liberating Women's History*. Chicago: University of Chicago Press, 1976.

Johnson, Warren R. *Human Sexual Behavior and Sex Education*. Philadelphia, PA: Lea and Febiger, 1968.

Jordan, Joan. *The Place of American Women*. Boston: The New England Press, 1969.

Jung, Carl G. *Contributions to Analytical Psychology*. New York: Harcourt, Brace, 1928.

Kagan, Jerome. "Acquisition and significance of sex-typing and sex-role identity. Pp. 137–167 in M. L. Hoffman and L. W. Hoffman (eds.), *Review of Child Development Research*, vol. 1 New York: Russell Sage Foundation, 1964.

Kahn-Hut, Rachel; Daniels, Arlene Kaplan; and Colvard, Richard (eds.), *Women and Work: Problems and Perspectives*. New York: Oxford University Press, 1982.

Kamerman, S. B. *Parenting in an Unresponsive Society: Managing Work and Family*. New York: The Free Press, 1980.

Kaminski, Donna M. "Where are the female Einsteins? the gender stratification of math and science." Pp. 350–357 in Jeanne Ballentine (ed.), *Schools and Society: A Reader in Education and Society*. Palo Alto, CA: Mayfield, 1985.

Kanowitz, Leo. *Women and the Law: The Unfinished Revolution*. Albuquerque: The University of New Mexico Press, 1969.

Kanter, Rosabeth Moss. *Men and Women of the Corporation*. New York: Basic Books, 1977.

———. "Work in a new America." *Daedalus: Journal of the American Academy of Arts and Science* 107 (1978): 47–48.

Kaplan, M. "A woman's view of DSM-III." *American Psychologist* 38 (1983a): 766–92.

Kaplan, M. "The issue of sex bias in DSM-III: comments on the articles of Spitzer, Williams, and Kass." *American Psychologist* 38 (1983b): 802–807.

Kash, Sara D. "A 12 year old challenges her church." *Ms.*, December 1984: 21.

Katz, David. "Faculty salaries, promotions and productivity at a large university." *American Economic Review* 63 (1973): 469–477.

Kay, Herma Hill. *Text, Cases and Materials on Sex-Based Discrimination in Family Law*. St. Paul, MN: West Publishing Co., 1974.

Kelly, Alison. *Changing Schools and Changing Society: Some Reflections on the Girls in Science and Technology Project*. New York: The Open University, 1984.

Kelly-Gadol, Joan. "The social relation of the sexes: methodological implications of women's history." *Signs* 1 (1976): 809–823.

Kendall, Diane, and Feagin, Joe R. "Blatant and subtle patterns of discrimination: minority women in medical schools." *Journal of Intergroup Relations* 9 (1983): 6–9.

Keskiner, A.; Zaleman, M.; and Ruppert, E. "Advantages of being female in psychiatric rehabilitation." *Archives of General Psychiatry* 23 (1973): 689–692.

Key, Mary Ritchie. *Male/Female Language*. Metuchen, NJ: The Scarecrow Press, 1975.

Kirschner, Betty, and [Walum], Laurel Richardson. "Two-location families: married singles." *Alternative Lifestyles* 1 (1978): 513–525.

Klatch, Rebecca. "Gender ideology, feminism, and women and the new right." Paper presented to the Eastern Sociological Society Meetings, New York, 1986.

Klein, Dorie. "The etiology of female crime: a review of the literature." *Issues in Criminology* 8 (1973): 3–30.

Klein, Ethel. *Gender Politics*. Cambridge, MA: Harvard University Press, 1984.

Klein, Susan (ed.). *Handbook for Achieving Sex Equity in Education*. Baltimore, MD: Johns Hopkins University Press, 1985.

Kochman, Thomas. "The kinetic element in black idiom." Pp. 160–169 in Thomas Kochman (ed.), *Rappin' and Stylin' Out*. Urbana, IL: University of Illinois Press, 1972.

Koedt, Anne. "The myth of the vaginal orgasm." Pp. 284–289 in Sue Cox (ed.), *Female Psychology: The Emerging Self*. Chicago: Science Research Associations, 1976.

Kohlberg, Lawrence. "A cognitive-developmental analysis of children's sex-role concepts and attitudes." Pp. 82–166 in Eleanor Maccoby (ed.), *The Development of Sex Differences*. Stanford, CA: Stanford University Press, 1966.

Korda, Michael. *Male Chauvinism: How It Works*. New York: Random House, 1973.

Korner, A. F. "Neonatal startles, smiles, erection, and reflex sucks as related to state, sex, and individuality." *Child Development* 40 (1969): 1039–1053.

Kramerae, Cheris. "Women's speech: separate but unequal?" Pp. 43–56 in Barrie Thorne and Nancy Henley (eds.), *Language and Sex: Difference and Dominance*. Rowley, MA: Newbury House, 1975.

————. *Women and Men Speaking*. Rowley, MA: Newbury House, 1981.

Kramerae, Cheris; Thorne, Barrie; and Henley, Nancy (compilers). "Sex communication: an annotated bibliography." Pp. 153–331 in Barrie Thorne; Cheris Kramarae; and Nancy Henley (eds.), *Language, Gender and Society*. Rowley, MA: Newbury House, 1983.

Kuhn, Manfred. "How mates are sorted." In Howard Becker and Rueben Hill (eds.), *Family, Marriage and Parenthood*. Boston: D. C. Heath, 1955.

Labov, William. "Rules for ritual insults." Pp. 265–314 in Thomas Kochman (ed.), *Rappin' and Stylin' Out*. Urbana, IL: University of Illinois Press, 1972.

Lahof, Bruce. "The higher meaning of Marlboro cigarettes." *Journalism Quarterly* 52 (1975): 309–321.

Lake, Alice. "Are we born into our sex-roles or programmed into them?" *Woman's Day*, January 1975: 24–25.

Lakoff, Robin. *Language and Woman's Place*. New York: Harper Colophon Books, 1975.

————. "Stylistic strategies within a grammar of style." Pp. 53–80 in Judith Orasanu, Miriam K. Slater, and Lenore Loeb Adler (eds.), *Language, Sex and Gender: Does La Difference Make A Difference?* New York: New York Academy of Sciences Annals, 1979.

Lamb, Michael E. "The development of parent preferences in the first two years of life." *Sex Roles* 3 (1977): 495–497.

Lambert, Phillip. "Mathematical ability and masculinity." *The Arithmetic Teacher* 7 (1960): 19–21.

Lancaster, Jane Beckman. "In praise of the achieving female monkey," Pp. 5–9 in *The Female Experience*. Del Mar, CA: Communications Research Machines, 1973.

————. *Primate Behavior and The Emergence of Human Culture*. New York: Holt, Rinehart and Winston, 1975.

Lang, Gladys Engel. "The most admired woman: image-making in the news." In Gaye Tuchman; Arlene Kaplan Daniels; and James Benet (eds.), *Hearth and Home: Images of Women in the Mass Media*. New York: Oxford University Press, 1978.

LaRue, Linda J. M. "Black liberation and woman's lib." *Transaction* 61 (1970): 59–64.

Laws, Judith Long. "A feminist review of marital adjustment literature: the rape of the locke." *Journal of Marriage and the Family* 33 (1971): 483–516.

Lear, Martha Weinman. "You'll probably think I'm stupid." *The New York Times Magazine*, April 11, 1976.

Leavitt, R. *Peaceable Primates and Gentle People: Anthropological Approaches to Women's Studies*. New York: Harper & Row, 1975.

Lehman, Edward C., Jr. *Women Clergy: Breaking Through Gender Barriers*. New Brunswick, NJ: Transaction Books, 1985.

Leibowitz, Lila. *Females, Males, Families: A Biosocial Approach*. North Scituate, MA: Duxbury Press, 1978.

LeMasters, E. E. "Folklore about parenthood." Pp. 295–303 in Judy Blankenship (ed.), *Scenes from Life: Views of Family, Marriage and Intimacy*. Boston: Little, Brown and Co., 1976.

Lemon, Judith. "Dominant or dominated? Women on prime-time television." In Gaye Tuchman; Arlene Kaplan Daniels; and James Benet (eds.), *Hearth and Home: Images of Women in the Mass Media*. New York: Oxford University Press, 1978.

Lenski, Gerhard E. *Power and Privilege: A Theory of Social Stratification*. New York: McGraw-Hill, 1966.

Lerner, Richard M. "Some female stereotypes of male body build-behavior." *Perceptual and Motor Skills* 28 (1969): 363–366.

Leshin, Geraldine. *EEO Law: Impact on Fringe Benefits*. Los Angeles: Institute of Industrial Relations, University of California, 1979.

Lester, Julius. "Being a boy." Pp. 270–276 in Deborah S. David and Robert Brannon (eds.), *The Forty-Nine Percent Majority: The Male Sex Role*. Reading, MA: Addison-Wesley Publishing Co., 1976.

Lever, Janet. "Sex differences in the games children play." *Social Problems* 23 (1976): 478–487.

———. "Sex differences in the complexity of children's play and games. *American Sociological Review* 43 (1978): 471–483.

Levin, Ira. *The Stepford Wives*. New York: Random House, 1972.

Levine, Joe. "Help from the unborn." *Time*, January 12, 1987: 62.

Lewis, H. B. *Psychic War in Men and Women*. New York: New York University Press, 1976.

Lewis, Michael. "State as an infant-environment interaction: an analysis of mother-infant interactions as a function of sex." *Merrill-Palmer Quarterly of Behavior and Development* 18 (1972): 95–121.

Lewis, Sasha Gregory. *Sunday's Women: A Report on Lesbian Life Today*. Boston: Beacon Press, 1979.

Leznoff, Maurice, and Westley, William A. "The homosexual community." Pp. 184–197 in John H. Gagnon and William Simon (eds.), *Sexual Deviance*. New York: Harper & Row, 1977.

Libby, R. W. "Creative singlehood as a sexual lifestyle: beyond marriage as a rite of passage." In R. W. Libby and R. N. Whitehurst (eds.), *Marriage and Its Alternatives: Exploring Intimate Life Styles*. Glenview, IL: Scott, Foresman, 1977.

Lipmen-Blumen, Jean. *Gender Roles and Power*. Englewood Cliffs, NJ: Prentice-Hall, 1984.

Lloyd, Cynthia B. "The division of labor between the sexes: a review." Pp. 1–24 in Cynthia B. Lloyd (ed.), *Sex, Discrimination and the Division of Labor*. New York: Columbia University Press, 1975.

Lockheed, Marlaine E. "Sex equity in classroom organization and climate." Pp. 189–217 in Susan S. Klein (ed.), *Handbook for Achieving Sex Equity through Education*. Baltimore, MD: Johns Hopkins University Press, 1985.

Lopez, Lisa. "A study of rape." Unpublished paper. Columbus, Ohio: The Ohio State University, 1974.

Lorber, Judith. "Trust, loyalty and the place of women in the informal organization of work." Pp. 371–381 in Jo Freeman (ed.), *Women: A Feminist Perspective*, 2d ed. Palo Alto, CA: Mayfield, 1979.

Lougee, Carolyn C. "Review essay: modern European history." *Signs* 2 (1977): 628–650.

Lowe, Marian. "Sociobiology and sex differences." *Signs* 4 (1978): 118–125.

Lowi, Theodore J. *The Politics of Disorder*. New York: Basic Books, 1971.

Luker, Kristin. *Abortion and the Politics of Motherhood*. Berkeley, CA: University of California Press, 1984.

Lynn, David B. "Fathers and sex-role development." *Family Coordinator* 25 (1976): 403–409.

Lynn, Naomi. "Women in American politics: an overview." Pp. 364–385 in Jo Freeman (ed.), *Women: A Feminist Perspective*. Palo Alto, CA: Mayfield, 1975.

MAC (Men Against Cool). "Men against cool." Mimeographed. Chicago, IL, 1970.

MacArthur, Leslie, and Eisen, S. "Achievements of male and female storybook characters as determinants of achievement behavior by boys and girls." *Journal of Personality and Social Psychology* 33 (1976): 467–473.

Maccoby, Eleanor. "Women's intellect." Pp. 24–39 in Seymour Farber and Robert Wilson (eds.), *The Potential of Women*. New York: McGraw-Hill, 1963.

———. *The Development of Sex Differences*. Stanford, CA: Stanford University Press, 1966.

Maccoby, Eleanor, and Jacklin, Carol Nagy. *The Psychology of Sex Differences*. Stanford, CA: Stanford University Press, 1974.

MacHaffie, Barbara J. *Her Story: Women in Christian Tradition*. Philadelphia: Fortress Press, 1986.

MacKay, Donald G. "Prescriptive grammar and the pronoun problem." Pp. 38–53 in Barrie Thorne; Cheris Kramarae; and Nancy Henley (eds.), *Language, Gender and Society*. Rowley, MA: Newbury House, 1983.

Macke, Anne; Richardson, Laurel; and Cook, Judith. *Sex Typed Teaching Styles of University Professors and Student Reactions*. Final Report. Washington, D.C.: National Institute of Education (Grant # NIE-G-78-0144), 1980.

MacKinnon, Catharine A. *Sexual Harassment of Working Women*. New Haven, CT: Yale University Press, 1979.

Macklin, E. D. "Nonmarital heterosexual cohabitation." *Marriage and Family Review* 1 (1978): 1–12.

Major, B. "Gender patterns in touching behavior." Pp. 92–113 in C. Mayo and N. Henley (eds.), *Gender and Nonverbal Behavior*. New York: Springer-Verlag, 1981.

Maltz, Daniel N., and Borker, Ruth A. "A cultural approach to male-female miscommunication." Pp. 195–216 in John Gumperz (ed.), *Language and Social Identity*. New York: Cambridge University Press, 1983.

Mander, Anica Vesel, and Rush, Anne Kent. *Feminism as Therapy*. New York: Random House, 1974.

Markle, Gerald E., and Nam, Charles B. "The impact of sex predetermination on fertility." Paper presented at the annual meetings of the Population Association of America, April 1973.

Marmor, Judd (ed.). *Homosexual Behavior*. New York: Basic Books, 1980.

Marshall, Hannah, and Knafl, Kathleen. "Professionalizing motherhood: La Leche league and breast feeding." Paper presented at the American Sociological Association, New York, August 26–30, 1973.

Martin, Susan Ehrlich. "Sexual harassment: the link between gender stratification, sexuality, and women's economic status." Pp. 54–69 in Jo Freeman (ed.), *Women: A Feminist Perspective*. Palo Alto, CA: Mayfield, 1984.

Martyna, Wendy. "What does 'he' mean? Use of the generic masculine." *Journal of Communication* 28 (1978): 131–138.

———. "Beyond the 'he/man' approach: the case for nonsexist language." *Signs* 5 (1980): 482–493.

Marx, Karl. *Early Writings*. Translated and edited by T. B. Bottomore. New York: McGraw-Hill, 1964.

Masters, William H., and Johnson, Virginia E. *Human Sexual Response*. Boston: Little, Brown and Co., 1966.

McArthur, Leslie Z., and Resko, Beth G. "The portrayal of men and women in American t.v. commercials." *Journal of Social Psychology* 97 (1975): 209–220.

McClelland, David C. *The Achieving Society*. Glencoe, IL: Free Press, 1961.

McClelland, D. C., and Watt, N. F. "Sex role alienation in schizophrenia." *Journal of Abnormal Psychology* 73 (1968): 226–239.

McCombs, Maxwell, and Eyal, Chaim H. "Spending on mass-media." *Journal of Communication* 30 (1980): 153–158.

McConnell-Ginet, Sally. "Intonation in a man's world." Pp. 54–68 in Barrie Thorne; Cheris Kramarae; and Nancy Henley (eds.), *Language, Gender and Society*. Rowley, MA: Newbury House, 1983.

McC. Dachowski, M. "DSM-III: sexism of societal reality?" *American Psychologist*, 39 (1984): 702–703.

McGhee, Paul, and Grodzitsky, Phyllis. "Sex-role identification and humor among preschool children." *Journal of Psychology* 84 (1973): 189–193.

McKee, J., and Sherrifs, A. "The differential evaluation of males and females." *Journal of Personality* 25 (1957): 356–371.

McNally, Fiona. *Women for Hire: A Study of the Female Office Worker*. New York: St. Martin's Press, 1979.

McNeil, Jean C. "Feminism, feminists and the television series: a content analysis." *Journal of Broadcasting* 19 (1975): 259–271.

McNeil, John. "Programmed instruction versus visual classroom procedures in teaching boys to read." *American Educational Research Journal* 1 (1964): 113–120.

Media Report to Women Index Directory. 3306 Ross Place, Washington, D.C.

Mehrabian, A. *Nonverbal Communication*. Chicago: Aldine-Atherton Press, 1972.

Mencken, H. L. *The American Language*, 4th ed. and two supplements. Abridged and edited by Raven I. McDavis, New York: Alfred A. Knopf, 1963.

Merton, Robert K. *Social Theory and Social Structure* (rev. ed.). New York: The Free Press, 1957.

Meyer, Katherine; Seidler, John; and Aveni, Adrian. "Woman's image in fourth of July cartoons: a 100 year look." *Journal of Communication* 30 (1980): 21–30.

Miller, Mark M., and Reeves, Byron. "Dramatic t.v. content and children's stereotypes." *Journal of Broadcasting* 20 (1976): 35–50.

Miller, S. M. "The making of a confused middle-class husband." Pp. 374–381 in Judy Blankenship (ed.), *Scenes from Life: Views of Family, Marriage and Intimacy*. Boston: Little, Brown and Co., 1976.

Millet, Kate. *Sexual Politics*. New York. Doubleday, 1970.

Mills, C. Wright. *The Sociological Imagination*. New York: Oxford University Press, 1959.

Millum, Trevor. *Images of Women: Advertising in Women's Magazines*. Totowa, NJ: Rowman and Littlefield, 1975.

Minton, Cheryl; Kagan, Jerome; and Levine, Janet A. "Maternal control and obedience in the two year old." *Child Development* 42 (1971): 1873–1894.

Mitchell-Kernan, Claudia. "Signifying, loud-talking and marking." Pp. 315–336 in Thomas Kochman (ed.), *Rappin' and Stylin' Out*. Urbana, IL: The University of Illinois Press, 1972.

Money, John, and Ehrhardt Anke A. *Man, Woman, Boy and Girl*. Baltimore, MD: The Johns Hopkins University Press, 1972.

———. "Rearing of a sex-reassigned normal male infant after traumatic loss of the penis." Pp. 46–51 in Jack Petras (ed.), *Sex: Male/Gender: Masculine*. Port Washington, NY: Alfred Publishing Co., 1975.

Money, John, and Wiedeking, C. "Gender identity/role: normal differentiation and its transpositions." Pp. 261–284 in B. Wolman and J. Money (eds.), *Handbook of Human Sexuality*. Englewood Cliffs, NJ: Prentice-Hall, 1980.

Morris, Desmond. *The Naked Ape*. New York: Dell, 1967.

———. *Intimate Behavior*. New York: Random House, 1971.

Morris, Jan. *Conundrum*. New York: Signet Books, 1974.

Morrison, Toni. "What the Black woman thinks about woman's lib." *The New York Times*, August 15, 1971: 64.

Mortimer, Jeylan T., and London, Jayne. "The varying linkages of work and family." Pp. 20–35 in Patricia Voydanoff (ed.), *Work and Family: Changing Roles of Men and Women*. Palo Alto, CA: Mayfield, 1984.

Moss, E. A. "Sex, age and state as determinants of mother-infant interaction. *Merrill-Palmer Quarterly of Behavior and Development* 13 (1967): 19–36.

Mowbray, C. S. Lanir, and Hulce, M. (eds.). *Women and Mental Health*. New York: Haworth Press, 1984.

Mt. Vernon News. "Baptists oppose women's ordination." Mt. Vernon, Ohio, June 16, 1984.

Nagel, S. S., and Weitzman, L. J. "Women as litigants." *The Hastings Law Journal* 23 (1962): 171–198.

National Education Association. *Status of the American School Teacher*. Washington, D. C.: National Education Association, 1977.

National Organization for Changing Men. "National organization for changing men." Broadsheet, n.d.

Ness, Evaline. *Sam, Bangs and Moonshine*. New York: Holt Rinehart and Winston, 1967.

Newton, Niles. "Trebly sensuous woman." Pp. 22–25 in *The Female Experience*. Del Mar, CA: Communication Research Machines, 1973.

Nonkin, Lesley Jane. "Fear-of-power-dressing." *Vogue*, September 1986: 316–317.

NOW (National Organization for Women). "Bill of rights adopted at NOW's first national conference." Washington, D.C. Also Pp. 512–514 in Robin Morgan (ed.), *Sisterhood is Powerful*. New York: Vintage Press, 1967.

Oakley, Anne. "A case of maternity: paradigms of women as maternity cases." *Signs* 4 (1979): 607–631.

O'Connor, Lynn. "Male dominance: the nitty-gritty of oppression." *It Ain't Me, Babe*. 1 (1970): 9–11.

O'Hara, Robert. "The roots of careers." *Elementary School Journal* 62 (1962): 277–280.

Oppenheimer, Karen. "Demographic influence on female employment and the status of women." *American Journal of Sociology* 78 (1973): 184–199.

Orr, W.; Anderson, R.; Martin, M.; and Philpot, D. "Factors influencing discharge of female patients from a state mental hospital." *American Journal of Psychiatry* 3 (1955): 576–582.

Orthner, D.; Brown, T.; and Ferguson, D. "Single parent fatherhood: an emerging family life style." *The Family Coordinator* 25 (1976): 429–437.

Palmer, Edward L., and McDowell, Cynthia N. "Program/commerical separators in children's television programming." *Journal of Communication* 29 (1979): 197–201.

Papachristou, Judith (ed.). *Women Together: A History in Documents of the Women's Movement in the United States.* New York: Alfred A. Knopf, 1976.

Papanek, Hannah. "Men, women and work: Reflections on the two-person career." *American Journal of Sociology,* 78 (1973): 852–872.

Parcel, Toby L.; Zorn, Jenny; and Mueller, Charles W. "Comparable worth and occupational labor market explanations of occupational earnings differentials." Paper presented to the American Sociological Association Meetings, New York, 1986.

Pearce, Diane. "The feminization of poverty: women, work and welfare. Pp. 103–124 in K. F. Feinstein (ed.), *Working Women and Families.* Beverly Hills, CA: Sage, 1979.

Pederson, F. A., and Robson, K. S. "Father participation in infancy." *American Journal of Orthopsychiatry* 39 (1969): 466–472.

Pedgug, Robert A. "Sexual matters: on conceptualizing sexuality in history." *Radical History Review* 20 (1979): 3–23.

Pellegrini, R. J., and Emprey, J. "Interpersonal spatial orientation in dyads." *Journal of Psychology* 76 (1970): 67–70.

Petchesky, R. "Antiabortion, antifeminism, and the rise of the New Right." *Feminist Studies* 7 (1981): 206–246.

Petro, Carole Smith, and Putnam, Barbara A. "Sex-role stereotypes: issues of attitudinal changes." *Signs* 5 (1979): 41–50.

Phillips, Brenda. *Sex Role Socialization and Play Behavior in a Rural Playground.* Unpublished M.A. thesis, Ohio State University, 1982.

Piaget, Jean. *The Construction of Reality in the Child.* New York: Basic Books, 1954.

Piotrkowski, C. S. *Work and the Family System.* New York: The Free Press, 1978.

Pleck, Joseph H. "Psychological frontiers for men." *Rough Times* 6 (1973): 14–15.

———. "The work-family role system." *Social Problems* 24 (1977): 417–427.

Pleck, Joseph, and Brannon, Robert. "Male roles and the male school experience." *Journal of Social Issues* 34 (1978): 1–4.

Pogrebin, Letty. "The secret fear that keeps us from raising free children." Pp. 36–40 in Laurel Richardson and Verta Taylor (eds.), *Feminist Frontiers: Rethinking Sex, Gender, and Society.* New York: Random House, 1983.

Pollak, Otto. *The Criminality of Women.* Philadelphia: The University of Pennsylvania Press, 1950.

Poloma, Margaret M. "Role conflict and the married professional woman." Pp. 197–198 in Constantina Safilios-Rothschild (ed.), *Toward a Sociology of Women.* Lexington, MA: Xerox Publishing Co., 1972.

Poloma, Margaret M., and Garland, Neal T. "The myth of the egalitarian family: familial roles and the professionally employed wife." Pp. 741–761 in Athena Theodore (ed.), *The Professional Woman.* Cambridge, MA: Schenkman Publishing Co., 1971.

Polatnick, Margaret. "Why women don't rear children: a power analysis." *Berkeley Journal of Sociology* 18 (1975): 45–86.

Ponse, Barbara. *Identities in the Lesbian World: The Social Construction of Self.* Westport, CT: Greenwood Press, 1978.

Prisuta, Robert H. "Televised sport and political values." *Journal of Communication* 20 (1979): 94–103.

Probber, Joan, and Ehrman, Lee. "Pertinent genetics for understanding gender." Pp. 13–30 in Ethel Tobach and Betty Rosoff (eds.), *Genes and Gender.* New York: Gordian Press, 1978.

Pyle, R. L., et al. "Incidence of bulimia in freshmen college students." *Journal of Eating Disorders* 2 (1983): 75–85.

Quarforth, Joanne M. "Children's understanding of the nature of television characters." *Journal of Communication* 29 (1979): 210–218.

Quintinalles, Mirtha. "Friendship and family amongst Latina lesbians." Ph.D. dissertation prospectus. Columbus: Department of Anthropology, Ohio State University, 1980.

Ramey, James. "Experimental family forms—the family of the future." *Marriage and Family Review* 1 (1978): 1–9.

Rapoport, Rhona N, and Rapoport, Robert. *Dual-Career Families.* Hardmondsworth, England: Penguin, 1971.

———. "The dual-career family: a variant pattern and social change." Pp. 216–244 in Constantina Safilios-Rothschild (ed.), *Toward a Sociology of Women.* Lexington, MA: Xerox Publishing Co., 1972.

———. *Dual-Career Families Re-examined.* New York: Harper & Row, 1976.

———. "Dual-career families: progress and prospects." *Marriage and Family Review* 1 (1978): 1–13.

Rawlings, Edna I., and Carter, Dianne K. "Comparative case analyses of sexist and feminist therapies." Pp. 77–98 in Edna I. Rawlings and Dianne K. Carter (eds.), *Psychotherapy for Women: Treatment Toward Equality.* Springfield, IL: Charles C. Thomas Publishers, 1977.

Raymond, Janice. "Transsexualism: the ultimate homage to sex-role power." *Chrysalis* 3 (1978): 11–23.

———. "Feminist ethics, ecology and vision." Pp. 427–437 in Rita Arditti, et al. (eds.), *Test Tube Women: What Future for Motherhood?* London: Pandora Press, 1984.

Reckless, Walter, and Kay, Barbara. *The Female Offender.* Report to the President's Commission on Law Enforcement and the Administration of Justice. Washington, D.C.: U.S. Government Printing Office, 1967.

Reitz, Roseta. *Menopause: A Positive Approach.* Radnor, PA: Chilton Book Company, 1977.

Remick, Helen (ed.). *Comparable Worth and Wage Discrimination: Technical Possibilities and Political Realities.* Philadelphia: Temple University Press, 1984.

Reskin, Barbara (ed.). *Sex Segregation in the Workplace: Trends, Explanations and Remedies.* Washington, D.C.: National Academy Press, 1984.

Reskin, Barbara, and Hartman, Heidi I. (eds.). *Women's Work, Men's Work: Sex Segregation on the Job.* Washington, D.C.: National Academy Press, 1986.

Reuther, Rosemary Radford. *New Woman/New Earth: Sexist Ideologies and Human Liberation.* New York: The Seabury Press, 1975.

Rheingold, H. L., and Cook, K. "The content of boys' and girls' rooms as an index of parents' behavior." *Child Development* 46 (1975): 459–463.

Rheingold, Joseph. *The Fear of Being a Woman*. New York: Grune and Stratton, 1964.

Richardson, Laurel [Walum]. "Sociology and the mass media: some major problems and modest solutions." *The American Sociologist* 19 (1975): 28–32.

———. "The 'other woman': the end of the long affair." *Alternative Lifestyles* 2 (1979): 397–414.

———. "Secrecy and the construction of intimacy: relationships between single women and married men." Paper presented at the North Central Sociological Association Meetings, Dayton, Ohio, May, 1980.

Richardson, Laurel. *The Dynamics of Sex and Gender: A Sociological Perspective*, rev. 2d ed. Boston: Houghton Mifflin, 1981.

———. "No, thank you!: A discourse on etiquette." Pp. 5–7 in Laurel Richardson and Verta Taylor (eds.), *Feminist Frontiers: Rethinking Sex, Gender, and Society*. New York: Random House, 1983.

———. *The New Other Woman: Contemporary Single Women in Affairs with Married Men*. New York: The Free Press, 1985.

Richardson, Laurel; Cook, Judith A.; and Statham, Anne. "Down the up staircase: male and female university professors classroom management strategies." Pp. 280–287 in Laurel Richardson and Verta Taylor (eds.), *Feminist Frontiers: Rethinking Sex, Gender, and Society*, 1st ed. Reading, MA: Addison-Wesley, 1983.

Rickles, Nathan K. "The angry woman syndrome." *Archives of General Psychiatry* 24 (1971).

Rivera, Rhonda R. "Our straightlaced judges: the legal position of homosexual persons in the United States." *The Hastings Law Journal* 30 (1979): 799–952.

Roberts, Barbara. "Psychosurgery: the final solution to the women problem?" *The Second Wave* 1 (1972).

Robertson, Ian. *Sociology*. New York: Worth, 1981.

Rodman, H. "The textbook world of family sociology." *Social Problems* 12 (1965): 445–457.

Rosenkantz, Paul; Vogel, Susan; Bee, Helen; and Broverman, Donald. "Sex-role stereotypes and self-concepts in college students." *Journal of Consulting and Clinical Psychology* 32 (1968): 287–295.

Rosenthal, Robert, and Jackson, Lenore. "Pygmalion in the classroom: an excerpt." Pp. 115–240 in Melvin Silberman (ed.), *The Experience of Schooling*. New York: Holt, Rinehart and Winston, 1971.

Ross, Catherine E. "The Division of Labor at Home." Unpublished paper. University of Illinois, 1986.

Rossi, Alice. "Equality between the sexes." Pp. 98–143 in Robert Jay Lifton (ed.), *The Woman in America*. Boston: Houghton Mifflin, 1964.

———. "Sex equality: the beginnings of an ideology." Pp. 344–353 in Constantina Safilios-Rothschild (ed.), *Toward a Sociology of Women*. Lexington, MA: Xerox Publishing Co., 1972.

———. *Feminists in Politics: A Panel Analysis of the First National Women's Conference*. New York: Academic Press, 1982.

———. "Gender and Parenthood." *American Sociological Review* 49 (1984): 1–19.

Rothman, Barbara Katz. *The Tentative Pregnancy*. New York: Viking Penguin, 1986.

Rothschild (ed.). *Toward a Sociology of Women*. Lexington, MA: Xerox Publishing Co., 1972.

———. "A biosocial perspective on parenting." *Daedalus* 106 (1977): 1–31.

Rowbotham, Sheila. *Hidden From History: Rediscovering Women in History from the 17th Century to the Present*. New York: Vintage Books, 1973.

Rubin, Jeffrey Z.; Provenzano, Frank J.; and Lurra, Zella. "The eye of the beholder: parents' views on sex of newborns." *American Journal of Orthopsychiatry* 44 (1974): 512–519.

Ruether, Rosemary Radford. *New Woman/New Earth*. New York: The Seabury Press, 1975.

Runciman, Walter Garrison. *Relative Deprivation and Social Justice: A Study of Attitudes to Social Inequality in Twentieth Century England*. Berkeley, CA: University of California Press, 1966.

Rupp, Leila J. "Women, power, and history." Unpublished manuscript. Columbus: Department of History, Ohio State University.

———. "Imagine my surprise: women's relationships in historical perspective." Unpublished paper. Columbus: Department of History, Ohio State University, 1980.

Rupp, Leila J., and Taylor, Verta A. "The American women's movement in the post Second World War period." Unpublished research proposal. Columbus: Ohio State University, 1980.

———. "The woman's movement since 1960: structure, strategies, and new directions." Pp. 75–104 in Robert H. Bremmer; Richard Hopkins; and Gary W. Reichard (eds.), *American Choices: Social Dilemmas and Public Policy since 1960*. Columbus: Ohio State University Press, 1986.

———. *Survival in the Doldrums: American Women's Rights Movement, 1945–1960*. New York: Oxford University Press, 1987.

Russo, Nancy Felipe. "Sex-role stereotyping, socialization, and sexism." Pp. 150–168 in Alice G. Sargent (ed.), *Beyond Sex Roles*, 2d ed. St. Paul, MN: West Publishing, 1983.

Ruth, Sheila. *Issues in Feminism: A First Course in Women's Studies*. Boston: Houghton Mifflin, 1980.

Ryan, Barbara E. "Ideological purity and social movement division: the women's movement from 1966–1975." Paper presented to the American Sociological Association Meetings, New York, August, 1986.

Ryan, Patricia, and Schirtzinger, Marie. "A look at women in religion: Catholicism and Judaism." Unpublished paper. Columbus: The Ohio State University, 1974.

Saario, Terry; Jacklin, Carol; and Tittle, Carol. "Sex role stereotyping in the public schools." *Harvard Educational Review* 43 (1973): 386–416.

Sachs, Jacqueline. "Cues to the identification of sex in children's speech." Pp. 152–171 in Barrie Thorne and Nancy Henley (eds.), *Language and Sex: Difference and Domination*. Rowley, MA: Newbury House, 1975.

Sachs, Jacqueline; Lieberman, Philip; and Erickson, Donna. "Anatomical and cultural determinants of male and female speech." Pp. 74–83 in Roger W. Shuy and Ralph W. Fasold (eds.), *Language Attitudes: Current Trends and Prospects*. Washington, D.C.: Georgetown University Press, 1973.

Sachs, Oliver. *The Man Who Mistook His Wife for a Hat and Other Clinical Tales*. New York: Summit Books, 1985.

Sadker, David, and Sadker, Myra. *Year 3 Final Report, Promoting Effectiveness in Classroom Instruction*. Washington, D.C.: National Institute of Education, 1984.

Sadker, Myra P., and Sadker, David Miller. "Sexism in teacher education texts." *Harvard Educational Review* 50 (1980): 36–46.

———. *Effectiveness and Equity in College Teaching: Final Report*. Washington, D.C.: National Institute of Education, 1985.

Sadker, Myra; Sadker, David; and Klein, Susan S. "Abolishing misconceptions about sex equity in education." *Theory into Practice* 25 (Autumn 1986): 219–226.

Safilios-Rothschild, Constantina. "Family sociology or wives' family sociology?" *Journal of Marriage and the Family* 31 (1969): 290–301.

Safron, Claire. "What men do to women on the job: a shocking look at sexual harassment." *Redbook*, November, 1976.

Sahli, Nancy. "Smashing: women's relationships before the fall." *Chrysalis* 8 (1979): 17–27.

Sanday, Peggy Reeves. *Female Power and Male Dominance: On the Origins of Sexual Inequality*. New York: Cambridge University Press, 1981.

Sattel, Jack W. "Men, inexpressiveness, and power." Pp. 242–246 in Laurel Richardson and Verta Taylor (eds.), *Feminist Frontiers: Rethinking Sex, Gender, and Society*. New York: Random House, 1983.

Scanzoni, Letha, and Hardesty, Nancy. *All We're Meant To Be*. Waco, TX: World Books, 1978.

Scanzoni, Letha, and Scanzoni, John. *Men, Women and Change: A Sociology of Marriage and Family*. New York: McGraw-Hill, 1978.

Schaller, George. *The Mountain Gorilla: Ecology and Behavior*. Chicago: The University of Chicago Press, 1963.

Scheff, Thomas J. *Being Mentally Ill: A Sociological Theory*. Chicago: Aldine, 1966.

Scheflen, A. E. *Body Language and the Social Order*. Englewood Cliffs, NJ: Prentice-Hall, 1972.

———. *How Behavior Means*. Garden City, NY: Doubleday-Anchor, 1974.

Schneider, Beth E. "Political generations and the contemporary women's movement." Paper presented to the American Sociological Association Meetings, New York, 1986.

Schneider, Joseph, and Hacker, Sally. "Sex role imagery in the use of the generic 'man' in introductory texts: a case in the sociology of sociology." *American Sociologist* 8 (1973): 12–18.

Schulz, Muriel R. "The semantic derogation of women." Pp. 64–75 in Barrie Thorne and Nancy Henley (eds.), *Language Sex: Difference and Domination*. Rowley, MA: Newbury House, 1975.

Schur, Edwin M. *Labeling Women Deviant*. Philadelphia: Temple University Press, 1983.

Science News. "The third sex." *Science News* 102 (December 9, 1972): 376.

Scott, Hilda. *Working Your Way to the Bottom: The Feminization of Poverty*. London: Pandora Press, 1984.

Scully, Diane. *Men Who Control Women's Health: The Miseducation of Obstetrician Gynecologists*. Boston: Houghton Mifflin, 1980.

Scully, Diana, and Bart, Pauline. "A funny thing happened on the way to the orifice: women in gynecology textbooks." Unpublished paper. Chicago: University of Illinois at Chicago Circle, 1972. Abbreviated version, pp. 283–288 in Joan Huber (ed.), *Changing Women in a Changing Society*. Chicago: University of Chicago Press, 1973.

Seager, Joni, and Olson, Ann. *Women in the World Atlas*. New York: Simon and Schuster, 1986.

Seaman, B., and Seaman, G. *Women and the Crises in Hormones*. New York: Rowson Associates, 1977.

Sears, R. R. "Development of gender role." Pp. 133–162 in F. A. Beach (ed.), *Sex and Behavior*. New York: Wiley, 1965.

Seeman, Jeanette. "The hidden curriculum: gender stereotyping in sixth grade mathematics books: 1963–1974." Unpublished paper. Columbus: The Ohio State University, 1974.

Seidler, John. Personal Communication. 1976.

Seifer, N. *Absent from the Majority*. New York: American Jewish Committee, 1973.

Seneca, Gail. "The social meaning of maternity: where do we go from here." Unpublished paper. Geneseo: Department of Sociology, State University of New York at Geneseo, 1980.

Shakeshaft, C. "Strategies for overcoming the barriers to women in educational administration." Pp. 124–144 in Susan Klein (ed.), *Handbook for Achieving Sex Equity Through Education*. Baltimore, MD: Johns Hopkins University Press, 1985.

Shapiro, N. "The Shapiro report: an analysis of salaries of men and women faculty at Ohio State University." Columbus: Ohio State University, 1976.

Sheehy, Gail. *Passages: Predictable Crises of Adult Life*. New York: E. P. Dutton, 1976.

Sherfey, Mary Jane. "A theory of female sexuality." Pp. 220–230 in Robin Morgan (ed.), *Sisterhood is Powerful*. New York: Vintage Books, 1966.

Sherman, Julia. "Problems of sex differences in space perception and aspects of intellectual functioning." *Psychological Review* 74 (1967): 290–299.

———. "Effects of biological factors on sex-related differences in mathematics achievement." *Psychological Review* 8 (1977).

———. "Therapist attitudes and sex role stereotyping." In A. Brodsky and R. Hare-Mustin (eds.), *Women and Psychotherapy*. New York: Guilford, 1980.

Shorr, Alvin, and Moen, Phyllis. "The single parent and public policy." Pp. 288–297 in Patricia Voydanoff (ed.), *Work and Family: Changing Roles of Men and Women*. Palo Alto, CA: Mayfield, 1984.

Shostak, Arthur B. "Blue-collar work." Pp. 98–106 in Deborah David and Robert Brannon (eds.), *The Forty-Nine Percent Majority: The Male Sex Role*. Reading, MA: Addison-Wesley Publishing Co., 1976.

Shulman, Alix. "Organs and orgasms." Pp. 292–303 in Vivian Gornick and Barbara Moran (eds.), *Women in Sexist Society: Studies in Power and Powerlessness*. New York: New American Library, 1972.

Shuster, Janet. "Grammatical forms marked for male and female in English." Unpublished paper. Chicago: University of Chicago, 1973.

Signorelli, Nancy. *Role Portrayal and Stereotyping on Television: An Annotated Bibliography of Studies Relating to Women, Minorities, Aging, Sexual Behavior, Health and Handicaps*. Westport, CT: Greenwood Press, 1985.

Silveira, Jeannette. "Thoughts on the politics of touch." *Women's Press* 1 (1972): 13.

Simon, Rita. *The Contemporary Woman and Crime*. Rockville, MD: National Institute of Mental Health, Center for Studies of Crime and Delinquency, 1975.

Skolnick, Arlene. *The Intimate Environment: Exploring Marriage and the Family*. Boston: Little, Brown and Co., 1973.

Slocum, Sally. "Woman the Gatherer: male bias in anthropology." Pp. 36–50 in Rayna R. Reiter (ed.), *Toward an Anthropology of Women*. New York: Monthly Review Press, 1975.

Smith, Don D. "The social content of pornography." *Journal of Communication* 26 (1976): 16–24.

Smith, E. R., and Kluegel, J. R. "Beliefs and attitudes about women's opportunity: comparisons with beliefs about blacks and a general model." *Social Psychology* 47 (1984): 81–94.

Smith, M. "Sex bias in counseling and psychotherapy." *Psychological Bulletin* 87 (1980): 392–407.

Smith, M. A.; Kalvelage, J.; and Schmuck, P. *Women Getting Together and Getting Ahead*. Washington, D.C.: Women's Educational Equity Act Program, 1982.

Smith, Robert Rutherford. "Mythic elements in television news." *Journal of Communication* 29 (1979): 75–82.

Smith-Rosenberg, Carroll. "The female world of love and ritual: relations between women in nineteenth century America." *Signs* 1 (1975): 1– 29.

Sokoloff, Natalie. "Theories of women's labor force status: a review and critique." Paper presented at the National Women's Studies Association Meetings, Bloomington, Ind., May 1980.

Solanis, Valerie. "Excerpts from the SCUM (Society for Cutting Up Men) Manifesto." Pp. 514–519 in Robin Morgan (ed.), *Sisterhood is Powerful*. New York: Vintage Books, 1970.

Sommer, Robert. *Personal Space: The Behavioral Basis of Design*. Englewood Cliffs, NJ: Prentice-Hall, 1969.

Spanier, Graham. "Married and unmarried cohabitation in the United States: 1980." *Journal of Marriage and the Family* 42 (1983): 277–278.

Spence, J., and Helmreich, R. *Masculinity and Femininity*. Austin, TX: The University of Texas, 1978.

Spender, Dale. *Man Made Language*. London: Routledge and Kegan Paul, 1985.

Spitze, Glenna, and Huber, Joan. "Effects of anticipated consequences on ERA opinion." *Social Science Quarterly* 63 (1982): 323–332.

Spock, Benjamin. *Raising Your Child in a Different Time*. New York: Norton, 1974.

Stangler, R. S., and Printz, A. M. "DSM-III: psychiatric diagnosis in a University Population." *American Journal of Psychiatry* 137: 937–940.

Stanley, Julia P. "Paradigmatic woman: the prostitute." In David L. Shores (ed.), *Papers in Language Variation*. Birmingham: University of Alabama Press (reprinted by Know, Inc.), 1977.

Statham, Anne [Macke]; and Richardson, Laurel; with Cook, Judith A. *Sex- Typed Teaching Styles of University Professors and Student Reactions*. Washington, D.C.: National Institute of Education, 1980.

Stearns, Peter N. "Problems of change in emotions research: new standards for anger in 20th century American childrearing." Paper presented to the American Sociological Association Meetings, New York, August, 1986a.

———. "Historical analysis in the study of emotions." *Motivation and Emotion* 10 (1986b): 185–193.

Stein, Peter J. "Singlehood: an alternative to marriage." *The Family Coordinator* 24 (1975): 489–503.

———. *Single*. Englewood Cliffs, NJ: Prentice-Hall, 1976.

———. "The lifestyles and life chances of the never-married." *Marriage and Family Review* 1 (1978): 1 ff.

Stein, Peter. "Understanding single adulthood." Pp. 9–21 in Peter Stein (ed.), *Single Life: Unmarried Adults in Social Context*. New York: St. Martin's Press, 1981.

Steinberg, Ronnie. *Equal Employment Policy for Women: Strategies of Implementation in the United States, Canada, and Western Europe*. Philadelphia: Temple University Press, 1980.

Steinmetz, Suzanne. "Wifebeating/husbandbeating—a comparison of the use of physical violence between spouses to resolve marital fights." Pp. 63–72 in Maria Roy (ed.), *Battered Women*. Cincinnati, OH: Van Nostrand Reinhold, 1977.

Sternglanz, S. H., and Serbin, L. A. "Sex-role stereotyping in children's television programs." *Developmental Psychology* 10 (1974): 710– 715.

Stiehm, J. "Women, men and military service: is protection necessarily a racket?" Pp. 292– 292 in E. Boneparth (ed.), *Women, Power and Policy*. New York: Pergamon, 1982.

Stohler, Robert. *The Transsexual Experiment*. London: The Hogarth Press, 1975.

Stoll, Clarice Stasz. *Female and Male*. Dubuque, IA: William C. Brown, 1974.

Stoller, R. J. "Effects of parents' attitudes on core gender identity." *International Journal of Psychiatry* 4 (1967): 57.

Stoltenberg, John. "Forum on sado-masochism." Pp. 85–117 in Karla Jay and Allen Young (eds.), *Lavender Culture*. New York: Jove/HBJ Books, 1978.

Stone, Pauline Terrelonge. "Feminist consciousness and Black women." Pp. 575–588 in Jo Freeman (ed.), *Women: A Feminist Perspective*. Palo Alto, CA: Mayfield, 1979.

Strauss, Murray; Gelles, Richard; and Steinmetz, Suzanne. *Violence in the American Family*. New York: Doubleday/Anchor, 1979.

Strouse, Jean (ed.). *Women and Analysis: Dialogues on Psychoanalytic Views of Femininity*. New York: Grossman Publishers, 1974.

Sussman, Marvin. "Marriage contracts: social and legal consequences." Plenary address presented at the 1975 International Workshop on Changing Sex Roles in Family and Society, July 17, 1975.

Swacker, Marjorie R. "The sex of speaker as a sociolinguistic variable." Pp. 76–83 in Barrie Thorne and Nancy Henley (eds.), *Language and Sex: Difference and Dominance*. Rowley, MA: Newbury House, 1975.

Szasz, Thomas. *The Myth of Mental Illness*. New York: Harper & Row, 1961.

———. *The Manufacture of Madness*. New York: Harper & Row, 1970.

Tanner, Donna, M. *The Lesbian Couple*. Lexington, MA: Lexington Books, 1978.

Tanner, Nancy, and Zihlman, Adrienne. "Women in evolution, part 1: innovation and selection in human origins." *Signs* 1 (1976): 585–608.

Tavris, D., with Baumgartner, A. I. "How would your life be different?" *Redbook*, February 1983: 92–95.

Taylor, Verta. "Review of *A Group Called Women: Sisterhood and Symbolism in the Women's Movement* by Joan Cassell." *Women's Studies Review* 1 (1979): 4–6.

———. "Review essays of four books on lesbianism." *Journal of Marriage and Family* 42 (1980): 224–228.

———. "The future of feminism in the 1980s: a social movement analysis." Pp. 434–450 in Laurel Richardson and Verta Taylor (eds.), *Feminist Frontiers: Rethinking Sex, Gender, and Society*, 1st ed. Reading, MA: Addison-Wesley, 1983.

———. *Mental Health Implications of the Post-partum Period*. Report to the Ohio Department of Mental Health, March, 1987.

Tennov, Dorothy. *Psychotherapy: The Hazardous Cure*. Garden City, NY: Anchor Books, 1976.

Thomas, W. I., and Znaniecki, Florian. *The Polish Peasant in Europe and America*. Boston: Gorham Press, 1918. 2d ed. New York: Alfred A. Knopf, 1927.

Thompson, Wayne N. *Quantitative Research in Public Address and Communication*. New York: Random House, 1967.

Thorne, Barrie. "Women's self-help: a new medical concept." Discussion presented at the meetings of the North Central Sociological Society, Windsor, Canada, May 3, 1974.

———. (ed.). *Rethinking the Family: Some Feminist Questions*. New York: Longman, 1982.

———. "Crossing the gender divide: what 'tomboys' can teach us about processes of gender separation among children." Paper presented to Ohio State University Sociology Lecture Series, Spring 1986a.

———. "Boys and girls together—but mostly apart: gender arrangements in elementary schools." Pp. 167–184 in Willard W. Hartup and Zick Rubin (eds.), *Relationships and Development*. Hillsdale, NJ: Lawrence Erlbaum, 1986b.

————, and Luria, Zella. "Sexuality and gender in children's daily worlds." *Social Problems* 33 (1986): 176–190.

————, Kramarae, Cheris, and Henley, Nancy. "Language, gender and society: opening a second decade of research." Pp. 7–24 in Barrie Thorne; Cheris Kramarae; and Nancy Henley (eds.), *Language, Gender and Society*. Rowley, MA: Newbury House, 1983.

Thorne, Barrie, and Henley, Nancy. *Language and Sex: Difference and Dominance*. Rowley, MA: Newbury House, 1975.

Tiger, Lionel. *Men in Groups*. New York: Random House, 1969.

Tiger, Lionel, and Fox, Robin. *The Imperial Animal*. New York: Holt, Rinehart and Winston, 1971.

Tomizuka, C., and Tobias, S. "Mathematical ability: is sex a factor?" *Science* 212 (1981): 114.

Trudgill, Peter. "Sex, covert prestige and linguistic change in urban Bristish English of Norwich." *Language in Society* 1 (1972): 179–195.

Tuchman, Gaye. "Introduction: the symbolic annihilation of women by the mass media." Pp. 3–38 in Gaye Tuchman; Arlene Kaplan Daniels; and James Benet (eds.), *Hearth and Home: Image of Women in the Mass Media*. New York: Oxford University Press, 1978.

————. "Women's depiction by the mass media." *Signs* 4 (1979): 528– 542.

Tudor, W.; Tudor, J. F.; and Gove, W. R. "The effect of sex role differences on the social control of mental illness." *Journal of Health and Social Behavior* 18 (1977): 98–112.

Tumin, Melvin M. *Social Stratification: The Forms and Functions of Inequality*. Englewood Cliffs, NJ: Prentice-Hall, 1967.

Turnbull, Colin M. *The Forest People*. New York: Simon and Schuster, 1961.

————. *The Mountain People*. New York: Simon and Schuster, 1972.

United States Bureau of the Census. Current Population Report (1981), Series P-60, Nos. 105 and 127.

————. Current Population Report (1983), Series P-60, No. 140, pp. 49, 50, 53.

————. Special Demographic Analyses, CDS-80-8. *American Women: Three Decades of Change*. Washington, D.C.: U.S. Government Printing Office, 1984.

————. Statistical Abstracts of the United States Department of Commerce. *Household and Family Characteristics: March 1984*. Series P-20, No. 398, 1985.

United States Department of Commerce. *Statistical Abstracts of the United States, 1987*. Washington, D.C.: Bureau of the Census, 1986.

United States Department of Labor, Bureau of Labor Statistics. *U.S. Working Women: A Databook*. Washington, D.C.: U.S. Government Printing Office, 1977.

United States Department of Labor, Women's Bureau. *The Earnings Gap Between Women and Men*. Washington, D.C.: U.S. Government Printing Office, 1979.

United States Department of Labor, Bureau of Labor Statistics, Employment and Earnings, January, 1983, p. 157.

Vanderbilt, Amy. *Amy Vanderbilt's Etiquette*. Garden City, NY: Doubleday and Co., Inc., 1972.

Vann, Barbara H. "Self-perception and eating behavior in a college population." Paper presented to the National Women's Studies Convention, University of Illinois, June 1986.

Vogel, Susan; Broverman, Inge; and Gardner, Jo-Ann. *Sesame Street and Sex- Role Stereotypes*, revised. Pittsburgh: Know, 1970.

Voyandoff, Patricia (ed.). *Work and Family: Changing Roles of Men and Women*. Palo Alto, CA: Mayfield, 1984.

Wall Street Journal. August 9, 1977, p. 1, col. 5.

Walley, D. *What Boys Can Be*. Kansas City: Hallmark, n.d.

———. *What Girls Can Be*. Kansas City: Hallmark, n.d.

[Walum], Laurel Richardson. "A content analysis of La Leche League newsletters." Unpublished paper. Columbus: The Ohio State University, 1972.

———. "The changing door ceremony: some notes on the operation of sex-roles in everyday life." *Urban Life and Culture* 2 (1974a): 506– 515.

———. "The etiquette of bondage." *Newsday*. Long Island, New York, May 1974b.

———. "Sociology and the mass media: some major problems and modest proposals." *The American Sociologist* 10 (1975): 28–32.

———. "Ethnomethodology and social organization." Pp. 40–62 in Ronald Corwin and Ray Ederfelt (eds.), *Perspective on Organizations,* vol. III. Washington, D.C.: American Association of Colleges for Teacher Education and the Association of Teacher Educators, 1978.

[Walum], Laurel Richardson, and Franklin, Clyde, Jr. "Structural components of wives' working." Report prepared for Center for Human Resources, Columbus: Ohio State University, 1972.

Warren, Mary Anne. *Gendercide*. Tottowa, NJ: Rowman and Allheld, 1985.

Washingtonian. "The women's network: shortcut to the top." January 1980: 179–183.

Weber, Max. *From Max Weber*. Edited by Hans H. Gerth and C. Wright Mills. New York: Oxford University Press, 1946.

———. *The Theory of Social and Economic Organization*. New York: The Free Press, 1969.

Weeks, Jeffrey. *Coming Out: Homosexual Politics in Britain*. London: Quartet Books, 1979.

Weissman, M.; Pincus, C.; Radding, N.; Lawrence, R.; and Siegel, R. "The educated housewife: mild depression and the search for work." *American Journal of Orthopsychiatry* 43 (1973): 565–573.

Weisstein, Naomi. "Kinder, kuche, kirche as scientific law: psychology constructs the female." Pp. 205–220 in Robin Morgan (ed.), *Sisterhood is Powerful*. New York: Random House, 1971.

Weitzman, Lenore J. *Sex Role Socialization: A Focus on Women*. Palo Alto, CA: Mayfield, 1979.

———. *The Divorce Revolution*. New York: The Free Press, 1985.

Weitzman, Lenore J.; Eifler, Deborah; Hokada, Elizabeth; and Ross, Catherine. "Sex-role socialization in picture books for preschool children." *American Journal of Sociology* 77 (1972): 1125–1150.

Welch, Renate L., et al. "Subtle cues in children's commercials." *Journal of Communication* 29 (1979): 202–209.

West, Candace. "Against our will: male interruptions of females in cross-sex conversation." Pp. 81–100 in Judith Orasanu; Miriam K. Slater; and Lenore Loeb Adler (eds.), *Language, Sex and Gender: Does La Difference Make a Difference?* New York: New York Academy of Sciences Annals, 1979.

West, Candace, and Zimmerman, Don H. "Small insults; a study of interruptions in cross-sex conversations between unacquainted persons." Pp. 103–119 in Barrie Thorne; Cheris Kramarae; and Nancy Henley (eds.), *Language, Gender and Society*. Rowley, MA: Newbury House, 1983.

———. "Doing gender." *Gender and Society* 1 (1987): (in press).

West, Rebecca. "Review of *Conundrum*." *The New York Times Book Review*, April 14, 1975: 5.

Westoff, Charles; Potty, Robert G.; Sage, Phillip C.; and Mishler, E. *Family Growth in Metropolitan America*. Princeton: Princeton University Press, 1961.

Whittaker, Susan McDargh. "Male vs. female newscasters—a study of the relative effectiveness, believeability and acceptance." Paper presented to the Annual Meetings of the Association for Education in Journalism, 1975.

Williams, Brett. "1930's animals as hard time heroes in American children's books." *Central Issues in Anthropology* 6 (1986): 43–51.

Williamson, Nancy. *Sons or Daughters*. Beverly Hills, CA: Sage Publications, 1976.

Willis, Frank N., Jr. "Initial speaking distance as a function of the speakers' relationship." *Psychonomic Science* 6 (1966): 221– 222.

Wilmore, Jack H. "They told you, you couldn't compete with men and you, like a fool, believed them. Here's hope." *Womensports*. June 1974: 40– 43.

Wilson, Edward O. *Sociobiology: The New Synthesis*. Princeton, NJ: Princeton University Press, 1975.

Wilson, Everett K. *Sociology: Rules, Roles and Relationships*. Homewood, IL: Dorsey Press, 1966, 1972.

Wolf, Deborah Coleman. *The Lesbian Community*. Los Angeles: University of California Press, 1979.

Women's Equity Action League (WEAL). "Sports fact sheet." Washington, D.C., 1978a.

———. *Washington Report* 7 (1978b).

Women's Equity Action League (WEAL), and Legal Defense Fund. "What WEAL and WEAL FUND have done for women and girls in sports." Washington, D.C., 1978.

Wood, Marion. "The influence of sex and knowledge of communication effectiveness on spontaneous speech." *Word* 22 (1966): 112– 137.

Yarrow, L. J.; Rubenstein, J. C.; and Pederson, F. A. "Dimensions of early stimulation: differential effects on infant development." Paper presented at the meetings of the Society for Research in Child Development," 1971.

Yinger, Milton J. *Religion, Society and the Individual*. New York: Macmillan, 1957.

Zeldow, P. B. "Effects of nonpathological sex role stereotypes on student evaluations of psychiatric patients." *Journal of Consulting and Clinical Psychology* 44 (1976): 304.

Zimmerman, Don H., and West, Candace. "Sex roles, interruptions and silences in conversations." Pp. 105–129 in Barrie Thorne and Nancy Henley (eds.), *Language and Sex: Difference and Dominance*. Rowley, MA: Newbury House, 1975.

□ □ Name Index □ □

Abrahams, Roger, 30, 32, 251
Abzug, Bella, 163, 251
Acker, Juan R., 176, 251
Adams, Abigail, 229, 251
Adams, Harold J., 138, 251
Adamsky, Cathryn, 19, 251
Almquist, Elizabeth M., 175, 251
Alpert, Jane, 145, 251
Altman, I., 25, 251
Alvin, Duane F., 56, 252
Amir, Nebachem, 115, 252
Amundsen, Kirsten, 161, 252
Angrist, Shirley, 136, 251, 252
Arditti, Rita, 126, 252
Ardrey, Robert, 152, 252
Arkin, B., 251, 252
Armstrong, Christopher F., 57, 58, 252
Atkin, Charles K., 81, 252
Atkinson, Ti-Grace, 233

Bachofen, Johann Jacob, 151, 252
Baldridge, J. Victor, 228, 252
Bandura, Albert, 38, 252
Banner, Lois W., 26, 252
Barash, David, 154, 252
Bart, Pauline, 131, 133, 136 fn., 252
Baumgartner, A. I., 54, 279
Baxter, Sandra, 163, 253
Beach, Frank A., 42, 133, 260
Becker, Howard, 17, 180, 253
Bell, Alan F., 222, 223, 253
Bell, Tony, 247, 253
Bem, Daryl, 20, 253
Bem, Sandra, 25, 253
Benbow, C., 61, 253
Bendix, John, 18, 253
Benedict, Ruth, 182
Benokraitis, Nijole V., 64, 70, 253

Bentzen, Frances, 56, 253
Berger, Peter, 31, 253
Bernard, Jessie, 182, 216, 253
Bernstein, Barton E., 106, 253
Best, Raphaela, 39, 55, 254
Bettelheim, Bruno, 135, 254
Bienen, Leigh, 67, 254
Bird, Phyllis, 88, 254
Black, Joan, 101 fn.
Blau, Francine D., 165, 167, 175, 254
Blaxall, Martha, 175, 254
Bleier, Ruth, 151, 254
Blotnick, Srully, 254
Blumberg, Rae Lesser, 150, 152, 153, 155, 254
Blumstein, Philip, 214, 215, 220, 222, 223, 225, 226, 254
Boas, Frank, 182
Bodine, Ann, 20, 21, 254
Booth, Alan, 216, 254
Boren, Jerry, 203, 254
Borker, Ruth A., 55, 269
Boserup, Esther, 156, 254
Boswell, Sally L., 61, 254
Brabant, Sarah, 70, 254
Brend, Ruth M., 28–29, 254
Brenton, Myron, 187, 188, 255
Briscoe, Anne M., 148, 149, 255
Brody, Leslie, 42, 255
Broverman, I. K., 9, 10, 11, 136, 255, 280
Brown, Penelope, 30, 255
Brown, Rita Mae, 233, 255
Brown, Roger, 25, 255
Brownmiller, Susan, 26, 60, 115, 116, 117, 139, 255
Bruner, Jerome, 59, 255
Bunch, Charlotte, 221, 255

Burgess, Ann Wolbert, 114, 115, 265
Burton, Sydney G., 69, 255

Cameron, Paul, 23, 255
Cargan, Leonard, 208, 256
Carroll, Jackson W., 91, 92, 256
Carter, Dianne K., 136, 138, 273
Carter, Ellin, 73
Cassell, Joan, 221, 230, 256
Chafetz, Janet Saltzman, 145, 256
Chase, Stuart, 148
Cheles-Miller, Pamela, 81, 256
Chesler, Phyllis, 135, 136, 137, 256
Chisholm, Shirley, 241, 256
Chodorow, Nancy, 49, 198–199, 256
Christ, Carol P., 94, 98, 99, 256
Cicourel, Aaron, 112, 256
Clancy, E. K., 137, 256
Cleaver, Eldridge, 241, 256
Cline, Carolyn Garrett, 179, 256
Coleman, J., 138, 256
Collins, Randall, 178, 183, 256
Condry, John, 41, 257
Condry, Sandra, 41, 257
Cook, Beverly Blair, 103, 181, 257
Cook, Blanch W., 223, 257
Cook, K., 39, 273
Cooley, Charles Norton, 17, 37, 257
Cordes, C., 57, 59, 257
Coser, Lewis A., 172, 257

Dalton, Katharina, 154, 257
Daly, Mary, 18, 90, 93, 98, 257
Davis, Angela Y., 244, 245, 257
Davis, Elizabeth Gould, 145, 146, 257
Davis, Madeline, 220, 257
Deaux, K., 9, 12, 258
Deckard, Barbara, 230, 258
DeStefano, Johanna S., 18, 19, 30, 32, 258
Diamond, Timothy, 91, 98, 258
Dizard, Jan E., 196, 215, 226, 258
Dobrofsky, L., 215, 252
Domhoff, G. William, 70, 164, 165, 258
Dornbusch, Sanford, 63, 258
Douglas, Priscilla Harriet, 167, 258
Draper, Patricia, 153, 258
Duberman, Lucile, 208, 258
Dunham, Jan Michele, 115, 116, 265

Durham, Leona, 138, 251
Durkheim, Emile, 101, 258
Dweck, Carol S., 59, 258

Eagly, A., 9, 12, 258
Edelsky, Carole, 34, 259
Ehrenreich, Barbara, 73, 74, 259
Ehrhardt, A., 5–6, 12, 46, 271
Ehrman, Lee, 5, 273
Eichler, Margrit, 13, 14, 259
Eisen, S., 20, 269
Eisenberg, Sue, 106, 259
Ekstrom, R., 57, 59, 259
Ellsworth, P. C., 26, 259
England, Paula, 192, 259
Epstein, Cynthia Fuchs, 70, 180, 215, 217, 259
Erickson, S. Nancy, 101 fn., 119–120, 259
Ernest, John, 61, 63, 259
Etzioni, Amitai, 36, 259
Evans, Sara, 222, 259

Falk, Gail, 181, 184, 259
Farkas, George, 192, 259
Farley, Lin, 185, 259
Farmer, H. S., 33, 259
Farrell, Warren T., 75, 247–258, 259
Fasteau, Marc Feigen, 184, 240
Fausto-Sterling, Anne, 153–154, 260
Feagin, Joe R., 64, 70, 253
Felshin, Jan, 57, 260
Fennema, Elizabeth, 62, 260
Fernberger, S., 9, 260
Ferraro, Geraldine, 160
Ferree, Myra Marx, 193, 235, 236, 237, 247, 249, 260
Festinger, Leon, 239, 260
Fields, Rona M., 53, 260
Filene, Peter, 196, 197, 260
Firestone, Shulamith, 232
Fishel, Anne, 138, 260
Fishman, Pamela, 31, 260
Fiske, Shirley, 57, 260
Fleener, Marilyn G., 220, 260
Flemming, J. B., 105, 260
Folb, Edith, 32, 260
Fonda, Jane, 140
Fonow, Mary Margaret, 174, 184, 185, 260

Ford, Clellar S., 42, 133, 260
Fox, Greer Litton, 213, 260
Fox, Lynn H., 63, 260
Fox, Mary Frank, 192, 260
Fox, Robin, 152, 280
Franklin, Clyde, 239, 247, 260, 261
Franks, Violet, 138, 261, 262
Frazier, Nancy, 56, 59, 261
Freeman, Jo, 119, 227, 228, 230, 231, 232, 261
Freud, Sigmund, 134, 135, 136, 261
Friedan, Betty, 231, 233 fn., 261
Friedl, Ernestine, 153, 155, 156, 157, 194, 200, 261

Gagnon, John, 58, 261
Galbraith, John Kenneth, 156, 261
Garcia-Zamor, M. A., 28, 261
Garfinkel, Harold, 7, 261
Garland, Neal-T., 217, 272
Gerbner, George, 69, 77, 78, 79, 80, 81, 261
Gerson, Kathleen, 192, 261
Gifford-Jones, W., 131, 261
Gillespie, Dair L., 194, 195, 261
Gilligan, Carol, 49, 261
Ginsberg, Ruth Bader, 102, 262
Glazer, Nona, 74, 75, 262
Glick, P. C., 191, 201, 262
Goffman, Erving, 25, 26, 27, 28, 76, 178, 262
Goldenberg, Naomi Ruth, 94, 262
Gomberg, Edith S., 137, 262
Goodall, Jane, 151, 262
Goode, William H., 194, 262
Goode, William J., 195, 262
Gove, Walter R., 137, 256, 262, 280
Grauerholz, Elizabeth, 47, 48, 262
Greeley, Andrew M., 92, 263
Greenberg, S., 56, 59, 262
Greiff, Geoffrey L., 202, 203, 262
Griffin, Susan, 115, 116, 263
Griffiths, M., 105, 263
Gringold, Judith, 106, 263
Grønseth, Erick, 197, 215, 263
Gross, Edward, 175, 263
Gross, Harriet Engel, 217, 219, 263
Gross, Larry, 69, 77, 78, 79, 80, 81, 261
Grunden, Rickie Sue, 60, 61, 263
Gundry, Patricia, 95, 96, 263

Guning, Rosemary, 119
Guttentag, Marcia, 208, 263

Hacker, Sally, 18, 276
Hall, Roberta, 64, 263
Halmi, K. A., 139, 263
Hamilton, N., 18, 263
Hardesty, Nancy, 95, 96, 97, 191, 276
Hardin, Garrett, 118, 263
Harding, Esther, 135, 263
Hare-Mustin, R., 138, 264
Harris, Ann Sutherland, 65, 264
Hartley, Ruth E., 45, 264
Hartman, Heidi, 165, 175, 176–177, 264, 273
Heckler, Margaret, 162
Heidensohn, Frances, 111, 264
Heller, Joseph, 188, 264
Helmreich, R., 9, 278
Henley, Nancy, 19, 24, 25, 26, 30, 33, 264, 267
Henning, Margaret, 181, 264
Henry, Alice, 181, 264
Herschberger, Ruth, 123, 124, 125, 264
Hess, Beth B., 235, 236, 237, 247, 249
Hesse-Biber, Sharlene, 192, 260
Hiller, Dana, 195, 264
Hochschild, Arlie Russell, 26, 264
Hoffman, L. W., 192, 264
Hole, Judith, 89, 97, 98, 264
Holland, David, 224, 264
Holmstrom, Lynda Lytle, 103, 114, 115, 217, 264, 265
Hooker, Evelyn, 223, 265
Hooks, Bell, 244, 245, 265
Horney, Karen, 135, 265
Houseknecht, Sharon, 216, 265
Howe, Louise Kapp, 175, 265
Hubbard, Ruth, 124, 126, 127, 265
Huber, Joan, 111, 155, 156, 157, 158, 192, 197, 201, 213, 216, 236, 265, 278
Hudnell, Terese Connerton, 115, 116, 265
Hutchins, Grace, 189, 265
Hutner, Frances C., 178, 265

Inazu, Judith, 213, 260
Iritani, Bonita, 21, 265

Jacklin, Carol Nagy, 40, 41, 43, 44, 46, 269

Jackson, Jacqueline I., 239, 265
Jackson, Lenore, 54, 274
Jackson, Phil, 56, 265
Jaquette, Jane S., 163, 266
Jardin, Anne, 181, 264
Jefferson, Thomas, 102
Johnson, Virginia E., 128, 131, 270
Johnson, Warren R., 127–128, 266
Jordan, Joan, 189, 266
Jung, Carl G., 135, 266

Kahn-Hut, Rachel, 192, 266
Kamerman, S. B., 213, 266
Kaminski, Donna M., 62, 266
Kanowitz, Leo, 102, 104, 105, 112, 113,
    266
Kanter, Rosabeth Moss, 175, 178, 179,
    181, 266
Kaplan, M., 136, 266
Kash, Sara D., 92, 266
Kay, Barbara, 111, 273
Keller, Helen, 17
Kelly, Alison, 63, 266
Kendall, Diane, 64, 266
Kennedy, John, 231
Kirschner, Betty, 217, 218, 219, 266
Kitsuse, John, 112, 256
Klatch, Rebecca, 236, 267
Klein, Dorie, 111, 267
Klein, Ethel, 160, 230, 234, 267
Klein, Susan, 52, 267, 275
Kluegel, J. R., 236, 277
Knafl, Kathleen, 133, 270
Kockman, Thomas, 32, 267
Koedt, Anne, 129, 267
Kohlberg, Lawrence, 38, 267
Korda, Michael, 179–180, 181, 267
Korner, A. F., 40, 267
Kramerae, Cheris, 16 fn., 18, 22, 30
Kuhn, Manfred, 208, 267

Labov, William, 32, 267
Lahaderne, Henriette, 56, 265
Lahof, Bruce, 75, 76, 267
Lake, Alice, 40, 41, 267
Lamb, Michael E., 41, 267
Lancaster, Jane Beckman, 151, 267
Lang, Gladys Engel, 71, 267
Lansing, Marjorie, 163, 253
LaRue, Linda J. M., 243, 268

Lear, Martha Weinman, 119, 268
Leavitte, R., 151, 268
Lehman, Edward C., Jr., 91, 268
Leibowitz, Lila, 147, 148, 149, 150, 151,
    152, 268
LeMasters, E. E., 216, 268
Lenski, Gerhard E., 155, 157, 174, 268
Lerner, Richard M., 122, 268
Lester, Julius, 58, 268
Lever, Janet, 55, 57, 268
Levine, Ellen, 89, 97, 98, 264
Levine, Joe, 124, 268
Lewis, L., 9, 12, 258
Lewis, Michael, 41, 268
Lewis, Sasha Gregory, 220, 221, 222,
    268
Leznoff, Maurice, 224, 268
Lipman-Blumen, Jean, 57, 61, 63, 64,
    268
Lloyd, Cynthia B., 175, 268
Lockheed, Marlaine E., 54, 269
London, Jayne, 91, 191, 192, 194, 195,
    271
Lopez, Lisa, 113, 269
Lorber, Judith, 13, 185, 269
Lowe, Marian, 150, 152, 269
Lowi, Theodore J., 227, 269
Luckman, Thomas, 31, 253
Luker, Kristin, 118, 269
Luria, Zella, 55, 280
Lynn, David B., 45, 269
Lynn, Naomi, 161, 162, 269

MacArthur, Leslie, 20, 269
Maccoby, Eleanor, 40, 41, 43, 44, 46,
    159, 269
MacHaffie, Barbara J., 88, 91, 92, 94,
    269
MacKay, Donald G., 18, 19, 269
Macke, Anne, 179, 269
MacKinnon, Catharine A., 185, 269
Macklin, E. D., 213, 214, 269
Maltz, Daniel N., 55, 269
Mander, Anica Vesel, 138, 269
Marshall, Hannah, 133, 270
Martin, Susan Ehrlich, 185, 186, 270
Martyna, Wendy, 18, 19, 270
Marx, Karl, 84, 90, 270
Masters, William H., 128, 131, 270
McClelland, David C., 47, 270

McConnell-Ginet, Sally, 28, 29, 270
McDowell, Cynthia N., 70, 272
McKee, J., 9, 270
McNeil, John, 56, 270
Mead, Margaret, 46
Mencken, H. L., 23, 270
Merton, Robert E., 9, 270
Meyer, Katherine, 70, 270
Michelson, Avra, 220, 257
Miller, Mark M., 81, 270
Miller, S. M., 215, 216, 270
Millett, Kate, 136, 233, 271
Minton, Cheryl, 41, 271
Moen, Phyllis, 201, 202, 203, 277
Money, John, 5–7, 12, 46, 271
Morgan, Marabel, 236
Morris, Desmond, 152, 271
Morris, Jan, 13–14, 271
Morrison, Toni, 241, 242, 271
Mortimer, Jeylan T., 191, 192, 194, 195, 271
Mosmiller, Tom, 247, 260
Moss, E. A., 41, 271
Mowbray, C. S., 137, 271
Munter, P. E., 194, 263

Nagel, S. S., 112, 271
Nelson, P. A., 25, 251
Newton, Niles, 130, 271
Nonkin, Lesley Jane, 26, 271

Oakley, Anne, 129, 271
O'Connor, Lynn, 26, 271
O'Connor, Sandra Day, 162
O'Hara, Robert, 59, 272
Olson, Ann, 65, 173, 276
Oppenheimer, Karen, 115, 272

Palmer, Edward L., 70, 272
Papachristou, Judith, 220, 272
Papanek, Hannah, 194, 272
Parcel, Toby L., 215, 272
Pearce, Diane, 169, 236, 272
Pederson, F. A., 41, 272
Pedgug, Robert A., 223, 272
Pescosolido, Bernice, 47, 48, 262
Petchesky, R., 237, 272
Petro, Carole Smith, 52, 272
Philiber, William, 195, 264
Phillips, Brenda, 55, 272

Piaget, Jean, 38, 272
Piotrkowski, C. S., 194, 272
Pius XII, Pope, 90
Plaskow, Judith, 94, 98, 99, 256
Pleck, Joseph, 195, 245, 272
Pogrebin, Letty, 42, 272
Polatnick, Margaret, 198, 199, 273
Pollak, Otto, 111, 272
Poloma, Margaret M., 217, 272
Ponse, Barbara, 220, 273
Printz, A. M., 139, 278
Prisuta, Robert H., 69, 273
Probber, Joan, 5, 273
Putnam, Barbara A., 52, 272

Quarforth, Joanne M., 70, 273
Quintinalles, Mirtha, 221, 273

Rapoport, Rhona N., 215, 217, 273
Rapoport, Robert, 215, 217, 273
Rawlings, Edna I., 136, 138, 273
Raymond, Janice, 12, 14, 124, 273
Reagan, Barbara, 175, 254
Reagan, Nancy, 71
Reagan, Ronald, 162, 163
Reckless, Walter, 111, 273
Reeves, Byron, 81, 270
Reitz, Roseta, 133, 273
Remick, Helen, 177, 273
Reskin, Barbara, 165, 175, 273
Reuther, Rosemary Radford, 89, 96
Rheingold, H. L., 39, 273
Rheingold, Joseph, 135, 274
Richardson, Laurel (Walum), 27, 33, 39, 66, 67, 71, 130, 133, 178, 179, 185, 201, 208, 210, 217, 218, 219, 239, 274, 278, 281
Rickles, Nathan K., 136, 274
Rivera, Rhonda R., 106–107, 274
Robertson, Ian, 90, 274
Robson, K. S., 41, 272
Roosevelt, Eleanor, 71
Rosenberg, Bernard, 172, 257
Rosenberg, S., 194, 259
Rosenkrantz, Paul, 9–10, 274
Rosenthal, Robert, 54, 274
Ross, Catherine E., 195, 274
Rossi, Alice, 41, 48, 145, 146, 249, 274
Rothman, Barbara Katz, 124, 126
Rubin, Jeffrey Z., 40, 275

Ruffin, Josephine St. Pierre, 244
Runciman, Walter Garrison, 239, 275
Rupp, Leila J., 223, 230, 234, 235, 236, 237, 250, 275
Rush, Anne Kent, 138, 269
Russo, Nancy Felipe, 41, 275
Ruth, Sheila, 229, 251, 275
Ryan, Barbara E., 234, 275
Ryan, Patricia, 90, 275

Sachs, Jacqueline, 28, 275
Sachs, Oliver, 24, 275
Sadker, David, 52, 56, 275
Sadker, Myra, 52, 53, 56, 57, 59, 64, 65, 261, 275
Safron, Claire, 109, 276
Sahli, Nancy, 223, 276
St. John, Margo, 113
Sanday, Peggy Reeves, 154, 276
Sandler, Bernice, 64, 263
Sattel, Jack W., 42, 276
Scanzoni, John, 222, 276
Scanzoni, Letha, 95, 96, 97, 191, 222, 276
Schaff, Thomas J., 17, 276
Schaller, George, 150, 151, 276
Scheflen, A. E., 17, 276
Schirtzinger, Marie, 90, 275
Schneider, Beth E., 237, 238, 276
Schneider, Joseph, 18, 276
Schulz, Muriel R., 22, 23–24, 276
Schur, Edwin M., 140, 170, 276
Schwartz, Pepper, 214, 215, 220, 222, 223, 225, 226, 254
Scott, Helda, 169, 276
Scully, Diane, 131, 276
Seager, Joni, 65, 173, 276
Seaman, B., 31, 276
Seaman, G., 131, 276
Sears, R. R., 38, 276
Secord, Paul R., 208, 263
Seidler, John, 93, 276
Seneca, Gail, 129, 277
Shakeshaft, C., 53, 277
Sherfey, Mary Jane, 131, 277
Sherman, Julia, 62, 63, 137, 138, 277
Sherrifs, A., 9, 270
Shorr, Alvin, 201, 202, 203, 277
Shostak, Arthur B., 186, 187, 188, 277
Shulman, Alix, 132, 277

Shuster, Janet, 22, 277
Signorelli, Nancy, 79, 277
Silveira, Jeannette, 25, 277
Slocum, Sally, 152, 277
Smith, Don D., 72, 277
Smith, E. R., 236, 277
Smith, Howard, 231
Smith, M., 137, 277
Smith, M. A., 53, 277
Smith, Margaret Chase, 162
Smith-Rosenberg, Carroll, 223, 278
Sokoloff, Natalie, 176, 278
Solanis, Valerie, 146, 278
Sommer, Robert, 24, 278
Spanier, Graham, 213, 278
Spence, J., 9, 278
Spender, Dale, 132, 278
Spitze, Glenna, 155, 192, 201, 213, 216, 236, 265, 278
Spock, Benjamin, 38–39, 278
Stangler, R. S., 139, 278
Stanley, Julia P., 22, 278
Stanton, Elizabeth Cady, 94
Statham, Anne (Macke), 67, 278
Stein, Peter J., 208, 209, 278
Steinberg, Ronnie, 177, 278
Steinmetz, Suzanne, 105, 278, 279
Stiehm, J., 236, 278
Stohler, Robert, 12, 278
Stoll, Clarice Stasz, 188, 278
Stoller, R. J., 43, 279
Stoltenberg, John, 225, 279
Stone, Lucy, 94
Stone, Pauline Terrelonge, 243, 279
Strauss, Anselm, 180, 253
Strauss, Murray, 105, 279
Strouse, Jean, 136, 279
Swacker, Marjorie R., 30, 279
Szasz, Thomas, 136, 279

Tanner, Donna M., 220, 222, 223, 279
Tanner, Nancy, 151, 279
Tauber, Cynthia M., 166
Tavris, D., 54, 279
Taylor, Verta A., 136, 220, 223, 230, 234, 235, 236, 237, 250, 275, 279
Tennov, Dorothy, 134, 137, 279
Terrell, Mary Church, 244
Thomas, W. I., 239, 279
Thomas Aquinas, St., 89

Thorne, Barrie, 6, 30, 34, 49, 54, 55, 131, 133, 191, 264, 267, 279, 280
Tiger, Lionel, 151–152, 280
Tobias, S., 61, 280
Tomizuka, C., 61, 280
Trudgill, Peter, 30, 280
Truth, Sojourner, 229, 244
Tuchman, Gaye, 10, 78, 280
Tumin, Melvin M., 144, 280
Turnbull, Colin M., 153, 280

Valdisera, Victor, 166
Vanderbilt, Amy, 18, 280
Vann, Barbara H., 139, 280
Voyandoff, Patricia, 192, 281

Walters, Richard H., 38, 252
Walum, Laurel Richardson, *see* Richardson, Laurel (Walum)
Warren, Mary Anne, 36, 281
Weber, Max, 30, 172, 281
Weeks, Jeffrey, 223, 226, 281
Weinberg, Martin S., 222, 223, 253

Weissman, M., 138, 281
Weisstein, Naomi, 134, 136, 281
Weitzman, Lenore J., 45, 47, 62, 63, 105, 112, 202, 271, 281
West, Candace, 5, 21, 32, 265, 281
West, Rebecca, 14, 282
Westler, William A., 224, 268
Wiedeking, C., 12, 271
Williams, Brett, 47, 282
Williamson, Nancy, 36 fn., 282
Wilmore, Jack H., 60, 282
Wilson, Edward O., 146, 282
Wilson, Everett K., 85, 101, 282
Wolf, Deborah Coleman, 220, 282
Wood, Marion, 30, 282

Yarrow, L. J., 41, 282
Yinger, Milton J., 90, 282

Zihlman, Adrienne, 151, 279
Zimmerman, Don H., 5, 32, 281, 282
Znaniecki, Florian, 239, 279

□ □ Subject Index □ □

Abortion, 117–118, 237
Adultery, 88
Advertisements, 72, 75–77
Aggression, 43–44
AIDS, 225
Amniocentesis, 36, 126
Androcentrism, 14
Androgen, 148–149
Anorexia nervosa, 138, 139
Antifeminism, 236–237
Arapesh, 3
Artifacts, children's, 46–49

Bible, 86–99
Biocultural theory, 145, 154–158
Biogenetic theory, 145–154
Biological deterministic thinking, 145,
    147
Black Liberation Movement, 240
Black Power Movement, 228
Blacks, 238–245
Body types, 122–123
Bonding
    male, 151–152
    socioemotional, 182–186
Bottle feeding, 157
Boys, school experience of, 56–59
Breastfeeding, 129, 130
Bulimia, 138–140
Bureaucracy, 172

Caldecott Medal books, 47
Change, social and political, 205–250
Chauvinism, male, 14
Childbirth, 129–130
Child care, 197–201
Child custody, 105
Child support, 105

Churches, *see* Religion
Citizens' Advisory Committee on the Sta-
    tus of Women, 231
Civil Rights Act (1964), 107, 231
Civil Rights Movement, 230
Cognitive-development model, 37, 38
Cohabitation, 106, 213–214
Communication, 15, 17
    nonverbal, 24–28
    verbal, 8–24
Congress, U.S., 161–162
Couples, dual-location, 217–219
Criminal law, 111–117
Culture
    defined, 3
    sex and gender and, 3–15

Demeanor, 26–27
Dependency, 43, 44
Determinism, biological, 1, 145, 147
Differentiation, sexual, 1
Divorce, 105, 191–192
Domestic relations, law and, 104–107
Dominance, male, 153, 154–158
Dual-location couples, 217–219
Dual market model, 176, 177

Eating disorders, therapy for, 138–140
Ectomorphs, 122
Education, 50–68
    law and, 109–111
Employment, law and, 107–109
Endomorphs, 122
Equal Employment Opportunity Commis-
    sion, 231, 233
"Equal pay for equal work," 107
Equal Rights Amendment, 119–120, 160
Establishment, the, 160

Etiquette, 27–28
Evolution, human social, 151–154

Family, 191, 192
Family of orientation, 37
Federally Employed Women (FEW), 230, 234
Femininity, 7, 9–14, 27
Feminism
    Marxist, 176–177
    passive, 237–238
Feminist movement, 160, 229–238
    future of the, 248–250
Feminist therapy, 138–140
Feminist Women's Health Center (Los Angeles), 133–134
Fertility, decline in, 157, 158
First Ladies, 71
Foreplay, 132

Gay Rights Movement, 223, 224
Gender, 4–7
    learning, 7–9
Gendercide, 36
Gender gap (voting behavior), 163
Gender identity, 6, 7, 37–38, 43
Gender stereotyping, 16, 24, 27
Girls, school experience of, 59–61
Government, 160–162
Groups, primary, 37
Gynecologists, 131

Harassment, sexual, on the job, 109, 185–186
Health systems, medical and mental, 121–140
Hermaphrodites, 4
Hierarchical networks, 178–180
Higher education, 64–68
Home, linkages between work and, 191–203
Homophobia, 42
Homosexuality, 129, 219–226
    gender identity and, 7
    homophobia and, 42
    law and, 106–107
Hormones, 147–149
Horticultural societies, 156
Human social evolution, 151–154

Hunting-gathering societies, 152–153
Hysterectomy, 131

Identity, gender, 6, 7, 37–38, 43
Impotence, 128–129
Income discrepancies, 165–166
Inequality, sex-based, 141–203
Infant socialization, 38–43
Intercourse, misconceptions about, 129
Interest groups, 160
Intimate relationships, changing, 207–220
Intonation (speech), 28–29

Judeo-Christian tradition, 86–90

!Kung, 153

Labeling, 17
    division of, 143, 151, 154, 158, 172
    specialization of, 172
Labor force, 165
Lactation, 130
La Leche League, 133
Language, as socializer, 16–34
Law, 83–84, 101–120
    criminal, 111–117
Legal system, 101–120
Lesbians, 219–223, 233
    See also Homosexuality

Magazines, 72–75
Male bonding, 151–152
Male chauvinism, 14
Male dominance, 153, 154–156
Manu, 3
Marquesan, 147
Marriage, 191, 193–197, 208, 214–219
Marvin v. Marvin, 106
Marxist feminism, 176–177
Marxist model, 176
Masculinity, 7, 9–14, 27
Mass media, socialization and the, 69–81
Masturbation, 127, 128
Mathematics, 61–64
Matriarchy, 153
Mbuti, 153
Menopause, 131
Men's Movement, 240, 245–248
Mesomorphs, 122

Metacommunication, 17
Mobility, social, 172
Modeling, 49
Modern Language Association, 20
Mundugomor, 3

National Organization for Changing Men, 246–247
National Organization for Women (NOW), 230, 231–234
National Women's Political Caucus, 231, 234
Navajo, 4, 28
New Right, 236
Newspapers, 70–71, 75
Norm
    prescriptive, 4
    proscriptive, 4
Normal, concepts of, 123 fn.
Nsdle, 4
Nursing, 130

Occupational segregation, 166–169, 175–190
Organizational structure, 180
Orgasm, 128, 129

Parents, single, 201–203
Parturition, 130
Patriarchalism, 14
Penis, size of, 128
Physiology, gender and, 147–149
Picture books, 47–48
Politics, 160–163
Poverty, 169
Power, 144, 159–163
Preschool socialization, 43–49
Prescriptive norm, 4
Prestige, 144, 170–171
Primary groups, 37
Primates, 149–151
Progesterone, 148
Property, 144, 163–169
Proscriptive norm, 4
Prostitution, 112–113
Psychiatry, 134–138
Psychology, clinical, 134–138
Psychosexual development, 135

Rape, 113–117, 154
Religion, 83, 85–100
Reproduction, 123–127
Reproductive rights, 117–119
Roles, gender and, 6–7

Schools, *see* Education
Science, 84, 121–140
Segregation
    occupational, 166–169, 175–190
    sex, 54–55, 167, 175–178
Self-categorization, 38
Self-help movement, 133–134
Sex
    as an ascribed status, 4–6
    biological, 5
Sex change operations, *see* Transsexualism
Sex differences, speech and, 28–34
Sex discrimination, law and, 104
Sexism, 14
Sex saliency, 174
Sex segregation, 167, 175–178
    in schools, 54–55
Sex stereotypes, 9–15, 20
Sexual differentiation, 1
Sexual harassment on the job, 109, 185–186
Sexuality, 127–129
Sharing, 153
Single life style, 208–213
Single parenting, 201–203
Social change, 205–250
Social control, institutions of, 83–140
Social evolution, human, 151–154
Socialization, 15
    early, 35–49
    education and, 50–68
    language and, 16–34
    mass media and, 69–81
Social-learning model, 37
Social mobility, 172
Social movements, 227–250
Social shaping, 1
Social space, 24–25
Socioemotional bonding, 182–186
Space, social, 24–25
Sponsor-protégé system, 180–182
Status attainment model, 176

Status inconsistency, 173–175
Statutory rape, 113
Stereotypes, sex, 9–15, 20
Stereotyping, gender, 16, 26, 27
Stratification, sex-based, 143–190
Stress, 4
Students for a Democratic Society, 232

Tasaday, 153
Tcambuli, 3
Television, 69–70, 77–81
Therapy, 134–140
Toda, 3
Touching, 25
Toys, 48–49
Traditionalism, 86–90
Traits, 9–12

Transsexualism, 7–9, 12–15

"Velvet Ghetto, The," 179
Violence
   crimes of, 112
   domestic, 105–106
Voting behavior, 162–163

Wealth, 163–164
Women's Equity Action League (WEAL),
      230
Women's Movement, 160, 229–238
   future of the, 248–250
Work, linkages between home and, 191–
      203
Work world, organization and process in
      the, 172–190